Autobiography

Journey East, Journey West

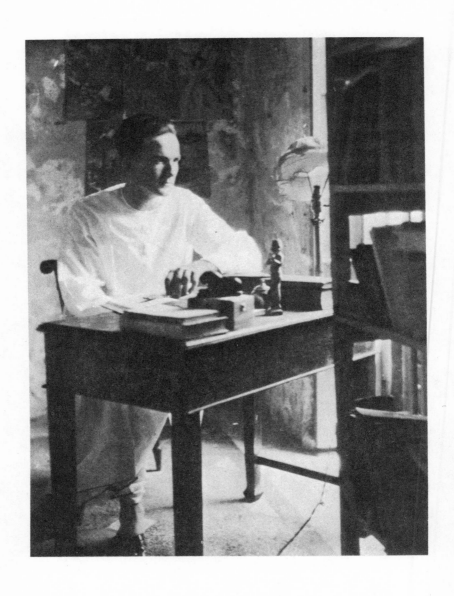

MIRCEA ELIADE

Autobiography

Volume I: 1907–1937
Journey East, Journey West

TRANSLATED FROM THE ROMANIAN BY

Mac Linscott Ricketts

The University of Chicago Press
Chicago & London

Photograph facing title page: the author in 1930 at the home of
Surendranath Dasgupta in Calcutta.

English translation originally published in 1981 by Harper & Row,
Publishers, Inc.

The University of Chicago Press, Chicago 60637
The University of Chicago Press, Ltd., London
© 1981 by Mircea Eliade
All rights reserved. Published 1981
University of Chicago Press edition published 1990
Printed in the United States of America
98 97 96 95 94 93 92 91 90   54321

Library of Congress Cataloging-in-Publication Data

Eliade, Mircea, 1907–1986
    Autobiography / Mircea Eliade : translated from the Romanian by
    Mac Linscott Ricketts.
        p.   cm.
    Reprint. Originally published: San Francisco : Harper & Row,
    c1981–c1988.
    Includes bibliographical references.
    Contents: v. 1. Journey east, journey west, 1907–1937.
    ISBN 0-226-20407-3 (v. 1 : alk. paper)
    1. Eliade, Mircea, 1907–1986.   2. Religion historians—United
States—Biography.   I. Title.
[BL43.E4A315   1990]
281'.092—dc20
[B]   89-27991
                                                          CIP

This book is printed on acid-free paper.

Contents

Translator's Preface

THE PUBLICATION of this English translation of the first three parts of Mircea Eliade's autobiography is the culmination of an effort I began a decade ago. It was in June of 1971 that Professor Eliade first proposed that I help him prepare an English translation of *Amintiri: I, Mansarda*, the portion of his autobiography that had been published as a book in 1966 in Romanian (equivalent, with minor emendations, to Part I of this volume).

Eliade began writing his memoirs in the summer of 1960, as indicated in his journal excerpts published as *No Souvenirs: Journal, 1957–1969* (Harper & Row, 1977). The first journal reference to the autobiography, dated July 25, 1960, states that he is writing that day of his childhood in Cernavodă; evidently, he had begun the project a few days earlier. Eliade undertook the autobiography with an overall plan, and it is plain that he wrote it chronologically. After the initial entry there are no additional notes in the journal about the memoirs until April 5, 1963, when we learn that he has begun the second volume (Part II). By this time, Volume I was being published by a Romanian emigré house, Destin, in Madrid. Other references to the writing of the autobiography appear in entries for April 9 and 21, 1963, and August 3 and 15, 1964. By the last of these dates, Eliade had reached 1935 and the writing of *Huliganii*, which is recounted here in Chapter 13. While Volume II has not been published in Romanian, two chapters, 9 and 14, appeared in the Romanian emigré review *Ființa românească*, published in Paris, in 1964 and 1966 respectively. (They have been emended slightly for publication here in translation.)

Because virtually all documents of Eliade's life in Romania except the books published during that era were lost to him when he left the country during World War II, the writing of the autobiography was largely a process of recollection. Eliade was astonished and gratified to remember so much of his past that he had feared forever lost. He accorded much significance to this anamnesis and gave high priority to the writing of his memoirs during these years.

My personal acquaintance with Mircea Eliade began during this time, when I was a student of the history of religions at the University of Chicago. I do not believe that any of us who were his students then were aware that he was writing his memoirs. After my graduation in 1964, I continued to read extensively in those of Eliade's writings that were accessible to me, and to present papers and occasionally publish articles about him. In the winter of 1971, while on the faculty of Duke University, I conducted an undergraduate seminar on Eliade's works (in English and French) and was further stimulated to plumb the depths of my former professor's thought. The publication in 1969 of the Eliade Festschrift, *Myths and Symbols: Studies in Honor of Mircea Eliade* (edited by Joseph M. Kitagawa and Charles H. Long; The University of Chicago Press), made me aware of the existence of an important body of "Eliade materials" in the Romanian language, including fictional and autobiographical works. In 1971 I wrote to Eliade, asking if he could send me certain of these materials, although at that time I had no idea how I should be able to read them. He responded generously, as always; but then, quite unexpectedly, he offered to send me an English translation of *Amintiri: I,* a rough translation by Juliana Geram, a Romanian-American. The translation, he said, needed revision to make it read smoothly in English. Would I be willing to revise it? At the same time, he encouraged me to learn Romanian, saying, "The language is not difficult, and there are grand Romanian poets who are untranslatable." And so I began, working first with the overly literal translation of *Amintiri.*

What began as a revision became, eventually, a new translation (although I remain forever indebted to the first translator). To the original nine chapters five more were added, detailing the crucial "Indian adventure" and the little-known years (1932–1937) immediately following Eliade's return to his homeland. Altogether, then, we have here the memoirs of Mircea Eliade's first thirty years: the *illud tempus* of the scholar known to the West for what he has done since 1945, when he settled in Paris.

In making this translation, I have striven to reproduce the literary quality of Eliade's story of himself. While Romanian may not be a "difficult" language (such as, I suppose, Tibetan or Navajo might be), it presents to the translator, as does any foreign language, certain problems: there are terms and expressions that simply cannot be rendered adequately in English. Fortunately, the style of the original is basically straightforward; it possesses a cleanness and simplicity, avoiding unusual "effects" (in contrast to some of Eliade's early literary creations). I have endeavored to render this translation in English of a comparable style.

The readers of this volume will wish to express with me deep gratitude to Mircea Eliade for sharing with us so frankly these recollections of his youth, thus enabling us to know him better—not only as a scholar but also as a human being. Readers will also join me in expressing appreciation to Harper & Row for undertaking to publish this important work, and especially to John B. Shopp, editor, and his staff in San Francisco.

MAC LINSCOTT RICKETTS

PART I

The Attic

1. *Earliest Recollections*

I WAS born in Bucharest on March 9, 1907. My brother Nicolaie ("Nicu") had been born the year before, and my sister Cornelia ("Corina") came four years later. Father was a Moldavian from Tecuci. Born Ieremia, he had changed his name to Eliade. His French-Romanian dictionary, which I carried throughout lycée, was signed "Gheorghe Ieremia." He was the eldest of four children. The second son, Costica, was—like my father—an army officer; but he had attended military school and had become a staff officer and later division-general, while my father, owing perhaps to less intelligence—or more—never rose above the rank of captain. The youngest of the brothers, Pavel, after some adventures the family never discussed, became an employee of the railroad. The last time we heard from him, he was a station master. I hardly ever saw him. He was dark, like Father, but he had not lost his hair and looked more handsome.

Their only sister had died not long after marrying a school teacher. I never knew what she had looked like, where she had lived, or what she had done. Once, around 1919 or 1920, when we were living on Strada Melodiei in Bucharest, a blond and rather awkward young man clad in the green uniform of the School of Forestry showed up at our door. My father introduced him to us as Cezar Cristea, his sister's son. I took an immediate liking to him because he had read some literature, used choice words, and was a poet.

Uncle Costica lived in Bucharest in a large, luxurious apartment on Bulevardul Pache Protopopescu. He had married Hariclia, a wealthy Greek woman from Galați, and they had two sons, Dinu and Gicu. Costica was blond, shorter than my father, but more handsome and—I thought—quite elegant, even coquettish, because he always smelled discreetly of cologne. No matter how deeply I descend into my memory, I always see him looking just the same: a portly army major, twisting and curling his moustaches, speaking with a trill, punctuating his sentences with short laughs.

I never knew for certain why Father and Uncle Costica had changed their names from Ieremia to Eliade, nor why the other brother insisted on remaining Pavel Ieremia. My father said that they did it out of admiration for the writer Eliade-Rădulescu. I was quite young when I stayed for the last time with my paternal grandparents at their home in Tecuci, and it never occurred to me to ask them what they thought of the name change.

Of my grandparents and their home I still have very clear memories. Grandfather was tall, gaunt, stiff, and white-haired. Every afternoon he would take me along with him to the coffee shop to watch him play backgammon. I was allowed to eat candy and Turkish delights, and when Grandfather won a game I would get an extra piece of candy. Toward evening we would return home along Strada Mare.

I think that I was four or five years old, and was clinging to my grandfather's hand as we walked down Strada Mare one evening, when I noticed among the trousers and dresses that were passing us a girl about my own age, also holding her grandfather's hand. We gazed deeply into each other's eyes, and after she had passed I turned to look at her again and saw that she too had stopped and turned her head. For several seconds we stared at each other before our grandfathers pulled us on down the street. I didn't know what had happened to me; I felt only that something extraordinary and decisive had occurred. In fact, that very evening I discovered that it was enough for me to visualize the image from Strada Mare in order to feel myself slipping into a state of bliss I had never known, and which I was able to prolong indefinitely. During the months that followed, I would call up that image several times a day at least, especially before falling asleep. I would feel my whole body draw up into a warm shiver, then stiffen; and in the next moment everything around me would disappear. I would remain suspended, as in an unnatural sigh prolonged to infinity. For years the image of the girl on Strada Mare was a kind of secret talisman for me, because it allowed me to take refuge instantly in that fragment of incomparable time. Never have I forgotten the face of that girl: she had the largest eyes I have ever seen, black, with enormous pupils. Her face was pale brown and seemed paler still because of the black curls that fell to her shoulders. She was dressed according to the fashion for children of that time: a blouse of dark blue and a red skirt. Many years later I would still be startled whenever I chanced to see someone on the street wearing those two colors.

That year—1911 or 1912—I believe I stayed in Tecuci for a whole month. I searched for that girl on every street that I walked with my grandfather, but in vain. I never saw her again.

Grandmother was slight, pale-eyed, and kept her ashen hair pulled back tightly from her temples. I remember her better from the second vacation I spent in Tecuci, which was during the summer of 1919. I was almost twelve then, and had recently rediscovered an appetite for reading. I would sit next to the window almost all the time, engrossed in my books. Whenever Grandmother would pass, she would ask me to read aloud to her. I tried to explain that she could not understand very much by hearing only disconnected fragments, but Grandmother insisted. "That's how Costica reads to me," she said. "He reads from any book he has in front of him, even if it's a physics or chemistry textbook." I had to give in. I remember that I read her pieces from *The Travels of a Romanian Man on the Moon* (whose author I have long since forgotten) and from *Ilderim* by Queen Marie.

That year I saw both my grandparents for the last time. I never returned to Tecuci again. The grandparents from Moldavia (as I used to call them) passed away a few years later. Grandfather was almost ninety when he died.

I was born in Bucharest, but that same year my father was moved with his garrison to Rîmnicu-Sărat, and my first memories are of that town. We lived in a large house with many rooms, and there were willow trees opposite the windows in front. In the back was a courtyard and a park-like garden that seemed huge to me, overshadowed as it was by prune, peach, and quince trees. My earliest memory (I believe I was less than three) is of being in the garden with my brother and our big white dog, Picu. All three of us are rolling in the grass. Next to us on a stool is Mother, talking with a neighbor. Right after this image, another: I am on the platform at the train station, in the evening, waiting for an aunt from Bucharest. There are many people. I have a crescent roll, which I had not dared to eat because it seemed so enormous. I hold it in my hand, contemplating it, displaying it, congratulating myself for having it. When the train arrives at the station our group begins to move, and I am left alone for a second. Out of nowhere there emerges a little boy of about five or six who snatches away my roll! He watches me for a second with a mischievous smile, then thrusts the roll into his mouth and disappears. I am so startled that I can neither speak nor move. That event revealed to me the terrible power of skill and daring.

Other memories from the age of three or four include the carriage rides to the forest and to the vineyards around the Rîmnic. When the carriage would stop in the middle of the road under the heavily laden trees, I would climb up on the box and gather the silvery-gray prunes. Once, in the forest, creeping on all fours through the grass, I unexpectedly found myself in front of a glittering blue-green lizard. Both of us were dumbfounded, and we just stared at each other. I was not afraid and yet my heart was throbbing. I was overwhelmed by the joy of having encountered, for the first time, a creature of such strange beauty.

But I remember especially a summer afternoon when the whole household was sleeping. I left the room my brother and I shared, creeping so as not to make any noise, and headed toward the drawing room. I hardly knew how it looked, for we were not allowed to go in except on special occasions or when we had guests. Besides, I believe that the rest of the time the door was locked. But this time I found it open and entered, still crawling. The next moment I was transfixed with emotion. It was as if I had entered a fairy-tale palace. The roller blinds and the heavy curtains of green velvet were drawn. The room was pervaded by an eerie iridescent light. It was as though I were suddenly enclosed within a huge grape. I don't know how long I stayed there on the carpet, breathing heavily. When I came to my senses, I crept carefully across the floor, detouring around the furniture, looking greedily at the little tables and shelves on which all kinds of statuettes had been carefully placed along with cowry shells, little crystal vials, and small silver boxes. I gazed into the large venetian mirrors in whose deep and clear waters I found myself looking very different—more grown-up, more handsome, as if ennobled by that light from another world.

I never told anyone about this discovery. Actually, I think I should not have known what to tell. Had I been able to use adult vocabulary, I might have said that I had discovered a mystery. As was true also of the image of the little girl from Strada Mare, I could later evoke at will that green fairyland. When I did so I would remain motionless, almost not daring to breathe, and I would rediscover that beatitude all over again; I would relive with the same intensity the moment when I had stumbled into that paradise of incomparable light. I practiced for many years this exercise of recapturing the epiphanic moment, and I would always find again the same plenitude. I would slip into it as into a fragment of time devoid of duration—without beginning and without end. During my last years of lycée, when I struggled with prolonged attacks of melancholy, I still succeeded at times in returning to the golden green light of that afternoon in Rîmnicu-Sărat. But even though the beatitude was the same, it was now impossible to bear because it aggravated my sadness too much; by this time I knew the world to which the drawing room belonged—with the green velvet curtain, the carpet on which I had crept on hands and knees, and the matchless light—was a world forever lost.

*   *   *

In 1912, when I was five, Father was moved with his garrison to Cernavodă. We stayed there two years. In my memory, that time spent there between the Danube and the brick-colored calcinated hills, where wild roses and tiny flowers with pale dry petals grew, is always lighted with sunshine. When we arrived, we were housed for a few months in one of the regimental barracks. This was the only place where there were other trees than willows. I remember prowling among the pines and the maritime fir trees, and I remember the lawns with blue flowers. As I recall it was only there, in the regimental park, that there was really any shade. The rest of Cernavodă was always bathed in sunshine.

Soon we moved into a little house on the hillside. We had a garden with archways and grape arbors. One day the boxes of furniture from Rîmnicu-Sărat began to arrive, and I studied with fascination how my father, with the help of the orderly, opened each one.

He would lift up the cover with great care, touch the straw hesitantly, and reach for the mysterious objects enveloped in newspapers. He would remove each one slowly while we all held our breath till we saw if it had arrived intact. One by one there appeared glasses of all colors, plates, cups, teapots. Periodically, my father would frown and swear at length in a whisper, biting his moustache, then place the broken object in a nearby box as if he did not have the heart to throw it away.

That autumn I entered kindergarten. I was proud when I put on the gray uniform, and I went to school alone. I had already learned the alphabet, but still I did not know what its use might be. Neither did it seem very interesting when I could syllabize *o-u, ou; bo-u, bou,* nor even when I could read "Our country is called Romania," without pronouncing it syllable by syllable. But once I stumbled upon my brother's *Primary Reader,* and after the first page I could not put it down. I was fascinated, as if having found a new game. For with each line I read I discovered unknown and unexpected things. I learned the names of districts, rivers, and towns, and many, many other things that overwhelmed me with their vastness and mystery. But after a week, when I had finished Nicu's book, I suddenly discovered that things were not as simple as I had expected—for there was no other book available for me to take up next. My father had about one or two hundred books beautifully bound in leather, but they were locked in a case with glass windows. I could read only the titles, and even those I did not always understand. There were some volumes entitled "Novel," and my parents had a long discussion about whether or not they should explain the meaning of this word to me. For many years, my father forbade me to read novels. For him, the novel was somehow an immoral book, since it involved either adultery or adventures in a world one could only talk about in whispers. He did not even allow me to read short stories. The only books he permitted me were those bearing the title or subtitle "tales."

I had been allowed to read *Fairy-tales* by Ispirescu, and the tales and childhood memories of Creangă, when an episode occurred that cast gloom over my entire childhood. I had entered the first grade, and my father had invited the teacher to consult him about the books I could read. We were all three standing in front of the bookcase. The teacher seemed enthusiastic about the books, and especially about their leather bindings. Leafing through a volume by N. Iorga—I can still see it, it was *Pe drumuri departate* (On Distant Roads)—he said, pointing at me: "But don't let him read too much or he'll tire his eyes. He doesn't have very good sight. I put him in the front desk, and he still doesn't always see what I'm writing on the blackboard." "I can see if I squint my eyes!" I interrupted. "That means you have weak eyes and you'll be nearsighted," the teacher replied.

This discovery was a real catastrophe. Father decided that I must not strain my eyes reading books other than school texts, so I was no longer allowed to read during my leisure time. The source of my extracurricular readings had dried up anyway: my father closed the glass-windowed bookcase and no longer allowed me to browse through those beautifully bound volumes. Later, I realized that those years that followed were truly wasted. My thirst for reading had to be quenched at random. I read whatever fell to hand: serial novels, mystery stories, the *Psalm Book*, *The Key to Dreams*. I read in secret, far back in the garden, in the attic, or in the basement (as I also did in Bucharest, after 1914). With the passage of time, this random reading began to bore me. One day I discovered that street games could be just as exciting as adventure stories, and I began spending all my free time roaming the streets and vacant lots of Bucharest. The Townhall Tract, the Old Market, the hill of the Metropolitan Cathedral, the Cemetery of Oatu—I knew them all, and I had friends among all the ruffians and urchins from every lower-class neighborhood in town. But this was to happen later, after 1916, when my father had encamped with his regiment in Moldavia.

I remember the hills around Cernavodă. Father sometimes took us with him on hikes there. We climbed the parched, dusty paths, winding through thistles and wormwood, until we reached the top. From there the Danube could be seen in the distance, lying amidst thickets of willows and bluish haze. My father was not a very articulate person. While he could be very tedious, boring us with his lengthy "moralizing" (as he liked to call it), he became speechless whenever we found ourselves in new and unfamiliar situations outside the context of family relationships. We would sit on a flat rock and Father would remove his cap, wipe his forehead with a handkerchief, and begin to twist his moustaches. When we could tell by his smile that he was content, we would ask him all sorts of questions. Sometimes we asked him things we knew he was expecting from his sons. We knew he considered us intelligent and gifted with all sorts of talents. (He believed, for instance, that we both were musicians—near prodigies with great futures.) He was happy when our questions seemed to verify once more his faith in our intelligence. Nevertheless he answered succinctly, almost monosyllabically, and sometimes rather awkwardly.

We would return by another path, so that we would descend close to the bridge over the Danube. Sometimes we had the good fortune to see a freight train passing slowly by, like a huge caterpillar. Once when we were coming down from the hills, a Tartar girl of about our own age suddenly stepped out from a ravine, and without a word handed my father a bunch of blue flowers. The three of us stared at her in astonishment. This was the first time we boys had ever seen a Tartar girl at close range. Her hair and nails were dyed red, and she was wearing Turkish trousers. Father managed to smile, stammered out a word of thanks, patted her on the shoulder, stroked her hair once, and finally, not knowing how else to show his gratitude, doffed his cap several times, saluting her.

We climbed these hills often in the spring with the whole school. I remember an excursion we took around the end of March. It was unusually warm. When we reached the top of the hill I was thirsty, and since no one had brought any water, I ate some old snow that still remained in the gullies and between the cliffs. I was sick afterwards for about two weeks.

Whenever I came home from school I was thirsty. I always ran home, usually getting into a scuffle or two along the way, so I was perspiring and dirty when I reached the house. Before anyone saw me, I would gulp down several cups of water, fresh from the pump. I lost the liberty to do this when my parents decided to hire a French-speaking governess who would help us learn the language. One day my father asked for the carriage and went to the train station. He came back with a very dark-complexioned woman who had a big black mole on her face and smelled strongly of tobacco. She spoke *Romanian* perfectly well, and she was constantly rolling cigarettes over a box of golden tobacco. I felt even that evening that my parents were disappointed with her. She was too old, smoked too much, and was far from fluent in French. She stayed only a few weeks. I think that I unwittingly created the pretext on which she was dismissed. The governess had decided that I had no right to drink water when I came home from school, on the grounds that I was perspiring. I was not allowed to go near the pump any more, nor to enter the kitchen or the dining room until dinner time. I had to stay in my room, which my brother and I shared with the governess. I suffered horribly from thirst. One day, taking advantage of the fact that I was left alone in the room, I began to search. In the closet I stumbled over a bottle labeled "boric acid." I knew that this solution was used as a disinfectant, but I was too thirsty to care. I drank almost half the bottle. I did not feel sick until later, and then I told my mother what I had done. Lying in bed and pretending to be more ill than I really was, I heard, as a consolation, the sharp, bitter dialogue between Mother and the governess.

In Cernavodă, as in Rîmnicu-Sărat, we had a carriage with horses. Although my father was an infantry officer, he had a great weakness for horses. He seldom told us about his childhood and adolescence in Tecuci, but when he did he never forgot to speak about the horses he rode without a saddle, and about the lizards that he would hide in his shirt and bring home. Quite possibly, the passion that I had from the time I was a small child for all kinds of animals was inherited from him. And it is strange that the only serious accident he had was caused by his favorite horse. During the campaign of 1913 he was slightly wounded in the shoulder, but the horse, frightened, jerked abruptly and threw him down. For several months my father carried his arm in a cast as a result.

My most dramatic childhood memory is connected with our horse-drawn carriage. Mother was coming from Bucharest, and we had gone to the train station to meet her. We were all returning in the carriage, laden with suitcases and packages. The road to our house passed in front of a bridge. It was a rugged road, with dust a foot deep, and at one point it sloped quite sharply downward. I do not know now why the horses became frightened, but they started to run just where the road began to descend. In vain the driver and my father tried to stop them by pulling on the reins. The carriage seemed to have gone crazy. It raced downhill creaking and groaning, leaning first on two wheels, then on the other two, bouncing and bumping into the horses, making them go even faster. Mother started to yell, and not knowing what to do, she held us with one hand and began throwing out the packages with the other. This gesture seemed so insane to me that I caught her knees and begged her not to throw them away—because I suspected there were goodies and gifts hidden in them. Nicu was hanging onto Mother's arm, too scared to cry. Mother caught me with her other arm and pulled me to herself. Then I saw that the carriage was heading directly toward the ravine that plunges down into the Danube beside the bridge. For years I was haunted by those long moments when we were expecting to reach the brink of the precipice and fall in. I was frightened, but at the same time I was fascinated by the ravine and could not believe that all would end there. Later, when we were remembering and commenting on that event, Mother told me that, without my knowing it, I had believed in a miracle and was waiting for it to happen.

The guard at the bridge understood that it was absolutely impossible to stop the horses from inside the carriage, and so he ran in front of them. He lifted his gun in the air with both arms and began shouting. Two more soldiers from the bridge leaped to help. Together, they managed to stop the carriage a few yards from the ravine. My father jumped down and embraced them. The horses were trembling and jerking their heads from one side to the other, as if trying to drive away a ghost.

I believe this was our last ride in the carriage. We spent that summer in Tekirghiol, near the coast; in the autumn of 1914, shortly after the war broke out, Father was moved to Bucharest.

From what I could understand later, my father decided that we must spend the summer in Tekirghiol taking mud baths, after he had chanced to encounter some scrofulous children. The sight depressed him terribly. He immediately thought of his own children, especially since the doctor of the regiment told him we were "lymphatic." To prevent the possibility of scrofula, he took us to Tekirghiol. I was five years old when, as we were approaching the train station at Constanţa, I had my first sight of the sea. I was still reeling from this discovery when my father made us board the bus for Tekirghiol. Very soon we entered a field of poppies and bottle-flowers, and the air began to smell like dried flowers, dust, and salt. Surprised, I inhaled deeply of this exotic atmosphere. Then the smell of the marsh began to strike us—a powerful, heavy odor of sulfur and tar, but just as exhilarating. After about an hour, the bus stopped at Vidrighin's Inn, at the entrance to Tekirghiol. In the salt marsh nearby, the water was low and oily, exposing the mud flats. A carriage passed close by us, raising a cloud of dust through which the bus made its way with difficulty. All the passengers pressed handkerchiefs to their faces. In such fashion we arrived at Tekirghiol.

At that time, in 1912, Tekirghiol was still a village, having only a few notable buildings: one modern hotel, several inns, the establishment for hot mud baths, the somber buildings of the summer vacationers, and four or five villas. Up on the hill, out of sight from the highway, the mud huts of the Tartars were situated. That summer, my father had rented for two months a spacious room in a villa. The whole family took hot mud baths every morning. We would then return quickly to the villa and go back to bed, to perspire. In the afternoon we had to sleep again, or at least to rest for an hour. The miraculous quality of the baths, my father said, lay in the fact that they tired a person down to his marrow, forcing him to rest; afterwards, he would be stronger and healthier.

My father was so taken by this first experience that he decided on the spot that we must have our own villa, where we could spend the whole summer. In that same year he found and bought a lot, up on the hill, and when we returned the next summer, the beginning of a villa was waiting for us: two rooms with a veranda, and a kitchen in the backyard. The well was not yet finished, and for a few weeks we were forced to carry water from a neighbor's place. The ground contained limestone and it had to be blasted with dynamite; we reached water only after digging more than fifteen meters. Only then did Mother realize that Father had been much too hasty when he bought a lot situated so far uphill. The well cost him almost as much as a room. It is true that we had the coldest water in the village, but it was so full of sediment that we had to let it stand awhile before we could drink it. The slope was so steep that no carriage could get up it. It was a quarter of an hour's climb on foot from the bus stop—quite a walk when carrying luggage, packages, and boxes! On dogdays, or coming back from the mud baths, the ascent was torture. If we forgot to buy something from the market below on the highway, we had half an hour's wait until one of us could go down and come trotting back again.

But my father's enterprising spirit did not stop here. He calculated that if he built another suite of rooms, he could rent them during the summer. And after he had recovered the cost of building them, from the extra money he could accumulate a dowry for our sister Cornelia, who had been born a few years before. The next year "Villa Cornelia" had come into being, with six rooms. I do not know when or how they were furnished, but a short while after we came, the tenants began to arrive too. In vain Mother tried to put up a resistance, but my father had big plans: vegetable gardens, a flower nursery, an orchard with fruit trees. During the course of the year, he came whenever he could get away from Cernavodă or from Bucharest to plant trees and to enlarge the garden. He had bought another lot lying to the back and one side of the villa, on which he planned to build kitchens and servants' rooms (believing that in this way he would attract rich tenants).

This enthusiasm was cut short by Romania's entrance into World War I. For two years we heard nothing about "Villa Cornelia." When we went to Tekirghiol again, in the summer of 1919, we found only the walls. One of the neighbors said the villa had been occupied and then destroyed by the Bulgarian troops. But part of the furniture we later found scattered among the houses of the village.

From those first summer vacations in Tekirghiol, I still have the memory of the late sunsets, which I would await sitting up on the hillside among euphorbias and cockles. The salt marsh could be seen as far as Eforia and Tuzla, and beyond it, like a giant dam supporting the sky, rose the Black Sea. Not very far away on the right were the truck gardens, from which we bought watermelons and cantaloupes. On the other side, out of sight, the Tartar mud huts were situated. At the fall of evening you could hear their dogs, and a sour smoke of burnt dung mixed with straw came from that direction. For many years that oppressive Turkish smoke always embodied the presence of Dobruja for me—a prologue to *The Thousand and One Nights.*

When we arrived in Bucharest in the beginning of the autumn of 1914, the house on Strada Melodiei was still being repaired. For a few weeks we stayed with my grandparents at the end of Bulevardul Pache Protopopescu. The fabulous homes of that neighborhood were already familiar to me from early childhood. Memories of an enormous courtyard surrounded by stables and granaries, and of an endless orchard have remained with me. The orchard seemed truly endless; I ventured to its limits only after I was eight years old. I went there with Nicu and the youngest of my mother's sisters, Viorica, who was just a few years older than we. There, at the end of the orchard, we came upon some mounds on which weeds were growing, a few old hen houses, piles of crumbling forgotten bricks, and a wooden fence ready to collapse, supported here and there by thick props stuck into the ground. When we arrived, all three of us climbed one of the mounds and looked over the fence. We could see nothing but apricots, prunes, and quinces—the same kinds of trees that were in my grandparents' orchard. But we could hear no chickens or dogs, only the buzzing of bees and all kinds of strange little noises.

"Once this was ours also," said Viorica. Fifty years before, all that land had belonged to my great-grandfather. Bulevardul Pache Protopopescu had not yet been built, and there was nothing but orchards and vegetable gardens. The stockyard was close by. The old house in front had once been an inn. Still preserved in the large room were parts of the counters and shelves where crockery, bottles, and glasses stood. In a corner of the room, behind the counter, was the stairway to the cellar. My grandfather still went down there before supper each night to fetch fresh wine from one of the barrels.

Later, I found out from stories my maternal uncles told me that after my great-grandfather gave up keeping the inn, he had contented himself for ten years operating it as a tavern. Uncle Mitache still remembered the days when he would come home from primary school and find the tavern full, and his father (my grandfather) would make him recite poetry to amuse the horse dealers. Then, a few years after my great-grandfather's death, my grandparents gave up the tavern too. The family had grown considerably and they had to build extra rooms. My grandparents had fourteen children, but three died in infancy. Their eldest daughter, Didina, had been married for several years when my grandmother bore her last two children, Viorica and Traian. When we came to live on Bulevardul Pache Protopopescu, a house had just been built in the back of the former inn as a residence for three of my uncles.

I later learned a part of my great-grandfather's story. His father had come to Bucharest as a child, had worked for a few years as a groom at the stables, had become a carriage driver, then a horse dealer, and finally he had bought quite a number of acres of garden land and had built his inn. No one knew exactly where my great-grandfather had come from. From Dunărea, said Uncle Mitache. From the Olt, held one of the aunts, and she told me even the name of the village: Arvireşti. As proof, she reminded me that my mother's name was Ioana Arvira. At any rate, I liked knowing that I was descended from a family of Moldavian yeomen and an innkeeper from Dunărea or the Olt. The father of my grandfather from Tecuci had been a yeoman, and I was proud of the fact that I was only three generations removed from peasants—that, although born and bred in a city, I was still so close to the "soul of the country."

When, as an adolescent, I experienced moods of deep melancholy, I would tell myself that it was part of my Moldavian heritage. Sometimes I would rebel against this propensity for reverie and contemplation, for returning into the past and letting myself be overwhelmed by memories. I would rebel against my Moldavian blood and would call upon the deposits of energy bequeathed to me by my mother's family: the spirit of adventure, the capacity for work, and the stubbornness and the almost vulgar vitality of the horse breeders from Dunărea.

In one of these revolts against melancholy I wrote and published in *Cuvântul* in 1927, when I was a university student, a piece called "Impotriva Moldovei" (Against Moldavia), which aroused a lengthy polemic. Of course, I oversimplified things too much. But I continue to believe that these two hereditary dispositions have constantly fought each other within the depths of my being, thus helping me to grow and teaching me not to identify myself with either of them, ultimately forcing me to find a different kind of equilibrium by starting from the opposite disposition and using the opposite means.

I do not know how my parents met. When they were married, my father had been an eligible bachelor for some time; he was fifteen years older than my mother. In the wedding picture taken about 1904, my father did not look his thirty-five years, although he was already bald. Swarthy, thin, with black handlebar moustaches, heavy eyebrows, and steely eyes, my father seemed never to grow old. He had a strong constitution. At seventy he would walk from one end of Bucharest to the other and could not be still for a moment; he was constantly finding things to do in the house, the cellar, or the yard. He was frugal by nature, but at parties he ate and drank as much as five. After he retired and decided to occupy himself seriously with our education, he lacked the energy for it—although he seemed to think he had to teach us constantly how to behave, and especially to "moralize" to us. During my last years in the lycée, at almost every meal he gave us a long sermon, which was constantly interrupted by my mother's exasperated interjections and interpretations.

When we finally settled in Bucharest, my mother was still very young; she had not reached the age of thirty. At that time she was quite beautiful and elegant, but a few years later—during the German occupation and just after the war, when we became poor—my mother gradually forsook elegance and coquetry. At thirty-five she decided she had ceased to be young, that she had growing children for whose welfare alone she should live. She no longer wanted to buy anything for herself, and she took care of the house by herself for about ten years, giving up even the servant girl from the country in order to be able to keep her children in the lycée and in the university. On the other hand, she always gave me as much money as I wanted whenever I asked to buy books. I guessed later that through me she was satisfying, in a way, her own thirst for reading, which she had had in her youth. She had always liked to read, but during the war, when my father was with his regiment in Moldavia and she was left alone with us, her leisure time for reading grew less each day. She nevertheless kept a few books by her bedside, and she never went to sleep without opening the *Psalm Book*, *Anna Karenina*, or Eminescu's *Poems*.

Throughout my childhood and adolescence, my mother's family was for me an inexhaustible universe, full of secrets and rich in surprises. There were, first of all, the houses on Bulevardul Pache Protopopescu. Those rooms of different styles and centuries, all the way from the large room, which had been the inn's dining hall and later a tavern—a dark, smoked room with a low ceiling and wood-paneled walls, smelling of wine, kerosene, and sheepskin (my grandfather still wore a sheepskin coat and fur hat)—to the new rooms in the back, built with windows looking eastward, bathed in sunlight, with ugly "modern" furniture. There were also the three rooms of my aunts, connected to the old dining hall by a narrow, dark corridor. During that autumn of 1914 my five aunts, ranging in age from ten to twenty, slept there. A new world began at their doors. It was a microcosm of pillows and down, of whole baskets of silk veils and ribbons, illustrated magazines, colored postcards, and all kinds of books, from the youngest girl's classical textbooks to the novels by Radulescu-Niger, the *Decameron*, and the serial novels of the eldest, who were hoping soon to be married. (But soon the war broke out, their brothers encamped in Moldavia, and the eldest sister, Marioara, was not married until 1919.)

I was especially fond of the large old cellar. It was filled with wine barrels, casks of lard or pickles, buckets, and countless other objects whose identity I tried to guess by the dim light of the candle when my grandfather took me with him to fetch some wine. In the courtyard were abandoned storehouses, the granary, and the remains of the stables, which had become cart-houses. In a corner I had discovered a cabriolet, around which I invented all sorts of games. But by the time we came to live there the horses had been sold, and a few years later, during the war, the cabriolet also disappeared.

My mother's brothers Mitache, Petrică, and Nae ran a foundry on Calea Moşilor, near the Church of St. Gheorghe. It was an enormous building with entrances on two streets. Every time I went there I saw truckdrivers loading or unloading sheet metal, bars of iron, or kegs of nails. Uncle Mitache was then about thirty years old. He was blond, not too tall, and had a reddish moustache. He was to gain weight later, since he liked choice foods, good wines, and endless feasts with friends and fiddlers. He got along well with my mother, and after he returned from Moldavia in 1918 he lived with us on Strada Melodiei for about twelve years, until he married. But his marriage did not last long, and around 1935 Uncle Mitache returned to live in the little house where my parents had found refuge.

To this uncle I owe more than I could ever repay. Throughout my years in the lycée he was my confidant and patron, and when I left for India he gave me travel money. Until around 1916, he was a rich man. The war (and later the iron trust) impoverished him gradually. His destiny was, indeed, that of our whole family. When my father returned from Moldavia and left the army, he realized that we would not be able to keep three children in school on a retired captain's pension. Fortunately, we had our house on Strada Melodiei. Very soon we rented it out, and all five of us moved into the two little rooms in the attic. This happened in 1919, when I was twelve years old. Actually, we were used to it already, since my mother and the three of us children had lived there ever since Bucharest had been occupied by the Austro-German troops and the whole house had been requisitioned. That attic had a decisive importance in my life. It is hard for me to imagine the person that I became later and am today without those two low-ceilinged rooms, with their whitewashed walls and tiny windows—one of them round like a porthole—and an incredible stove: its mouth in one room and its body in the other. It was the great fortune of my youth that I was able to live there for twelve years, and especially that I could live the last five or six years there alone.

2. The War at Age Nine

THE HOUSE on Strada Melodiei, demolished about 1935, stood on a plot that fronted on three streets. The main entrance was through a paved courtyard; on the right was the garden, on the left the new wing of the house. To enter the latter, one climbed several stone steps protected by a glass awning that resembled a transparent fan. But the only people who used that entrance were the officers we billeted during the Austro-German occupation and (after the war) the tenants. The family and our friends entered by a more modest set of steps that led into a long hallway. Along this corridor on the left were the bathroom, the kitchen, a little room that later became my parents' bedroom, and the dining room. This last was a part of the new wing, which included an enormous parlor, a guest room, and two large bedrooms. On the right of the corridor was a door leading to a separate apartment consisting of a large square room and a bath. Here Uncle Mitache lived.

The two wings of the house formed a right angle, and between the two sides of that angle lay the garden, which was an unusually large one for that neighborhood. It was surrounded by a low cement wall, topped by an iron fence of spear-like rods. Lilac bushes, as tall and dense as trees, created a bower in the farthest corner of the garden. Protected, as behind a curtain, were a bench, iron chairs, and a table.

When we moved into this house on Strada Melodiei, the remodeling was not yet finished. In the rooms of the new wing the walls were being painted, and in the dining room the parquetry was being changed. When I would come home from school, there were always new things for me to discover: another room freshly painted, other pieces of furniture unloaded, empty trunks and boxes ready to be carried down to the basement. At this house there were two cellars. One of them was located under the new wing. It was deep, had a dirt floor, and was divided into several rooms. In the first, firewood, charcoal, barrels of wine, and pickles were kept. But in the back there was one more room, in which candles flickered briefly and died out, a cellar full of mysteries and fears, which I learned to know in detail only many years later.

The other cellar had been divided in two, the larger part having been made into rooms. In the back was a room with a cement floor, which served as washroom, and in which I later set up my laboratory. It had a large zinc bathtub with only cold water piped to it. During my last years in the lycée, on summer afternoons, when the attic became so hot that I could not endure it even entirely naked, I sometimes went down there and immersed myself for a few moments in a tub of freezing water. It was like having thrown myself into a lake in a mountain cave.

I remember only vaguely the room in which I slept for almost two years, before we moved to the attic. It was one of the large, well-lit rooms, later occupied by an officer of the Austrian Army. I remember nothing but the smell of fresh paint, and the sunlight that awakened us in the morning. .

I had entered the second grade at the primary school on Strada Mântuleasa. It was a large, sturdy building flanked by chestnut trees, with a wide courtyard in the back where we played during recesses. The principal had a hunchbacked son, a medical student, whom I often met on my way home. He was the first to notice that I was rather nearsighted and he tried to teach me how to read without tiring my eyes. I was now reading anything that fell into my hands, because Father's glass-windowed bookcase was forbidden to me. But slowly, almost unconsciously, my passion for reading began to abate, because I had many other things to interest me.

The horse-drawn tram passed in front of our house and made a turn at the corner. Nicu and I and a few friends of our age would wait quietly in front of the gate, pretending to be talking. But once the car turned the corner, we would run after it and catch hold of it, hiding so that the conductor wouldn't see us. We were always careful to be bareheaded, lest the conductor confiscate our school caps. For years this game fascinated me. I became a great expert, and later I began to learn how to climb onto even the electric tram while it was in motion. I would ride hanging on, while the car made a circuit of several blocks. Sometimes the conductor would catch me and pull my ears, but I accepted this risk proudly. Only once was I made to feel guilty and humiliated: when Mother came home one day, sad and upset, saying: "There were two gentlemen sitting next to me on the tram-car today, and when they saw you two boys one of them said, 'There go the Captain's brats!' I was very ashamed," she added, and sighed.

But this was to happen later, after my father had gone away with his regiment into Moldavia. I remember how upset I was. I would have preferred any other punishment. But in a few days the episode was forgotten—and I was back at my favorite sport.

During the two years my father stayed with us in Bucharest, he had enough time to discover that in addition to my talent as a pianist—which he considered exceptional—I also had a unique voice. He was continually bringing me love songs *(doine)* and operatic arias, which I learned to sing while accompanying myself at the piano. He was so enthused over my soprano voice that he decided I must begin to take voice lessons. I don't know what teacher he went to see, but he came home quite depressed. The maestro had advised him to wait until my voice changed, and to return with me after I was sixteen or seventeen.

In those years my father liked to believe (and sometimes I too believed it) that I should someday become a great concert pianist. He insisted that I practice at least an hour or two every day, imagining that it is possible to develop into a virtuoso that easily. As a matter of fact, my talent was rather modest.

As I later learned, I had a perfect ear (I could detect a wrong note even in the fifty-piece band of the Lycée Spiru-Haret), and I had sensitivity and imagination enough, but I totally lacked the ability to memorize. I would repeat a simple melody ten or fifteen times, and still I could not memorize it without error. Perhaps even more serious was the fact that I could never develop the technique of a true pianist. I did not have enough patience, and I spent as little time as possible on scales and exercises. As soon as I was able to play Beethoven's sonatas, I began to sight-read Rachmaninoff's concertos, and then I fell into the habit of spending hours at the piano improvising variations on some Rachmaninoff melody.

By the time I was playing Rachmaninoff concertos from beginning to end, I knew that I would never become a good pianist; but I loved music too much to give up those several hours at the keyboard each day. When I was attending Spiru-Haret I "performed" at every school function, but at length my father decided that Nicu and I should give a concert of our own. I believe this concert was my father's last act of authority. It was after his return from Moldavia. I had a rather generous piano teacher who let himself be persuaded by my father's enthusiasm and agreed to help me prepare for a public concert. Father rented a hall, printed announcements, and took charge personally of ticket distribution. I believe that the majority of the tickets were bought by relatives, friends, and former associates of his from the army. However, on the afternoon of the concert, the hall was half empty. In the first part of the concert, Nicu and I presented several pieces, and then I played the *Pathétique*. I played it not nearly as well as I usually did at home, and this discouraged me. The second part was really terrible, and I was ashamed. Yet there were a few reviews of the concert that mentioned a promising talent!

Later, while a student at the university, I felt that the time I had devoted to the piano had been hours lost from study. At that time I was forcing myself to work at a feverish pace, and I did not know how to find more time, even though I slept only a few hours a night. On the other hand, I felt I was spreading myself too thin and I was afraid that this frenzied dispersion might be fatal to me. It was then that I decided to abandon the piano. At first, it was a hard thing to do. I would come down from the attic, go to the living room, and linger beside the instrument. Sometimes I would open it and play a few lieder. In time, however, I began to get used to not playing, especially since rather soon after that I went to Italy for three months. But about 1929 or 1930, when I was in Calcutta, I could bear it no longer. At Mrs. Perris's boarding house on Ripon Street there was a piano, and as soon as I saw it I sat down at it for several hours, playing everything I could remember and whatever I could improvise after three or four years of almost total interruption. After that I wrote home to have scores of my favorite pieces sent to me. That was the last throbbing of my vocation as a pianist.

,   ,   ,

I liked attending the Mântuleasa School. I studied there things I already knew—because, a week after school started, I had already finished reading the textbook. But in the fall of 1916 things turned out differently. I was in the fourth grade, and before school opened Romania entered the war. Like everyone else, I marked with little tricolored flag pins on a map the advance of Romanian troops into Transylvania. My uncles had been mobilized, but (with the exception of the youngest) they had all remained in Bucharest. Then we found out about the disaster at Turtucaia. At that time, a friend from Cernavodă was living with us; she had just lost her husband, a retired colonel. Her son, recently made second lieutenant, was at the garrison in Turtucaia. One day the news came that he was dead. I no longer remember what her first reaction was. She stayed with us for a few more weeks, then she moved to the other side of Bucharest. But she often came to see us and she continued talking about her son, the second lieutenant: "Now he would have been twenty-four. Now he would have been on leave. Now he would have found a girl, he would have been engaged. Now he would have been promoted to the rank of lieutenant. . . ."

At night, we heard the sergeant shouting on the street: "Turn off the light!" And then, one night, the bells from the Metropolitan Cathedral started to ring and soon we heard antiaircraft fire. The zeppelin was coming. It kept coming that way every night. It would float lazily above the city, drop a few bombs, then disappear in the direction of the Danube. My father and uncle stayed in the garden, to watch for it to be shot down by antiaircraft guns. One night they called us boys to see the zeppelin. As the search lights caught and followed it on its lazy course in the sky, it looked like a giant cigar. One day the rumor came that it had been hit by a shell and had fallen in flames on the Bulgarian bank of the Danube.

When the German planes came, Mother would make us go down to the cellar. The signal was given by the bells from the Metropolitan Cathedral, and afterwards bells resounded from the other churches too, just as on Easter night. Usually the planes came late in the morning, shortly before noon. We would notice them, like silvery pigeons, glittering in the bright September sun, followed by the little white clouds of the exploding shells. A few batteries were set up on the Townhall Tract, about one kilometer from our house. We would hear the short, muffled poppings of the antiaircraft guns, and sometimes we heard shell fragments fall on houses and the pavement.

Once I had gone to buy something from a shop on Bulevardul Brătianu. When the alarm sounded I quickly started home, with the full basket under my arm. But soon the shell fragments began to fall, and a sergeant whistled at me. I went into an archway. A few other passersby were sheltered there. From time to time, someone dared to step out on the sidewalk, look up at the sky, and tell us what was going on. Suddenly I felt an explosion, entirely different from all the others, as if the bomb had fallen very close by. When I returned home half an hour later, I saw that it had landed on the porch of a house on our street. A few people were wounded, and one man killed. A piece of shrapnel had cut off his head. I went the next day with my mother to see him. He was laid out on a table, among flowers, his head clumsily attached to the body, and bandaged.

I kept hearing about defeats, but I had no doubts about the final victory of the Romanian troops. Like everyone who had gone through primary school, I believed that our army was invincible. The defeats, if they were indeed real, were due exclusively to the errors of the generals.

My father would come home more and more depressed. When I found out that Uncle Costica had left the capital, I understood that the situation had worsened considerably. Because he was assigned to be Colonel Sideri's driver, Uncle Mitache believed that he had reliable information. He encouraged us, assuring us that a great battle was in preparation. If we won it, the capital would be saved. My father told us that there would be fighting even near Bucharest, but that it would be necessary to resist, at the very worst, only a few days, before we should drive off the attackers.

We boys were ready for the siege. In fact, for several weeks I had had the feeling that I was participating in the war. Around the middle of September we had been called to school. We had been told to bring old newspapers, needles, and white thread. A young man asked us if we could sew, and then he explained to us what it was about. Soon the winter will come, he told us, and our soldiers need warm clothing. It has been proven that paper keeps away the cold. We must make paper shirts, he said, and he explained to us how to cut them and how to sew them. At first, for a few days, he was the only one who cut them. He took several newspapers, placed them carefully in a stack, then cut out a semicircle at the top. Next we sewed the margins together (there were sometimes five or six sheets, and it was difficult: we pricked ourselves, we tore the paper). Two such sides were then sewn together, so that it constituted a sort of corselet.

I often saw Boy Scouts wearing on their arms a white band with a red cross, a sign that they were trained to give first aid. I wished that I were a few years older so I too could be used in a campaign hospital. The temptation was too great, and in the end I could no longer resist it. I found somewhere a piece of red cloth, cut out a cross, and sewed it on a white band. Sometimes I put it on my arm and slipped stealthily out into the street. It seemed to me that the passersby looked at me and were impressed.

Thus I was standing once at our gate, when a car stopped in front of me. Uncle Mitache jumped out quickly, without having seen me, and ran into the courtyard. Later, I heard myself being called. I realized that Mother had been crying, but I pretended not to notice anything. My uncle kissed all of us, then took his suitcase and went to the car. "It is a great disaster!" he said to us as the car was leaving.

My father left the next day, also in haste. I had hoped until the last moment that he would take us with him to Moldavia, as it had been decided when the news first started spreading in Bucharest concerning the atrocities of the Bulgarians. I also knew that the Boy Scouts were ready to retreat with the troops, and I suffered deeply for not yet being ten years old (I had heard that you could not become a Boy Scout before you had reached the age of ten). I no longer remember what happened at my father's farewell. I was trying to feel sad, crushed. But in fact I was proud of him, of his campaign uniform, of the revolver he wore at his belt. The orderly had driven the army truck into the courtyard and was waiting beside it. In front of the gate, my father did not forget to give us more advice, to tell us how to behave.

All that night we heard explosions. In several places the sky had reddened and begun to flicker. The forts and the arsenal had been blown up, as we found out the next day. It was a long, weary night, one which it seemed would never pass. But when morning came, everything appeared just as before. In school the classroom was half empty, and after about an hour of waiting, the principal came and told us to go home. He also told us that Bucharest had capitulated and that quite possibly the entrance of the enemy troops would take place the next day.

That afternoon a sergeant brought us the proclamation of the major, which said—among other things—that all arms had to be deposited at the commissariat in the next twenty-four hours, and that certain houses would be requisitioned for the billeting of the Austro-German troops. We talked at great length—Mother, we children, and Lina (one of Mother's sisters, who had come to live with us)—wondering what to do with the hunting rifle and the old pistols we had. We decided to keep the rifle and to throw away the pistols. Late that night, with fear and elation, we dropped them into the mouth of a sewer.

The next morning, the Austro-German troops began entering Bucharest. I saw the head of the column when it reached the Rosetti statue near our house: a detachment of ulans on big white horses came first, their spears propped against their boot legs. They looked tired as they smiled at the group of children and curious people on the pavement. Did I imagine it, or did I really see a little girl step forward and give them a bunch of flowers? I felt that the crowd around me was fretting, a bit confused. "She must be German," someone whispered.

Heavy, stonelike, the horses' hooves could be heard cutting through the silence on the boulevard. After they had passed on and the Bavarian battalions came, I went home.

That afternoon, I discovered that I could be consoled and could even get revenge. It happened this way. I imagined that a few Romanian soldiers were hiding in a cornfield near Bucharest. At first they were unarmed, or nearly so: they had a single carbine, a few bayonets, and a revolver. But I soon gave up this image, and I armed them to the teeth. In the beginning, there were only three or four soldiers and an officer. But very quickly I discovered that in the same cornfield others were hiding too. I started to bring them together, to organize them. I lay on my back in bed, with eyes half open, not quite knowing what was happening to me or whence this secret—almost guilty—happiness had sprung. I was captivated by my own visions, bound as if by an invisible thread, for when Mother called and I came to my senses, I could feel the thread breaking and I found myself in the everyday world, still excited by the memory of the things seen in my imagination, but without the former feeling of bliss.

That afternoon I learned how to regain contact with my secret army. It was enough for me to be alone—isolated in a room, in the cellar, in the attic—and to visualize the field from the beginning, waiting to see the tremblings of the first cornstalks. The action would start immediately. I kept discovering hidden soldiers, making their way with great care toward the place of assembly. By evening almost a hundred fighting men were gathered there, and they were becoming better and better equipped. The former second lieutenant was now captain; and a few other young officers had come to help him. One of them knew a great secret (my heart had almost stopped as I discovered it): the arsenal had not been blown up in its entirety, as we had believed! In the last moment, one of the lieutenants had succeeded in hiding a considerable number of carbines and machine guns inside an enormous subterranean storehouse, known to him alone, and—as I found this out my heart beat faster—there were even field cannons with ammunition.

I was so excited by this discovery that I had to interrupt my vision and return to my senses. I felt I was participating in a secret that could change the course of the war. To be sure, I knew that everything had sprung from my own mind, and that the secret army had come out of a field that—at least in the beginning—I had invented. But on the other hand, I felt I was not in control of my imaginings. Actually, I did not imagine it; rather, I *saw* what was happening, as if it were on an inner movie screen. Often I did not anticipate at all what turn of events the growth and organization of the secret army was to take. It was not I who discovered that the arsenal had not been blown up; this was told me by one of my lieutenants. And in the beginning I did not even know the name of this lieutenant. Everything that I found out later about him and about his family I learned from him. The story was modified and amplified as often as I relived it again from the beginning. The excitement with which I saw it unfold was due to the fact that it invented itself, sometimes even contrary to my knowledge or wishes. In the beginning, my soldiers only attacked the sentinels or small German detachments to procure arms and ammunition. But very soon things took a different turn. Instead of attacking small groups, the secret army was content to grow through its own means (the subterranean arsenal) and to organize in the forest, preparing for an attack.

For a few days I lived in a different world. I took no notice of my mother's tears when the sergeant came with an interpreter and an Austrian noncommissioned officer to see the commandeered rooms. Nor did the disastrous rumors that circulated succeed in depressing me. I hid whenever I could and immersed myself in contemplation of the secret army until one afternoon, about a week after I had seen the first ulan heading toward the Rosetti statue, I could restrain myself no longer and I exploded. Unexpectedly, the detachments, the companies, the regiments that I had watched for so many days preparing and organizing themselves attacked the enemy troops by surprise. As soon as I heard the first cannon shots and saw the first waves of soldiers starting to charge with bayonets, I lost the relative calm with which I had so far observed the preparations for battle. Almost panting, I whispered over and over: "Fire! Attack! Charge! Fire!" These were the commands my officers were giving. I could not remain still. I left my hiding place and started to walk along the sidewalk, with eyes lowered, in order not to interrupt my visions. I could not stop what was happening. And yet I knew that I had to stop it, to be able to inform the real Romanian troops, which were in the process of retreating to Moldavia, about *our* victories—those being won behind the front lines! When the two Romanian armies—the real one and the secret one—should meet, the war would start again under different conditions!

The campaign of my army lasted for several months. I continued it every day. Usually, it was only a matter of skirmishes among patrols or detachments, because I liked to prolong, as much as I could, the preparations for the battle. Sometimes I would announce to myself, with a certain solemnity, the precise day and hour of the attack. A few hours before the battle I would return to my hiding place. I savored every move my officers made. The attack always surprised the enemy troops.

My brother had noticed rather quickly that something was

wrong, and he started questioning me. It was hard for me to explain to him. I told him that I was writing a war story. In fact, a few weeks after I had first seen the cornfield where those few soldiers had been hiding, I *had* started to describe the incident in a notebook. To my great disappointment, the writing did not keep pace with the events I was contemplating on my inner screen. I would fall behind, and soon the joyous thrill I had felt while writing the first lines was gone. I would wake up listless and discouraged. I had started to work in a sort of trance, and now I looked with detachment and indifference at the notebook in which I had written barely a page.

I did not know at the time that I was on my way toward making my first experiments as a writer.

,   ,   ,

The autumn seemed more bitter that year. It was a long, unending November. We were almost glad when the first snow flurries fell. At that time we were billeting a German second lieutenant who was a banker from Hamburg, and a Bukovinian lieutenant from the Austrian army. They were both over fifty and as genial as they could be. The banker spoke French, was an enthusiastic stamp collector, and was always smoking cigars. As for the Bukovinian, I remember my great surprise when I came home from school one day to find in the dining room an Austrian officer who spoke Romanian. Before them we had billeted, for only a few days, three German officers. They were always considerate and discreet, so we hardly saw them, but their presence paralyzed us. We had all withdrawn into the garret, and Marioara, another aunt from Bulevardul Pache Protopopescu, had come to live with us. When all six of us— Mother, the two aunts, and we children—went down the first morning to examine the rooms, we found them just as we had left them: the beds were made and the spreads pulled over them. Only the smell of boots and tobacco reminded us that officers of an enemy army had been sleeping there. The banker and the Bukovinian were just as neat. But they were also friendly, jovial, and helpful (they brought us sugar, coffee, biscuits). The Bukovinian stayed with us until the next spring. Because he was Romanian, we did not consider him to be a soldier in an enemy army. He spoke Latin well. When he left, he took us boys aside and told us: "I will come back after the war, to see if you have learned your Latin." We never heard from him again, however.

The banker from Hamburg had been assigned to auxiliary service, so he remained with us over a year. He was blond, fat, and smelled of cologne and cigars. He was very vain about his hands and nails. He gave them much care and was always looking at them. He polished his nails with a tiny brush. Sometimes, in the evening, he allowed me to sit next to him and look at his stamps. He conversed very little and by preference spoke only in French. The next year when I would go to him for help with my German, he would lose his patience. *"Mais c'est de l'allemand, ça!"* he exclaimed after he opened the notebook.

During the winter, the occupation began to make itself felt. Wood could be found only with difficulty. The bread was mixed with cornmeal and the lines at the bakeries began to form around four in the morning. Mother would wake Nicu and give him three pairs of socks and his boots, because there were drifts of snow and each night the snowstorms became more severe. Dressed in a woolen coat and hat, Nicu went down the wooden stairs from the attic (and only then would his boots wake me), opened the gate (sometimes he had to shovel the snow away to be able to budge it), and started for the bakery. Mother boiled water for tea over the fire in the stove, then helped Corina and me to wash ourselves. The bakery did not open until six. If Nicu was there in time—that is, before five—he was among the first and he came back with the bread around half past six. After I drank the tea, I went down together with my two aunts, and shoveled the snow on the sidewalk so we should not have to pay a fine. At last, with my book satchel on my back, I started to school.

That year I didn't learn a great deal. I was in the fourth grade and all my interests were concentrated upon the new subjects that Nicu was learning in the first class of the lycée. I was especially fascinated by zoology and ancient history. At the school on Strada Mântuleasa I continued to be a prize student, somewhat by force of inertia, but both the principal and I felt that something was wrong. I did not like school any more, I did not write my papers with as much pleasure and care as formerly, and my grades in deportment had fallen off. Without the strong bond of my father's supervision, I had discovered the natural playgrounds of the city—the vacant lots. At the very beginning of that autumn, we children played cops and robbers in a lot on Calea Călăraşi led by some shoemaker's apprentices who had taught us all kinds of tricks (such as how to leave secret chalk signs on walls without being caught). Then we would join a gang of urchins in back of the Church of St. Gheorghe, where we could hide in a big courtyard that apparently was abandoned. When the winter came, we gathered on the vacant lot for snowball fights. I would return home toward evening, wet and dirty, with my clothes torn. In the beginning, my mother was not too worried. She knew I was playing with the boys, and she was delighted that at least she did not have to spy on me to keep me from reading too much. For my father had given strict instructions: she must make sure that I did not tire my eyes too much. But soon, when the snow-banks had become as high as a man, my friends from the streets appeared with sleds. Most of them were put together clumsily out of little boxes, but there were also some true sleds with glittering runners, like skates. I was among the few who had no sled, and I had to find all kinds of ways to borrow one for a few hours or even for a whole afternoon. Usually I paid the rent in buttons, marbles, or lead soldiers.

One glassy January morning, when school was closed because there was no more fuel, I went sledding with the whole crowd on the hill of the Metropolitan Cathedral. It was a long journey from the Rosetti statue to the church, but we got there quickly because we raced with one another. From the top of the hill we could see a great distance, and from up there the descent looked like a ski slope. We did not dare go down it with sleds, but we contented ourselves with starting from the point on the hill near the bell tower, down the long and slightly curving street which was almost deserted at that hour, descending to Strada Șerban-Vodă. Then up the hill we would climb again, our sleds behind us. In order to avoid being struck by those who were coasting pell-mell downhill, we walked along the side of the street in the snowdrifts. After a few hours I began to feel a tingling in my feet, and because I could not scratch I would kick myself gently with my boot. When the tingling became unbearable, I stood with all my weight first on one foot and then on the other.

I arrived home toward evening, exhausted, famished, and nearly unable to feel my feet. Mother had planned a suitable punishment for me, but when she saw my dreadful condition, she postponed it. Only after I took off my shoes and socks did she realize my feet were frozen! The skin was broken, bloody, and in places it had been torn off by the sock. The toes were purple, and when I went near the stove the tingling returned with such fury that one of my aunts had to hold my hand to keep me from scratching myself. The family doctor was old and lived rather far away, but my mother had recently noticed the sign of a woman doctor nearby. She dressed quickly and soon returned with her. Dr. Buttu had just received her M.D. and was at that time interning at Colţea Hospital. When she saw my feet she frowned. Asking for a pan of snow, she knelt in front of me and began massaging my feet in it. I groaned with pain, but she continued rubbing my feet all over until they began to bleed profusely. In the morning Mother went through the same operation again. I was not allowed to go near the stove, and I had to lie at the foot of the bed with my feet all bandaged. Some member of the family was near me at all times to see that I did not scratch myself or approach the fire.

I did not attend school for several weeks. It was not necessary to amputate any of the toes, but all that winter the rubbing with snow each morning was torture. For many years thereafter the tingling sensation would return whenever I would enter an overheated room in winter.

Thus was I cured of sleds, and perhaps that is why I was never in later years tempted by winter sports. Mother forgave me. Thanks to my frozen toes, she found a new family doctor. Dr. Buttu remained our physician and friend for almost twenty years.

That winter seemed endless to me. The snow on the ground in the garden still had not melted by March. By some means, which I no longer remember, we received news from my father around Easter. He had arrived safely in Moldavia, but he did not tell us exactly where he was or what he was doing. The bread was becoming steadily worse and more yellowish because of the cornmeal in it. And yet when it was fresh and we spread lard over it, it seemed tasty. During those years of occupation we kept, involuntarily, quite lengthy fasts. For whole weeks we ate nothing but beans, pickles, and fried potatoes. Each of us had found something to do in the kitchen. I liked frying potatoes. I learned how to cut them and how to turn them from one side to the other in order to brown them without scorching them. On rare occasions Mother would receive news from my grandparents that someone had secretly butchered a pig—and we would all go out to Bulevardul Pache Protopopescu so that we could bring home lard, rinds of bacon, and sometimes a big piece of meat, without arousing suspicion.

And yet, eventually, spring came also that year. We awoke one morning to find our peach tree in bloom. From our street all the way to school we walked beneath blossoming apricot and cherry trees. I could hardly stay home in the afternoons. The vacant lots and games were calling me again.

That year the observance of the Tenth of May, which was Romanian Independence Day, had been prohibited by the Occupation. We were obliged to attend school as usual. (The principal had warned us that, by order of the military authorities, only absences due to illness would be excused, and only with a note from the doctor.) May Tenth had to be a day like any other. But I still remember the sad, intense expression on the face of the instructor when he took a book from his pocket and called on one of the boys, the most talented in the art of recitation. "You're old enough now," he said to us, "and you can keep a secret." He opened the book and showed the boy a poem. "Go out into the courtyard and learn it by heart," he whispered to him.

Perhaps less than a quarter of an hour elapsed before he returned, but to us it seemed like an eternity. The instructor remained at his desk, staring vacantly into space. In the classroom there was no sound but the buzzing of bees at the upper part of the windows, trying to find a way through the glass out into the garden. At last our classmate appeared. Approaching the teacher's desk, he began to recite solemnly. I'd give anything to be able to remember what poem he recited then. It was not, of course, one of the traditional verses dedicated to the Tenth of May, nor a patriotic poem, because these were familiar to the whole class. It was, perhaps, one by Octavian Goga or Ș. O. Iosif. I remember only our trembling silence and our tears of proud happiness. For we understood from the poet's allusions that this time again Romania would emerge victorious.

After the boy had finished reciting, the instructor put his hand on his shoulder. Turning to us, he said with a smile, "Sit still for fifteen minutes longer, and then you may go home."

′   ′   ′

The tears with which I finished reading *Cuore* assured me that I was not a bad boy; I discovered once again that I loved my country and my family (especially Mother); I discovered also that I loved even school. But how hard it was for me to remember all these things when I found myself back on the streets, with so many trams on which I could hitch rides, with endless sidewalks on which I could rove for hours without getting lost; how hard especially when I returned to the vacant lots or the garden on Bulevardul Pache Protopopescu.

In the summer of 1917, Mother could no longer hold me in check. She had tried everything: a bamboo stick (my father usually had threatened us with a belt), hiding my shoes so I couldn't go out on the street (but, seemingly, I liked to run barefoot on the hot pavement even better), locking me up in a room (from which I would manage to escape by jumping out the window). Rather tardily, Mother came to discover the only means of keeping me off the streets: giving me a book. But even this was not a perfect solution, because by evening, or at most by the middle of the night, I would have finished reading it, and Mother did not have another book ready. And besides, she kept remembering my father's order: not to let me strain my eyes. Other superstitions were now invoked: that I was still a child and that excessive reading might "fatigue my nerves" (the expression belonged to one of my aunts). I had hoped to find an ally in Dr. Buttu. But she also subscribed to the same idea, that the mind must not be tired in "the growing years," and that it is fed sufficiently by school books and piano lessons.

I found consolation on the vacant lots. Summer had come, I had finished primary school, and while waiting for the lycée entrance examination (which I was to take in September) I was totally free. I played on the grass by the Townhall where the antiaircraft guns had been the previous year. There was an enormous vacant tract near the Brătianu statue on which the stone blocks for the new wing of the university had been deposited. The construction had been interrupted by the war, leaving a maze of cellars into which countless cartloads of sand had been dumped and bricks and lime sacks stored. I was to begin exploring those underground chambers soon, right after entering lycée. For many years those mysterious cellars, with their weak scaffolding on which rats played, would constitute one of my secret universes. Together with a few of the new friends I made in lycée, I explored them with much excitement until the day we were discovered by a group of police looking for vagabonds.

I do not know how, but toward the end of summer we learned of the Romanian victories at Mărăşeşti and Mărăşti. For several days rumors circulated about the lightning advance of some famous divisions toward Rîmnicu-Sărat. Awakened by these victories, I tried to throw my secret army into the fray also. But the game was no longer the same. That primordial field proved incapable of producing, in a few days, the forces necessary to cut the retreat of the German divisions. I tried to imagine something else: Romanian regiments hidden in the mountains, having spent the winter of 1917 in caves and forests, attacking German ammunition depots by night. But I had too many other things to do. Soon we learned that the advance of the troops had been permanently arrested due to the breakup of the Russian army. News reached us of villages behind the front lines that had been pillaged and burned by troops who had quit fighting and were heading back to Russia.

Then one September morning, on going to the Lycée Spiru-Haret to see the results of the entrance examination, I read my name on the list of those admitted. I returned home, quite somber, to give the news to Mother. I had the feeling that something very decisive had occurred, that I was about to begin a new life.

3. *"How I Found the Philosopher's Stone"*

AT FIRST everything about the lycée fascinated me. What I especially liked was having a different teacher for each subject. Nicolaie Moisescu captivated me from the very first lesson, and he remained my favorite until his death several years later. He was the teacher of biological sciences. Tall, quite thin, almost gaunt, he seemed older than he was because of his white hair and moustache. He spoke slowly and distinctly, as if conserving his strength. While he lectured he would pace back and forth in front of the room, taking small light steps, which he interrupted from time to time with short pauses in order to look deeply into the eyes of some student. He smiled after each sentence, as if he wanted to emphasize the period and pause that must separate it from the next one. His lectures were accompanied by broad, deliberate gestures, and watching these you understood how perfectly he had succeeded in saving the small amount of energy he had available.

He had the habit of coming to class with a microscope and calling us all to look through it, one after another; then he would have us draw on the blackboard what we had seen. Rarely did one of us manage to reproduce very approximately those strange iridescent, madreporic forms we discovered. (We would blur the images, lose them, and discover them again by slowly turning the screw of the microscope.) Moisescu noticed me, I believe, because I was among those few who proved capable of sketching what they saw. From that time onward, his interest in me never wavered. He always looked me straight in the eye, and he was continually asking me questions, almost as though he wanted my opinion. Gradually, I became aware that there were secrets which we could understand. They were the secrets of that mysterious force which Moisescu called "Nature." I understood why butterflies of the forest have wings the color of bark, why the porcupine has quills, why the male birds of many species are much more brilliantly decorated than the females. "Nature" has done all these things to camouflage them, to protect them, to select them. There are, then, certain laws that can be deciphered. Suddenly, everything acquired meaning and purpose. The world no longer was seen to be a conglomeration of unrelated creatures and happenings; rather, it showed itself to be the result of a unique and irresistible will. As she revealed herself to me in Moisescu's lectures, "Nature" was animated by a single impetus: that of creating and maintaining life, in spite of all obstacles and disasters.

That winter I learned what is meant by the instincts of preservation of the individual and of the species. But above all I learned to distinguish and love various animals, particularly reptiles and amphibians, and insects. Nicolaie Moisescu showed them to us on colored plates, stuffed or preserved in bottles of alcohol, or in insectariums. Then I contemplated them, along with the rest of the class, at the Museum of Natural Sciences in Șosea. After that, I visited the museum regularly each Sunday the entire winter. And with great impatience I waited for spring to come so that I could, at last, go hunting for insects in the forests around Bucharest.

Perhaps it was this passion for the natural sciences that saved me and helped me to pass through the crisis that had come upon me almost without my being aware of it. It was not just puberty, because (with the exception of zoology) nothing interested me. I did not do my homework, I spent all my time on the Townhall Tract and in the cellars at the university construction site. I remained friends with the same urchins from the slums, while I became close only with the laziest and most cantankerous of my new classmates at the lycée. It is true that, as soon as the snow had melted, I managed to persuade them to roam around the woods in Șosea, in search of plants and insects. In May of 1918, I began going early each Sunday morning to the monasteries outside Bucharest. I would return about midnight, tired, sunburnt, dirty, and laden with jars full of insects, lizards, frogs, and snails. Out of a little box with a glass cover I made myself a "terrarium." Whole hours were spent following closely the quiet, gloomy life of all sorts of insects, frogs, and lizards. I made plans for summer excursions along the banks of the Dîmbovița all the way to the Danube to investigate the mud flats and swamps so rich in larvae.

This dream was suddenly canceled by the surprise I received at the year's end. I found that I had failed in three subjects: Romanian, French, and German. I was indignant; three failures meant that the grade must be repeated. But Moisescu insisted that I be given another chance. I was his best student. It was a profound embarrassment to me to read my name on the list of failures. It is true, I had been a bit apprehensive about German. As a matter of fact, we should not have had to begin studying it until the second year of the lycée, but the Occupation authorities had imposed it also on the first year students. For that reason the whole class had sabotaged it as much as possible. But I was truly surprised when I saw I had failed French, and even more so Romanian.

Iosif Frollo was our French teacher. It would be useless for me to try to eulogize him: he was well-known by whole generations of lycée students. But he had a great penchant for grammar, and at that time I thought grammar absurd and unimportant, seemingly invented expressly to prevent a student from savoring the text he is translating. Frollo was satisfied with what I knew, but he had warned me that I could not pass the course if I did not know all the conjugations by heart. I took his threat as a joke, since (as was his habit) he had said this very sweetly, looking me in the eye and smiling. But he kept his word and this provoked a true break between us. I remained aloof from him from then on. A few years later, when I had become involved in reading books without number, I forced myself to read the complete works of the French authors we were studying in class. Frollo tried several times to advise me and guide me; but I always listened to him with a hostile smile on my lips, continuing to read what I liked and as I liked.

Apparently, Frollo understood very quickly what was taking place in the mind of the frustrated and anarchic adolescent that I was, and he left me alone. But he also had a sophisticated method of getting revenge. During my last year in lycée, whenever he was discussing one of the authors he knew very well that I had read—because, impertinently, I came to school with the complete works and placed them on my desk, leafing through them occasionally with a feigned nonchalance—Frollo would ask the class questions that I probably could have answered better than anyone else; but he always refused to call on me, although I raised my hand. Eventually, I gave up raising my hand and listened, smiling ironically, to the stupid and inept answers of my fellow students. Only once did Frollo come down from his dais to see the books I had arranged provocatively on my desk. He had spoken to us about Port Royal, and I had brought *Les Provinciales* and all the volumes on Pascal that I could find in the library. He thumbed through them with an amused expression, then clapped me on the shoulder. But even then he didn't ask me a question that would have given me the chance to show I knew more than anyone else in the class.

Failing Romanian I considered a huge injustice. It is true I had not studied, but I was sure I had nothing else to learn, because I had read the textbook on the Romanian language before entering lycée. I was also convinced that I read and wrote better than all my fellow students. But the teacher of Romanian at that time, D. Nanul, was also the principal of the school, so he knew what an undisciplined and incorrigible pupil I was. Oftentimes I would run away from school, escaping through the window, and play games on the Townhall Tract. At other times I did not come to school and lied that I had been ill. I tore pages out of my notebook so that Mother would not see what bad marks I was getting, and at school I would pretend I had forgotten and left it at home or lost it. D. Nanul was certainly justified in trying to make me repeat the grade, even in trying to persuade my mother to take me out of the lycée. I was, as he liked to put it, "an undesirable element." But to me it seemed that my failure in Romanian was due to his personal vengeance, and that actually I should have deserved a prize or at least honorable mention!

Thus the idea slowly began to creep into my mind that I was persecuted, that the principal and all the other teachers with the exception of Moisescu—for reasons I was unable to fathom— protected some students and persecuted others, especially me. This discovery wounded me deeply, but at the same time it gave me a strange satisfaction. It seemed to me that I was entirely different from all my classmates, that I was predestined to remain on the fringes of society, that the roads of others were forbidden to me, and that I would be forced to find a new path for myself. And so, when I read my name on the list of those who had failed, my first thought was that I would run away into the wide world. I started out for Şosea and I walked aimlessly for hours without noticing hunger or fatigue. Towards evening, however, I returned home. Mother had difficulty hiding her happiness at seeing me back. She had learned from my brother that I had not passed three subjects, and she was afraid I might have done something foolish. She tried to console me by promising to get me tutors in French and German.

In a way, failing those courses worked to my advantage. That summer, whenever Mother saw me with a book in my hand, she did not remind me as before that I mustn't tire my eyes; she assumed I was studying in preparation for the autumn exams. For the first time in my life I did not read in secrecy and fear. On the other hand, the conviction I had formed that I was "persecuted" gave me, in my own eyes, a martyr's halo and also a certain responsibility. As much as I loved the games of the streets, I felt now that I must not give the impression of being good for nothing else. It seemed to me that "others" were watching me—especially the principal and certain teachers. I told myself: they think I'm a no-good, and they're sure I'll never amount to anything. Someday I'll give them a surprise!

But it was impossible for me to decide then, in that summer of 1918, what that surprise would be. Would I become a great zoologist, a great pianist, a great doctor—or an inventor, or an explorer; or should I decipher a dead language? Of one thing I was certain: that I would never be a prize student. I made up my mind that I would barely pass from one grade to another. In those summer afternoons, with one of the three grammar books in front of me, I discerned what later proved to be characteristic of my temperament: that it was impossible for me to learn something on demand; that is, to learn as everyone else does, in conformity with an academic schedule. From the first grade of lycée to the last, I always felt attracted to the subjects that were not in the curriculum for that year, or to subjects and authors that were not taught in school. A few years later, when I became interested in physico-chemical sciences, I studied chemistry when physics was in the schedule, and vice versa. Sometimes it was enough that a discipline I loved should appear in the curriculum for me to lose interest in it. This happened with logic, psychology, and biology. Everything I was *forced* to study lost its interest for me and became a "subject" like any other, good for memorization by "grinds" and prize students. My aversion for textbooks and programmed studies took, as time went by, pathetic proportions. Several years later, when I undertook the study of Latin and mathematics, I was not satisfied with the textbooks from which all my classmates studied, but I bought the books of Meillet, H. Poincaré, and Gino Loria from used bookstores, though it was only with great difficulty and by enormous effort that I made headway in them.

,   ,   ,

I have no idea how I passed my examinations in the autumn. I had succeeded in learning the conjugations in French and German and declensions in the latter, but at the oral exam, in front of Nanul, I was so intimidated that I forgot the gender of even the most common nouns. It is probable that the written examinations turned out better, because both Frollo and Nanul passed me. I was waiting to take my German exam when the German teacher, Papadopol, announced that since the German language had to be studied only starting in the second year of lycée, all failing grades were canceled. But he added with a piercing gaze, "Those of you who failed are expected to distinguish yourselves this year!"

So far as I was concerned, I did unquestionably disappoint him. German was one of the terrors of my adolescence, not so much because of its difficulty, but because Papadopol became principal of the lycée the next year. Thereafter, I had to deal with him every time I broke a windowpane, or whenever he caught me jumping out of a window, or discovered I had signed the excuse for my own absence. And yet, unexpectedly, in the fourth year we were reconciled, and later we even became good friends. In his class that year he assigned several research topics in literary history, and to me there fell *Sturm und Drang*. We each had to give a twenty-minute oral report. Working day and night, I had read all the monographs I could find, and I had written a whole notebook. My introduction alone lasted for almost an hour. I began with Nibelungen and Minnesänger. On the blackboard I wrote all the names, titles, and dates I considered to be important. Of course I had copied these out of the textbooks and monographs I had read. But, with visible delight, Papadopol was refreshing his memory on Minnesänger and some minor authors about whom, undoubtedly, he had not thought since he had received his degree.

I had entered the second class without much enthusiasm. But around the end of October, rumors began to circulate about the disasters of the Central Powers. The teachers were in a better mood during classes and they seemed even more absentminded. One morning we learned that Germany had asked for an armistice. I had started out for school, but I found myself going down the boulevard toward the Brătianu statue. As I proceeded, I encountered increasingly noisy groups of people, some carrying small Romanian or French flags, several in faded, ragged uniforms. I heard a young fellow shout, "To the Kommandant's!" and he started running with the whole crowd following. I began to run too, holding my schoolbag against my back with one hand to keep it from bouncing. But I did not reach the Kommandant's. Somewhere near the Colțea Hospital I came across other shouting, threatening groups, and I stopped to see what was happening. Someone had climbed onto the roof of a building and was trying to fasten up a flag. "Tie it with your belt," I heard someone shout. Then several people next to me burst out laughing. Some applauded till their hands were blistered. "He's going to lose his pants on the roof!" someone said.

But the next moment there were shouts of "Watch out!"—and the people began to disperse. From a window someone was throwing sticks into a pile on the pavement. There were hundreds and hundreds of white sticks, about two meters long, which seemed all the more precious to me because I didn't know what they were good for. The people were hurrying to pick them up, and they brandished them over their heads like swords. With some difficulty I made my way through the crowd and managed to get hold of one. "They're tent poles," someone next to me said. But then I heard the sound of windows being smashed, and at one of them I saw two men struggling to lift a sack to the window ledge. "Step aside, it's sugar!" shouted one of them, who was trying to rip open the bag with a pocket knife.

Soon a dense cascade of granulated sugar was pouring onto the pavement and the people crowded in again, stooping, crouching, scrambling to gather the sugar in their hands, filling their pockets, handkerchiefs, hats—all the while shouting, threatening, swearing. "Watch out!" came the cry again from other windows, and more sacks spilled their contents—sugar, lentils, flour—onto the sidewalk. Only a few minutes had passed, but already the street was full of people. From out of nowhere women had appeared, crowding beneath the broken windows and emerging again from the mob with skirts caught up, immodestly carrying in them the sugar mixed with lentils and mud.

When I started for home with my white stick under my arm and a handkerchief full of sugar in my right hand, I learned that the looted building had been a warehouse for the German army. The guards had disappeared during the night.

My father returned from Moldavia soon after that. During the last months we had received news from him quite frequently. He had told us that all our relatives were alive, except for Traian, my mother's youngest brother, who had died of typhus. In Moldavia, Father had exchanged his wages for articles of immediate usefulness: shoe-sole material, linen, lard, flour, and biscuits. For years Nicu and I went clothed in the same ash-colored army jackets, the same military tunics of dark, rough cloth, and the same enormous boots. We were not to be freed from these gifts, which our father had collected with much difficulty in Moldavia, until the upper grades of lycée, when all students were required to wear the school uniform and the cap with the mauve ribbon of Spiru-Haret. Besides, during those years when there was almost nothing for sale, the boys came to school dressed as best they could. Almost everyone wore something military: an officer's cap, a tunic, a khaki shirt, or at least boots and puttees.

A few days after the Armistice was signed, we started going to school an hour earlier and staying one or two hours later in the afternoon in order to learn, as quickly as possible, the anthems of the Allies. Almost all of us knew the "Marseillaise," but we had to learn "God Save the King" and "It's a Long Way to Tipperary." We also had to learn the American and Italian national anthems. Soloveanu, our music teacher, had written the respective texts phonetically on the blackboard, and we tried to memorize them as best we could. It all had to be done very hurriedly, because the triumphal entry of the Allied detachments and some parts of General Franchet d'Esperey's army from Salonica seemed imminent. However, the parade was postponed several times.

At last we were called together one morning, and before it was fully light we started for Calea Victoriei. From the Mogoşoaia Bridge to Bulevardul Elisabeta, the pupils of all the primary and secondary schools of the capital were assembled, holding flags of various sizes. First came the children of the elementary schools, then those of us in the first years of the lycée followed by the older lycée pupils, and finally the university students. I no longer recollect which were the first detachments that paraded in front of us. I remember the cheers we heard in the distance, growing like a giant billow as the troops approached us. I remember the company of Englishmen with their round, flat helmets and their inimitable smiles when they heard us pronouncing an elongated and accentuated "Tip-per-ra-ry." I also remember the detachment of Senegalese and the astonishment with which we greeted them and followed them with our gaze, so that we forgot the words of the "Marseillaise" and were just making sounds at random, until Soloveanu came up behind us and tapped us on the shoulders with his baton, as if trying to waken us from a dream.

It was another long and severe winter. But this time we did not have to rise at dawn and stand in line for bread. We drank tea with the dry biscuits Father had brought and trudged off to school through drifts of snow. Moisescu was teaching us botany now. He came with the microscope and made each of us look at a grain of pollen or a cross-section of a pistil or a stamen. One day I discovered in the window of a bookstore his *Vegetal Physiology,* and I bought it. I read it almost in a frenzy, but I don't think I understood a great deal. Now I awaited spring with great impatience so I could go looking for plants and set up my own herbarium.

But before spring came, something else happened: I discovered a new game. At school, several of us would come with such and such a book and propose to exchange it for another. The game quickly captivated me because of the innumerable surprises to which it gave rise. It was like having visits of a mobile library: I discovered all sorts of books. I especially liked the little volumes from *Biblioteca pentru toţi* (Everyone's Library) and *Minerva;* there was everything from Darwin's *The Origin of the Species* to Silvio Pellico's *Le mie prigioni* (My Imprisonment). It was my great discovery of that winter that there was available to me a great number of books on all manner of topics—above all, foreign, exotic books written by authors·I had never heard of—from which I could learn all sorts of things about other worlds and people in faraway places: not only the books of Camille Flammarion or Victor Anestin about astronomy and the mysteries of the universe, but also the worlds of Tolstoy and Gorki, the characters of Balzac, of strange people who have lost their shadows or have traveled to the moon or have spoken with the dead.

Before I realized what was happening, I found I had become interested not only in the natural sciences but also in all these new universes that the foreign literature, biographies, and popular books revealed to me. I came to read a book a day, but I soon discovered that at this pace I should never be able to finish. Every morning I was tempted by three or four volumes, and in order to be able to borrow them I had to bring to school at least as many to exchange. I had bought books before, but only after I became caught up in this new game did I begin to sense the advantages of having a library. Only that way could I choose any volume I wished and read everything that tempted me. That winter of 1919 there were precious few books in the bookstores, and the dealers in second-hand books with whom I was then acquainted bought and sold school texts primarily. That is why, while making the rounds of the bookstores, I would buy any cheap book, even if I didn't understand the title very well.

That winter the fear of frostbite kept me at home in the attic all the time. Since my father's return, only we children continued to live in the garret, so I was not constantly supervised as before. I could read to my heart's content. As a precaution, I always kept a school textbook open in front of me. When I heard footsteps on the wooden staircase I hid the book I was reading and pretended to be doing my homework. Father would come in from time to time, put on his glasses, pick up the book and read the title aloud, in order to convince himself that it was a serious schoolbook and that I was not wasting my time with something else. He knew, of course, that I had a "library," because I had neatly arranged the seventy or eighty volumes on a shelf, but I had persuaded him that I read them only during my spare time.

Little by little I obtained permission to read even at night. I had a work table and a large lamp with a shade, but because my eyes still watered and I could never find glasses that fit me, my father had bought me a blue bulb. Someone had told him that a blue light is less tiring for the eyes. At first the light was so weak that after about half an hour of reading my eyes would blur and begin to water. But after a while the bulb lost its color and the light became tolerable. I was allowed to read until 11:00 P.M., but every time Father would come to turn out the light, he would find me working some math problem or writing a theme for the next day (because I would start my homework only a few minutes before eleven), so he would have to allow me half an hour more! But oftentimes he would not come up to check on whether or not I had gone to bed, and then I would continue to read until overcome by sleep.

That year, 1918–1919, I had a different teacher for Romanian, Mazilu. We all liked him from the start because he was so droll. He liked to read our compositions out loud and make amusing comments on them. He lectured us constantly about literature and urged us to read the Romanian classics "to enrich the mind and the vocabulary," as he had the habit of saying. In March he gave us a topic for a composition to be written at home: "How have I sensed the coming of spring?"

This time I didn't postpone the writing of the paper until the last moment. I began writing early in the afternoon and I did not stop until Mother called me from the bottom of the stairway to come to dinner. There were about twenty notebook pages, and I had written them with a strange, hitherto unknown joy, as if I had suddenly awakened in one of those worlds of the books I had been reading— the only real and meaningful worlds for me. I felt as though I were writing like one of those true authors—those we had not yet studied at school—and as though I were writing for someone like myself to read, not for a teacher or for a grade.

Mazilu had the habit of looking at us directly and pleasantly while apparently trying to guess who would be the author of the most picturesque text, the one that would give him the opportunity to correct us while making a lot of jokes that would throw the class into convulsions. He would select several notebooks, return to his desk, and begin to read. I don't know how I knew it, but I was sure that this time he would choose mine. I looked at him with the smile of an accomplice. Probably this audacious act made me blush, because after hesitating a moment in front of a neighboring desk he turned and asked for my notebook.

I recollect only vaguely that first lucky composition. I only know that I related how, one day at the beginning of March, I had fallen asleep while looking at a few snowflakes on my attic window sill. I had witnessed then a number of fantastic happenings: how the gypsies who had gone to gather snowbells in the forest were caught by a snowstorm, and how each had taken shelter under a tree and had become one with the bark of the tree. I described the battle that followed between the rear guards of winter—creatures of hoarfrost, with cheeks of ice and long, transparent fingers like stalactites—and those first spies of spring who struggled to make their way up through the snow from subterranean realms. They emerged into the light one after another, half men, half flowers, with fingers of snowbells. They were blowing continually on the melting snow and whistling: "Where is the North-Wind Emperor? Where is the North-Wind Emperor? If I could embrace him once, only once!"

After reading the first page, Mazilu raised his eyes from the notebook and asked me, "From where did you copy this?" When I started to protest he added, "I mean, what inspired you? What book?" I reddened and shrugged helplessly. Mazilu discerned my embarrassment and resumed his reading with a curious smile on his face. From time to time, in order to avoid leaving the impression that this was a masterpiece, he pointed out an adjective that was too harsh and interrupted his reading to explain that I had made an error. But when he finished, he looked me straight in the eye and said, "Bravo! I'm obliged to give you an A!"

It was my first victory: the acknowledgment, in front of the whole class, that I was no longer last year's failure in Romanian literature. Apparently, Mazilu was so surprised by my story that he talked about it in the faculty office, because at the end of recess Moisescu came to me and asked for my notebook. He wanted to read for himself about my oneiric adventures with the North-Wind Emperor and all those other characters that I have long since forgotten. It was a real triumph, and one that I related in great detail as soon as I arrived home; but I don't know if I succeeded in overcoming the reserve and skepticism of my parents. (My father said that he would let himself be convinced only when he saw the A transferred onto my notebook—that is, at the end of the trimester!)

But for me that experience had far deeper consequences. I had discovered that if I were "inspired," I could write with the same ease—although not with the same speed—with which a few years before I had visualized on my inner screen the adventures of my secret army. Several times since then I had tried to write, but after a few pages I would find myself suddenly bored. I would read over the last lines with consternation and disgust, then furiously tear the pages out of the notebook, crumple them, and throw them into the fire. Now I seemed to have discovered the secret: I could write well only if I were "inspired." And I knew what that meant: it was like a kind of pleasant narcosis that I sensed penetrating my whole being, until I was left gazing fixedly upon an object or a point on the wall opposite for uncounted minutes that passed without my feeling their duration; I sensed only that I had passed into another space, somewhere close by, right in front of me, where those events that I was to relate were taking place. I knew now from experience that I must not begin to write until this reverie had attained an almost unbearable intensity and beatitude. Then I would dip my pen deeply into the ink and start to write.

Sometimes this unnatural enchantment would become deeper as I continued writing. In the majority of instances, however, the "inspiration" lasted an hour or two, then faded, suffering who knows what incomprehensible transformations, until it disappeared entirely, leaving me frustrated and depressed. I could not recover it again until the next day or several days later, while rereading certain lines that I knew I liked, and which I felt certain were perfect.

That spring I began to write stories regularly. Their themes I recall only vaguely now. I know only that almost all of them were fantasies. One of them began something like this: Today I met God on the street. He wanted to make himself a switch. He broke a branch off a tree and asked me: "Do you happen to have a pocketknife?" But I don't remember what came after that. The main character of another story was a humble functionary in a small provincial town. He is uneducated, almost illiterate. One day he feels an impulse to write, and he writes several books, one after another. He takes the manuscripts to the teacher of literature in the local lycée. The teacher leafs through them, reads a paragraph or so here and there, and then asks him, "Whatever possessed you to copy all these famous books—*Madame Bovary, The Kreutzer Sonata*, etc.?" The young man swears he had never heard of those books, that he does not like to read literature, and that he wrote without knowing what was happening to him. The teacher is skeptical. He advises him to try something else, a play for instance. A few weeks later the man returns with two more manuscripts. They are *The Barber of Seville* and *The Sunset* by Delovrancea.

Sometimes my inspiration came from my father's war stories. But I chose to write exclusively about strange, mysterious happenings. I remember that I wrote a long novella on the subject of a brilliant officer who had been ordered to blow up a bridge. He waits, hidden among the reeds, in water up to his knees. He does not explode the dynamite until the first German troops are on the bridge; then he tries to slip away stealthily through the swamp. But after the explosion he hears something fall with a heavy splash just ahead of him in the water, and he stops in his tracks, transfixed. After a few seconds he gropes around in the water, finds the object, and lifts it up. It is the head of a young soldier, blown off just under the chin, looking at him wide-eyed as though surprised to meet him there. Long after midnight the officer succeeds in reaching his unit in a half-deserted village. Exhausted, he throws himself on the bed and falls asleep. But soon he is awakened by a loud knocking at the door. He thrusts his hand under the pillow, finds his revolver, and fires all the bullets at what he thinks is the head of that German soldier. At least, this is his testimony when he is brought before the court-martial. Actually, it had been an orderly. The order had been given to evacuate the village and he had come to waken him. The orderly, too, had died with his eyes open, with an expression of great surprise on his face.

I copied these stories into a thick notebook on the cover of which I inscribed: *Novellas and Tales, Vol. I.* I did not doubt that some day I should be able to publish them, and that there would even be several volumes. But literature constituted only a part, and not the most important part, of my production. I could write literature only in hours of "inspiration." But I had discovered that in the remainder of the time I could write other things: for instance, résumés of books I had read, or critical presentations of scientific theories, or detailed descriptions of the animals and plants I collected, observed, and studied. I had all sorts of notebooks: on plant morphology, on entomology, on résumés of evolutionary theories, and others. To differentiate them from school copybooks, which seemed cold and impersonal to me, I used the notebooks my father made for me from unlined, better-grade paper, sewn together with white thread and bound with various colored covers. In subsequent years the number of notebooks was to grow considerably because I gradually became enthusiastic about new subjects: physics, chemistry, the Orient, occult sciences, philosophy. I kept them all. By the end of my lycée years I had filled a footlocker with them.

That year I passed the grade without failing a single subject. My father seemed rather pleased with me, because he believed I was destined to become a great pianist. That summer we spent at Săcele, one of the Seven Villages near Braşov. Our villa at Tekirghiol was too dilapidated to be inhabitable. What a thrill when I first crossed the Carpathians and discovered the mountains, Transylvania, and rural life! We lived in a clean, sunny house with a family who had a swarm of children. Among them was a girl a few years older than I. She was blond, freckled, and bore the fragrance of milk and hay. I've never forgotten her, because she had a crush on Nicu and kept trying to kiss him. Once, when the three of us were sitting on a haystack and she was caressing his hair, she said, "How I love boys with hair like the raven's feather!" I smiled skeptically. It was impossible for me to believe her. I had known since the days when I had heard my first fairy tales that Prince Charming was always blond. Though I was a redhead in those days, I considered myself closer to Prince Charming than Nicu was. Deep down I had long pitied him for having been born with dark hair. I thought that no one would ever fall in love with him and that when the time came, all the girls would be attracted to me, because I was blond. Besides, I believed myself to be quite handsome. I knew very well that I had small, nearsighted eyes, and I wore wire-rimmed glasses, but I considered that this gave me a touch of distinguished severity, that it announced my future as a scientist: a great doctor, for instance, or a naturalist.

At last, seeing how passionately our host's daughter was caressing Nicu, I could no longer restrain myself and I told her what I thought, namely that she was making a mistake. I made it clear that I was glad she liked my brother so much, whom I also loved, but that she was wrong in praising his dark hair. Boys with dark hair are, as a matter of fact, ugly, and consequently later on they will all be unlucky and no one will love them. The really handsome one, the one who deserved to be loved, I said, is I, because I am blond like Prince Charming!

The girl listened to me at first with moderate interest, but very soon she burst into laughter, and she laughed long and hard until the tears streamed down her cheeks. I still believed she was joking, and I smiled. But eventually, after hearing her describe the difference between boys with hair "black as the raven's feather" and the "faded ones," like herself and me, the blonds and the redheads, I became convinced that she was serious and it made me sad. A whole world of values began to crumble. I understood that having been born looking very nearly like Prince Charming was not considered by everyone as an exceptional gift. You could be judged ugly, or you could pass unobserved, even though you resembled a fairy-tale hero.

A few years later I began to think of myself as truly ugly. And probably I *was*—due to the transformations of puberty, my myopia, and the regulations of the Lycée Spiru-Haret: close-cropped hair, thicker and thicker lenses, a face covered with pimples and a downy reddish beard. But I saw myself even more ugly than I was, and this explained a number of my ideas and some of my behavior at that time: I wanted to isolate myself at all costs, to be *"le veuf, l'inconsole,"* to know absolute loneliness. This happened around 1922–1923, when I was writing *Romanul adolescentului miop* (The Novel of the Nearsighted Adolescent).

The revelation that the daughter of our host had made to me, quite unintentionally, did not spoil the joys of that summer vacation at Săcele. I would set out each morning with a book and some boxes for insects, examine the osiers near the stream, climb through raspberry bushes looking for *Cetonia aurata*, linger for hours over an ant colony, or lie in wait for lizards and snakes. I read without plan, whatever fell into my hands. I had brought with me two volumes of Fabre's *Souvenirs entomologiques*, and I began to translate several chapters. I learned by heart the *Dictionary of Medicinal Plants* by Zaharia Pantu. I made plans for short stories.

In that autumn of 1919 I entered the third year of lycée and began to study physics, while Nicu started chemistry. I liked physics, especially since the year before I had learned already the rudiments from Nicu's textbook and with his help. But chemistry fascinated me as no other science had before—so much so that I believed I had found my true vocation. In the course of the school year, 1919–1920, I made myself a laboratory. In the beginning it was a rather modest affair in the loft beside our attic rooms. On a table with a metal top I set up a retort, a dozen test tubes, an alcohol lamp, and a few bottles of "substances." When school friends would drop in, I would show them a few classical experiments: phosphorus burning with a sizzle when dropped into water, the mysterious transformations of burning sulfur, and so on. The following year when it came our turn to study chemistry, some of my fellow students tried to imitate me and they, too, improvised laboratories. We would take turns gathering in one another's homes and perform experiments, beginning with those in the fourth year textbook and going on to those in more technical volumes. The teacher of physics and chemistry, Voitinovici, soon observed how enthusiastic I was and how much I knew for my age, and he entrusted to me the key to the school laboratory. I went there whenever I could in the afternoons, alone or with one of my classmates, and attempted all sorts of experiments.

Through my interest in chemistry I became friends with several of my new classmates. Cărpişteanu was, like myself, both a pianist and a lover of chemistry. At that time he was a handsome, though pale boy, with a broad forehead. He wore the bitter, melancholic smile of one who suffers from a chronic disease (he was afflicted with coxalgia). He was the only one who had put together a decent lab, and he majored in chemistry almost until the end of baccalaureate studies. Then he left for France to study medicine, and I never heard from him again. With Dinu Sighireanu I had become friends the previous year, but the laboratory drew us closer together. Soon, however, Dinu gave up chemistry and he passed along to me everything that remained usable from his lab. But he continued to be interested in insects, and from his family estate in Ialomiţa, near the village of Sighireni, he would bring me each autumn rare butterflies and strange coleoptera. I was to become even closer to Dinu in the last years of lycée when the two of us discovered many new authors in his sister's library. And several times I was to spend unforgettable weeks at his place in the country. But concerning Dinu, as well as other friends, I shall write in greater detail further on.

Finally, due indirectly to chemistry, I was to find in those years a new friend, Mircea Mărculescu, and a new passion, Balzac. Attracted by the scientific interest of the subject, I had read *La Recherche de l'absolu*. Mărculescu, who did not like chemistry but was a fan of Balzac, lent me *La Peau de chagrin*. Enthused, I next reread *Le Père Goriot* and immediately afterward *Gobseck*, and thus I discovered the reappearance of characters, a method that delighted me. Together with Mărculescu, I started going through new and used bookstores looking for volumes by Balzac. What joy when we came upon *Histoire des Treize* and *La Cousine Bette*, because in the first months we had found only random volumes from *Oeuvres pour la jeunesse*, and with all our enthusiasm we had been impressed only by *Le Centenaire*.

But these things happened two years later when I was, as they say, "a published author."

I still remember very well my first published article: "The Enemy of the Silkworm," which appeared in *Ziarul Ştiinţelor Populare* (The Newspaper of Popular Sciences) in the spring of 1921. I had entered the fourth year of lycée and was living alone in my little attic room, because Nicu had gone to attend military school at Tîrgu-Mureş. I had spent the summer with the whole family at the half-rebuilt "Villa Cornelia" at Tekirghiol. I had been bored, having come with few books; and after finishing them I sought desperately for something to read—anything. In a closet I found Vasile Conta's *Complete Works*, and I stubbornly read through them all, without always understanding them. The rest of the time I collected plants, snails, and insects. I began writing a study about the fauna and flora of Tekirghiol, which I later reworked and published in the winter of 1922 in *Ziarul Ştiinţelor Populare*.

I don't know what made me choose as the subject of my very first article the "enemy of the silkworm." The subject did not particularly attract me, and at that time I knew enough about entomology to have written something more significant. Probably I told myself that, since the subject had its practical aspect, it would have a greater chance of being published. It was signed "Eliade Gh. Mircea." When I saw my name in print—in the abstract and again at the end of the article—my heart began to pound. All the way home from the stand where I had bought the paper, it seemed to me that everyone was looking at me. In triumph I showed it to my parents. Mother pretended not to have time to read it. Probably she wanted to savor it at leisure, the way I know she read some of my articles later. But Father put on his glasses and read it on the spot (it was no longer than a column). "It doesn't have much value," he said. "It's a patchwork."

So it was, indeed. I tried to explain to him that in this article I was not doing "science" but "popularization," something just as important and necessary as original research. However, I don't think I convinced him.

A few months later *Ziarul Ştiinţelor Populare* announced a contest for lycée students. With great excitement I read the rules. It was exactly what I had dreamed of doing: a scientific topic to be treated in a literary fashion. I composed a brief fantasy entitled, "How I Found the Philosopher's Stone." It began something like this: I am in my laboratory, and for some reason or other I have fallen asleep (but of course the reader didn't know this, because I did not tell him). There appears a strange character who talks to me about the Philosopher's Stone and assures me that it is no legend, that the stone can be obtained if you know a certain formula. He tells me about a lot of operations performed by famous alchemists, which he has witnessed, and he proposes that we reconstruct the experiment together. He has not convinced me, but I agree. The stranger mixes different substances in a crucible, places it over the fire, then sprinkles some powder on it and exclaims: "Watch closely now! Watch!" In truth, the substances in the crucible are transformed into gold before my very eyes! In my excitement I make an abrupt gesture, knocking the crucible to the floor. At that instant I awake and find myself alone in the laboratory. But for a moment the dream seems to have been a reality: a crucible really is lying on the floor, and beside it is a piece of gold. Only after I pick it up do I realize that it is pyrite or "fool's gold."

I never reread that story, but when I thought about it, decades later, I realized that it was not without significance. When I wrote it I was enthusiastic about chemistry and knew almost nothing about alchemy. At that time I loved matter, I believed in it; I knew the immediate utility of different substances, but I was also fascinated by the mystery of chemical structures, the countless combinations possible among molecules. Not until several years later did I discover, in the library of the King Carol I Foundation, *Collection des anciens alchimistes grecs* by Marcellin Berthelot. Soon after that I felt strongly attracted to alchemy, and since then I have never lost interest in the subject. In 1924-1925 I published my first articles about Alexandrian and Medieval alchemy in *Ziarul Ştiinţelor Populare*. While studying at the university, I wrote to Prophulla Chandra Ray, and he sent me from Calcutta his two volumes on Indian alchemy. When I was in India (1928-1931), I collected a rich body of material that I used in the series of articles first published in *Vremea* and republished as a monograph, *Alchimia Asiatică* (Asian Alchemy), in 1935. Then followed *Cosmologie şi Alchimie Babiloniană* (Babylonian Cosmology and Alchemy) in 1937, *Metallurgy, Magic, and Alchemy* in 1938, and *The Forge and the Crucible (Forgerons et Alchimistes)* in 1956—this last book resuming and developing the themes of the earlier works. At that time I knew nothing about Jung's researches. I tried to demonstrate, nevertheless, that alchemy was not a rudimentary chemistry, a "pre-chemistry," but a spiritual technique, seeking something entirely different from the conquest of matter; seeking, at bottom, the transmutation of man: his "salvation" or liberation.

What I wouldn't give to be able to read that story again now, to find out what that mysterious character revealed to me, what alchemistic operations he had witnessed! I had found, *in dreams*, the Philosopher's Stone. Only decades later was I to understand, after having read Jung, the meaning of that oneiric symbolism.

/ / /

My story received first prize and was published at the end of 1921. From that time on, I felt that I was really an author. The prize was 100 lei, or about $20.00. On my way to collect it I met Professor Dan Dimiu, the managing editor of *Ziarul Ştiinţelor Populare*. He congratulated me and asked me to contribute regularly to the review. I had—practically in a finished state—a number of articles about various insects, which I had entitled "Entomological Conversations." I began submitting them and they appeared regularly for several years. As I have not reread them since, I am not aware of how "original" my entomological contributions were. I had studied from cover to cover the books of Brehm and Fabre, and I had made a number of observations for myself. I had seen through Moisescu's microscope all that could be seen concerning the anatomy and physiology of insects. Ever since I had set up an aquarium, I had spent many hours setting down in a notebook observations concerning the behavior of *Nepa cineraria.* Nevertheless, a few years later when I abandoned entomology once and for all, I realized rather sadly that I had discovered nothing really new or previously unobserved by others with respect to all those creatures I had propagated, watched over, and loved so many years.

But then again, perhaps there *were* indeed things that only I had seen. In any event, during that year, 1921–1922, I wrote, using several notebooks, *The Journey of the Five Cockchafers in the Land of the Red Ants,* a sort of adventure novel in which I mixed entomology with humor and fantasy. What excited me most in the writing of it was describing the various places in the way the cockchafers saw them while passing through them or flying over them. It was, as a matter of fact, an imaginary microgeography, which I created as I went along. I discovered a paradoxical dream world that was at the same time both larger and smaller than our world of everyday. I sensed how the little stone becomes as large and cold as a boulder to the cockchafer which bumps against it. But a few seconds later, when the beetle flies away, the "boulder" becomes for him just a pebble again—that is, according to the scale of my eyes, something no bigger than a grain of sand.

I no longer remember whether or not I ever finished the tale of the travelers in the land of the red ants. But before I took full leave of entomology (in 1923–1924), I decided to develop several previously published articles about bees, hornets, and ants, and collect them in a little volume for *Biblioteca pentru toţi.* I wrote to the Alcalay Publishing House without, of course, mentioning the fact that I was a lycée pupil, asking them if they would be interested in such a book. Very soon I received a post card inviting me to submit the manuscript. With the very best handwriting of which I was capable, I transcribed the text into two thick notebooks. Not for a single moment did I think that they might guess my age from my immature script. And because I did not dare send the notebooks by mail, I asked one of my friends, Radu Bossie, to deliver them directly into the hands of the managing editor.

I waited for him impatiently, pacing back and forth on the sidewalk a few doors from the Alcalay offices. "What did he say?" I asked. "He said, 'All right, leave the notebooks here—to be examined.'"

I never heard anything more about them. But I was soon consoled. A few years later I should have been chagrined to have seen in some window a little book by myself on the subject of bees, hornets, and ants. I was a university student then, and I wanted to publish other kinds of books—and above all, *Romanul adolescentului miop.*

4. *The Temptations of the Nearsighted Adolescent*

IN THE autumn of that year, 1921, I entered the fifth year of lycée. I had completed the gymnasium, and having passed the so-called "examination of ability," I began the upper-level course. At that time the advanced course was divided into three areas: "Real," which included a considerable amount of mathematics and no Latin; "Modern," with very little mathematics and considerable Latin; and "Classic," without mathematics, but with Latin and Greek. Convinced that I would major in the physical sciences in the university, I chose Real. But it didn't take me long to realize that I was mistaken and had been wrong in my choice. I had given up Latin and especially the Latin teacher, Nedelea Locusteanu, whom I greatly admired because he taught us history, literature, and philosophy in addition to grammar and vocabulary, and he talked to us in class about Pythagoras and Omar Khayyám, Novalis and Leonardo da Vinci. I had chosen mathematics, which interested me only sporadically. But I knew that without a background in math, I could never become a good chemist.

It so happened, however, that I did not get along very well with the mathematics instructor, Banciu. Everyone—teachers, pupils, and parents alike—considered Banciu a model teacher. They had a saying: "It is impossible not to understand it when Banciu explains it to you!" I knew this also. Every time I heard him teach, not only did I understand, but I felt a fascination for mathematics. But as it always happened with me, when something interested me—a book begun at home and unfinished, an article that I was getting ready to write, a plot for a novella—I could not listen to the teacher's explanations. First I tried to see if I could skip class without being missed. When I saw that would be unwise, I stayed for the lectures, but did not listen. Most of the time I managed to continue my reading without the teacher's noticing it.

Once he called me to the blackboard, and when he saw I didn't know how to solve the problem, he thought I hadn't understood. He explained all over again, just for me, what he had explained a few sessions earlier. He became convinced then that I was capable of understanding if I paid attention, and he began to take special notice of me. Soon afterward he caught me reading *Le Rouge et le noir* during class. He gave me an F, confiscated my book, and warned me that if he caught me reading again he would suspend me for a week. I thought he was joking. But some time later Banciu caught me again—and he kept his promise. Not only did he give me an F and suspend me, but he called me to the faculty office and slapped me a couple of times.

This happened in the spring of 1922. I was fifteen, and I knew now what humiliation and hatred meant. Those slaps created an unbridgeable gulf between us. In vain did Banciu try to be amiable and friendly when I returned to school after a week. I locked my feelings inside and became like a block of stone. But during that week I had gone through the whole algebra textbook, and I had solved a number of problems. When next he called me to the blackboard, Banciu was so surprised he was ready to congratulate me. Probably he told himself that I had taken to heart the lesson he had given me. But he was mistaken. The fact was, I had broken completely with mathematics. I continued to study out of fear, and especially just before examinations, but I never became a good mathematician. Because Banciu kept threatening to fail me, saying that if I didn't study for the make-up examination he would have me repeat the grade no matter how brilliant I was in other subjects (referring to physical sciences and natural sciences), mathematics soon became a real terror. However, I managed to pass every subject that year and the next. But in view of the discoveries I had made during those two years, I knew that I would not major in chemistry at the university, so I decided in the seventh year to switch over to "Modern." In the middle of that year, after a short preparation, I took an examination with Locusteanu and was transferred to the Modern division. When we said goodbye, Banciu told me: "After two years of Real you'll be, undoubtedly, the best mathematician among your Latinists. Don't forget that math is taught in Modern too, although only one hour a week. If you don't work up to your best, I'll fail you!"

And he kept his promise this time also.

*   *   *

I see myself in the attic during those years, seated at the wooden table covered with blue paper. I see the lamp with the white shade, beneath which I kept pushing the book farther and farther, the more my eyes blurred and the more difficult it became to make out the letters. Those were the days of the "galloping myopia," as one of the oculists I was seeing at the time called it. The diopters were growing more rapidly than he could change the lenses. There was, the doctor said, only one solution: not to tire my eyes by reading too much by lamplight. But how could I (or *anyone*) have spared my eyes at a time when almost every week I was discovering a new author, other worlds, other destinies? I tried, nevertheless, to protect myself, reading without glasses, with my chin right against the book, by closing first one eye and then the other or pushing the glasses down on my nose, or by changing the light bulb—first blue, then white, now weak, now very strong. And when my eyes watered and became totally blurred, I would go to the next room and rinse them with cold water. Then I would lie stretched out on the bed with my eyes closed, trying not to think about anything.

In memory I see the bed—a wooden one, painted red. Above it, fastened tight to the wall, the glass-topped box in which I kept the most beautiful coleopteras and several large butterflies with immaculate wings. On the wall opposite, a bookcase that my father had made out of boards. By the sixth year I had already accumulated about five hundred books, most of them from *Biblioteca pentru toţi*, *Minerva*, and *Lumea*. But there were also some more valuable volumes: *Souvenirs entomologiques* by J. H. Fabre, *Die Insekten* by Brehm, treatises on chemistry, "classics" of transformism, and almost all that I could find from *Bibliothèque scientifique*, volumes with red covers from Flammarion, and *Bibliothèque philosophique* by Felix Alcan.

Every week Mother would give me a small sum of pocket money, but she never refused me when I would tell her I wanted to buy myself a rather expensive book. Often she asked me not to say anything about it to my father. The war had impoverished them, and in order to be able to keep us in school they had rented out almost the whole house. The first tenants were two French teachers, members of the Cultural Mission. Later there were some Hungarian employees of a Transylvanian firm, and finally we rented to the Italo-Romanian Chamber of Commerce. This was how I came to know Giovanni Costa at the very time I was studying Italian. Thanks to him, I was able to order all the Italian books I thought I needed.

I had the attic all to myself now, and it was filled with my things. Between the bed and the desk was a small stand where I kept collections of periodicals: *Ziarul Ştiinţelor Populare, Revista Muzicală, Orizontul,* and others. To prevent the wind from blowing them away when the windows were open, I put on top of them the most beautiful specimens from my geological collection: a piece of iron pyrite, one of granite, and fragments of stalactites. Above the stand I had pinned to the wall copies of Egyptian tomb frescoes, executed in different colors of ink: vestiges of the enthusiasm with which I had read the books of Maspero and Alexandre Moret. Under the stand was a little brown box in which I kept correspondence from friends, filled notebooks, and at the very bottom, camouflaged so my father wouldn't find it—*The Journal.*

I don't remember now how I started to write my journal. At first, in 1921, I recorded only what I was working on and how long I had worked every day: how many hours I had spent in the laboratory or with insects and plants, and how many hours I had devoted to reading, plus the titles of the books read and short commentaries on them. Soon after, I began to set down observations about my teachers and friends. But I wasn't content with that: I attempted to reproduce conversations verbatim, to describe in detail certain happenings from school or parties (starting in the sixth year we began to hold parties at the homes of different students, where we met girls of our own age). In time I came to write ten to fifteen pages about a single party, trying to reproduce dialogues with as much fidelity as possible, using expressions characteristic of each person. When I began *Romanul adolescentului miop* I used many of these pages. For instance, in describing our society, the Muse, I directly transcribed whole passages. Eventually, during the final two years of lycée, the journal became the confidant of all my attacks of melancholy, and it is likely that these excesses of lyricism and lamentation came one day to disgust me, so that I abandoned the journal. I did not resume it again until the summer of 1928, a little while before leaving for India.

I wrote in my diary mostly at night, sometimes long past midnight, when I was sure my father would not be coming to check on me. From the fifth year on, until I had completed my university studies, I accustomed myself to sleeping less and less. Sometimes three or four hours per night sufficed. I arrived at this point only after a long process of self-discipline. For several months I would go to bed each night a few minutes later than on the previous night, and I would set the alarm one minute earlier. When I had succeeded in robbing sleep of one hour, I would call a halt and not change the alarm for a few weeks. Then I would start the whole procedure again, limiting my allowance of sleep by one or two minutes every night.

I can't say that it was easy. Sometimes, when I went on reading until after 2:00 A.M., I could not fall asleep and kept tossing in bed. But I forced myself not to take these periods of insomnia into account, and I continued counting the hours and minutes allotted for sleeping from the moment I turned off the light and went to bed, even if I was still awake an hour or two later. At other times I would be sleepy after lunch, especially during the summer, and if I saw that all the coffee I drank and all the cold water I splashed on my face had no effect, I would lie down for half an hour with the alarm clock at the head of the bed. But I wouldn't forget to subtract half an hour from my sleep that night!

Eventually, I accustomed myself to a ration of four hours, and even if I had wished I would not have been able to sleep more. Later, when in addition to the endless reading and hours of writing there were also the other excesses of youth, I sometimes experienced curious blackouts, which frightened me terribly. I still remember two of those incidents, undoubtedly brought on by overwork. One night (I believe I was in the seventh year of lycée) I undressed, set the alarm for five, and went to bed. A few minutes later I awoke to find myself fully clothed, seated at my desk, with a book open in front of me. I was unable to remember anything—even whether or not I had been reading. I looked at my watch and saw that it was past three. The second scare of this kind happened to me when I was a university student. I suddenly came to my senses outside my house, on the street, without being able to figure out what I was doing there, whether I was going out or coming home. I could not even clearly remember my name or who I was! It was an afternoon in July, unspeakably hot. I recognized the house, however, and had enough strength to climb up to the attic, which at that hour was like an oven. I threw myself naked on the bed and slept until late in the evening. I had locked the door and I was awakened by my father's loud knocking. He had come to see what was wrong, since I had not appeared for supper.

Such accidents, although rather rare, really frightened me. I didn't tell anyone about them, but they worried me. The last incident of this sort happened to me in Calcutta, also on a terribly hot day.

I was forced to resort to such measures. I had a great need for "time"—not only to be able to cope with the reading of all the books that had piled up on my desk and shelves, but especially because, besides the journal and the many other notebooks in which I had come to write daily (résumés, critiques, articles), I had begun a fantasy novel projected with gigantic dimensions: *Memoriile unui soldat de plumb* (Memories of a Lead Soldier). I worked at this novel for some two years, in the fifth and sixth classes; and when I finally broke it off, I copied neatly in several notebooks those portions that I considered the more successful and gave them to certain friends to read. (Some years later, when I lent the entire manuscript to a friend, he failed to return it.) It was a novel of reckless proportions, encompassing not only global history but also the whole history of the Cosmos, from the beginning of our galaxy to the formation of the earth, the origin of life, and the appearance of man!

So far as I can remember, it began like this: a Boy Scout—that is, myself—is in a terrible train wreck at Valea Largă. At the moment of the crash, the Scout hides his head in fear inside his knapsack, and due to this instinctive gesture he escapes unharmed. Inside his bag he was carrying a lead soldier, one of the many lead soldiers with which he had played as a child and which he now as a teenager kept as a sort of "good luck charm." In that endless moment of the crash, the Boy Scout listens to the protracted, interminable life story of the lead soldier, told by that talisman itself! For the particles of lead out of which the toy soldier was made had witnessed the most important events of human history: the conquest of India by the Aryans, the destruction of Nineveh, Cleopatra's death, the crucifixion of Christ, the devastation of Rome by Alaric, Mohammed's life, the Crusades, and so on, up to our own times, including such recent events as the battle of Mărăşeşti. But before history, the lead (in gaseous form) had been part of various cosmic conflagrations that had led to the formation of the solar system and the earth, and it remembered countless millions of lifeless years, the appearance of living creatures, combats between prehistoric monsters, and so on until the coming of man and the inception of the first civilization.

It was a kaleidoscopic fresco made like a mosaic, in which I wanted to include everything I thought I knew, everything I had fed upon without always having digested from the cafeteria of my readings. But this fantastic novel was pervaded by a certain pessimism. Through the sarcasm attributed to the lead soldier I showed, in fact, what ephemeral and inconstant beings people really are, how quickly they forget, betray, and kill one another, and how blind is the destiny that rewards undeserving individuals and mediocre peoples, but destroys without a trace whole nations of heroes (like the Getae, early inhabitants of what is now Romania, and so many other prehistoric races) and truly great personalities. (One of the theses of the novel was this very idea: that the true heroes, the creative geniuses, and the authentic prophets never had the possibility of fulfilling their vocations, fate having paralyzed them or eliminated them before their time.) The source of this pessimistic vision of universal history (besides the melancholia caused by my having read about so many horrors and historical catastrophes, and the biographies of several martyrs of thought such as Giordano Bruno or T. Campanella) were of course my own experiences. I now felt superior to all my fellow students, if only because of the enormous effort I had expended to broaden and deepen my education. And yet, although I had been noticed by a few teachers, I had never received a prize, not even in biology or physical science, and at the end of every year I anxiously read the list of students who had passed their courses, to see if my name was there.

But there was something else besides that. I was now in the midst of a "puberty crisis." I found myself each morning uglier and clumsier. Most of all I realized, when girls of my age were around, how timid and unattractive I was compared with some of my friends. This mental state, which began around the sixth year with my *Memoriile unui soldat de plumb,* continued to worsen until I finished lycée. It was probably because of it that I was unable to complete the novel. At a given moment I felt that I could no longer write except in the first person, that any other kind of literature except the directly or indirectly autobiographical had no meaning. And so I began *Romanul adolescentului miop.*

From the first years of lycée, I had been friends with Dinu Sighireanu and Radu Bossie. Now, in the upper grades, Dinu had become a handsome boy, dark, green-eyed, the heartache of many a girl. He liked French history, which he knew as none other in our group, and also the books of Kipling. We met almost every day, usually at my attic, which seemed to be the ideal gathering place for my friends. During the last year in lycée as well as later, when I was in the university, not a day passed without one or more of my friends coming up, until I was forced to post a note on the door specifying the times when I would welcome visitors.

Radu Bossie remained unchanged from the moment I met him in the first years of lycée until his sudden, absurd death at age twenty-three. He was the son of the famous prosecutor Bossie. His mother, of English origin, was blond, beautiful, and eccentric; she obtained a divorce and died soon after at a poor little rundown country house. Radu was nearsighted like myself, and rather homely with his thick lips and large bulbous nose, but he had a sense of humor and an incomparable charm. He did not like to study, and in the higher grades, when he was in danger of failing, he was sent to a boarding school in Braşov. I was always glad to see him when he came home on vacations. He was jovial, optimistic, and indifferent to the boredoms of school life. Though he was almost cynical, he possessed a great kindheartedness and he was a perfect friend. He had great faith in my future as a scientist and read all my articles, whereas Dinu Sighireanu, Haig Acterian, and Jean-Victor Vojen were my literary confidants. After I had gone to India he stopped by my home often to find out from my mother what I was doing. He would come with a large pack of cigarettes, accept coffee gladly, and cheer up the whole house telling stories of his belated student life. Then, one day, he went on business to Craiova, fell ill, and died a few days later. I learned of it in November of 1930, in my little hut at Svarga Ashram in the Himalayas. He was the first among us to leave.

With Haig Acterian I became friends rather late, but the friendship was one that continued and deepened, especially after university years. In the first years we both "performed" in lycée shows—I with some piano sonata and he, a precocious baritone, singing *Le Grenadier*. Then, together with J-V. Vojen (with whom he attended the Conservatory of Dramatic Art), he discovered his vocation as an actor. Also in the lycée shows—held during the last years at the National Theater—they both received leading roles in a comedy by Valjean (in which I played the part of an under-commissar), and in *Sarmală, Friend of the People*, by Nicolae Iorga.

Haig had a rather dark, swarthy complexion and an indolent, Oriental kind of good looks; while Vojen was blond, and even during adolescence he rivaled Dinu Sighireanu in looks, elegance, and success with the fairer sex. He told us about his father whom he had never known, who had disappeared under mysterious circumstances, and whom he liked to imagine as a great adventurer, a genuine Don Juan. To this group of friends was later added the tall, proud, ironic Petre Viforeanu. Somehow he managed to be a prize student without pedantry, being interested in many things at once: literature, Latin, social life, and politics. He was the first person to reveal to me what true ambition is, when he confessed one day that he would consider himself a failure if by thirty he had not become a university professor, by forty a deputy minister, and by age fifty prime minister!

During the sixth year this group of friends, plus a few others, began to get together on Sunday afternoons at the home of our classmate Mircea Moschuna-Sion. A few girls came too, and in order to distinguish these afternoon meetings from ordinary social gatherings, we decided to establish a "cultural and artistic society" that we named the Muse. The program was rather ambitious: lectures followed by discussions, "concerts," and—above all—dramatic performances. One of our first efforts was a fragment from *Don Juan* by Victor Eftimiu, in which I had the role of a monk and Vojen that of

Don Juan. I also played the piano on several occasions: Rachmaninoff, Grieg, Debussy. But I never consented to play any arias from *Tomiris*, the "opera" I was writing at that time, about which only a few friends knew anything. My "opera" was, as a matter of fact, a very ambitious project, and I progressed with it rather slowly. Since writing out the score took too much time, I contented myself with memorizing the melodies I composed; and inasmuch as my musical memory was somewhat imperfect, these melodies were modified from one working session to another.

I did, however, agree to give a lecture about . . . the god Rama! The documentary material I extracted entirely from a book I had recently discovered, *Les Grands initiés* by Schuré. Knowing next to nothing about ancient India, I believed that everything Schuré said was true. (And great was my surprise and fury upon learning soon afterward that it was a case of a "mystical" story that Schuré himself had invented! I think that at that time there arose within me a mistrust of dilettantes, a fear of letting myself be duped by an amateur, an increasingly insistent desire to go directly to the sources, to consult exclusively the works of specialists, to exhaust the bibliography.) The lecture was long, prolix, probably pretentious, and I remember only that the small group of boys and girls listened to it with amusement, mostly out of fear of being bored.

At the time when I was participating diligently and enthusiastically in the gatherings of our society, I had already begun to take seriously my homeliness and my singularity—the latter largely imagined. I was the only one who came to meetings of the Muse wearing the school uniform; all the others had long ago started wearing "civilian" clothes. I was the only one who didn't try to camouflage his short-cropped hair—on the contrary, I set the clippers for the closest cut possible. I had recognized some time previously that, in the company of all my handsome friends, seldom was a girl willing to talk with me. This fact had brought me suffering at first, but now it gave me great satisfaction, since it confirmed my belief that I was hideous and repulsive. In vain did my friends try to convince me of the contrary; I refused to listen to them. Dinu Sighireanu pointed out to me that if I wouldn't agree to grow a beard, I should at least put some powder on my face (as he did) to hide the freckles and pimples. Vojen was convinced that my heavy eyebrows, broad forehead, and small ears made me, in my own way, a handsome boy, but he thought I needed to accentuate these traits: I must, as he said, create a "type" for myself.

I felt, however, that it was not only a question of nearsightedness and homeliness. Radu Bossie was just as nearsighted and perhaps even homelier, and yet the girls sought his friendship, and at our gatherings his exuberance was much appreciated. But, unlike him and almost all my other friends, I was timid and awkward with girls. When I was left alone with one of them, I didn't know what to say. I didn't know how to flirt. I had the impression that this activity called for a certain kind of person, like Vojen or Sighireanu, or at least some sort of sharp, ironic conversation like Viforeanu's, or the humor of Bossie. In addition, I had a great shortcoming: I didn't know how to dance. Probably I could have learned, as did my fellow students and friends at our Sunday gatherings, if I hadn't always volunteered to play for them to dance—fashionable foxtrots and tangos. From then to the end of lycée, I was invited to all the parties because I had proved myself the best and most indefatigable pianist.

But, as I said, I took greater and greater pleasure in this situation, which seemed to be an intrinsic part of my destiny as an exceptional adolescent. I felt that all my social failures, like the humiliations I suffered in school, were meant to isolate me from the world, to preserve me exclusively for the "oeuvre" I was called to write—the first item of which, most certainly, was to be *Romanul adolescentului miop*.

The "galloping myopia" coincided with my discovery of Balzac, Voltaire, and Hasdeu—all of them prolific authors who fascinated me particularly for their breadth and diversity. I read approximately a book per day by Balzac. He became almost an obsession with Mircea Mărculescu and me, and we advertised him and tried to convince as many of our friends as possible to read him. We persuaded Jean-Victor Vojen to do this for a few months. It was a sort of ritual: during school recesses we discussed the latest discoveries, and we tried, to the best of our abilities, to reconstitute the repertoire of characters from *La Comédie humaine*. We reread some of the novels that we hadn't especially liked on first reading, only because we didn't remember exactly some response or observation of Horace Bianchon. After we had exhausted our recent discoveries from used bookstores or the libraries to which we had access, we would read again each of our favorite books. I believe that during the lycée years alone I read five or six times *Le Père Goriot*, the book which, for me, has remained the most typical of Balzac's style—one to which I always returned with the same pleasure whenever, later on, the passion for Balzac came over me. (The last time this happened was in Paris in 1947, when I even began writing a biography of Balzac that I carried down to 1829, the year of the publication of his novel *Les Chouans*.) But what delighted me especially were his fantasies (*Séraphita, La Peau de chagrin, Le Centenaire*) and the lesser-known novellas (such as *La Vie des martyrs* and *Les Proscrits*). This giant who moved in so many worlds captivated me; he was not content to be "in the mainstream of current thought," but he introduced the androgyne into modern literature and invented a great many mythologies pertaining to the "will" and "energy" of the man of action.

Voltaire attracted me at first because he wrote everything—novels, pamphlets, historical monographs, letters, philosophy, and literary criticism—with the same unequaled perfection. I had read only a few of Voltaire's books when I bought at a used bookstore two unrelated volumes from Bengesco's *Bibliographie*. I skimmed over them with great excitement and enthusiasm. Recorded there were hundreds and hundreds of things of the greatest diversity—and this corresponded exactly with my secret hope that I would be allowed to write about a great many things, that I would not be forced to limit myself to science, for instance, or literature or history. Voltaire was my first encounter with an encyclopedist of genius, and I believe this was the reason I admired him: he confirmed my inclination to become a polyhistorian, he encouraged my dreams of a universal spirit. But, in fact, I never became a "Voltairian." And when I discovered other "universal" authors, especially Papini, and later Goethe and Leonardo da Vinci, I ceased to read him.

Hasdeu fascinated me because of his vast learning and his daring hypotheses concerning history. I had read him at the library of the King Carol I Foundation, but in the seventh year, when I announced that I wished to lecture on him before the class, Nanul gave me an introductory note to one of the librarians at the Romanian Academy. I went there one afternoon, and although I was wearing my school uniform I was admitted to the reading room of the Academy. In this way I was able to learn at firsthand about works from Hasdeu's youth, in particular the study that impressed me so much, *Perit-au Dacii?* (Did the Dacians Disappear?). I then wrote a long dissertation, which I read in two class sessions. From that manuscript I extracted my first articles about Hasdeu, published in *Universul literar, Foaia Tinerimii,* and *Cuvântul.* Since then, my admiration for Hasdeu's genius has never ceased. From 1934 to 1937, when I was Nae Ionescu's assistant in the Faculty of Letters, I spent many afternoons at the library of the Romanian Academy working on a critical edition of his writings, and in the spring of 1937 the Royal Foundations published in two volumes: *Scrieri literare, morale şi politice de B. P. Hasdeu.* The edition was far from perfect, but at that time there was no other, nor has a better one been published since.

Beginning in 1922 there appeared in *Ziarul Ştiinţelor Populare,* next to "Entomological Conversations," a series of sketches under the title, "From the Notebook of a Boy Scout." I do not think they were well-written, but they had a sentimental value for me. The series was a sort of fictionalized journal of my excursions in the Carpathians, to the monasteries in Prahova and Moldavia, and of my travels in Bukovina and Transylvania. I had become a Boy Scout at the ideal moment in my life. My bent for "adventure," satisfied for so many years on the streets and vacant tracts of Bucharest with ruffians and ragamuffins, had now found an outlet that allowed it to become disciplined and at the same time deepened. When I discovered that, as a Scout, I could wander for days through valleys and mountains without my parents' considering it to be "bumming around," I knew that I had discovered the key to freedom. All I had to do was to announce that our group was planning a new excursion of three or four days or a week, and Mother would ask how much money I needed!

In fact, my parents were delighted that I had become a Boy Scout. Mother especially was quite worried about my random and excessive reading. She was afraid that I would either lose my sight or ruin my health. It seemed abnormal to her that a boy my age, who had been used to spending so much time on the streets, should now shut himself indoors and read day and night, especially since I was reading books that, in her estimation, were much too difficult for my unripe mind. When I was with the Scouts, she knew at least that I wasn't reading, that I was breathing fresh air, that I was tiring my body and not my eyes and mind.

And tire myself I did. I will never forget the snow storm and the drifts we encountered one Easter when we went camping at Schitul Scheia in the Carpathians; or the cold, endless rains we endured for days on end, with only our short raincoats clumsily improvised out of tent-cloth to protect us, when we crossed over Cheile Bicazului into the Transylvanian valley. I shall never forget the bivouacs on Piatra Craiului, nor our first excursion in the Danube Delta—which so fascinated us that, although I was almost drowned in an arm of the warm swamp when my feet became entangled in the reeds, we decided to buy our own boat to use to travel from Tulcea to Constanța.

During the last three years of lycée I did not spend the summers with my family in Tekirghiol, but with the Boy Scouts. We would climb mountains for a week or two; then, for about a month, we would go to a Scout camp at Poiana Sibului or Mangalia. I would return to Bucharest around the end of August, and for the rest of the summer I would be on my own. The family, except for Nicu, were still in Tekirghiol. Nicu was supposed to look after me, cooking my meals or going with me in the evenings to a milk shop. I had the feeling of absolute freedom. I could read whatever I wanted and as much as I wanted, and although the attic was so hot that sometimes I could not bear even a shirt on my back, I *should* have been happy. But, as a matter of fact, I was not.

*   *   *

The attacks of melancholia, with which I was to struggle for many years to come, had started. It required a great effort of will for me to resist the first outbreaks of sadness. They would come upon me unexpectedly, toward sunset. At first I didn't know what was wrong; I thought it must be fatigue brought on by lack of sleep. But in vain did I try to rest, or even to go to bed; I could not fall asleep. I was not exhausted; I did not feel tired. There was only that terrible sensation of the irremediable—the feeling that I had lost something essential and irreplaceable. I felt there was no purpose in my life, that there was no reason for me to spend my time reading or writing. In fact, nothing held any meaning for me now: neither music nor camping trips, nor walks nor parties with my friends. I was trying desperately to identify what it was that I had "lost," and sometimes it seemed to me that it pertained to my childhood, the years at Rîmnicu-Sărat and Cernavodă, the first years in Bucharest, which now seemed fraught with beatitude and miracle. It was enough for me to recall an episode from childhood: a Christmas tree, the carriage we had at Cernavodă, one of Mother's dresses, Father's parade uniform—and my eyes would fill with tears. I detested crying, and I would never have forgiven myself had I begun to weep. I tried all sorts of things to defend myself from this humiliating experience, such as burying my head in a washbasin of cold water, or rushing downstairs and taking a walk on the streets, or trying to talk to myself out loud, making fun of my condition.

Soon, however, I discovered that my inexplicable sadness sprang from numerous other, unsuspected sources: for instance, the feeling of "the past," that simple fact that there have been things that *are* no more, that have "passed," such as my childhood or my father's youth; the thought that there were opportunities we missed and now it is too late, the chance is gone forever. Sometimes I regretted that I had not been reared in the country, that I did not know as a child the village life that seemed to me to be the only true kind, and that now I was severed irrevocably from that idyllic world.

Reading the nostalgic literature of the Moldavian authors—Sadoveanu, Ionel Teodoreanu, Cezar Petrescu—which hearkened back to childhood and the patriarchal way of life of other times, was also an occasion for sadness. And the fury with which I later wrote the article "Impotriva Moldovei" was nothing else but a supreme effort to shake off the depression that was slowly undermining the health of my soul. That was why I read so hungrily the stormy prose of Papini's early years. Here I found myself among "my kind"—among those whom I truly wished to be like: men of stone, like Dante and Carducci, not of honey, like Petrarch and the romantics. The long hybrid essay "Apologia virilitații" (In Defense of Virility), which I published in *Gândirea* during my student years, was also a protective gesture against the "Moldavia" that I carried in my blood.

It was so hard for me to defend myself against these moods because the springs of my sadness were many and hidden. Sometimes I found myself enveloped in melancholy just when I least was expecting it. For years I had gloried in my exaggerated sense of singularity, in the fact that ever since my childhood I had felt isolated, unusual, "unique." For a long time my "peculiarity" had protected me like an inner armor from all sorts of failures and humiliations. And at the same time my singularity, which seemed predestined, weighed on me like a tombstone. I would have tried anything to have broken free of it, to have been able to get close to someone who could "understand" me. That someone, obviously, could not have been one of my male friends, but one of those girls I met on Sunday afternoons at homes of classmates or at meetings of the Muse. Or, to be more precise, not exactly one of them, but a girl similar to them—endowed, however, with all the qualities I ascribed to an ideal woman, including a great musical talent, an encyclopedic education, and a prodigious knowledge of foreign literature and the occult sciences! But, on the other hand, the more clearly I envisioned the beauty, charm, and genius of that girl—a composite of all the actresses and heroines I knew—so much worse did my defects seem, especially my homeliness and my timidity.

I poured out my complaints about all this in my journal. The melancholy moods came upon me at dusk and held me prisoner as though in a gigantic net, from which I struggled desperately to escape until long after midnight. Then I would come to my senses feeling drained, exhausted, and yet resigned, almost reconciled, and I would dutifully take up my work again.

As time passed I learned to make fun of myself, especially for my imaginary, pulp-novel romances in which I was loved by my ideal heroine who combined all the beauty of my favorite actresses and the girls at whom I cast glances when I went to parties. Besides, I had discovered houses in the slum districts where I met another kind of woman, of flesh and blood, whose colorful reality had come to enchant me. In a chapter of *Romanul adolescentului miop* entitled "Saturday," I described later, from the notes in my journal, these nocturnal escapades on which Mircea Mărculescu often accompanied me, and which ended with long discussions in neighborhood bars, sometimes prolonged until dawn.

During the last years of lycée I became even closer to Mărculescu, that tall, lean, scraggy boy with the pointed nose. Thanks to him I came to know at firsthand the life of the poor Jews of Dudeşti. We got into the habit of spending holidays together: the Christian ones at my home, the Jewish ones with his family. He was a Balzac enthusiast, although his naive enthusiasm made him fall in love for a while with Anatole France. Later he discovered Freud, and this led him to decide to go to Paris to study psychoanalysis as well as medicine. Like me, Mărculescu had an unquenchable thirst for learning and he read enormously. With him I could talk about so many things that we made an agreement to meet only at night so we might have time to discuss all the problems that interested us, from *La Fille aux yeux d'or* to the origin of the Pentateuch or the book of Freud's we had read most recently. We were good friends, but although we confided in each other I never told him about my melancholy moods. I would have been ashamed to have him think that his friend, whom he believed to be so "scientific," could suffer in such an inexplicable way, and for no other reason than the fact that time passes, and in its passing something essential in us is irretrievably lost.

Soon after I became a Boy Scout, I tried to persuade Mărculescu to come with us on our outings. He agreed with a certain reluctance, because he was a city boy in the true sense of the word and nature left him indifferent. Once during an Easter holiday we took the train to Sinaia, and from there set off on foot from the chalet at Schitul Ialomicioara. But even before we reached Pietrele Arse, the weather changed abruptly and snow started to fall, soon turning into a blizzard. The five or six of us were dressed in spring clothes. Mărculescu was even wearing white canvas shoes. We had left Sinaia rather late, and because of the storm we lost our way. I don't remember how many hours we hiked, not knowing where we were headed, until we came across a cabin that probably was used during the summer by workers at one of the sawmills. We broke the lock and went inside. After kindling a fire, we prepared some tea and drank it with a lot of rum, and soon we were in good spirits. The storm had worsened, but what did we care? The next day we could scarcely open the door, and in order to walk through the drifts without sinking we had to fasten short lengths of boards to the soles of our shoes.

That night, however, soon after we had fallen asleep, we were awakened by a loud knocking at the door. We opened it to find two workmen carrying a corpse on an improvised sled. They were bringing it from the top of the mountain, and noticing the light through the windows of our cabin they had decided to leave it with us. They were workers who had to be at the factory early in the morning. They assured us that they would notify the police in Sinaia and that someone would be sent to pick it up. "If we leave it outside the door, the wolves will eat it before morning," said one of them who had noticed our reluctance to keep it.

They laid the body, which was wrapped in a raincoat, right beside the door. I don't think any of us slept at all the rest of the night. This incident cured Mărculescu of Scouting. The rest of us, however, once we returned to Bucharest, were very proud of having passed through such a dangerous situation. I even wrote a short story inspired by this adventure, called "Eva," which received a prize in a contest for young writers. It was about a young man who, like us, had daringly started up the mountain with his girl friend one spring day. But except for the snow and getting lost in the forest and breaking into the cabin, everything else was invented. After the hero has saved the girl by almost carrying her to the hut in his arms, and she has fallen asleep exhausted on the floor, the story ends with his saying: "And then I felt how impetuously I desired Eva's body . . ."

5. *Navigare Necesse Est...*

I HAD begun *Romanul adolescentului miop* somewhat earlier, but only in the winter of 1923–1924 did I "see" it as a whole, from one end to the other. This time I was certain I would finish it, and I was confident it would be an exceptional book that would create quite a stir. I imagined that through it I should get revenge on the teachers, the prize students, and all those beautiful but superficial girls who had not had the sense to notice me. I believed I was prepared to write a novel: I had published about fifty articles and literary sketches in several magazines, I had contributed regularly to the lycée review, *Vlăstarul*, and had even become the editor-in-chief (I gathered the material, took it to the printer, and spent hours with the typesetter to make sure he correctly deciphered certain manuscripts). In addition, I had at my disposal a voluminous journal. I was convinced that if I knew how to make use of this material, the novel would be ready in a few months.

It was more than an autobiographical novel. I wanted it to be at the same time a document exemplifying adolescence. I decided not to invent anything or to embellish it in any way—and I believe I held to my intention. Even the girls' love letters were authentic: I simply copied some of those Dinu Sighireanu had received! The chapters in which I described our society, the Muse, the parties with friends, the difficulties with Papadopol and Banciu were all constructed by following the journal closely and sometimes copying whole passages from it. I wanted the dialogues to be absolutely "authentic" and each character to use his own personal vocabulary. The value I accorded to *Romanul adolescentului miop* was, above all, documentary. I told myself that for the first time an adolescent was writing about adolescence, and his writing was based upon "documents." A few years later, when excerpts from the second volume of Teodoreanu's *La Medeleni* began to appear in *Viaţa Românească*, I knew I had not been wrong. Teodoreanu's adolescents were not the ones I had known. They belonged to another world—one that both fascinated and moved me, but one that I felt to be past and gone forever. My adolescents were from the *here and now*, from the Bucharest of the first years after the war, the years of jazz and *La Garçonne*. Aside from the inevitable self-flattery (for I was writing partly to avenge myself), the novel was as "realistic" as it was possible to make it. I did not blush from devoting a lengthy chapter to erotic discoveries, and almost everything that my classmates and I believed about sex, love, God, the meaning of life, and all the other problems that tormented us was noted there almost raw, without embellishment.

This was, besides, my great ambition: to show that we, the adolescents of that time, were not like the puppets we encountered sporadically in literature. We were alert, physically and spiritually, but the world we wanted to enter was not the world of our parents. We wanted something else and we dreamed of something else—although the only person who seemed to know anything precise about that "something else" was the author of the novel!

The plot was simple enough: a student from the Lycée Spiru-Haret was writing about himself, his fellow students, friends, and teachers. Those who knew me guessed from the outset that the student was I, because I talked about the attic, the insectarium, the books I liked, and my hopes of becoming a scholar, pianist, or writer. There were also some chapters unrelated to the others: about the melancholia that sometimes came over me at dusk (for instance, when I looked down at the empty street from the window of my attic, or when I heard a charwoman singing in the distance on a Sunday evening); about the German class and all the things that passed through my mind listening to Papadopol explaining *Die Räuber*; about the Muse and the girls who attracted me and intimidated me at the same time. But above all there were countless pages of confessions: what I wanted to be, what I wanted to do, endless analyses of my emotional states (of exultation, indifference, exhaustion, detachment, etc.), portraits of my friends, plots of short stories and novels I proposed to write and with whose characters I liked to converse (I believe I devoted a whole chapter to a conversation I had with Nonora, the heroine of a novella I never succeeded in finishing, because the more I wrote, the more the plot altered itself).

And yet, out of those disconnected chapters written in diverse styles (some lyrical and terribly sad, others almost humorous, some harsh and vehement), the "subject" quickly emerged: an adolescent who feels he has outgrown adolescence, who is torn by the melancholy that this era has brought (an era which, it seems to him, ought to have been full of bliss), and who at the same time is impatiently waiting to be freed from it so he can start his "true life." The whole book is pervaded by a curious ambivalence: the author insists time and again that adolescence is an essential moment in life, that *this* adolescence—his and that of his friends—constitutes a new spiritual phenomenon never encountered before and, as such, deserves to be prolonged in order to be correctly analyzed and interpreted; and on the other hand he appears exasperated by the difficulties of adolescence, especially by the melancholy, the regrets, and the timidity of which it seems to him to be composed.

But aside from all this, what a safety valve this novel was for me at that time! Even more than in the case of my journal (because I hoped to publish the novel), I could rid myself of writing in it of all my failures and humiliations. For many years I had participated in the contests sponsored by *Tinerimii Române* (Romanian Youth), and I had not received so much as an honorable mention. I remember, for example, the contest of the sixth year class. I no longer recall what topic we were given, but I was so "inspired" when I wrote and so enthusiastic after rereading the manuscript, that I had no doubt I would obtain first prize with honors. I couldn't believe it when I didn't find my name on the list of winners. I was sure there had been an error. That Sunday I went to the atheneum to see for myself how the prizes were distributed. When they came to the sixth year class, my heart began to pound. The first prize with honors went to another Mircea: Mircea Ionescu of the Lycée Matei Basarab. I had known this long before, of course, since the names of the winners had been published in the newspaper, but up to that moment I still believed there had been a typographical error!

My fury knew no bounds. I think I hated Mircea Ionescu (he was also nearsighted and even homelier than I). This injustice could not be buried in a private diary; it deserved to be denounced in public! I started walking toward Şosea, lost in thought. It was a Sunday in May, near dusk, the hour I most feared because the melancholy and sadness tempted me then. But this time I did not fear it. I was bleeding. What humiliated me most was the injustice of it all—I *knew* that Mircea Ionescu could not have written better than I had! I considered those inspired pages some of the best I had ever penned. And I believed that I could not be mistaken, because so many other sketches, short stories, and essays of mine had been judged good and published.

Sunk in contemplation, I walked for several hours. By the time I reached home it had become completely dark. That night I started writing a new chapter of the novel. I think I entitled it, "Mircea Ionescu, First Prize with Honors." Thus I managed to lift my spirits, and later I fell asleep, reconciled. Rereading it afterward, I was proud of it. But a short while later Ionel Teodoreanu published in *Adevărul Literar* an excerpt from the second volume of his trilogy, *La Medeleni*, entitled "Mircea Ionescu"—and so I discarded my chapter.

That was not the only chapter I sacrificed. During the course of those years I constantly added and eliminated pages and even whole chapters. The novel was almost finished, but when I would read it over it would seem to me that I had not said everything, or that I had not been sufficiently "authentic." This would send me back to check the notebooks of *The Journal*, and as a result I would correct something or introduce new passages. I labored especially to evoke the thrill of intellectual discoveries: to show, for example, that to realize the impossibility of belief in an anthropomorphic God is an experience as exciting as the first taste of physical love. I tried to describe as precisely and in as much detail as possible the process of thinking: for instance, what happened in my mind when I first read that "time and space are *a priori* perceptions"; or what happened when I closed my eyes and stopped my ears and said to myself, "I am myself, I am I, only I; but who is this 'I,' what is there inside me which I believe to be myself?"

I wanted, furthermore, to show how *alive* books are, what an extraordinary experience it is to discover in old bookstores some work you had sought for years. Sometimes such discoveries become even more dramatic due to the circumstances in which they are made. Thus I remember one summer afternoon I found at an antiquary's one isolated volume of Plutarch's *Morals,* and I discovered in it that mysterious treatise, *De Pythiae oraculis.* I could not wait to reach home to read it. I stopped at Cişmigiu Park and on a bench there I read it through in one breath. Then I realized the sun was setting, and all of a sudden *De Pythiae oraculis* seemed far away and futile. Indeed, all Plutarch's works seemed vain, as did all writings in general, all the books I loved, all the authors I admired; and one question kept returning to me like an obsession: What for? What good is it to *you* to know that the Pythia no longer answers in verses?

It was as if the whole world had suddenly turned to ashes and I found myself in a universe of shadows and vanities, without meaning or hope, where all things are essentially vain and empty. During those endless moments of despair I tried to regain myself and find an answer to the question: What for? Of what use is *De Pythiae oraculis?* Sitting there on the bench, with Plutarch's volume on my lap, I tried to smile. I wiped my glasses with a handkerchief and sought an answer. "To annoy you," I whispered, "you, the one who's asking me!" I felt this wasn't quite the right answer, but I insisted on it stubbornly. "It's just because Plutarch's treatise is useless and absurd that you ought to read it! And because nothing has any meaning, I laugh at both meaning and meaninglessness, and I'll do what I want, even if it doesn't have any meaning!" But I felt that all these were cries of helplessness. I sensed how false they were because, in those moments, I no longer wanted anything; and I certainly didn't want to read Plutarch.

Little by little, Cişmigiu sank into darkness and the coolness of the freshly watered flowers. The people no longer seemed the same. Gone were the pensioners, the orderlies, the governesses with children. The lights had not yet been lit, and those who came at this hour were making for the linden trees, which were blooming. Young couples, students, and soldiers on leave passed by. The trams going down to Bulevardul Elisabeta sounded closer than usual. I continued to smile and I decided that I had been wrong: that, although I didn't know the answer, the world *does* have a meaning, Plutarch deserves to be read, and *De Pythiae oraculis* was a true discovery.

That night I wrote down all these things in as much detail as possible, hoping at some later date to integrate them into a chapter of the novel. It seemed to me that such "experiences" were important. I did not consider myself a "cerebral" person (like the characters in Remy de Gourmont's novel *Sixtine*), but I wanted to show that, at least for me, books are sometimes more alive than people, that they also can be loaded with dynamite, and that from an encounter with certain books you can emerge either mutilated or else ten times stronger than you had believed you were. Such an encounter, which was decisive for me as well as for the destiny of *Romanul adolescentului miop*, was *Un uomo finito* (A Finished Man) by Giovanni Papini. I had read, as had most of my friends, his *Life of Christ*, but it didn't appeal to me. *Un uomo finito*, on the contrary, struck like a bolt of lightning. It had appeared in a Romanian translation and Haig Acterian had discovered it. He insisted I read it. "You'll like it," he told me. "The author's just like you!"

I should not have believed that I could be so much like someone else. I rediscovered myself throughout almost all of Papini's childhood and adolescence. Like him I was homely, very nearsighted, consumed by a precocious and unbounded curiosity, wanting to read everything, and dreaming that I would write about everything. Like him I was timid, loved solitude, and got along only with friends who were intelligent and studious; like him I hated school and believed only in what I learned by myself without the help of teachers. Later, however, I realized that the resemblance was not as extraordinary as it had seemed then. For instance, Papini had not had the mischievous childhood I had had, and he had not been attracted by the natural sciences and chemistry, nor was he a lover of music. Moreover, I had not wanted to write, as had he, an encyclopedia and a history of world literature. But it was still true that we were alike in our precociousness, our myopia, our thirst for reading, and our encyclopedic interests. I was struck by the fact that Papini spoke of adolescence not as a physiological or emotional phase, but as an era of intellectual discoveries, even as I did in my novel. On rereading *Un uomo finito*, I sometimes had the impression that I was a replica of Papini. But my enthusiasm gave place to doubt, jealousy, and fury because so many chapters of *Romanul adolescentului miop* would be considered copied from, or at least inspired by, *Un uomo finito*.

Naturally, this discovery was too important not to be recounted in the novel. I believe I rewrote that chapter several times, because I kept feeling I hadn't found the right "tone." It was necessary that I tell about everything I felt and everything that went through my mind while reading *Un uomo finito:* the joy of having found a friend, an older brother, a master who had experienced what I had experienced—but also the fury of suddenly having found myself the double of someone else. It was painful to discover that all my "originalities" belonged to another, that I was introducing nothing new in my novel, at least so far as the essential problem of the main character was concerned: the feeling of uniqueness and solitariness upon which so much of my peculiar behavior depended. A few years later, when I began publishing excerpts from my novel, the definitive version of this chapter appeared in *Viaţa Literară* under the title "Papini, Eu şi Lumea" (Papini, I, and the World). It was wholly Papinian in style, reminiscent of the pamphlets of Papini's first period. I spoke of myself as an unrecognized genius, an intellectual giant camouflaged as a lycée pupil, threatening to destroy all who dared stand in his way. The essay was so frantic and absurd that it received delighted comments from all my journalist friends of the time.

My passion for Papini induced me to learn Italian quickly so that I could read his other books. I shall never forget the thrill with which I took in my hands the Italian editions from Valecci, with their colored covers and titles printed in thick letters, as though carved in wood. I was elated as I read pages of criticism and polemics in *Stroncature, Maschilità, Ventiquattro Cervelli,* and others. In a few months I had managed to obtain all of Papini's books except for those that were out of print, which I was to read in 1927 at the Central Library in Rome. As I said before, Papini's prose—frantic and stormy yet sharp and caustic—helped me for many years in my struggle with melancholia. Only later did I come to realize that Papini was not a "great writer," of the stature of Leopardi, for instance, or Carducci. Much of his work is "dated," and it is probable that later generations will leave him far behind. But I have no doubt that *Un uomo finito* is and will remain an exceptional spiritual document, unique in modern literature.

I am grateful to Papini also for the fact that, through him, I became familiar even in lycée days with Italian literature, and thus I succeeded in freeing myself from the tutelage of the French book trade. He helped me indirectly, by revealing to me other preoccupations and nourishing me from other springs, to orient myself differently from the majority of the intellectuals of my generation who primarily read and discussed books and authors accessible in the French language.

After that I wrote several articles about Papini, and I translated several of his short fantasies. In 1926–1927, when I was in the university, I published in *Cuvântul* three articles on Papini, which I sent to him along with a letter in which, among other things, I told him that I was a student at the Faculty of Letters. A few weeks later I received a three-page reply. *"Cher ami inconnu,"* he wrote in his large sprawling script, and he lamented that I was studying philosophy, "the most futile of the sciences." He invited me to visit him, should I ever come to Florence. And visit him I did, that very spring, on my first trip to Italy.

Little by little during the seventh year I found myself becoming estranged from my beloved natural sciences, physics, and chemistry, and increasingly fascinated not only by literature, which I had loved since childhood, but also by philosophy, Oriental studies, and the history of religions. In the middle of that year I transferred to "Modern." Professor Nedelea Locusteanu helped me to arrive very quickly at the level of Latin my fellow students had already reached. Locusteanu was an excellent Latinist; he had translated Titus Livius and was richly and brilliantly cultured. I learned that in his youth he had majored in chemistry at the university. An explosion in the laboratory had snatched away his right hand and obliged him to give up chemistry. He knew all sorts of things unexpected in a professor of Latin. But his great passion was Anthroposophy, and I believe he really began to hold me in esteem after I told him that I had read several books by Rudolf Steiner. He knew only a little German and in order to learn it he had translated, slowly and for his own use only, certain works of Steiner that he had not been able to find in French. He was interested in the occult sciences and magic, and he even had some curious notions about the role of magical charms in Romanian political life.

I was now totally captivated by the ancient Orient. At the library of the King Carol I Foundation, to which I had gained access in the sixth year, I kept making discoveries in the enormous (and at the

time, for me, boring) *Geschichte des Altertums* by Ed. Meyer. I summarized it almost page by page, with long extracts, until the appearance of the publications of the Musée Guimet in which I found
translations from Sanskrit and Chinese, and *The Zend-Avesta* by
Darmesteter. (This last disappointed me because, after having read
Thus Spake Zarathustra, I had expected something entirely different.)
During those years of almost mystical admiration for the ancient
Orient, when I believed in the mysteries of the Pyramids, the deep
wisdom of the Chaldeans, and the occult sciences of the Persian
magi, my efforts were nurtured by the hope that one day I would
solve all the "secrets" of religions, of history, and of man's destiny
on earth.

Locusteanu only encouraged such a hope, and although he was
strict with me in Latin he did not push me to learn Greek (which I
started only in the first year at the university), but instead he directed me toward Oriental languages, advising me to begin with Hebrew. I bought myself the textbook published by our former instructor in religion, and undertook the study of Hebrew. As was my
habit, I studied several hours per day, but lacking experience and
assistance, and being more attracted to other Oriental languages, I
did not make much progress. Besides, Hebrew did not appeal to me.
Locusteanu assured me that there were Cabalistic texts of considerable importance, but his efforts were in vain. What I had read of
these in translation had not attracted me.

So I plunged into Persian and Sanskrit, using the Hoepli manuals of Pizzi and Pizzagalli. At first I liked Persian better, and I
dreamed that someday I would translate *Shah-nama* into Romanian.
I labored with the two handbooks for a few months, but I don't
believe I got very far. I was tempted by too many passions and I
wanted to do too many things at once. I had discovered, among
other things, in French translations, Frazer's *The Golden Bough* and
Folklore in the Old Testament, which had revealed to me the inexhaustible universe of primitive religions and folklore. Then too, that
summer of 1924, I finished school with even greater impatience
than usual because, at a modest shipyard in Tulcea, our little boat
was being built. We had picked a name for it long before: it was
called *Hai-hui* (Pell-mell).

It cost some 20,000 lei, and it was to be the property of eight of us boys who had been friends in Scouting for many years. We had gone on numerous camping trips and other outings together by this time. Our decision to purchase the boat had come after that unforgettable excursion to the Danube Delta of which I spoke earlier. One of the boys had relatives in Tulcea and he assured us that we could buy it there for less than half the market price.

That summer we did not climb the Bucegi as usual. Instead, we went to Tulcea to see how the construction of the boat was progressing. We set up a tent in our friend's back yard and ate wherever we were invited. Mornings were spent at the shipyard, trying to guess how many days it would be before we could put the boat in the water. Then we practiced rowing on the Danube and did some swimming. In the evenings we went strolling on the main street, dressed in our best and saluting collectively all the young ladies who smiled at us.

After about ten days the boat was ready. It was approximately twelve meters in length, and it had a cabin, a huge mast, and three pairs of oars. We registered it at the harbor-master's office; we took pictures of ourselves in front of it, together with the men who had built it; and then on a Sunday afternoon, in order to be admired by all our acquaintances in Tulcea, we embarked. There wasn't the slightest breeze, and we were forced to row with all our might. We labored thus until late evening, when at last we found a suitable spot among the willows to set up our tent. In Tulcea we had begun to get used to the mosquitoes, but here on the Danube whole colonies attacked us. We wrapped ourselves in our raincoats and hid our heads in towels, but still we had difficulty sleeping.

The next morning, and each day thereafter, we were greeted by the same hot, motionless atmosphere. It seemed as if nothing were breathing and not a leaf shaking in that enchanted Danube Delta. For a shortcut, we left the arm of the Danube called St. Gheorghe and plunged into the maze of canals that intersects the reeds. The year before we had left Sulina with a group of young people in five or six large boats, with two oarsmen per boat, and we had reached the sea in a few days. This time it took us a whole week because we had to row all the way. We arrived exhausted and starved because our supplies had given out except for a few watermelons and a little keg of drinking water, half empty.

As soon as we reached the sea, the wind started to blow. It was so strong that we debated whether or not we ought to undertake this adventure. Every day one of us was designated "captain." But that afternoon the "captain" did not dare take the responsibility by himself and asked us to decide together, by secret vote. Five of us including the "captain," who was named Livovski, were for leaving. Triumphant, singing, we spread the sails—and we could hardly believe our eyes. The boat leaned slowly to one side as if bending under the weight of the mast; then suddenly the wind caught the canvas and we shot off like an arrow straight for Russia. We kept trying to steer south, but the wind was so strong and we were so unskilled in manipulating the sails that we barely managed to direct it toward the southeast. Now it was going forward diagonally, heading toward the Caucasus. It cut the waves with a speed that made us dizzy. We had never imagined that a boat loaded as ours was could move so swiftly. Soon we lost sight of the shore, except that we could see far away, in miniature, the hills of Dobruja, painted and hazy in the afterglow of sunset.

Then the storm began. We saw the clouds gathering and the billows rising threateningly. Our boat would list heavily, first to one side and then to the other; hesitate a few seconds as if not knowing what direction to take; then catch the wind suddenly and be off again. It was totally dark when the storm burst upon us. The sky began to palpitate, cleft again and again by enormous bolts of lightning that sliced it from one end to the other. Thunderclaps resounded closer and closer to us. Sometimes we heard the lightning strike the water, sizzling as if a red-hot iron were piercing the surface.

In those days I loved the lightning. About two years earlier, an extraordinarily violent storm had overtaken us in the Carpathians on Pietrele Arse. When lightning started striking a dozen meters or so from us, I was elated. I climbed on a rock and began to sing, or rather to scream, the "Cavalcade" from *Die Valkyrie*. Even that night on the sea I was not afraid of the lightning. There again I sang the "Cavalcade."

As soon as it started to rain, the "captain" went inside the cabin to consult the map and compass. He became seasick because the boat was now rolling in the billows. We decided to fold our sails. That was no easy task, since we could scarcely get to our feet. At last we succeeded, but the mast was so tall and so heavy, on account of the wet sails being wrapped about it, that several times the boat

dipped threateningly. We would throw ourselves then to the opposite side and thus manage to bring it to a somewhat normal position. But the tiller hindered us terribly. No matter how we held it,
the boat zig-zagged forward, and several times it revolved as if
caught in a whirlpool. We changed helmsmen three times in less
than half an hour without any success. Then we gave up, took out
the tiller, laid it at our feet, and abandoned ourselves to the mercy
of fate.

Probably this act of desperation saved us. The boat had been
well-constructed and it had an unusually deep keel. Left to itself, it
floated like a nutshell. It rose on the billows and then plunged into
the phosphorescent abysses between the swells without capsizing,
since we were ready to shift from one side to the other in order to
counterbalance the mast. It was raining very hard, and we had also
taken on a great deal of water from all the waves that had broken
over us. We bailed madly with anything we could lay our hands on:
buckets, cans, mess-tins. The "captain" as well as his "mate," who
had gone to assist him, were both lying ill in the cabin. But since
there was really nothing to decide, the absence of a chief was not
particularly noticeable.

I shall never forget that night. Soaked to the skin, lying on the
bottom of the boat, dipping water with a mess-tin and throwing it
overboard as in a trance, I sometimes saw coming toward us a gigantic form, tall as a house. As it drew nearer, I could see it palpitate
and quiver. It appeared to be illuminated from inside by a phosphorescent light. It hesitated a few moments, then began to buzz metal-
lically and seemed ready to fall down. We came directly beneath its
belly, and watching from the bottom of the boat it seemed to me
that I was looking at a mountain of green gold. I would tell myself,
this time we won't make it!—and I would close my eyes. We would
feel the boat shaking violently, as if being pushed from underneath,
and then we would sense ourselves being lifted. When we opened
our eyes, we would find ourselves between the foam and the gold,
with an abyss on all sides. A few seconds later we would hear the
mast creaking and we would drop into the void, holding onto the
benches with both hands.

I was afraid, and yet I didn't feel paralyzed. One day, the year
before, when we were boating in the Danube Delta, we were all
exhausted from rowing and threw ourselves into the warm, stag-

nant waters of the canal. I felt my feet becoming entangled in the grasses; then all at once my body seemed to grow heavy and I began to sink—slowly, without struggling—into the depths. Those who had returned to the boat saw me, but they thought I was clowning, and they were admiring the skill with which I was simulating a drowning. I was saved at the last moment by a friend who swam under me and pushed me to the surface. This time, however, the fear of drowning did not paralyze me. I felt that we were abandoned to the will of fate, without hope of help from anywhere. The sense of absolute helplessness, which in a way reconciled me, also gave me a strange sort of peace. Since nothing more could be done, I had the feeling of complete freedom. Will, intelligence, and all my spiritual faculties were, for the first time, *free;* they no longer were straining after an immediately attainable goal.

The lightning continued to cleave the darkness, sometimes disclosing the troughs in which we lay and at other times the crests of the waves onto which we had been lifted, driven by the tempest that was still raging. Sometimes I looked at the tip of the mast and it seemed to me that it was lit by the same phosphorescence as the waves. I heard it whistling like some gigantic bird. Then, after midnight, the storm passed on, although the sea continued to boil and toss. When daylight came we found ourselves surrounded by purple-gray waves, but by now we were used to them. The wind was still blowing rather hard, and in that fact lay our hope. We decided to rest a few hours, with two of us always keeping watch, and then put up the sails and make for the shore. We did not see the shore, but we had a compass to direct us. As the light grew brighter we realized more and more what a desperate situation we faced. Part of our gear had been lost overboard; the rest was strewn all over the bottom of the boat amidst books, cameras, and watermelons. Very little drinking water remained in the keg, and what there was had become cloudy and stale. We were exhausted from our struggle and lack of sleep, but nevertheless we were happy, and above all proud, proud to have survived such an ordeal.

(We had a right to be proud, although we had done nothing to merit our escape. When we reached Constanţa a week later we discovered that during that stormy night many fishermen's boats had been sunk. We had survived because we had let the boat float by itself. We also learned in Constanţa that the leader of the Scouts in

Mamaia where we had been expected for several days had been so worried that he had sent out a seaplane from the naval base that had been searching for us the entire morning all along the coast.)

By taking turns we managed to get a few hours' sleep. But about two o'clock a sudden gust of wind bent our mast and broke it, almost overturning the craft. Our hope of reaching the shore that evening was now crushed. The sea had become calm, but we sensed the current drawing us toward the east—less quickly than the storm of the previous night, but just as certainly. We decided then to row. We put the tiller back in place and rowed, taking turns of an hour each, four of us at a time while the others slept. There were a few pieces of sugar left, and we rationed them out along with slices of watermelon.

After several hours we began to see the low mountains of Dobruja. But the current was strong and we were tired, so we progressed very slowly. It was getting dark and we rowed as in a trance, without talking, our eyes half closed. To gain some strength, I imagined myself at home in the garden or the attic. I tried to remember the titles of the books I had not yet read, and to take pleasure in the fact that they were waiting for me there in that attic, now hot as an oven.

Midnight passed and we rowed constantly, growing ever more exhausted, but we were at least comforted by the thought that the current was not carrying us backward. Around 3 A.M. it seemed that we saw ahead of us, not very far away, a black streak where there were no waves. Our spirits rose. We supposed it was a sandbank and we proposed lifting the boat onto it and resting there until morning. Soon the boat grounded. A few of us jumped over the side to see how large the bank was. We began to shout for joy: we had arrived! We were on the beach! What we had taken for the distant mountains of Dobruja were in fact those dunes of clay and sand that run along the shores a few meters inland.

We beached the boat and unloaded the tent, intending to set it up. But one boy slipped and was so overcome by fatigue and sleeplessness that he lay where he fell, fully clothed. The next minute we all followed suit. We went to sleep lying on the sand, only halfway inside the tent.

The next day, a little past noon, we were awakened by some fishermen. They had noticed a boat on the shore and had shouted, and when no one had answered they had come to investigate. Their village was a few kilometers away. We managed to row there and ate like ravenous wolves. By means of a drayman who was going to Megidia, we sent a telegram to the Scout Camp leader in Mamaia, saying that we were alive. When we entered Mamaia a week later, now fully recovered and sunburnt, rowing like true mariners, the whole camp turned out to cheer us.

Only later did we begin to realize the consequences of our adventure. Some of us were left with a phobia for water and since then have never wanted to bathe in the seà. In my case, the attraction I had formerly had as a child for lightning and thunderstorms was replaced by an irrational panic, of which I was cured only much later. I discovered how irrational it was when, that autumn, at the National Theater, I could not bear to hear the storm in *King Lear* and had to leave the auditorium. The doctor whom I consulted at the time said that it was just the effect of a "nervous shock" and that it would disappear with time. But it did not disappear so quickly, and I remember that in London in 1940 I felt much calmer during an air raid than I did when a storm was brewing.

More interesting was the interpretation of a Zurich psychoanalyst whom I told in 1950 about my adventure. According to him, what happened was that out on the sea that night I had been fully conscious of the danger of drowning, so I did not acquire a phobia for water; but I had not "realized" the other danger, that of being struck by lightning, and hence *that* fear had become lodged in my unconscious and for that reason could not be controlled by rational arguments or subjugated by the will.

In any event, our adventure on the sea raised us considerably in the esteem of our fellow lycée students and the Scouts. I did not dare tell anyone at home about the dangers we had undergone, but occasionally I alluded to the terrible storm that had taught me not to be afraid of death. The experience was too dramatic for me not to use it as a literary pretext. The following year I wrote a sketch called "Răsărit pe mare" (Sunrise on the Sea), which appeared in 1927 in the review *Est-Vest*. (This was a publication brought out by Radu Capriel, Ion Anestin, and myself, which ceased after the second number when Capriel, who in the meantime had gotten married, was unable to continue subsidizing it.) It was our adventure that I told about, and all who had been party to it assured me that in reading it they had relived that stormy night from start to finish. But the story had to do with a much smaller boat in which two friends had ventured forth. The narrator remained at the helm and his friend sat at the prow. When the storm subsided, the narrator suddenly realized that he was alone, that he probably had been alone all night, and that he had been talking all the while to a shadow—a motionless shadow he thought he saw at the other end of the boat.

That autumn of 1924 when I entered the eighth year class of lycée, I already felt like a university student. Several of my friends, Haig Acterian, Petre Viforeanu, and Vojen, had passed their eighth year examinations during the summer and were now enrolled in the university. They were telling me about the courses of Nicolae Iorga and Vasile Pârvan, and they were enthusiastic about a young professor of logic and metaphysics, Nae Ionescu, whose name I heard then for the first time. I had made up my mind to study classical philology and philosophy in the university, and I began to prepare by reading more and more books of philosophy.

I continued, however, to write and publish whenever I could. No longer was I contributing to *Ziarul Ştiinţelor Populare*, but articles of mine now were appearing in *Orizontul, Foaia Tinerimii, Universul Literar*, and *Lumea*. I was now writing articles on the history of religions, Oriental studies, and alchemy. Occasionally, I was paid for my contributions. One day I introduced myself to Em. Cerbu, the editor-in-chief of *Orizontul*, to see if I could earn some money by translating. Cerbu, who had published many articles and translations of mine without offering me any honorarium, was persuaded that I knew how to write. He proposed that I translate short articles from a wide variety of German, French, and Italian periodicals for *Orizontul* and *Oglinda Lumii*. For each hundred pages of manuscript he offered to pay me 1,000 lei. It wasn't much, but I could purchase ten or fifteen books with that money, so I agreed. Once a month I would present myself with a manuscript. Cerbu would read the titles of the articles, count the pages carefully, and sign a note for which the cashier would give me 1,000 lei. I remember that once he had made a snide remark to the effect that my handwriting was too large and that there were too few lines to the page. I blushed to my ears and vowed inwardly to get revenge. Indeed, the next month I brought one hundred pages written as minutely as possible, having crowded onto them what should have required two hundred pages. But I don't believe Cerbu realized I had done it to get revenge.

Of course, I neglected my schoolwork even more openly than before. But because I had published a number of erudite articles in *Vlăstarul*, the lycée review, and especially because I had written an article about N. Iorga that had pleased that great man and had impressed all the teachers, I enjoyed a certain prestige and my faults were overlooked. However, Banciu never forgot to remind me whenever I could not solve a problem that if I did not decide to study seriously, he would fail me. I couldn't believe him. It was my impression that I had several allies among the teachers. Besides the instructors in Latin and Romanian, there was also Alexandru Claudian, the young philosophy teacher, who had "discovered" me, so to speak, as the result of a test. In the seventh year, after a few lessons, he asked us to write about the importance of Greek and Latin classicism for the education of modern man. When he came to class the next week with the papers under his arm, he went to his desk and asked, "Which of you is Mr. Eliade?" I rose, blushing. He looked at me a while and smiled. "I suspected it was you. You wrote an excellent paper. Be so kind as to summarize it for your classmates." Of course, my oral summary was not nearly so good as the written text. I had not expected to have to speak extempore, and I did not know how to organize my exposition. One of my fellow students said to me after class, "That was more or less what I wrote. Why didn't he praise me too?"

Often I walked with Claudian on the way home from school. He told me once that he had guessed as soon as he had seen me that I was uncommonly intelligent, because of the shape of my forehead. He was a good friend and great admirer of H. Sanielevici, and his affinity for me increased all the more when he learned I had read all Sanielevici's books. "Soon he will be publishing his great opus on anthropology," he told me. "It's a work of genius, the first Romanian contribution to universal science!"

The friendship that Alexandru Claudian showed me assured me that, in the end, even lycée teachers are forced to recognize the merits of a student although he is not a prize-winner. How wrong I was! It was a period of euphoria for me. I learned English in order to be able to read Frazer, I bought more and more books on the history of religions and Oriental studies, and I put up additional shelves in the attic. My workroom began to resemble the study of a scholar from a bygone age. I had accumulated by this time over a thousand books. Besides the collection of periodicals, which I kept wherever I could—on the floor, under the bed, and on top of the chest of manuscripts—there were also in that little room an insectarium, a herbarium, a mineralogical collection, and a remnant of my laboratory. On the walls were hand-drawn copies of Egyptian hieroglyphics and bas-reliefs. Soon it became necessary to remove the bed to the adjoining room, and during my student years at the university I had to install shelves there too. When Nae Ionescu came to visit me in 1927, he was fascinated. "What a wonderful room!" he exclaimed, "Made expressly *for study.*"

And "study" I did, with ever increasing fury, but I did not study for school. A long time before this I had discovered Iorga, and I admired him, especially for his polygraphy. I dreamed of being able myself to write someday, if not the many hundreds of volumes I knew he had written, then at least a hundred. Some of them I already had in mind, and I even had made a list. At the head of it was *Romanul adolescentului miop.* This was to be the first of a short series of novels under the general title *Dacia Felix.* The next novel in the series was to portray the life of a university student, and the third one would take place in a barber shop.

But that list contained for the most part books of essays, philosophy, and cultural history. Because I recently had discovered Orphism and the theories of Vittorio Macchioro, I dreamt of a massive work in two volumes: *The Origins of Europe.* (I even dared to announce it—in an article about Heraclitus and Orphism published in *Adevărul Literar.)* I recall also a book about *The Education of the Will,* and another entitled *A Manual of the Perfected Reader;* also a book about Hasdeu, another about Iorga, and one more on Romanian folk-botany.

Of course, I kept count of the articles I published, and in the spring of the year 1925 I celebrated with a few friends the appearance of my one hundredth article. Mother prepared a feast for us in the attic. Vojen wished that I should celebrate soon the publication of my thousandth article! The others, however, insisted that I publish *Romanul adolescentului miop.* They knew that it had to do with their lives too, and they wanted to preserve fresh forever in a book the memory of the adolescence that had already passed without our being aware of its going. I was eighteen now, but almost all the others were a year older than I. We had ceased to consider ourselves adolescents long ago. Vojen, Sighireanu, and Viforeanu were involved in liaisons, and from Braşov, Radu Bossie had sent word recently that he was a father. Even I had begun to mingle more with other young people. I had stopped wearing the school uniform and the wire-rimmed glasses, and I no longer cut my hair short. When my hair had grown, Father made me have my picture taken. But I was photographed the way I wanted to be: frowning, with a bitter, sarcastic smile in the corner of my mouth.

Unexpectedly, that spring the Minister of Public Education reintroduced the baccalaureate examination. The news struck like a bolt of lightning. I envied those who had finished the eighth year class the previous year, and had not been required to take this examination, which threatened to be very hard. What was even worse, the baccalaureate was not to be given by instructors from our own lycée, but by a special committee headed by a university professor. This meant that we were to be judged by strangers and exclusively on the basis of academic criteria. But after a few days of uneasiness and hesitation, I decided to proceed as usual: that is, instead of starting to study seriously the subjects required for the baccalaureate, I continued reading and writing about whatever interested me. (That spring I was especially interested in Babylonian religions, Orphism, and the English language; I labored to read in the original the works of Bishop Berkeley and Walt Whitman, both of whom I had discovered through Papini.)

Summer seemed to come earlier than usual that year. I would stroll through the school courtyard during class breaks with Mircea Mărculescu, conversing as usual, completely detached from the collective case of nerves from which our class was suffering, in their terror of the approaching baccalaureate. It was quite warm that morning when we went to see the results of the final class examinations. Mărculescu had failed Latin, and I mathematics. Just as he had warned me so many times, Banciu had given me an F. In order to avenge ourselves, we held a party in a summer garden restaurant. I insisted on wearing my lycée uniform, which I had not put on for a year. I found it in a trunk, all wrinkled and smelling of mothballs.

My parents were worried, but I had long since acquired the freedom of taking care of myself so that, except for giving advice, they did not interfere in anything I did. I had made summer plans earlier with my friends, and I carried them out completely, including an excursion to Piatra Craiului and a session at the Boy Scout camp at Mamaia. In August, however, I started to study the mathematics textbook in earnest. As was my habit, I would work six or seven hours without stopping, then read a book of philosophy or history of religions, and return to the mathematics book for another four or five hours. Sometimes at night I took walks with Mărculescu or some of my classmates who had taken the baccalaureate in June and had failed it. They told us in great detail about the horrors of this examination, and quoted us extraordinarily difficult questions seemingly invented for the express purpose of demoralizing the candidate.

I took the makeup examination in mathematics at the beginning of September and passed it with flying colors. After congratulating me, Banciu added: "I knew what I was doing when I failed you. I've succeeded in convincing you that you *can* understand mathematics!"

A week later I began the baccalaureate examination. I was not apprehensive about the written parts, and as I expected, I was admitted to the orals. Now, for the first time in my life, I found myself before a committee of seven or eight professors who could, in principle, ask me about anything I had studied during my eight years in lycée. Fortunately, the professor of Romanian language and literature asked me extremely difficult questions (for instance, about the Byzantine lexicon in Romanian and the analysis of the Voroneţ Codex)—things I knew because they were not found in our textbooks—and I answered him correctly. Of the rest, I remember almost nothing. I only know that I would breathe very deeply each time one professor would say "thank you," and turn to his colleague to indicate that he could begin. It seemed to me the number of examiners was endless. After half an hour there were still two or three waiting their turn. For years afterward I suffered from a nightmare in which I discovered, all of a sudden, that I had to take the baccalaureate examination over again. Either the papers had been lost, or a new decree had been issued that invalidated all the old examinations and required everyone, of every age and station, to take them over again. The reasons varied, but the nightmare was always the same: I was again facing a baccalaureate examining committee; and I would wake up in a cold sweat.

When I went to see the results, I was prepared for anything. At that time I used a "spiritual exercise" that fortified me inwardly and made me invulnerable: I would lie on the bed, close my eyes, and imagine myself in one of those worlds that fascinated me—either the universes of Camille Flammarion's science-fiction books, or one of those lost civilizations, such as Egypt, Mesopotamia, Vedic India, or the Greece of the Orphic Mysteries. I would lie motionless, concentrating, for about half an hour, until I felt I had become completely *present* in one of those extraterrestrial or lost worlds. Then I would begin to live there, to move in a landscape that, to me, seemed entirely *real*, meeting extraordinary beings who were excited over truly *interesting* problems (they had, in other words, the same interests as I) and listening to them discuss only important and urgent questions (for instance: why can we know nothing about God? Why has no definite proof of the immortality of the soul as yet been found?). When I awoke after such a "spiritual exercise," I was perfectly indifferent to what had happened or was about to happen to me.

Detached, calm, invulnerable, I went to see the results of the examination. I found myself among those who had been admitted. I was hardly able to feel happy, and my joy was dimmed indeed when, on closer inspection, I failed to find the name of Mircea Mărculescu on the list. However, I sensed that this was a decisive moment in my life. I was free from the nightmare of the baccalaureate and free from a world which, for so many years, had seemed to me like a prison—the world of studying according to stereotypes, the world of teachers and schedules and fixed times. I knew that whatever might happen from now on, one thing was certain: I would never again have to study what didn't interest me, and best of all, I would never again have to be tied to a program imposed by others. I had become completely and at last what I had set out to become long before: my own master.

And yet I returned home in a pensive mood; I could not be fully happy. Despite myself, I felt that I should miss this lycée life that had ended as it had begun, on an October morning; I should miss my classmates and friends with whom I had been linked during those eight years, and from whom I realized I should now be severed permanently. I knew that I should even miss some of the instructors and the building itself, where I felt I had been so humiliated, and which I had grown to hate. (I despised that school so much that I used to say, perhaps partly in jest, that after the baccalaureate I would not even pass by it for ten years, until all memory of it should have faded from my mind.)

That afternoon I gathered up all the textbooks I still owned and went to the used book store to sell them. But I wasn't a Balzacian for nothing. Passing in front of the university I whispered, *"Et maintenant, à nous deux!"* (Now, we'll have it out!).

I never suspected that such a venerable institution would not let itself be conquered by one possessed of the weapons I believed I possessed then.

6. *Et Maintenant, à Nous Deux!*

OCTOBER, 1925. I was eighteen, a university student—and free. The only thing I had to do was go to the administrative offices of the university with my baccalaureate diploma and enroll in the Faculty of Letters and Philosophy. I had in mind to take a number of courses, but since attendance was not required I was content to go regularly only to the first few sessions. Then, almost without realizing it, I found myself coming to the university less and less frequently. Not all the professors disappointed me, but I had the impression that I could learn better at home, in my attic. I remember the first classes of Rădulescu-Motru. He was only about sixty at the time, but he looked much older. His voice was very weak, he could hardly see, and he walked with difficulty, bent over a cane; he didn't recognize faces and he didn't remember names. A few years later, as the result of an operation, he was completely rejuvenated. When I went to see him after my return from India in 1932, he looked ten years younger. But his lectures in the fall of 1925 discouraged me. I preferred to read carefully again his *Outline of Psychology*, which had appeared in print a few years previously.

P. P. Negulescu impressed me by his hieratic rigidity, which he undoubtedly considered the supreme expression of self-discipline. He smiled moderately and occasionally wiped his lips and forehead with a handkerchief that he took, with a calculated discretion, from the inside pocket of his suit coat. It was said that he tried to imitate his master, Titu Maiorescu. His course was called "Philosophical Encyclopedia," and in it he proposed to show the dependence of philosophical thought on the discoveries and progress of science. In the classes I attended he made reference to all the sciences, from astronomy to chemistry. This should have fascinated me, but there was something about the attitude of P. P. Negulescu that kept me at a distance. In the first place, I disliked his superiority complex, which he betrayed by his pale, sardonic smile and the casual way he spoke of metaphysics and great philosophical systems, letting it be understood that all these were nothing more than "speculations lacking contact with reality." He believed only in science; and that was commendable, except that he was no scientist; he got his information from reading books and articles of a popular variety. This I had done too—in lycée! In the lectures I heard him give, it seemed to me that I often recognized passages from some volume in *Bibliothèque scientifique*, the famous series with the red covers published by Flammarion.

In the second place, I quickly realized that I had no new facts and no original method to learn from Negulescu. He was an honest, forthright teacher and knew many things, but in listening to him I never had the impression that his learning was a response to an inner necessity. I could not discern in him Faust's thirst for knowledge, but only the persistent and methodical labor of someone who wants to be informed at any price, and then only because *his profession obliges him to be*. In fact, he resembled some of the prize pupils I had known in lycée. Had he been asked to teach comparative philology, he would have learned it with the same patience and competency—but out of textbooks. Calculating and meticulous, he would never have ventured to read specialized monographs and articles. He might have wasted too much time, he might have risked becoming involved in peripheral problems! He lacked any passion for scientific research. He was content to be "informed"—in most instances, from the abbreviated studies written for the nonspecialist.

During my first year at the university I did not have much to do with P. P. Negulescu. I remember only that at one session of his seminar on the pre-Socratics, I stood up in the back of the room and spoke about Oriental influences, which I then believed to have been very important. I think he noticed me, but my interruption did not leave a favorable impression. He didn't like students to bring into the discussion points of view that he, the professor, did not consider worthy of being discussed. And he certainly didn't like my manner of speaking: fast, enthusiastic, without a plan, sometimes with stammering, giving the impression that I thought what I was saying was extremely important for an understanding of the origins of Greek thought. Negulescu preferred young men who were cut on his own last: calm, controlled, colorless. Even during that autumn he had already taken notice of Posescu, who later became his assistant, and whom he would have liked to have seen become successor to his chair. Posescu never missed a class, smiled when the teacher smiled, followed him to his office, and walked a step behind him in the halls of the university. I kept running into Negulescu and his disciples repeatedly, both as a student and later, when I served as Nae Ionescu's assistant.

✓　　　✓　　　✓

Mircea Florian was at that time lecturer in the history of philosophy. I had read in the sixth year his *Introduction to Philosophy*, and I went to hear him like an old friend. He did not disappoint me, but neither did he captivate me. He was to lecture on Berkeley, and I was among the first to enroll in his seminar. I had the impression that he would have liked to know me better; he was amiable and he invited me to accompany him to bookstores to purchase books for the seminar library collection. At the time, Florian was a man of about thirty-eight or forty, blond, robust, almost fat, and always smelled of eau de cologne. Only vague memories remain of his courses and lectures. His voice was too weak for his weight, and he spoke as though he were choked by some secret, mysterious emotion. He liked to talk, as well as write, "beautifully." He would say, for instance, "The white lily of Nietzsche's philosophy." He was also a librarian for the King Carol I Foundation, and I used to see him sitting majestically at his desk, reading old volumes of the *Revue Philosophique*. I think I should have become closer to him had there also not been Nae Ionescu.

At that time Nae Ionescu, like Mircea Florian, was a young lecturer, having taught at the university for only a few years. He conducted classes in logic and metaphysics, and held a seminar in the history of logic. I shall never forget the first class in metaphysics I attended under him. He had announced a lecture on "Faust and the

Problem of Salvation." The large lecture hall was completely filled, and it was only with difficulty that I found a seat in the rear, on the last bench. There entered a dark-haired, pale-complexioned man; his temples were bare and his black, bushy eyebrows were arched almost diabolically. He had large somber eyes of steel blue, unusually bright; and when he glanced over the auditorium it seemed that lightning flashed in the hall. He was thin, rather tall, dressed soberly but with a careless elegance, and he had the most beautiful and expressive hands I had ever seen, with long, slender, nervous fingers. When he spoke, those hands modeled his thoughts, underscoring nuances and anticipating difficulties and question marks.

He was greeted, according to custom, with applause, but Ionescu stopped it by raising his arm quickly. "If you have the right to applaud," he said, "you should also have the right to boo when you don't like a class. But the law prohibits booing in university lecture halls—so please, don't applaud."

He sat down on the chair, looked over the audience all the way to the rear of the auditorium, and started to speak. Suddenly, there was an unnatural silence, as if everyone were holding his breath. Nae Ionescu did not speak like a professor: he was giving us neither a lesson nor a lecture. It was a conversation that he had begun, and he seemed to be addressing each of us directly and individually. It was as though he had told us something or had presented to us a series of facts, had proposed an interpretation, and now was awaiting our comments. You had the impression that the whole lecture was just a part of a continuing dialogue, that each of us was invited to participate in the discussion, to offer his opinions at the end of the hour. You felt that what Nae Ionescu had to say could not be found in any book. It was something new, freshly conceived and organized right there in front of you. It was an original kind of thinking, and if this sort of thought interested you, you knew that you could find it nowhere but here, at its source. The man at the desk was speaking straight to *you*: opening up problems, teaching you to solve them, and forcing you to think.

When the fifty minutes were over, I wondered where the time had gone. I had taken almost no notes, but I found myself at the end of the class struggling with questions and problems: Had Goethe been tempted by the Manicheistic anthropology of those medieval sects that had survived in camouflaged form until the late

Renaissance? Was the problem of evil as it appears in *Faust* wrongly posed, thereby making it insoluble in the framework of traditional philosophy, or did it presuppose other problematics and did it demand to be debated on a different plane? These and many other such questions were whirling in my mind.

I shall have occasion to speak frequently about Nae Ionescu and all that he meant to me in my youth. But of course I shall not be able to discuss here his thought and his work, nor the influence he had on my generation. I shall limit myself to brief notes, except that when my relations with him become more intimate, I shall write with greater detail. But this was to come later, after I joined the editorial staff of *Cuvântul*. Curious as it may seem, my enthusiasm awakened by the discovery of Ionescu's lectures did not give me courage to approach him. I also attended his classes on logic, although these did not appeal to me as much, because that year he was speaking on mathematical logic. I did not enroll in his seminar. It was to be a commentary on *Regulae ad directionem ingenii*, a text that did not interest me at the time.

By Christmas, I was going to the university only to hear Nae Ionescu's lectures. I felt, however, that I was living fully the true "student life." Every evening a group of students, both male and female, classmates of mine or Nicu's for the most part, would gather in our attic. The student society to which both Nicu and I belonged was preparing a choral concert for Christmas, and some of the rehearsals took place in our attic. Those early evening get-togethers seemed to me rich in meaning and mystery. In the beginning I didn't know everyone who came, especially my new classmates. The attic was lit only by the lamp on the desk. In its faint glow there appeared many strange faces. I saw them moving around, approaching the stove or the bed, staring at the bookshelves. I imagined that they were surprised and fascinated by these two little rooms crammed with books and curious objects: the insectarium, stones, retorts, etc. On rainy nights toward the end of November the newcomers, one by one, would step up close to the stove in the wall in order to dry their clothing. The presence of so many girls in my attic seemed to be a part of the student mythology. This was how I had imagined "student life," a mixture of *Scènes de la vie de Bohème* and Russian novels. The mythology included poor girls who were studying medicine or letters, reading until late at night by the weak light of an oil lamp, in love, threatened with consumption; also sons of peasants or workers, who earned their living by tutoring, lodged in dirty flats, studying their medical or engineering books until dawn, resisting all temptations of getting a job through politics, clean and naive, "idealistic," determined to "bring light" to godforsaken villages where they would live out their lives, fighting malaria, working for justice, building schools, and so on.

Of course, this student mythology was not entirely invented from my readings. It was part of the spirit of the times, and I found it also in contemporary literature, the magazines I read, and the student papers. However, I elaborated it continually by introducing new elements: for instance, the character of the overworked student, threatened by insanity, but not daring to interrupt his work because it always seemed to him that he was on the verge of a "discovery" that would revolutionize human thought.

Among the girls who came to the rehearsals at the attic I still remember Ica. She was blonde and so nearsighted that her pale blue eyes could hardly be seen under the thick lenses of her pince-nez. Ica was short and slender and wore her hair braided around the temples, in the style of my grandmother's era. A student in the Faculty of Letters, she was preparing to be a history teacher. Her friend Gigi was almost ugly, but her coarseness made her attractive. Her mouth was too large, her teeth were irregular, and she spoke with a nasal whine because of an adenoid condition. But she was daring, witty, talked and laughed constantly, and when Gigi was around newcomers quickly became friends. There was also a Miss Fârtatu, who was exceptionally tall, so that I always had the impression that if she were to make an abrupt movement she would bump her head against the ceiling. One December evening when the first snow had fallen, there appeared a girl with violet-colored eyes, bobbed hair, and bangs. To me she seemed beautiful but distant, as though descended from another world, because she did not resemble any of the girls I had known before. Her name was Rica. I was impressed by her grave, low-pitched, sensual voice, which contrasted with a face that seemed to belong to a character from an English novel.

I felt a special attraction for a dark Greek girl, Thea, whose lips were extraordinarily red and full. She was a student at the Conservatory of Dramatic Arts, but she said she was also enrolled in Law. I discovered later that she had not passed her baccalaureate and that she had entered drama school after having failed the violin examination. I felt an even greater sympathy for her after I learned she lived in a miserable slum and that her father was a worker in a pipe factory. It was by chance that I discovered this fact. Once, at one of our parties at a tavern, she became ill and agreed reluctantly to let me take her home in a cab. Of course she didn't give the correct address. She told the driver to stop in front of a certain fine house, where she got out, insisting that I return at once to the party. I pretended to leave, but actually I followed her at a distance. She hid behind the house for a few minutes, then crossed the street, stepping with some difficulty around the mud puddles, and turned into a blind alley. The pipe factory was at the far end of the alley: a curious, crudely constructed shop that looked like a shack on top of which several dog kennels had been piled. Somewhere in the bowels of this hovel Thea had learned to play the violin and had dreamed of becoming a great artist.

The president of our student society was "Doctor" Zissu. We called him "doctor" because he was in his last year of medical school and because he was at least five or six years older than the other students. He was almost bald, and his manner was calm and deliberate. We all heeded his advice because he always seemed to find the right answers. His constant companion was a girl, also a medical student, who had a rather bony, masculine face. She even carried herself in a mannish way, and it was she who gave medical care to all the students in our group. The leader of the chorus was Pârvulescu, a thin, shriveled sort of fellow; and because he could not attend all the rehearsals he had a substitute, the son of a general, who was a dark young man, fully as tall as Miss Fârtatu. He would have been a handsome boy had it not been for a red birthmark that disfigured his neck and chin. Perhaps this defect determined his whole lifestyle. I have never seen such a cheerful and witty young man. No group could keep from laughing when he was around. No matter what he said it was always funny, partly because it was unpredictable, and especially because it seemed uncontrived. In a few minutes, no matter where he was, his disfigured face would become the center of attention.

I remember only vaguely the names and faces of other members of the chorus. Among them there was a student from the Polytech-

nic Institute, blond and glib, who always took advantage of the rehearsals to browse through my books. Later I found out that his
secret passion was Egyptology, especially papyrology. There were
also students in the second and third year of Philosophy. When
they saw my library they asked me if I knew Stelian Mateescu, a
student whose nickname was "the little Kant." They talked about
him as about a phenomenon, a second Pico della Mirandola, whom
even the professors feared! He was in the last year at the Faculty of
Letters, and his outbursts during the seminar on Romanian literature had already become a legend.

One day, accompanied by another student, I went to see him. He
was a very small, frail person with an enormous forehead and a
receding hairline; he wore frameless glasses that emphasized his
maturity and gave him a somber, professorial air. He spoke jerkily
in a high-pitched voice, and he often burst into a short laugh that
sometimes threatened to choke him. He nearly always carried with
him a black notebook, from which he occasionally read a sentence
or two, composed by himself or someone else. The black notebook
had become a legend, and Stelian Mateescu encouraged the legend,
appearing everywhere with it in his left hand, even when he lectured at the auditorium of the King Carol I Foundation. He recorded
in that book, in a small and precise hand, all sorts of observations
and reflections grouped under such headings as Aesthetics, Logic,
Metaphysics, etc. He lived in a poor neighborhood and his parents,
whom I once chanced to glimpse, looked quite ordinary. He had a
brother who was studying engineering in Switzerland and who,
like the rest of the family, considered Stelian a genius. And undoubtedly he was a genius, although he suffered from some mysterious nervous disorder that eventually destroyed him completely.

I became closer to Mateescu the following year, when I persuaded him to contribute to *Revista Universitară*, and especially in 1928,
during my last year at the university, when I became friends with
his colleagues Mircea Vulcănescu and Paul Sterian, the latter just
returned from Paris. But I still remember our first meetings in his
study room and in my attic. He had fewer books than I, but his
were all important and expensive ones: the classics of Western philosophy in the original languages; treatises on aesthetics, psychology, and sociology; the "great authors" of all literatures; luxurious
albums on the history of art. When he first set foot in my attic he

was pleased by my library and the entomological and geological collections, but he was disappointed by some of my favorite authors: Papini, Hasdeu, and Iorga. He approved only of Balzac, Fabre, and Oriental writers.

Almost everything interested him and he always read with a supreme and constant tension. I remember that I once lent him an offprint of an article by Pettazzoni, "L'Origine du monothéisme." Mateescu kept it several weeks, although it was only thirty pages long. One day, at his place, we were discussing it, and he sought it out from among other papers on his desk in order to cite a passage. I looked at the article in dismay. No longer did I recognize it. He had made notations all over its margins with a very fine pencil. There were hundreds and hundreds of lines, written so minutely that only he could read them. He assured me that I need not worry, that he would erase all his markings before he returned the article to me. Seeing my surprise, he explained how he read a text "responsibly": he tried to assimilate each piece of information that he considered essential and to examine every argument the author made. But this was only a preliminary exercise. When he had finished reading the text he started again, trying to see in what way he could integrate the central idea into his own personal system of thought. And if it could not be integrated, whose fault was it? All those microscopic notes on the margins of Pettazzoni's article showed that the fault was the great Italian scholar's, though I no longer remember for what reason. I realized then that each "responsible" reading—and he seldom read in any other way—was such a mental effort for Stelian Mateescu that he could not keep it up indefinitely. It did not surprise me to learn, on my return from India in 1932, that this exceptional mind had slipped into darkness a few years previously.

On Christmas Eve, 1925, we went to sing carols *(colinde)* at the Royal Palace, the Metropolitan Cathedral, and the homes of several professors. At the Palace, King Ferdinand and Queen Marie spoke with each of us while lackeys in golden liveries invited us to sample pieces of pound cake from sumptuous trays and to drink white wine from cheap green glasses. King Ferdinand would stop in front of each student and ask him what he was studying. "Interesting, interesting!" he kept repeating.

At the Cathedral and everywhere else we went we were enter-

tained lavishly, and before we left someone would seek out the trea-
surer of the society and discreetly hand him an envelope. Part of the
money we earned that night had been designated in advance for a
party at a tavern. Other friends joined us there, and we stayed till
almost dawn eating and drinking, but above all singing—and not
just Christmas carols! There were about forty or fifty of us students,
both boys and girls, gathered around several long wooden tables
under the low, smoky ceiling. We were happy to be together in that
cozy hall hidden under drifts of snow. I, especially, was happy. It
seemed to me that I was living at last the "student life" for which I
so long had yearned. Everything around me seemed "new," in contrast to our former amusements of lycée days. The presence of the
"coeds" transformed this party into an inexhaustible dramatic sce-
nario. Everything became possible when a girl was at your side:
romance, passion, adventure, friendship, "The Old Heidelberg," the
legendary life of the Romanian students from the early nineteenth
century. I felt that I would, at least, never have to regret later not
having lived the "student life." That evening I drank more than
usual, I kissed the girls, I learned to be "bold."

At that time, the young people learned boldness most frequently
in the movie theaters. During that winter I, too, went numerous
times to the movies, especially with Thea. And I liked, too, to spend
hours alone with her in the shadows of my attic. But aside from a
strong physical attraction and a great sympathetic compassion, Thea
inspired no deep sentiment in me. Sometimes I thought I could fall
in love with Ica. But whenever the door of the attic would open and
I would hear Rica's light steps and her short, solemn, sensual laugh,
my heart would begin to throb. Rica had the habit of coming at
infrequent intervals, always unexpectedly and on improbable pre-
texts: she wanted to borrow five lei for tram fare, or to have me
translate some Greek titles, or to ask me to play on the piano her
favorite tango, "Jalousie" (and then we would have to go downstairs, avoiding my parents, and shut ourselves quickly in the parlor; then, so that my mother wouldn't notice that we had come just
for "Jalousie," I had to start with other pieces and play at random
for about a quarter of an hour while Rica looked on in fascination,
as if I were some musical genius).

Once she came around dinner time to ask the meaning of the
word *katharsis.* I explained it to her as best I could, but I was ner-

vous and kept thinking I heard my father's footsteps on the wooden stairs, coming to inquire why I was late for dinner. I didn't dare invite her to eat with us because, although my parents had given me complete freedom in my attic and outside the house, Mother did not encourage my inviting fellow students to dinner. She would have been especially embarrassed if I should have told her unexpectedly that Rica or Thea would be eating with us. She believed that the presence of a guest at dinner implied a number of responsibilities: our best silverware, special wines, etc. However, that evening, when I saw that Rica had no intention of leaving, I asked her if she wouldn't stay for dinner. "I'll stay on one condition," she said. "If you'll bring me some tea and cheese and let me take it here alone. I *love* tea with cheese," she added.

When Mother learned of my difficulty, she prepared some tea and I returned to the attic with a tray of ham, cheese, boiled eggs, and pound cake. Rica was forced to accept my company, although I ate almost nothing. I was surprised at how voraciously Rica consumed her food. At that time I knew almost nothing about her financial situation. I had learned only that she had lived for a while in a student dormitory and later in town with a girlfriend, but she had recently left that place. That evening she told me about a friend of hers, whom I later met, nicknamed Nishka because she looked Russian. Having gone to visit her one evening, Nishka invited her to dinner, but she had only one frankfurter and a single bun. As usual, Nishka put the frankfurter to boil over the alcohol stove in a coffee pot, but this time there was so little fuel that the water had not begun to boil when the fire went out. They began tearing sheets of paper out of notebooks and lighting them with matches. But before they realized it, their supply of matches was exhausted and the frankfurter was barely warm. Just then there was a power failure and they were left in the dark, afraid to move lest they tip over the pot! "We both burst into tears," Rica concluded.

,   ,   ,

In the winter of 1926, I read with fury several philosophers including Bacon, Kant, and Malebranche. But I felt myself increasingly drawn to the history of religions. I had discovered at the library of the Institute of Ancient History (established by Pârvan) the five volumes of *Cultes, mythes et religions* by Salomon Reinach, Frazer's annotated translations from Pausanias and *Fasti* by Ovid, and the works of Ridgeway and Jane Harrison. I would go early in the morning and anxiously await the arrival of the librarian. I read breathlessly and assimilated as much as my age and my frenzied manner of reading—jumping from one subject to another—would allow. Moreover, I was then under the influence of Hasdeu and fantastic hypotheses attracted me. I wasted several weeks trying to verify whether the mysterious word "Basarab" could not be explained by the Greek term *bássaros*, identical with *bassareus*, one of Dionysus' names, and deriving from *bassára*, fox. If so, then I thought that the origin of the Basarab dynasty might have been in a Thracian secret cult that had as its sacred animal the fox.

I continued to sleep four or at the most five hours a night. Perhaps I should have been content to stop with that if I had not read somewhere that Alexander von Humboldt had not required more than two hours of sleep. This set me thinking. For several years, ever since reading *L'Education de la velonté*, I had been convinced that a human being could do anything, provided he *wanted* to, and *knew how* to control his will. Long ago I had learned to master my sense of taste by forcing myself to unpleasant things: first toothpaste, then soap, and finally cockchafers, flies, and caterpillars. When I saw that I could chew and swallow an insect or larva without feeling the normal revulsion, I would go on to a more daring exercise. I believed that such self-discipline was the gateway to absolute freedom. The struggle against sleep, like the struggle against normal modes of behavior, signified for me a heroic attempt to transcend the human condition. I did not know then that this is precisely the point of departure of the techniques of yoga. But it is quite probable that my interest in yoga, which three years later was to lead me to India, stemmed from my faith in the unlimited possibilities of man. I did not realize at the time the consequences of this Faustian ambition. What I knew about the "magical pragmatism" of Papini before his conversion encouraged this tendency. The curiosity which, in my last years of lycée, led me to read Steiner's works and occult literature, undoubtedly had the same explanation.

But perhaps there was also something else, which I was only to realize later. The freedom I thought I could obtain by doing the opposite of the "normal" signified the surpassing of my historical, social, and cultural condition. In a sense I was no longer conditioned by the fact that I had been born a Romanian and thereby integrated into a provincial culture with a certain tradition—one in which Latin, Greek, Slavic, and—more recently—Western elements were mingled. I became open to any adventure in a foreign or even exotic spiritual universe. The fact that I almost never read the recent French books that my friends devoured, that I did not let myself be attracted by any of the contemporary cultural vogues, could be interpreted in the same way. Basically, I instinctively resisted any attempt to be molded according to current patterns.

I did not succeed, however, in cutting my sleeping time in half. I observed that, even when I managed to keep perfectly awake for twenty-two hours by drinking much coffee, my eyes tired rather quickly and watered so much that I had to rest them for long periods under wet handkerchiefs. My myopia had worsened again recently, and from Papini's experience I had learned that I was in danger of losing my sight. Therefore, I contented myself with holding to the schedule established in lycée: working until three or four A.M. and then rising between seven and eight A.M.

/   /   /

I continued to publish articles in various Romanian weeklies. I was writing now about Oriental authors, historical characters who interested me, and books that had given rise to endless controversies, such as Ossendowski's *Bêtes, hommes et dieux* and *Le Mystère de Jésus* by P. L. Couchoud. I also wrote the only article published in a bourgeois paper on the Romanian anarchist, Panait Muşoiu, after having paid him a visit that spring (the article appeared in the short-lived student publication *Curentul Studenţesc* and later was reprinted in several provincial papers).

In the spring I started preparing for examinations. I had decided to attempt those in logic, aesthetics, history of philosophy, and "Philosophical Encyclopedia." I took all of them, but I remember only the examinations with Nae Ionescu (logic) and D. Gusti (aesthetics). In the case of the latter, I chose as the special subject of my written examination Croce's *Estetica*. Gusti congratulated me, but for reasons I found puzzling. He was pleased, he said, that I had read the book in the original language, that I had given all the biographical information (the year, edition, number of pages), that I had written legibly and concisely and on only a part of the page, leaving plenty of room for the professor's comments. He gave me the highest mark, and we parted friends.

I took the logic examination with a certain amount of trepidation. Nae Ionescu did not require a written examination, but was satisfied with an oral one. I was a bit apprehensive, because I had not attended classes for several months and I had not read Goblot's treatise on logic with which all my fellow students had struggled. Ionescu had the habit of asking at the outset of the examination what books you had read. When my turn came, I replied that I had read Croce's *Logica* and *Sistema di logica come teoria del conoscere* by Giovanni Gentile. The professor looked at me with interest. "But I cannot say that I understood everything I read," I added cautiously. "Neither can I," he replied, consoling me. After that, he let me tell him what I had understood of Gentile's system of logic, assuring me that, for my age, what I was saying was "not so bad." He then posed a question: "You know the story about Newton's sitting in the garden and discovering the law of universal gravitation after seeing an apple fall. What sort of logical operation took place in his mind that allowed him to understand that an apple—that is, a particular object—illustrated a universal law?"

After a few seconds I said I could not answer immediately, but if he would give me a moment I might approach a solution. "There is no hurry," he encouraged me. I ventured: "Recently I read a book by Lucian Blaga called *Fenomenul originar* . . ." The professor nodded his head approvingly. "You are on the right track," he said. "Go on."

I told him what had impressed me about the facts cited and interpreted by Blaga. Certain minds see elements of unity in nature or culture, they see what is essential and fundamental, and this allows them to discover structures.

"That's the answer!" Ionescu interrupted. "It's a matter of *structure.* The logical operation effected in Newton's mind did this: it apprehended the structure of the phenomenon of universal gravitation."

Then he gave me a long look. My eyes were bloodshot and sleepy behind the thick lenses, I needed a haircut, I was carelessly dressed, and I certainly did not present an attractive appearance. "Vacation is coming," he commented. "Look at the sky once in a while. What do you intend to do this summer?"

"I'm going to climb in the Bucegi mountains, and go on to Piatra Craiului," I replied.

Ionescu was somewhat surprised by my answer. No doubt he found it hard to imagine me as a mountain climber. "Good idea," he said finally. "But don't take any books along!"

′   ′   ′

That summer passed more quickly than usual. I hiked for several weeks in the mountains with my old Scouting friends. For the first time I received letters from girls: Gigi, Thea, and Rica. And, just as during every previous summer, I read enormously, although not always things related to courses I would be taking the following year.

But, above all, I was haunted by the project of a new review. I had persuaded "Dr." Zissu and the committee of my student society to sponsor a publication to be called *Revista Universitară*. The first issue coincided with the opening of school that fall. Just as when I worked for *Vlăstarul*, I gathered all the material myself and took care of all the proofreading. But this time it was a matter of a periodical that had to be distributed to newsstands and bookstores. In this task I was assisted by Pârvulescu, the leader of the chorus, who had now become the business manager of the review as well. We succeeded in publishing three issues of the review under the direction of a committee of which I was a member; then after the fourth—and last—issue, I had to withdraw. Professors who contributed were Rădulescu-Motru and D. Gusti. I remember a short, concise, ironic text by Stelian Mateescu and a juridicial article by Petre Viforeanu. I published, among others, an article about the novelist Ionel Teodoreanu and a critique of the first volume of Nicolae Iorga's *Essai de Synthèse de l'histoire d'humanité.*

These pages played a decisive role in my youth. The review of Iorga's book was exaggerated and full of juvenilisms. In my unbounded admiration for the genius of that polyhistorian, I had been profoundly disappointed by the first volume of his *Synthèse*. It is true that Iorga was not a specialist in the history of the ancient Orient nor in Greco-Roman antiquity. But since the *Essai de Synthèse* was intended to be the masterpiece of our great historian, I expected it to be prepared and edited with greater care than the hundreds of volumes that had preceded it (Iorga had published by this time some eight hundred books). I assumed that Iorga would be obliged to state in these four volumes the essence of his historical thought. I had dreamed about this book for years; I had imagined it would be lucid, sharply focused, and concise—a true monument raised against the ages.

Instead, I had been sorely disappointed to find the same hasty, rambling prose that I knew from Iorga's other writings; I was also disappointed by the note on the back of the title page, which said that the author had not always had opportunity to consult the books that he quoted; and I was especially disappointed to discover that the most learned historian of the Romanian people had ignored recent bibliographies and had used monographs that were in fashion in his youth. Worst of all, he had not kept in touch with the latest developments in the problematics of Oriental and ancient historiography.

My critique was all the more harsh because I had been such a fanatic admirer of Iorga for many years. Between the lines of my review article one could read the iconoclastic fury of one who suddenly finds himself cheated, who discovers that the god of his adolescence is guilty of human faults and weaknesses. Moreover, the failure of Iorga's *Synthèse* struck me very personally. I had believed in his encyclopedic historical science, and *Essai de Synthèse* should have confirmed brilliantly my faith in the possibility of the appearance of a new type of Pico della Mirandola. To those who would have criticized the diversity of my own interests, I ought to have been able to reply: "But look at the results of such diversity, look at the *Synthèse* Iorga has achieved!"

As might have been expected, my article provoked a minor scandal. Professor Iorga telephoned Gusti, "Thank you, my dear colleague, for contributing to that review where I am cursed so crudely!" In his own newspaper, *Neamul Românesc*, he published a short article entitled "More Humanity!" in which, among other things, he made reference to "the gutter press where students sling mud at their own professors." Six or seven months later there appeared in a provincial review, *Cele trei Crişuri*, the last article of a great savant, V. Bogrea, ironically entitled: "What N. Iorga Has Not Read, But Has Been Read by Mr. Mircea Eliade, Student in Philosophy." It was a painful lesson given by a formidable scholar to an overly excited young man. So far as Iorga was concerned, he never forgave me, although as he mentioned in his autobiography, *O viaţă de om*, when he was Minister of Education in 1930 he did extend my fellowship of 180 pounds sterling per year, which I had obtained the previous year for study at the University of Calcutta. He also stated in the autobiography that my article was the only review of the first volume of his *Essai de Synthèse* published, a fact that I consider a great injustice to him. I should have expected all Romanian historians to discuss the *Synthèse* of the one who had been everyone's teacher.

It was a tragic paradox that, although I had barely entered the university, I had criticized violently and alienated permanently the professor I most admired, the man I had chosen as my model and whose life and work had played an almost "magical" role in my life, both during and after adolescence. Indeed, every time I had felt tired or depressed, it had been enough for me to look at the several dozen books by Iorga that I had collected on my shelves in order to regain my strength. And it was this giant, the man in whose shadow I had yearned to grow, whom I had deeply offended.

As a consequence of this article I had to withdraw from the editorial board of *Revista Universitară*. Soon afterward the review ceased publication. In the meantime, however, the youthful and popular journalist, Pamfil Seicaru, dedicated a eulogy to it in *Cuvântul*. He wrote: "Among all these names, one stands out: Mircea Eliade," and he went on enthusiastically, bringing out the good qualities he found in my writings. He had especially liked the pages about Ionel Teodoreanu, which he reprinted in *Cuvântul* a few days later. This success gave me courage. D. Gusti had told Viforeanu that I might have difficulty with the Rector, and that disciplinary measures might be taken against me. I don't know how much truth there was in these rumors. In any event, I had obtained a prize of several thousand lei for a paper I had written in Mircea Florian's seminar, and that prize was now withdrawn.

About a week later I presented myself at the editorial office of *Cuvântul* and asked to see Pamfil Seicaru. I had brought with me two articles, one about religious experience and the other concerning a book by C. Formichi, *Il pensiero religioso nell'India prima del Buddha*. In the room into which I was ushered were Pamfil Seicaru, Nae Ionescu, and a few other journalists, among whom I recognized the novelist Cezar Petrescu. For several months Ionescu had been writing not only his famous weekly religious editorials, but also short political articles, signed Skythes or Kalikles. The fact that my

professor of logic and metaphysics was on the editorial staff of *Cuvântul* assured me that this sort of journalism was not incompatible
with a rigorous scientific activity. Moreover, for me, as well as for
others of my generation, *Cuvântul* was a paper like no other. I considered it more a review because the articles were signed and because there were contributions by many writers, critics, and essayists.

When I entered the room in which the staff members were seated, I introduced myself to Pamfil Seicaru, and he again praised my
learning and literary talent. He asked me if I would not like to contribute to *Cuvântul*, and I showed him the articles I had brought.
Nae Ionescu approached and after going over the manuscripts he
said they could be published as feuilletons. Seicaru would have preferred articles of literary criticism. I promised him texts on Hasdeu,
Papini, and several contemporary Romanian authors.

The two pieces were published within the week, and when I
brought others to the secretary of the editorial board he told me to
go by the main office and pick up my check. I received 1,000 lei,
more than I had dared hope. At the beginning of December I became a regular contributor to *Cuvântul;* I had to produce two feuilletons per week, plus notes and information for the literary page, and
my salary was set at 4,000 lei monthly. Everything happened so
quickly that I hardly had time to be happy. Only when I cashed my
first paycheck did I understand what it meant to be rich. Now I
could invite Rica to a restaurant and I could order books from Italy
and England.

I stopped by the editorial office almost every evening, fascinated
by all I saw around me. I enjoyed listening to the impetuous outbursts of Seicaru, the discussions between Gongopol and Ionescu,
and the gossip of the journalists. I delivered my articles with a perfect punctuality; I was writing them without effort, sometimes "inspired," because I was free to write about anything I wished. Sometimes I touched on major problems, which in the robust confidence
of youth I considered already solved and easily explained: Orient versus Occident, History versus Documents, and others of this kind.

Around Christmastime the secretary of the editorial board, Ion
Dragu, asked me to give him "a literary piece, a short story or a part
of a novel," for the holiday issue. I was surprised. "But how did you
know I write literature?" I asked him. "I just guessed it. All students

write literature!" I brought him an excerpt from *Romanul adolescentului miop*, the chapter about our society, the Muse. It appeared as a whole page of *Cuvântul*. This manifestation of my literary talents puzzled some of my professors, but it exalted me in the eyes of my fellow students.

During recent months I had become good friends with Rica; sometimes I even wondered if I weren't in love with her. I always managed to convince myself to the contrary because, for me, in my conception of myself and my ambitions, love seemed to be an ill-omened weakness. I had promised myself, as I used to say, a series of "vital experiences": among other things, I would make a trip to the Orient or maybe even travel around the world, accepting any job I might be offered in order to earn my living from one stopover to another. If I were in love, I would no longer be myself, I would no longer be "free," "available."

On the other hand, I knew myself well enough to realize that I was really expecting to fall in love. In the first place, I could not imagine "student life" without a great love affair. Also, I hoped that by being in love I might become free from those attacks of melancholy, or that they might at least become bearable. This ambivalent attitude toward love was to remain with me until late in life. Rica managed marvelously to encourage it. Sometimes I felt that she regarded me as something more than a "good friend," that she was trying to attract and charm me (her incomprehensible silences, the happiness that came over her face when she saw me, and the like). At other times, on the contrary, she seemed distant, or she would declare that she had never had such a good *friend* as I, a true "confidant." And yet I knew very little about her or her past. I would encounter her frequently at the library of the King Carol I Foundation, surrounded by books, preparing papers for the Romance languages seminar. Even though she always passed her examinations, I never had the impression that she was really enthused over philology, literary history, or folklore. She was studying conscientiously for her degree and in order to become a teacher of Romanian language and literature. At first I had thought she was different from all the other girls because she had read several books by Romain Rolland and Remy de Gourmont. In time, however, I discovered lacunae which seemed to me inadmissible, and I would force her to read Dostoevsky, Novalis, and Knut Hamsun. Certain articles I wrote were intended to teach her and encourage her to like the authors I liked. Among other things, I published in *Cuvântul* a series of pieces entitled "Men from Books," which was about several characters who interested me at some point: Sixtine, Brand, Martin Eden—and even Adam and Eve from the book of Genesis!

By the middle of that winter of 1927, only two or three months after my first article had been published in *Cuvântul*, the director and the editors considered me one of them. I found out later that Titus Enacovici, the director, had wanted to "make a newspaper man" out of me, that is to ask me for nonliterary articles as well as literary ones, but Nae Ionescu had been against it. "Let him finish his studies first," he told him. I would not have accepted such an offer anyway, and I believe that Enacovici was easily persuaded that I was not ready for the profession of journalism. In the first place, I had no conception of what could and could not be published in a newspaper. When I wrote an article, I tried to say everything I thought would be worth saying, without thinking about the paper's "political line" or my own interests. Thus, for instance, I began a series of articles under the title "Reading Iorga." I wanted to collect them later in a book, to show how well I had read Iorga and how much I admired his genius. The first article, moreover, was entitled: "From Hermes Trismegistus to Nicolae Iorga," and in it I spoke in exalted terms concerning Iorga's polygraphy. I even proposed the founding of an institute for the study of the work and thought of this giant.

In the second article, however, I began to analyze Iorga's "method" and I showed, among other things, that for many years, Iorga had not been *reading* books but merely skimming them—which seemed to me perfectly natural for a scholar of such prodigious learning who was now approaching sixty. I said further that one of the deficiencies in Iorga's "method" was due to his lack of interest in philosophy; I commented on his confession that he had never been able to read Aristotle, although he had succeeded in reading Plato; I concluded by saying that this was a very serious matter and that Iorga's genius was asystematic.

Probably the article also contained other observations of this kind, which I made in perfectly good faith. I calculated that only after I had explained precisely the structure of Iorga's "method" would it be possible to show the originality of his historiographic conception, namely the fact that it constituted a prophetic view of culture unequaled in this century. But I had forgotten that the editors of *Cuvântul* were fanatic admirers of Iorga, who could by no means admit that the great savant "does not read," or that his cultural propheticism compensates for his philosophical naiveté. The day following the publication of the article, I went to the newspaper office and found Seicaru purple with rage. "You've done it now!" he hissed through his teeth. I was summoned into the director's office. Titus Enacovici was seated at his desk, dignified but furious. Gongopol, who was sitting in an armchair next to him, said that probably I had never read *Cuvântul* and was not aware of what Iorga meant to them, that a youngster like myself had no right to "abuse" the greatest scholar of the Romanian people, and so on. From now on I would no longer be allowed to write about Iorga in *Cuvântul*, and in the future all my manuscripts would have to be read by Gongopol himself or Nae Ionescu. I listened, standing, my face flushed, not uttering a word. After a pause Gongopol added, "That's all we have to say to you." I murmured, "Good evening," bowed, and left.

I didn't know what to do. I felt profoundly offended by Gongopol's reprimand, but I was sad also that out of all I had written about Iorga in the two introductory articles, only the negative elements had been noticed, and that I had been forbidden to continue the projected series, "Reading Iorga," which I had barely begun. I said to myself that after such an incident I ought to resign, but when I asked Nae Ionescu about it he patted me on the shoulder and smiled. "Do as you see fit," he said, "but if at your age you don't know how to take a lesson from an older man, that's not a good sign." Ionescu, who himself was a fanatic admirer of Iorga, added: "What you say about Iorga's method is correct, but something of that sort must be expounded in a scholarly study; in a newspaper column such a criticism could be taken as an attack."

So I stayed with *Cuvântul*, presenting my articles for censorship. It so happened, however, that everything I wrote in the following weeks pleased Gongopol and Enacovici greatly. A series of polemic articles about the writers Ion Minulescu, Mihail Dragomirescu, Paul Zarifopol, and Tudor Arghezi had especially great success, and Gongopol insisted on congratulating me in front of all the editors. I had become again a "promising young man" and my manuscripts were no longer subject to censorship.

But still I ran into trouble. I wrote a rather cutting article about the first volume of Cezar Petrescu's novel *Intunecare*, which angered Pamfil Seicaru. "Don't you know Cezar Petrescu is our friend?" he exclaimed. And when, after my violent article against Tudor Arghezi, Dem. Theodorescu published a rather nasty note in another paper, *Adevărul*, and I answered him impertinently, it was again Seicaru who reprimanded me: "Didn't you know that Dem. Theodorescu is a contributor? Didn't you know he writes for us under the pen name 'Rastignac'?"

I didn't know.

7. *The Lesson of*
Søren Kierkegaard

IN THE spring of 1927, the Lycée Spiru-Haret arranged a three-week tour of Italy that was also open to former students. It cost 20,000 lei, a considerable sum of money, but Mother did not hesitate to give it to me. She had visited Italy once in 1909, and she was happy that at least one of her children would discover it. For me, it meant more than it could have meant to any other young man of twenty. It was an opportunity to meet several of the writers with whom I was in correspondence: Papini, Buonaiuti, Macchioro, and others. Besides the cities with fabulous names, there were also the adventures I imagined, the Italian language I was preparing to speak for the first time, the bookstores and antiquaries in which I knew I would find works that were inaccessible in Bucharest.

Indeed, that first trip to Italy has remained in my memory as the perfect and most luxurious journey of my youth. Not until many years later did I again have the opportunity of spending the nights in good hotels or on a sleeping car, and eating in expensive restaurants. I had three weeks to rove from town to town with no other care than to pack my suitcase every morning. Since we were traveling in a sleeping car, I did not have to worry about a place to deposit the many books I was buying. There were five or six of us university students, twenty lycée seniors, and four or five teachers.

The only annoyance was the fact that I had to send two articles per week to *Cuvântul*. I had not suspected that it would be so difficult to write "travel impressions," either late at night when I was tired from all the art museums and walking, or in the morning, hastily, at a café table before the arrival of the guide who was to be in charge of us for the day. From Venice, I sent two rather mediocre columns. Ravenna impressed me so profoundly that I didn't dare write my impressions. Happily in Florence, where we stopped for three or four days, I visited Papini. He greeted me at the door, appearing much as I knew him from photographs: wearing a collarless shirt and no tie, with a cigarette in the corner of his mouth. He was somewhat better looking than I had imagined him to be, but the thickness of his glasses was quite noticeable.

We conversed in a tiny chamber, hidden among vast rooms with book-covered walls. He asked me whether I wished to speak in French or Italian, and I chose Italian. I wanted to hear him communicate in that rugged, colorful language that had fascinated me for so many years. I had sent Papini the three articles about him that I had published recently in *Cuvântul*, but the young man who usually translated Romanian articles for him had been out of town and Papini had not been able to read them. He encouraged me to talk about my plans and my studies. I confided that I had been greatly impressed by his book, *Un uomo finito*, and by the resemblance between us—so much so, in fact, that at first I was afraid that no matter what I did, people would think I was imitating his work. He smiled, revealing his large, irregular, nicotine-stained teeth. "Don't worry," he consoled me. "From one point of view, all intellectuals resemble one another. But from another point of view, no one resembles anyone else, not even himself."

I asked him if he would allow me to publish the conversation we were about to have, and since he consented, I began to question him. I especially wanted to know what his religious experience had been, and how he reconciled the artist's absolute freedom to create with his fidelity to the Church; what he believed now about the stormy, polemical, iconoclastic prose of his youth; how far he had progressed with *Adamo* (his masterpiece, later entitled *Giudizio universale* [The Last Judgment]); and other such questions. Papini answered with the candor and vehemence that I expected, but after he had exhausted my questions he talked about contemporary Italian authors whom I didn't know, in particular P. Zanfrognini and G.

Manacorda, whose books he brought from one of the adjacent rooms and showed me; about the baleful influence of Hegelianism on Italian philosophy (he said that although he didn't agree with Croce, he could understand him, but that he could not understand Giovanni Gentile—although in his youth he had read and understood Hegel); and about his great love for Dante. When I was ready to leave, he asked me which of his books I should like for him to give me, but I had almost all of them already, and those I lacked were long since out of print and he did not intend to reprint them. He gave me a photograph with a cordial dedication, which was later reproduced along with the interview in *Universul Literar*.

I had looked forward so much to this meeting, and had dreamed about it ever since I knew I was going to Florence, that in a way it disappointed me—although I was at a loss to explain why. Perhaps it was because I had seen my dream with my eyes. I could not say that I had expected something else. Papini was exactly the way I had imagined him, and he had received me more graciously than I ever had dared to hope. But when I left his house I didn't feel like shouting for joy or weeping out of deep emotion. If someone had told me a few years before, when I had just discovered *Un uomo finito*, that I would feel this way, I wouldn't have believed him.

We stayed in Rome for a whole week. Thus I had opportunity to attend a lecture by Giovanni Gentile, to meet the novelist Alfredo Panzini, and to introduce myself to Ernesto Buonaiuti. I made the acquaintance also of Claudio Isopescu. He was at the time lecturer in Romanian language and literature at the University of Rome; he was also in conflict with our country's press attaché and trade representative, Eugeniu Porn. He accompanied our group to Fori Romani, on the ancient Appian Way, and while the group was gathered around the guide, Isopescu took me aside and explained how Porn's presence in Rome was a great detriment to Romanian interests. I set down everything he told me in a little notebook. A few days later, no longer able to restrain my indignation, I wrote a violent and sarcastic article, "Mr. Porn's Rome." When it was published in *Cuvântul*, the article provoked quite a scandal at the Directory of the Press and even at the Ministry of the Exterior, so Porn had to return to Bucharest immediately to defend himself. I realized later, after I had come to know that hotheaded Bukovinian Isopescu better, that I should not have taken at face value everything he told me. He was at odds with almost all his colleagues and with other Romanians in Italy, and he really wanted Porn's job.

Of all the people I met in Rome, the one who impressed me the most was R. P. Ernesto Buonaiuti. He lived rather far out, at the edge of the city, in a little house crammed with books. His mother, a small, quiet old lady, answered the door. I found him dressed in a cassock because, although he had been forbidden to wear it on the street, he said that no one could stop him from wearing it at home. At that time, Father Buonaiuti was about forty-five. He was a tall, dark man, with gray temples and deep, extremely piercing eyes, which reminded me of Nae Ionescu's. He seemed to be consumed by an unquenchable inner flame; his speech, writing, and gestures were precipitate, nervous, abrupt, and yet continuous, like a cascade. We had corresponded for about two years, ever since I had read enthusiastically his famous profiles of saints (Augustine, Jerome, and others). I had written to him to request others of his works. He had sent me several packages containing books and copies of his bimonthly, *Ricerche Religiose*. Buonaiuti was a prolific and surprisingly versatile author, writing erudite treatises and newspaper articles with equal ease. He spoke to me about his difficulty with the Curia, adding that his book on Luther, which had just been published, would dispel all suspicions of "heresy" that were hovering over him. Becoming suddenly grave, he confided that his most difficult personal problem concerned his mother, whom he venerated as a saint, for it was from her that he had learned the meaning of Christian love and faith, and she had encouraged him and sustained him during the course of his theological studies. The greatest happiness his mother had ever known was on the occasion of his ordination. He knew that if he were to be excommunicated it could kill her.

He gave me copies of his most recent works, *Il misticismo medievale* and *L'origini dell'ascetismo cristiano*. While he was writing the dedications, his mother came into the room with a stack of new books that she deposited quietly on the table. Buonaiuti looked at them with a hungry eye. I asked him when he found time to read and write so much, and yet keep up such an extraordinary correspondence (he sometimes wrote fifty letters a week, some of them seven to eight pages in length). He told me that he began work at four A.M., that he never had any difficulty expressing what he thought or felt, that writing did not fatigue him, and that if he had meditated on a subject long enough he could finish a book on it in a few weeks or less.

As soon as I returned to the hotel, I quickly recorded everything that seemed to me important in my conversation with Buonaiuti. The interview was published in *Cuvântul*, but I unintentionally caused a great deal of trouble for this man whom I admired and loved so much. I had asked him what he thought about fascism, and Buonaiuti answered that so far he had not experienced any difficulties, because Mussolini persecuted antifascists but tolerated those who were apolitical; and he, Buonaiuti, had no political activities but only religious and cultural ones. But, he added smilingly, he had of course no sympathy either for Mussolini or fascism. In my great naiveté, I reported these private remarks as part of the interview. As a result, Father Buonaiuti was questioned by the state police, but he quickly realized it had been a matter of naiveté on my part and in his great goodness he forgave me.

I remained in correspondence with him until 1939 and contributed to his journal, *Ricerche Religiose*, but I never saw him again. When I sought to resume our correspondence after the war from Paris, in 1945, he was on his deathbed.

′   ′   ′

I made the same blunder, with much more serious consequences, in the case of Vittorio Macchioro, whom I visited in Naples. Macchioro was at that time Director of the Museum of Antiquities. Ever since lycée I had been acquainted with his books on Orphism and I had carried on a regular correspondence with him, since there was always something I wanted to ask him to send me, such as an older article of his, a book from his personal library, or studies and offprints of articles by his friends. Macchioro had taken it upon himself one day to write all his friends and colleagues, asking them to send me their publications. Thus it came about that I received whole bundles from A. Rostagni, E. Bignone, and other Italian scholars, and even a book of S. Angus, professor at the University of Sydney, about the Greco-Oriental and Christian Mysteries. In the winter of 1927 I had decided to write a critical article on the Mysteries, and I had asked Macchioro to lend me, from his personal library, a number of books inaccessible in Bucharest. He had dispatched to me a dozen volumes, which I was now returning to him in Naples.

His daughter Anna, who was about my age, answered the door and showed me to the library. Vittorio Macchioro was a man of about fifty, bald, bespectacled, lively, and loquacious. After we had discussed the critical article I was preparing, he asked me about Romania. I spoke enthusiastically about Iorga and Pârvan, and finally about Eminescu and the folk ballad "Miorița." Macchioro talked about his illustrious neighbor, Benedetto Croce, about the Villa of the Mysteries, which he considered to be an Orphic chapel (a violently controversial interpretation), and about his religious convictions—he confessed to me that his ideal of a religious community was that of the Quakers. (In 1950, I learned that he had converted to Catholicism some time previously, and that after the death of his wife he had retired to a monastery.) He spoke to me especially about the neo-paganism that fascism constituted, deploring the fact that the Church had not taken a stand against this terrible apostasy.

Subsequently, I described the visit with Macchioro in an article, relating the essence of our conversation, including his antifascist observations. Since they were only ideological objections and objective criticisms, I did not imagine that I would upset anyone by repeating them. At that time I did not know what a dictatorship means. My naiveté was to cost Macchioro his post as Director of the Museum. He was immediately interrogated by the police. Indignant at my lack of discretion, Macchioro declared that he barely knew me, that he had said none of the things I had attributed to him, and that probably the confusion stemmed from my inadequate knowledge of Italian.

That saved him. Later he sent me a sad and bitter letter, asking me how I could have struck him such a blow. This happened at the end of May, a few weeks after my return from Italy. Macchioro's letter brought me suddenly to my senses; I awoke frightened, in a cold sweat, as if startled out of a deep sleep by a thunderclap. I was shaken when I realized the consequences of my "sincerity." But this was only one instance. Recalling the Iorga "scandal" and the indiscretions concerning Buonaiuti, I told myself that there was something in my destiny driving me against my will to offend the very people I most admired and loved. I asked myself if it could be some strange demonic force, if I was cursed to repay with misfortune those I loved and who loved me.

For many months this thought kept haunting me, even after Macchioro had forgiven me. (I sent him several heartrending letters and following a long silence he replied that from my lines "there emerged such sincerity" that he could only forgive me.) I was afraid now that I might harm my best friends, might cause unhappiness to the women I should love. Eventually I was cured of this obsession that I was cursed to wound everyone I loved, but the Macchioro incident was not the last one of that sort in my life. Perhaps what I considered at that time a "demonic force" was only my obsession with frankness and "authenticity" pushed almost into the unconscious. Just as I never shied from writing and publishing anything about myself that seemed to me "authentic" and true, even though it might be embarrassing and indiscreet, so also when I found myself in front of a blank sheet of paper I had no inhibitions about recording the behavior, gestures, and thoughts of others. Besides, when I was writing, it was impossible for me to camouflage what I believed to be "true" or "authentic." Because Macchioro's daughter was plainly and almost shabbily dressed, it seemed to me that she looked like a young servant girl—and I wrote that. It never occurred to me when I sent him the article that Macchioro might give it to someone to have it translated (which is what actually happened), and that likening her to a "servant girl" might seem insulting.

Several years later, when my first novels began to appear, this inability to rise above or even to control the "authenticity" of the experiences I was relating was to provoke an endless series of difficulties.

,   ,   ,

I have never forgotten Italy. I was to see Milan, Verona, and Venice again that year, toward the end of summer on my way home from Geneva, and I had already decided to spend the following spring in Rome, in order to collect material for my thesis. The attraction I felt for the landscape, the Italian language, and the culture was quite spontaneous, inasmuch as I was neither a classicist nor an Italianist. On the contrary, I had by now become completely enthralled by Oriental religions and Indian philosophy. Moreover, my careless, random readings in "dangerous" subjects, my interest in alchemy and hermeticism, my recent discovery of Novalis and Kierkegaard, my passion for "experiments" in which life and its laws were subjugated or surpassed—all these things contrasted with the traditions that confronted me in Italy. But no doubt this attraction was for my good. I was fascinated by mysticism, and like many of my generation, I eagerly followed the reevaluation of medieval philosophy that triumphed in France with Gilson and Maritain. Nae Ionescu discussed it in his lectures, but without accepting it entirely; although he made us read St. Thomas, his preference was for Byzantine theology, especially for Origen, whom he considered to be the most profound philosophical genius of the East (this was some twenty years before Origen's "reconsideration" by Catholic theologians).

Despite all this, I chose for my thesis topic Italian Renaissance philosophy, especially that of Pico della Mirandola, Giordano Bruno, and Campanella. Without realizing it I was trying, through a serious study of neo-pagan immanentism, pantheism, and "philosophy of Nature," to counterbalance my passion for transcendence, mysticism, and Oriental spiritualism. But perhaps things were not as simple as they seem to me now, thirty-five years later. After all, I could find as much magic and occultism as I wished in Pico, plenty of Neoplatonic mysticism in Marsilio Ficino, and an abundance of the fantastic in Campanella. I rediscovered, furthermore, in the whole Italian Renaissance, faith in the unlimited possibilities of man, the concept of creative freedom, and an almost Luciferic titanism—that is, all the obsessions of my youth.

But above all I discovered the great importance of the fact that I was twenty. I understood that I had to enjoy every second, that there are gifts we are not given twice, that one day I might regret everything that I had not done and had not "lived" now, when all things seemed possible.

*   *   *

I returned to my attic one evening in May, arriving from the North Station in a cab laden with books. After a joyful reunion with my family and the first enthusiastic descriptions of the wonders of Italy, I went straight to my attic. Over the garden I could see the silhouette of Ambassador Djuvara's house, rising huge and mysterious, where the lights were turned on only a few days in a year, during the ambassador's rare visits in Bucharest. Suddenly I found myself thinking of Rica, as I had done countless times during the past three weeks in the Piazza San Marco, at Capri, at Amalfi. From every place we stopped I had sent her postcards with mysterious messages, fraught with allusions. But I myself did not know to what exactly I was alluding. I had realized some time previously that I was in love with her, and undoubtedly Rica had guessed it—perhaps even before I had. But of what was taking place in her heart, I had no idea. She had not concealed from me the fact that a handsome and likable cadet in the Naval Academy was courting her, and that he had already asked her to marry him as soon as he received his commission. She had added that she didn't love him and that she preferred to find another type of husband, one from "her world," which was, of course, the world of our circle at the university.

All these things seemed irrelevant; and besides, they were to be fulfilled in a future that seemed extremely distant. I had begun to rid myself of my adolescent complexes and had emerged transformed from my little adventure with Thea. I felt that my love for Rica had no future: not only was marriage or even a prolonged affair out of the question, but I knew that I would try to persuade myself that I wasn't in love, and that I would do everything in my power not to *be* in love any longer.

When she came to see me the next day, we embraced; and we would have stayed in each other's arms for a long time if I had not heard a timid knocking at the door. As usual, it was one of my friends, come to find out how I had liked Italy. But from that evening onward, everything about our behavior toward each other seemed to have changed. Soon our friends began to realize what we had hoped might remain a secret. We were together all the time, and in the evenings we shut ourselves away in the attic. But when I was by myself, I tried to fight against this passion that seemed to threaten my freedom and spiritual integrity. The articles I wrote at that time were part of my coded dialogue with Rica. Such was the article dedicated to Søren Kierkegaard, "fiancé, pamphleteer, and ascetic" (probably the first article on Kierkegaard to appear in the Romanian language), in which, speaking of his love for Regine Olsen, I did not fail to quote the famous fragment that says a fiancée can help the man she loves to become a genius, while a wife can only make him a "general." An article on Novalis was also full of secret allusions.

That summer I wrote several sketches and short stories, which I published in *Universul Literar, Sinteza, Viața Literară*, and *Est-Vest*. I have not reread them since, and so I cannot judge them. I remember only that the majority were fantasies, with strange characters and improbable incidents. I published in *Sinteza* a short story whose main character was extremely ugly, and the whole plot evolved from his complex about his ugliness. In *Universul Literar* there appeared some chapters from *Romanul adolescentului miop*, as well as a novella in which I tried to describe the loss of self-consciousness and the first reactions of one who has lost contact with the real world. (Soon afterward, I met Camil Petrescu and gave him this story to read. His comment: "Madmen are not interesting as literary subjects." He was right.)

Est-Vest, financed by Radu Capriel and directed by Ion Anestin, V. Stoe, and myself, had a short existence: two or three numbers; and yet, among our contributors was Nae Ionescu with "Introduction to Romanian Drama." That winter, Radu Capriel had written to me saying he liked my articles and wanted to meet me. He was some ten years my senior, dark, handsome, with a black, drooping moustache. We became friends quickly. He told me he had several stocks he wished to sell, in order to be able to bring out a review. He invited us to dine with him several evenings, and we discussed at length the "line" of the review. Then one day Capriel confessed that he was getting married, that he was leaving in a few days for Abbazzi, and that he could no longer underwrite the review. After that we saw each other rarely. He was so interested in all I had written that he even asked for my manuscripts from adolescence. My only copy of *Memoriile unui soldat de plumb* has remained with him.

,   ,   ,

During the examination period I learned that the League of Nations was offering several fellowships for two months in Geneva. I took the competitive examination that was required, and was one of five to be selected for the fellowships. I left Romania with Nicolaie Argintescu and Radu Cotaru. Cotaru was then a tall, handsome boy, interested in sociology and counting himself among the favorite pupils of Gusti. Argintescu was short, ash-blond, and pedantically affected (a trait that exasperated everyone else, but amused me greatly). Our first stop was Vienna. In Geneva we all took lodging at the same *pension* at first, but the bedbugs were so abundant there that we scattered to find shelter wherever we could, separately.

In principle, we had to attend a series of classes on the structure

and future of the League of Nations; but I was content to register at
the university library and read books that were unobtainable in Bucharest, especially works on Oriental studies. We ate at a student
canteen, but often in the evenings we would have nothing but coffee with cream, and with the money we saved we would buy books.
I discovered Léon Bloy and completed my reading of Remy de
Gourmont. His *Dialogues des amateurs* disappointed and exasperated
me. What I found fascinating about Gourmont was his dramatic personal history and his multifaceted erudition. However, his naive admiration for "science" and his cheap skepticism irritated me. I wrote
two columns about him for *Cuvântul*, the first rather sympathetic,
the second very critical and probably unjust.

In Geneva my time was entirely my own. During the walks I
took around Lake Leman and during the hours of solitude spent in
the parks, I tried to put some sort of order into my discoveries and
experiences of the last few years. Of course, I also continued to plan
gigantic projects: for instance, a comparative history of mysticism.
But I started writing a series of articles for *Cuvântul*, entitled "Itinerariu spiritual" (The Spiritual Itinerary), in which I proposed to examine all the crises and temptations through which I had passed.
But I did not speak now only for myself. I felt that everything that
had happened to me, above all my increasingly aggressive detachment from the ideals of my forebears, constituted—or would soon
come to constitute—a decisive experience for any young man of my
age. Thus I wrote those twelve articles as a spiritual pilgrimage of
the "young generation"—that is, of those who had been children or
adolescents during the war and were now, in 1927, between twenty
and twenty-five years of age.

As I saw things, the differences between the "young generation"
and those generations that had preceded it were due primarily to
the fact that our forebears had realized their historic mission: the
reintegration of the Romanian people who had been divided between the Austro-Hungarian and Czarist empires. But if the First
World War had allowed Romania to consolidate itself nationally, it
had also caused terrible contradictions for official Western ideology.
The myth of infinite progress, the faith in the decisive role of science and industry to establish universal peace and social justice, the
preeminence of rationalism and the prestige of agnosticism—all
these had been swept away on the battlefront. The "irrationalism"

that had made the war possible and had sustained it was now making itself felt in the spiritual and cultural life of the West: in the rehabilitation of religious experience, the impressive number of conversions, the interest in pseudo-spirituality and Oriental gnoses (Theosophy, neo-Buddhism, Tagore, etc.), the success of surrealism, the vogue of psychoanalysis, and so on. The crisis upon which the Occidental world had entered proved to me that the ideology of the war generation was no longer valid. We, the "young generation," had to find our own goals. But unlike our predecessors, who had been born and lived with the ideal of national reunity, we did not have a ready-made ideal. We were free, open to all kinds of "experiences."* In my belief at that time, these "experiences" were not meant to encourage dilettantism or spiritual anarchy. They were imposed upon us by historical necessity. We were the first Romanian generation unconditioned in advance by an objective to be realized in history. In order not to slumber in cultural provincialism or spiritual sterility, we had to know what was happening everywhere in the world, in our *own time*.

Thus I began to discuss what was happening to me, my "experiences," and the books, theories, and gnoses that had disturbed me and made me think. I wrote about Gourmont's dilettantism, about Theosophy and Anthroposophy, about neo-Oriental gnoses; then about the restoration of metaphysics, various mystical experiences, the offensive of Catholicism, and historicism. I concluded "Itinerariu spiritual" with an article on Orthodoxy. It was rather superficial, because I knew very little and understood even less about the subject. But it had the merit of being neither dogmatic nor programmatic. I said only that, for a part of the "young generation," the Orthodox heritage could constitute a total conception of the world and existence, and that this synthesis, if it could be realized, would be a new phenomenon in the history of modern Romanian culture.

This "Itinerariu spiritual" had the effect of exciting many members of my generation. A young critic, Şerban Cioculescu, reviewed it critically but with great sympathy in *Viaţa Literară*. He, as well as the philosopher Mircea Vulcănescu and the sociologist Paul Sterian, had returned from Paris in the autumn of 1927, and thanks to "Itin-

---

*Romanian: *experienţele*, which may also be translated "experiments."—Tʀ.

erariu spiritual" I made their acquaintance. I was to become increasingly close to Vulcănescu in subsequent years. Only after talking to Vulcănescu and Sterian did I realize how ignorant I was regarding Eastern Christianity and Romanian religious traditions, to say nothing of the "Orthodox experience," which I did not have at all. Orthodoxy had seemed to me very precious to Romanians because it was *there* and had been there for a very long time as an integral part of Romanian history and culture. Personally, although I felt attracted to this tradition, I did not *live* it. Now, at twenty years of age, I had barely freed myself from the consequences of my adolescent scientism and agnosticism. I was still struggling with a number of difficulties and temptations, of which I shall write later.

Even as far as I was from the conception of Orthodoxy shared by Nae Ionescu, Mircea Vulcănescu, and Paul Sterian, I understood the answer Ionescu gave me when I asked him what he thought of the conclusion of "Itinerariu spiritual." He said, "I believe you're mistaken. You say one is *born* a Catholic or a Protestant, but one *becomes* Orthodox. I think just the opposite: you can become a Catholic or a Protestant, but if you are Romanian, Greek, or Russian, you are born Orthodox. Orthodoxy is a natural mode of being in the world: one which you either have or do not have, but one which you can only with difficulty construct. I don't quite see how, if you were born Romanian, you could convert to Orthodoxy, but I understand the process of converting to Catholicism. However, with you I think it's another matter: you consider Orthodoxy to be like a shore to which you hope to return after a series of adventures on the sea. Yet you won't return to the shore of your own free will, but only when you escape from a shipwreck, or when you want to avoid a shipwreck. For me, every existence is equivalent to a shipwreck, so that a longing to return to the shore is virtually inevitable. For you, existence means in the first place a series of spiritual adventures. I think you're wrong, but that doesn't matter. The only thing that matters is what you will do, what you will create, before and after you have understood that you were wrong."

In "Itinerariu spiritual" I articulated and made specific what I had stated several times before in various articles: that there *was* a "young generation," and that so far as I was concerned I was addressing myself to it primarily; that I was much less interested in other readers, those of another age and background. For some of the older generation the whole idea was preposterous. Many of them were genuinely amused by what they took to be an obsession or eccentricity on my part. But in the bottom of my heart I knew I was not wrong. We *were* different from our forebears, not only because we were younger, but also because a war separated us. The same thing, I realized, would happen to us if, in ten or fifteen years, there should be another world war. We would then be considered—by the new generation—not only older but different from them. Moreover, I soon became aware that this "problem of the generations" was not peculiar to Romania: it had been discussed in other countries as well. Later Ortega y Gasset and his disciples Julián Marías and Laín Entralgo were to elevate the concept of "generation" to the rank of a fundamental category in the philosophy of culture.

That same autumn of 1927 I finished a pretentious and confused article, written in several different styles—philosophical essay, diatribe, litany—which I entitled "Apologia virilității." It was published soon afterward in the monthly *Gândirea*. The essay was an attempt to make "virility"—a cliché I had borrowed from Papini's *Maschilità*—a mode of being in the world and also an instrument of knowledge and, therefore, of mastery of the world. I understood by "virility" that which (as I was to discover later in India) Buddhist Tantra symbolizes in the *vajra*: pure consciousness. (And it is significant that *vajra*, literally "thunderbolt," also represents the phallus, or more precisely, the "spiritual" potentialities inherent in and specific to this organ.) I believed, therefore, that virility in its absolute form was equivalent to pure spirit. I accepted Eros only as totally subservient to "virility"; otherwise, the absolute unity of the spirit risked being shattered. Love, in all its modes, I saw only as an instrument for the reintegration of the Spirit.

This mixture of asceticism, metaphysical exultation, and sexuality (a mixture that again recalls India) was baffling to my readers. Almost no one knew what to make of that article. Now and then I would read criticisms of it or derogatory remarks about it in provincial periodicals. Stelian Mateescu seemed rather interested, but he could not accept what he called the "sexualization of the Spirit." Paul Sterian liked it especially for the "poetry" he discovered in that passionate prose. There was a passage in which the author screamed his fury at not being able to be *everything* at *one and the same time*.

Mircea Vulcănescu told me that it could also be used as an argument for demonstrating the necessity of a metaphysics.

After that, I wrote articles that were of an increasingly personal nature, such as "Impotriva Moldovei," mentioned earlier. I received enthusiastic letters in response to some of my essays, even from lycée girls. Sometimes I allowed myself fantasies that I considered quite bold. Recently, I had begun another series, "Scrisori către un provincial" (Letters to a Provincial) in which, in a sense, I was addressing the young people of my generation. From the many letters I had received, I constructed a "provincial" or parochial type, to which I added many of my personal traits: for instance, my melancholia (against which, of course, I thundered and lightninged). To this "provincial" I gave lessons in manliness and heroism, I summoned him to shake off clichés, indolence, and mediocrity, telling him to take his youth seriously—that is, above all, to work with all his might, to *do* something, to *create*. I was obsessed by the fear that our generation, the only *free* generation in the history of the Romanian people, would not have time to accomplish its "mission," that we would wake up one morning "mobilized," as were our parents, grandparents, and earlier ancestors, and then it would be too late and we should no longer be able to create freely, or do anything except what our forebears were fated to do: fight, be sacrificed, and be silent.

I remember one of these pathetic articles: "Anno Domini," which impressed the critic Perspessicius because, he said, he had found in it "the specter of war." I was not thinking, however, only about war when I wrote it, but about any natural catastrophe or historical calamity. The advice I gave to the "provincial" was this: to imagine the coming year, 1928, as *his last year*, and to strive to do, during those twelve months ahead, everything he had promised himself to do in his life. From whence sprang this apocalyptic vision? Certainly not from the political situation in Romania or Europe. At the beginning of 1928 I doubt that there were many who lived in the terror of an imminent world war. Besides, I was almost entirely ignorant of the domestic and international political situation. My fear was of a different order: I felt that time was against us, in the sense that for what we had to do we had too little time available; therefore, we must not waste it in vain activities. On another level, it was the same "struggle against sleep" that I had begun in lycée when I realized that for all I had to do—so many books to read, so many sciences to learn—being awake for sixteen hours simply was not enough. But this time, however, it was no longer a question of myself only. I felt a responsibility for the entire "young generation," which I imagined called to grand destinies: in the first place, I knew that we had the duty of expanding considerably the Romanian cultural horizon and of opening windows toward spiritual universes that until then had been inaccessible. If I had published essays about Milarepa and Aśvagosha, about Kierkegaard and Orphism, I had done it on the one hand because such men and problems had not interested the older generations, and on the other hand because I wanted to oppose our cultural dependence upon France, a dependence that I regarded as proof of intellectual sloth. I demanded from the "provincial," as I demanded from myself, a superhuman effort to learn and to do everything that our forebears had not had the leisure to learn or to do.

I am still convinced that I was not wrong. Actually, our generation had only about ten or twelve years of "creative freedom." In 1938 the royal dictatorship was established; then came the Second World War; and in 1945 the Russian occupation—and total silence.

*   *   *

During that autumn, 1927, Pamfil Seicaru left *Cuvântul*, taking with him a number of members of the staff, and founded *Curentul*. In the aftermath of this crisis, Nae Ionescu acquired a greater responsibility for the political orientation of the paper. I continued to write my two weekly columns, but Titus Enacovici kept trying to persuade the professor that I could take the place of one of the editors who had gone.

At the end of autumn I lectured in public for the first time. Stelian Mateescu, who was the secretary of the Aesthetics Society, had made arrangements for a series of lectures at the King Carol I Foundation to be devoted to romanticism, and he asked me to speak on "Religious Romanticism." He himself gave the opening lecture, which was about romanticism in the arts—quoting copiously from his black notebook. Immediately afterward he left for Paris. Among the other lecturers, if I remember correctly, were the philosopher Stefan Nenițesci and the art critic Oskar Walter Cisek. I accepted the invitation because I believed I had discovered an original interpretation of religious romanticism. I proposed to show the "romantic" character of all new religious movements that had opposed, in a more or less violent fashion, traditional and state religions. The latter I considered "classical." Thus, the opposition between Taoism and Confucianism, Buddhism and Brahmanism, Dionysianism or Orphism and the religion of the Greek cities, even the reform of Zarathustra and the fiery messages of the Hebrew prophets, I interpreted as being so many manifestations of the same type of "romantic revolt"; each in its own way insisted on a personal religious experience and neglected or minimized the collective religious values of the family, the city, or the state. All these "romantic" currents had been born out of a need for a more sincere and more profound religious experience, in the first place out of the desire of the individual for "salvation" or for a more direct and personal relationship with the divine.

This daring attempt to find elements of unity for so many currents of reform and renewal was not wholly wrong, but I exaggerated in considering them all "romantic." Rather, it was a matter of tension between two types of religious experience. Since the general theme was romanticism, I called "romantic" every religious movement that exalted the individual over the group.

I did not write out my lecture, but simply drew up a rather elaborate outline. A few days beforehand I tried, alone in my attic, to speak out loud the opening words of the lecture. I was convinced that if I knew what I wanted to say in the first five minutes, the rest would come by itself. Only one thing worried me: the thought that I might have stage fright when I found myself in front of that huge auditorium. That was why I kept repeating to myself, silently or aloud, the introductory sentences of the lecture. Some of my friends reminded me to speak slowly, to articulate each word, and to avoid making gestures.

I still remember everything that happened. I descended the stairs quickly from the director's box to the stage, but I was careful not to trip. While making my descent I sensed the rustling of the audience, I heard their applause, and a state of calm euphoria came over my whole being. As soon as I began to speak, I knew that everything would go better than I had imagined. I found without any effort the proper pitch and volume, and I was so sure that I would be able to say everything I wanted to say that I didn't even take out the out-

line and notes I had in my pocket. And that was a mistake. I became
so fascinated by the ease with which I was speaking that I didn't
follow the plan I had made at home. I let myself be carried away
with commentaries, I emphasized analogies that occurred to me as I
spoke and that were perhaps interesting and original, but certainly
did not concern the audience. On the other hand, by not consulting
the outline at all, I forgot to present a number of facts and ideas that
were essential to the thesis I was defending! It was, to be sure, more
an informal "talk" than a learned lecture and—perhaps just because
of the spontaneity and offhandedness of my speech—the public listened attentively and with delight to my remarks about Taoism and
Orphism, subjects that probably would not have interested them
otherwise.

The applause that followed me when I returned to the director's
box confirmed the impression I had had all along that I had "made
contact with the audience." But before five minutes had gone by, I
began to realize how many facts and ideas I had omitted, and this
cast a shadow over my happiness at having successfully survived
the ordeal. I hastened to supply the lacunae when I met my friends
who were waiting for me at the exit. "I didn't emphasize Orphism
enough," I began. Only later, in the bar where we all gathered, did I
explain to them at length in what sense Orphism could be considered "romantic."

′　　　　　′　　　　　′

In January of 1928 I decided to write a sequel to *Romanul adolescentului miop*, to be called *Gaudeamus*. "Student life" was coming to
an end, and I wanted to capture it and preserve it all in an autobiographical novel. This time I had no journal to which to refer, as in
lycée days. I did not intend to write a documentary novel anyway; I
was no longer dealing with a phenomenon so little known and so
difficult to understand as adolescence. In a sense, "youth" seemed to
me a rather banal state. The only thing that could save it from banality would be a great love—and only then if that love were renounced, "sacrificed." At the time I had a wholly original conception of the "great passion." It seemed to me that a love did not
deserve that name unless it ended in marriage—or if it were given
up as soon as it had achieved the maximum point of incandescence.
At twenty, I admired only those students who had married or else
renounced (as I was prepared to do) the women they loved. A pro-

longed romance, transformed into a "liaison," seemed to me as uncreative as a succession of more or less lasting affairs. Basically, this was another way I had of opposing myself to the "shallowness" of behavior that was normal for my age and station as a student. Student marriages were rather rare in those days, and they always entailed a certain amount of sacrifice. As I saw it, one of the two—usually the husband—gave up something: a career that might have been brilliant, or at least a carefree youth. The few student couples I knew at the time had much difficulty making a living. To choose poverty at the age of twenty seemed to me a gesture of truly exemplary greatness.

I felt that I had to write *Gaudeamus* then, in that winter of 1928, as quickly as I could. On the one hand I had to capture the atmosphere of those first months of my "student life," which was beginning to fade from memory already. On the other hand, I anticipated that I would renounce the "great passion" I was experiencing at the time, and I was beginning to prepare myself for this ordeal. I was preparing Rica also, helping her to understand that the most certain proof of love I could give her was this: to sacrifice myself to her, by sacrificing her. The theme of the novel was this love, which began in refusal and exultation, fulfilled itself in a sort of oneiric bliss, and in the end was stifled in the name of no one, and—at least for the average reader—without motive and without justification. The author of the novel was perhaps more in love at the moment of separation than he had been in the last months of union with his beloved. It was exactly what I felt that winter, writing the novel, and I had no doubt that things would happen just that way eight or nine months later when I knew I would be leaving the country. I would sever all relations with Rica, and once I was gone I knew she would accept the naval officer's proposal of marriage and would vanish forever from "our world," the world we and all the others had built together in our student years.

I wrote, as usual, at night. But I was so caught up in this novel that I could have written day and night without stopping. Since in the attic I could never be certain that I might not be interrupted by a friend or Rica, I asked a former lycée acquaintance, Marin Popescu, to let me spend a few days at his place at Clinceni. His parents had the remnants of an estate there, with a country house and a pond. He took me there one morning in a cabriolet. It was only about twenty-five kilometers from Bucharest, and although it was the end of January the roads were still in good condition. After a few hours he returned to the city and I was left alone, except for the servants. A fire had been kindled in a small, freshly painted room where I set up my work table beside a window. A servant woman brought me food twice a day and made coffee for me whenever I asked. I began working that very afternoon, and I continued writing until late at night, by oil lamp.

I had promised myself I would finish the novel in a week. Almost a hundred pages were already written, and according to my calculations *Gaudeamus* would require about 250 pages in all. Twenty pages per eighteen-hour day didn't seem too many. But the further I progressed with the writing, the more I was oppressed by a feeling of great sadness. It seemed at times that I was writing an obituary of the "student life" that I loved so much, which—only two years before—I had hailed as a fabulous new existence. I believe there were whole pages written while my eyes were blurred by tears. When recalling the choral rehearsals in the attic and the first dates with Rica, I had the feeling that all this might be prolonged if I had not decided that I *must* give it up. But, at any rate, I had to free myself from this new reservoir of melancholy, constituted by the memories of student life, and especially by the history of my romance. I had to finish *Gaudeamus* in a week. Its eventual publication was of less concern to me, although I was thinking of showing it to a publisher, together with *Romanul adolescentului miop*.

After three or four days it started to snow. The storm developed into a blizzard that blew for about a day and a night without stopping. I remember drifts as high as a man, because just then I ran out of ink and there was no way I could get to the village to buy another bottle. I began to add water to the residue left in the inkwell, and I wrote the last chapters, which were increasingly shorter and more dramatic, with paler and paler ink. The last pages were almost illegible. When I gave Rica the manuscript to read, she asked me if those pages had been written with tears.

I don't know if Rica ever understood fully what *Gaudeamus* meant for me. The novel ended with her wedding and my departure. Our whole group of students scattered to the four winds, and my attic was destroyed not long afterward. Thus the source of our memories disappeared forever. In my desire to burn up the past utterly and to defend myself from the present, I even anticipated the event that seemed to me a veritable sacrilege. For I could not imagine myself in Bucharest without my attic on Strada Melodiei. I knew I would be out of the country for several years, but I was sure that when I returned the attic would still be there—that place where I had grown up and where the mysterious metamorphosis had taken place that had transformed me, in less than a decade, from the "Captain's brat" to the somber author of *Gaudeamus*. During those nights of exhausting labor at Clinceni, I cruelly forced myself to anticipate the destruction of the house on Strada Melodiei, which actually was to happen seven or eight years later, in 1935.

Rica did not try to conceal the fact that, although she liked the novel very much, it grieved her deeply. We discussed it as a literary work, almost without relating it to ourselves. I kept her informed about the impressions of other readers. There was only the original manuscript, but it was a manuscript almost devoid of corrections, and with the exception of the pages written in pale ink, it was legible enough. I gave it to Ionel Teodoreanu, hoping he would like it and present it to the venerable publishing concern, Cartea Românească. I had met Teodoreanu a year previously, in Iaşi, and although I had published some rather cautious articles about the last two volumes of his *La Medeleni*, we had remained good friends; he contacted me every time he came to Bucharest on business. After a few weeks, Teodoreanu returned my novel together with a short but cordial letter. He said it had to be taken in one gulp, like a glass of new wine. But, he added, good old wine is not to be drunk like the new, but sipped slowly. He left it to be understood that the novel was not yet a literary work, but was only the cry of a young man suffering for many reasons he did not understand.

Of course, he was right. When I reread *Gaudeamus* four or five years later, it seemed then both lyrical and frenzied, too pretentious, timidly indiscreet, and quite lacking in grandeur. But during that spring of 1928 I was so drunk with the "popularity" I believed I had gained from my two years of contributing to *Cuvântul*, that I introduced myself one day to Meny Toneghin, the chief editor at Cartea Românească. When I saw him, I looked at him with an expression of wonderment, and I believe he never forgave me for that. At that time he was a small young man, with thin hair slicked down on his head in a scholarly fashion. His movements were slow and he wished them to appear solemn and distinguished, especially when he was admiring his enormous signet ring. He wore, moreover, a pearl stickpin in his tie. I showed him the manuscripts of the two novels and asked him whether he would be willing to read them for possible publication. He gave me a weary smile and answered that Cartea Românească published only classical authors like Mihail Sadoveanu and a few others, or successful young novelists such as Ionel Teodoreanu—and that at the moment Ionel Teodoreanu was the only young author who could be considered a success. He added that the public was not reading Romanian literature, but preferred foreign novels, and that it was useless therefore for me to try at this time. Still, if I insisted he said he would be willing to leaf through the manuscripts, but he promised me in advance that I had no chance of being published by Cartea Românească.

I returned home with the manuscripts and I did not look for another publisher. I was content to let *Gaudeamus* circulate among my friends. (I did publish an excerpt from it in the weekly, *Viaţa Literară*.) Then I laid the two manuscripts in a drawer, alongside the many others. The last time I set eyes on *Gaudeamus* was in 1937 or 1938. I still remember it very clearly. There were 220 pages written in a precise, careful hand, which I was never able to duplicate afterward. The last ten or fifteen pages were faded, as if they had been left lying in the sun for a whole summer. They could still be read, but only with great difficulty.

8. *A Letter from the Maharaja of Kassimbazar*

AT THE beginning of April, 1928, I left Romania for a three-month stay in Rome. I had written to our press attaché, Theodor Solacolu, asking him to find me a room in a cheap *pensione*. He had found something even more convenient: a room in a private house, where the only food I was given was coffee in the mornings. This left me free to eat wherever I wished. I often took dinner at Theodor Solacolu's, but the majority of the time I ate at a trattoria near the library. Isopescu and his wife and members of the Romanian School in Rome often dined there too.

Since I wanted to do many things at once, I slept hardly at all. Days I spent at the university library, evenings I strolled about the city, and nights I worked at home, preparing my licentiate thesis or writing articles for *Cuvântul* or the Italian press. Around midnight I would go out for some coffee, which would keep me awake until dawn. I had brought with me the works of Giordano Bruno edited by Gentile, a few volumes by Campanella, and everything I had been able to buy relative to the philosophy of the Italian Renaissance. At the library I was struggling with the folio edition of Pico della Mirandola, transcribing as many passages as I could. But I always asked for other books and periodicals. I read *Leonardo*, the review founded by Papini, in which he started his prodigious career. I discovered Menéndez y Pelayo, although at first I stumbled upon a book from his early youth, *La ciencia española*, which did not especially interest me. But soon afterward I found his *Historias de las ideas estéticas en España* (Aesthetic Ideas), *Historias de los heterodoxos españoles* (Heterodoxies), and *Orígenes de la novela* (The Origins of the Novel), all huge compositions consisting of five or six volumes each, which I read in great haste. I was amazed at the fantastic erudition of Menéndez y Pelayo, and at the same time fascinated by the clarity of his thought and the richness of his prose. That's how Iorga should have written his *Essai de Synthèse*, I said to myself. I noticed very quickly how similar these two giants were and how comparable were their positions in the history of their respective cultures. But Menéndez y Pelayo had succeeded in mastering the immense quantity of materials he had gathered, and I took him as a model. When I discovered that he had also published a volume of poetry, my enthusiasm knew no bounds. I wrote, with veneration and envy, a long article about him in *Cuvântul.*

Polygraphs had always attracted me, even in adolescence. Menéndez y Pelayo encouraged my incursions into Spanish bibliography, and thus I discovered the learned volumes of Adolfo Bonilla y San Martín. I wrote an article on him also, probably the only one ever published in Eastern Europe concerning this encyclopedist. As for Arturo Farinelli, he was an old acquaintance. In my last year in lycée I had read the two volumes *Episodi di una vita* and *Petrarca, Manzoni, Leopardi: il sogno di una letteratura mondiale,* and since then I had tried to keep in touch with his prodigious output, buying everything I could and asking for the rest in enthusiastic letters.

The way I set about to work in Rome, I might never have finished anything I began. I was aware of the danger, but the temptation was too great. For the first time I was *living* in a great Western library, among publications inaccessible in Bucharest. I wanted to see everything, read everything, transcribe everything. I took copious notes, not daring to leave uncopied a page I knew I would never set eyes on again. My thesis threatened to become a comparative history of Italian Renaissance philosophy. In special folders I gathered supplementary documentation concerning Hermeticism, occultism, and alchemy, and their relations with the Orient. What didn't I plan? I was going to translate into Romanian a collection of fragments from Leonardo da Vinci, write a commentary on Michelangelo's sonnets, compile an anthology of Pico della Mirandola, and many other things.

And all this feverish activity was only a part of my adventures in the libraries of Rome. At the same time I added to my knowledge of India and especially of Indian philosophy. From the review *Bilychnis* I had found out, a few years earlier, about the journey of Carlo Formichi and Giuseppe Tucci to India. I was in correspondence with the professor of Sanskrit, Formichi, and I had received books and articles from him. When I went to see Tucci at the University of Rome, I was told he was still in Dacca, but I was given permission to work in the library of the School for Indian Studies.

I shall never forget that afternoon in May when I opened *A History of Indian Philosophy* by Surendranath Dasgupta. Earlier that winter I had purchased his book on Yoga, and I knew he was the most celebrated historian of Indian philosophy. But I had not yet seen this, his first volume of what later became his five-volume masterpiece. I had not dared to order it (it cost two guineas, or about $9). In the preface, Dasgupta acknowledged that without the help of the Maharaja Manindra Chandra Nandry of Kassimbazar his book would never have appeared. The subsidies of this patron had allowed Dasgupta to study five years at Cambridge, and it was also the Maharaja who had assumed the cost of the printing at Cambridge University Press. Dasgupta added that the name of the Maharaja of Kassimbazar was linked to all cultural and educational works in Bengal.

With great excitement I copied the name and address of the Maharaja; then, on the spot, I began composing a letter to him in French. I told him that I was preparing a licentiate thesis in the field of Renaissance philosophy, but that I was just as much interested in Indian philosophy and that I should like to go to Calcutta to work for two years with Dasgupta. I was willing to live quite modestly, the way an Indian student lives, and I asked him whether, once I arrived in Calcutta, I might be able to obtain a scholarship from him. That night, at home, I copied the letter and dispatched it the next day.

I have no doubt that my life would have been very different had I never written that letter. I knew that the best place to learn Sanskrit and to study Indian philosophy was at a university in India, but I did not dare to hope that I would get there so soon. I told myself that, very likely, I would obtain a fellowship from one of the Western European universities. In that case, I had decided to study comparative philosophy. Therefore, my researches into Renaissance philosophy were not entirely pointless. They would be completed later with a thorough study of Oriental philosophy. I believed I knew enough about pre-Socratic thought and the origins of Greek philosophy, and I planned that someday I would undertake an intensive study of the Classics. This was more or less how I saw my next five years of study: comparative philosophy was to be a preparation for research into the comparative study of religions. For that reason I was not much interested in post-Renaissance philosophical thought. For what I had in mind, Giordano Bruno and Campanella were more valuable than Descartes or Kant. All these plans, even the general orientation of my studies, were to be overturned by the Maharaja's reply. But the reply was not to arrive until some three months later. I was to receive it one summer morning, at Strada Melodiei, when I had lost almost all hope that it would ever come.

Sometimes in the evenings I would meet with a few Romanian students and we would go for a good time to the "Biblioteca" or some trattoria in Trastevere. We would return home singing. In vain did I stop at the bars still open to drink coffee. Once back in my warm room on Via della Scrofa, I had to struggle to stay awake.

Around the middle of June I decided to return to Romania. I had to be back in Bucharest by the end of the month to take my final examinations. I also had the unpleasant surprise of not receiving my salary from *Cuvântul*. Titus Enacovici had died recently and the paper, now under the direction of Nae Ionescu, was confronted with greater and greater financial difficulties. From home I received a money order that enabled me to pay my boat fare from Naples to Constantinople. Our consul had given me a letter addressed to his colleague in Istanbul, assuring me that I would receive there free passage on a Romanian ship. With great difficulty I managed to pack my notes, manuscripts, and books into two suitcases. I had written only fragments of my thesis, and much of what I had written was to be left out of the final draft, in which I had to restrict my study to three philosophers. A good portion of the material I gathered I never used. Those hundreds of pages on which I had transcribed and summarized rare texts were to find their place soon next to other manuscripts, on one of the shelves of a glass-fronted bookcase my father had given me as a gift.

I saw Naples again, but not Macchioro. The day after my arrival there I embarked on an Italian steamer. I spent as much time as possible on deck, reading *La conscienza di Zeno* by Italo Svevo. But the stifling nights spent in the bowels of the ship, where the third-class cabins were located, seemed endless. I had enough money left to afford a two-day stopover at Athens. I stayed at some sort of inn where I paid very little, and I also ate there sometimes because the prices were ridiculously low. Even after nearly three months in Italy, Athens thrilled me to the depths. In front of the Parthenon, I suddenly felt like crying. Ashamed, I bent over and began to search around me, as if I had lost something. I discovered a little flower, small as a lentil seed, of a pale faded blue color, and I plucked it passionately and pressed it in my notebook, determined never to part with it. And thus I was able to gaze upon the Parthenon in brighter spirits.

From Piraeus I took a Greek steamer to Constantinople, where I stayed for three days. Here, too, my delight knew no bounds. I walked all day, and every time my eyes came to rest on the Golden Horn, I would promise myself that I would never write travelogues again. In the bazaar at Istanbul I felt my heart pounding. Would the Maharaja answer me? I was almost afraid to hope. I felt that the Orient meant, for me, much more than a fairy-tale landscape or an object for study, that it was a part of the world that deserves to be known for its secret history or for the grandeur of its spiritual creations. It held a strange attraction for me, in which I seemed to read my fate: a mysterious enchantment sprung from unknown sources. I sensed it in a minaret discovered unexpectedly at the end of a street, a shadow beneath an old wall, the sky glimpsed between cypress trees.

Our consul obtained a free ticket for me on one of our Romanian ships, and one glorious morning late in June I arrived in Constanţa. With great difficulty I carried my two heavy suitcases to the train station. I had money left for a ticket and a meal. I contented myself with tea and bread, so I could take a cab home when I arrived in Bucharest.

,   ,   ,

That summer, the last one of my student years in Bucharest, lingers in my memory as a fabulous interlude. I had little difficulty passing the final examinations, but it was absolutely impossible for me to finish my thesis, so I postponed it until autumn. Rica, on the contrary, had succeeded in obtaining her degree and had applied to the Ministry of Education for a teaching position. The two of us lived now as in a dream, fearful that someone might waken us and remind us that the die had been cast long ago, that everything was already decided. Sometimes we seemed to question each other with our eyes: why did it *have* to happen this way?—but neither of us dared seek an answer.

I readily persuaded Nae Ionescu of the necessity for my trip to India. It could not have been otherwise with a professor who always encouraged us to go to the sources, not to be satisfied with "books about," but to read, whenever possible, a text in the original. Being aware of my sincere and continued interest in the Orient, especially India, the professor kept repeating to me whenever he had occasion that nowhere could a philosophy be better understood than at the place where it was conceived. In India, for example, he added, you can see how a man behaves, how he walks down the street, who does not believe in the ontological reality of the world.

That summer, Nae Ionescu carried almost singlehandedly the burden of *Cuvântul*. Very few of the editorial staff were left, and inasmuch as salaries were paid only occasionally and in part, even the remaining editors did not write their articles regularly. There were days when the professor wrote practically the entire front page of the paper, signing it with various names and pen-names. Sometimes he even signed the name of the editor who had neglected to submit his manuscript. I remember Perspessicius told me once that one day, upon opening the paper, he had been startled to find his name underneath an article he knew very well he hadn't written. He was even more amazed to read it: it sounded just like something he might have composed!

Even though I had little hope of being paid my salary, I continued bringing two feuilletons every week, and sometimes other articles also. No matter when I went to the editorial offices, I found Nae Ionescu there, bent over his desk, writing. He kept his smile, his calmness, and his sense of humor, but he lost weight and always looked tired. After spending a week in the Bucegi mountains, I went to see him at the end of July, and he admired my tanned, rested face. "I'd love to go myself, for a day or two, to the mountains," he said. "I've shrunken here, tinkering at this paper."

I met often with Stelian Mateescu, Paul Sterian, Mircea Vulcănescu, and Sandu Tudor. Together we planned a journal of religious philosophy, for which Tudor had found a title: *Duh și Slovă* (Spirit and Letter). The review was to take the place of and continue the two volumes of *Logos*, which Nae Ionescu had published in French in collaboration with several Russian theologians who were living as refugees in Germany and Paris. In *Logos* I had published my first studies in French: a long review article on Greco-Oriental Mysteries and the essay "La Vision chrétienne d'Ernesto Buonaiuti." But after only two volumes, *Logos* had ceased to appear. Vulcănescu and Tudor considered it our duty to take up the torch, publishing a journal in Romanian and addressing the youth especially. The first issue was to appear around Christmas. To me had fallen the responsibility of presenting the structure of magical philosophies and of showing to what extent magic constitutes one of the greatest temptations of the spirit. Stelian Mateescu was to demonstrate the invalidity of magical philosophies, and Vulcănescu was to present the specific characteristics of Christian religious experience. I don't know whether or not the other contributors sent in their articles on time. I managed to finish mine around the first of December, on board the S.S. *Hakone Maru*, shortly before arriving in Ceylon, and I mailed it to Vulcănescu from Colombo. But *Duh și Slovă* did not appear, and that text, "Faptul magic" (The Magic Deed), which certainly was not devoid of interest, was lost among Vulcănescu's papers. I never found a trace of it.

Through Mihail Polihroniade, one of my classmates at Spiru-Haret, I had made the acquaintance of Ionel Jianu and Petru Comarnescu. Jianu had just returned from Paris, and because he was interested in philosophy of religion we became friends quickly. He was at that time a tall, thin, timid young man, who sorely regretted having to leave Paris. Comarnescu had made a name for himself by means of the chronicles he wrote for the weekly, *Lumea*, in which he discussed art exhibits, concerts, lectures, and books. He had a great facility for writing, being able to compose several articles in a single afternoon, sometimes even about the same play or book. With Mihail Polihroniade I had become friends in the last years of lycée. We took the same streets home and always walked together and talked. Even in those days Polihroniade was interested in politics, and published reports on foreign affairs in the conservative newspaper, *Epoca*. In the first two years at the university we saw each other less frequently, but in 1928, especially due to our mutual acquaintances, we renewed our friendship. In this group also the idea of a review was taking shape. They were thinking about a series of quarterly issues in which all the great problems that interested young people—from our country as well as from Western Europe—would be discussed. Unlike *Duh și Slovă*, this review would not be limited to religion and philosophy; it would be called *Acțiune și Reacțiune*, and it would take into consideration all the ideologies and currents, both cultural and political, that had become established since the war. And again, unlike *Duh și Slovă*, the first issue of *Acțiune și Reacțiune* did see the light of day, although not until almost two years later. The principal contributors were Petru Comarnescu, Polihroniade, and Ionel Jianu.

One August morning I received an envelope franked with an Indian stamp. I opened it with trembling hands. The Maharaja Manindra Chandra Nandy of Kassimbazar had actually written to me! He congratulated me on my decision to study Indian philosophy with Surendranath Dasgupta, but he added that two years would not suffice. I would require at least five years to be able to learn Sanskrit and penetrate the mysteries of Indian philosophy. He was ready to offer me a five-year scholarship. But since he did not believe it possible for a European to live the life of an Indian student, he asked me to tell him how much I would need per month!

I read and reread the letter. It was like a dream. Then I ran to give Mother the news. That same evening I answered the Maharaja, assuring him that I should be very happy to study five years with Dasgupta in Calcutta. As to the amount of money I would need per month, I left that for him to decide. I recopied the letter very carefully, because my hand was trembling with excitement. And I fell asleep quite late, worrying about plans and questions: how much would the fare to India by steamer cost? And by what route should I go? Should I travel to Bombay and cross India by train, or should I wait for a ship circling the subcontinent that would take me to Calcutta?

When I told Nae Ionescu the great news the next day, he replied that before fall things *had* to improve, and when *Cuvântul* had been rescued he would be able to help by contributing to the expenses of the trip. He was thinking, of course, about the National-Peasant government, for which *Cuvântul* together with a large part of the country was calling and which no longer could be denied. But until then *Cuvântul* was surviving almost miraculously, thanks to the devotion of the editors and the steel will of Nae Ionescu.

Toward the end of August I spent a week in Bran at the villa of my old friend Mihail Puşcariu. Most of us who were gathered there had become friends in our last years at the lycée: Radu·Bossie, Petre Viforeanu, Dinu Sighireanu, Haig Acterian, and a few others. Almost all of us were about to receive our licentiate degrees and were preparing to go abroad for doctoral work. They were going to Paris and I was hoping to go to India. It was a time to reminisce about the beginnings of our friendship in the lycée and the predictions we had made, five or six years earlier, about one another. We also confessed the ideals or goals we had set for our lives, and we promised to meet again in Bran the first summer after we had returned from abroad, and every five years thereafter, to see to what extent each had held to his purpose.

Recently I had begun keeping my journal again. This time I did not spend long hours over it, writing down everything that went through my mind, analyzing myself and complaining, as I had done in lycée. Instead, I made brief entries that seemed significant for later use, ideas and observations related to things I was planning to write, and so forth. Above all, it was a private diary, written for myself exclusively. I did not hesitate to record indiscretions, although I planned to tear out a few pages now and then, especially if I suspected that someone else might see it. With a few interruptions, I have continued that journal to the present day.

*   *   *

In October I decided to wind up the thesis; otherwise, it threatened to remain unfinished forever. P. P. Negulescu and Mircea Florian read it, and soon afterward I received my Licentiate in Philosophy. But I had no time to be happy about being freed of that burden. The weeks that preceded my departure were perhaps the most dramatic of my life up till then. Rica had been given a teaching appointment at a lycée in Strehaia, and from there she sent me despondent letters every day. I answered her, also daily, not understanding why I was writing with such frenzy, because the irremediable had already happened. She had become engaged to the naval officer who two years before had asked her to marry him, and I had received a second letter from the Maharaja, assuring me that I would have a scholarship as soon as I arrived in Calcutta. Moreover, Dasgupta had written me that he would be happy to supervise my studies in Indian philosophy and my doctoral thesis on yoga. There was nothing left for me to do except obtain a British visa for India and find a suitable ship to take me there. But in 1928 these matters were not so simple for a Romanian citizen. I could obtain a British visa only with a letter of recommendation from Sir John Woodroffe (who, writing mostly under the pseudonym "Arthur Avalon," had introduced Tantrism to the Western world), and after showing that I possessed one hundred pounds sterling.

Matters might have dragged on for many more weeks if Mircea Vulcănescu had not discovered that at the beginning of December an international conference of the YMCA was going to be held in Poonamallee, near Madras, and Romania was invited to send a representative. It so happened that Vulcănescu was the secretary of the Romanian division of the YMCA, and since he could not participate in the congress, he appointed me! When I confronted the British Consul with the official paper confirming me as a delegate, he yielded and gave me a three-month visa. (However, during my three years in India, no one ever inquired about the validity of my visa.) My being a delegate to the congress at Poonamallee forced me, however, to modify my itinerary. I had to catch a ship in Egypt to take me to Ceylon, and from there go by train to Madras.

It was equally difficult to obtain the hundred pounds. I had hoped to be able to recover part of my salary from *Cuvântul* and perhaps even receive a significant advance, but the financial condition of the paper had not improved. Eventually, Uncle Mitache lent me the sum.

Then suddenly, in November, things began to happen. The democratic leader, Iuliu Maniu, was called to form a new government. It was, in a way, the "revolution" for which Nae Ionescu had called and had paved the way through his editorials in *Cuvântul*. The whole editorial board experienced the euphoria of victory. But I hardly had time to go to the editorial office to share in the general happiness. Rica had come to see me again. I was almost afraid I would give it all up—that I would jerk the engagement ring off her finger and fling it away, and that we would go off somewhere together, without plans or vows.

However, at night, alone in my attic, I would awake. *Now,* I said to myself, at least *for the time being,* there's nothing else I can do. I would open several books on Indian philosophy or travelogues on Oriental lands, and let myself be transported in thought. India fascinated me, it drew me like a mystery through which I seemed to foresee my destiny. It was necessary that I tear myself away from everything and everyone, at any cost, in order to go there. I felt that in a way it was a premature rupture. Nothing had come of my work of the past three years. I had not succeeded in publishing my novels (Nichifor Crainic had promised to publish "Itinerariu spiritual" in his series, Cartea Vremii, but actually the manuscript lay forgotten in a drawer, and soon afterward it was lost completely); I wanted to collect in one volume a large number of my columns that had appeared in *Cuvântul;* I also wanted to prepare a volume of short stories and another one of essays (to begin with "Apologia virilitaţii"). If I were to remain for another few months, perhaps at least one of these projects would have been realized. I knew that by leaving for India all these works would remain buried, like those files on Renaissance philosophy. But on the other hand, I knew that if I did not tear myself away from everyone and everything—from Rica, from *Cuvântul,* from my "works," finished or in the process of gestation—and if I did not do it *now,* when the wounds of my separation were still bleeding, I would not get there in time to encounter the mystery that was waiting for me somewhere in India, that mystery of which I knew nothing except that it was there for me to decipher and that in deciphering it I would at the same time reveal to myself the mystery of my own existence; I would discover at last who I was and why I wanted to be what I wanted to be, why all the things that had happened to me had happened to me, why I had been fascinated in turn by material substances, plants, insects, literature, philosophy, and religion, and how I had gotten from the games on the vacant lots to the problems that perplexed me now.

A few days before leaving I started to hide the notebooks in which I had kept my journal from adolescence under the piles of books for which there was no more room on the shelves and which I had stacked on top of one another in the glass-windowed bookcase. Most of the other manuscripts were in the chest where I had kept them ever since lycée. These, along with other little boxes full of notes and letters, I carried to the storage area of the attic. Now and again my eyes came to rest on some manuscript or letter whose existence I had nearly forgotten. Thus I found and leafed through (I believe for the last time) the notebook where I had compiled in lycée a history of the decipherment of hieroglyphics.

Then, one morning, I learned that I must leave the following day. I had obtained a free ticket on the Romanian steamer to Alexandria, and the ship was leaving the next day, November 20. I told my friends the news and packed my bags. In two suitcases I placed a few shirts, some sheets, Dasgupta's books, and the journal I had started that summer. The suitcases were small and fairly light, and I could carry them for a long time without becoming tired. As a matter of fact, I did carry them by myself until the day I took up lodging at Mrs. Perris's boarding house at 82 Ripon Street, Calcutta.

I no longer remember whether November 20 was a cloudy or sunny day. The night before I had said goodbye to Nae Ionescu. He had assured me that during the winter I would obtain a stipend from the Romanian government. I said goodbye to Mother and Nicu at home. Only my father and Corina accompanied me to the station. Corina was now in her last year in lycée, and I hoped that she would soon move into my place in the attic. On the train platform several friends were waiting for me: Radu Bossie, Haig Acterian, Ionel Jianu, and Polihroniade. The others had already gone to Paris. Ionel Jianu had brought me a carton of cigarettes and a book by Jacques Rivière, with a cordial dedication. Then on the platform he told me once again how much he admired my courage to be "going on a great adventure."

Time dragged by. At last there came the signal for departure, and the train began to move slowly away from the station.

PART II

India at Age Twenty

9. *From Ripon Street to Bhawanipore*

I SHALL never forget that evening in December, 1931, in the harbor of Bombay. I was waiting on the deck for the steamer to leave the pier. But when I saw the lights of the city begin to fade in the distance, I could stand it no longer and went below to my cabin. The cabin was to be shared with two Indian students, but I knew that for at least a half an hour I would have it to myself; for who else could have endured being shut in a cabin at that moment of twilight, with the ship gliding slowly across the calm waters?

I was leaving India against my will, and I had agreed to leave only because I had promised myself to return in a year or two, after I had done my military service. A pathetic letter from my father made me decide to return home. Because recently in my letters to him I had been telling about plans and projects that would take many more years, Father had not again requested a postponement of my military service, as he had done three times before, to allow me to continue my studies. In the fall of 1931, in Calcutta, I received a long letter imploring me to come back because, by not presenting myself for conscription, I would be called a deserter, and this would be the worst disgrace my father, a former army officer, could suffer. Of course, I had to obey.

I did not realize how much I had changed in those three years of Indian life until I arrived home. No longer was I the youth who, having disembarked at Alexandria on a November morning with two suitcases in hand, had set off casually along the docks to look for a ship to take him to India. It was as though a whole lifetime separated me from that week spent in Alexandria, Cairo, and Port Said. It amused me now, but also embarrassed me, to recall how naive and enthusiastic I had been then: riding to the Pyramids perched on the back of a camel, exploring the native quarter on my first night in Cairo, gazing with pride from the motor launch at Port Said at the S.S. *Hakone Maru,* which was to carry me to Ceylon. In the days spent on shipboard, I tried to express myself in English and write my first "travel impressions" of Egypt, the Red Sea, and the Indian Ocean. I made the acquaintance of two fellow-travelers: a young Japanese novelist who claimed to be a nihilist, and Bhimi Chandra, an Indian from Gujarat, with whom I was to travel from Colombo to Madras.

Ceylon captivated me even before I set foot on it. While we were still some distance from shore, the strong odors and aromas of the jungle intoxicated me. But only after seeing Kandy and Anuradhapura did I have a true revelation of the jungle: trembling in awe and exultation before cataracts of fresh sap and unrestrained vegetal cruelty. Millions of plants crushed and buried from sight under half-decayed tree trunks, gigantic ferns and lichens struggling to make room for themselves among spider webs, fungi, and mosses of all colors. Memories of that week in Ceylon and of my first days in South India have continued to haunt me.

I entered India through Danushkodi, at the southernmost point of the peninsula, and I spent the night in Rāmeshwaram in the house of a Brahman, Ramchandra Gangadhar. The excitement of the first Indian hospitality; the deep emotion as I approached the large and famous temple at Rāmeshwaram; its savage, nonhuman glory that overwhelmed me. . . . On the train to Madurai, Bhimi Chandra and I had the good luck to meet a young man who invited us to stop at the home of his brother, a merchant. The next day our host took us on a tour of the gigantic temple of the goddess Mīnakṣhī, where I saw my first sacred elephant, and he showed us the palace of the last king, Tirumal Nayak. Then we left for Madras, where I spent several days in the home of Swedish missionaries, and on Christmas Day I arrived at Poonamallee. Here, in an old abandoned army camp, the International Congress of the YMCA was being held.

Concerning all these discoveries and happenings, I had written hasty and enthusiastic reports that I dispatched regularly to *Cuvân-tul*. But for a long time, these first experiences in India had been pushed deeply into the past, into a time that now, in December, 1931, seemed to me a fabulous era: the time of my naiveté and ignorance, when I spoke bad English and did not understand Hindustani at all, when I scarcely could syllabalize Sanskrit and had not yet discovered the beauty of South Indian sculpture; the time when I carried my two suitcases and traveled third class in overcrowded coaches, being then, probably, the only European who had dared to undertake such an adventure. Concerning the camp at Poonamallee, I remember the bats I heard in the night, beating about in the room next to mine; the fires with young people from all over the world dancing around them and singing; a Romanian-American Baptist missionary stationed for fifteen years in Rangoon, who persuaded me that we ought to sing a few national songs, but he could not remember any except *"Pe-al nostru steag e scris unire"* (On our flag is written union). I had not thought about my "experiences" in South India for a long time, perhaps not since I had recalled them briefly in the summer of 1929, when I was writing the first chapter of *Isabel și Apele Diavolului* (Isabel and the Devil's Waters).

My journey, begun on November 20, did not end until six weeks later in Calcutta, after I had taken up lodging in the boarding house of Mrs. Perris at 82 Ripon Street. It was Dasgupta who suggested the boarding house. I had met him by chance at Adyar, in the library of the Theosophical Society. He had come there to examine certain Sanskrit manuscripts that he needed for the third volume of his *History of Indian Philosophy*. At that time he was about forty-five; he was short, almost fat, and his round face was lighted by a big smile. When I landed one morning in Calcutta after two days and nights on the train, I hailed a taxi and asked the driver to take me to a hotel. But when I discovered the price of a room was 20 rupees a day, I returned to the taxi and gave the driver Dasgupta's address. We crossed a good part of the city to reach Bhawanipore, situated in a neat Indian quarter where I should have liked to live and where, as a matter of fact, I was to reside later. But Dasgupta assured me that, at least in the beginning, it would be hard to accustom myself to Bengalese life, and he advised me to stay in an Anglo-Indian boarding house. That very evening a cousin of his escorted me to the Park Street section, where he knew a number of boarding houses were located. He asked Mrs. Perris the price and decided that it was reasonable: 90 rupees per month, room and board.

It was a large, two-story building surrounded by a lawn and garden, which I thought at first enormous. There was a wide hall that served as the lobby and dining room; in it were also several armchairs and sofas. To the right and left of the lobby were entrances to three large rooms with their windows facing the garden, one of which was mine. Three other young men shared the room with me: Mrs. Perris's two sons and an Anglo-Indian from Goa, named Lobo. To install myself, I had only to bring in a bed and table. The next day I purchased an army cot, equipped it with poles at the four corners, and on these poles I hung up a sheet in the evening to provide myself a little privacy when the other men were there. Mrs. Perris found a writing table for me. To the wonderment of everyone, I would spend the whole day and sometimes the better part of the night at that table. Dasgupta had told me which textbooks and which Sanskrit dictionary to buy, and had added that I would have to take up my studies in earnest in order to catch up with his Bengalese students.

Perhaps Dasgupta did not suspect how blindly I would follow his advice. Ordinarily, I would devote myself entirely to Sanskrit grammar and Indian philosophy from morning till night. I would study for several hours from a book on Sanskrit, read next from an Indian philosophical text in English translation, and then turn back to the Sanskrit grammar. I read nothing else. This went on for about three or four months, until I felt that I was beginning to become oriented in Sanskrit grammar—which seemed like a labyrinth to me then. I would interrupt my work for a few hours at nightfall and take a walk in the native quarter. And, of course, I regularly attended Dasgupta's classes at the University of Calcutta. I was the only European, and for my sake Dasgupta gave his lectures in English for almost two years. That winter he was lecturing on post-Śaṅkarian Vedānta and Sāṃkhya philosophy. There were about ten or twelve male students, plus one girl, all Vedānta enthusiasts. Dasgupta would read a passage of a text, most of the time reciting it from memory very rapidly, with his eyes closed; then he would translate it, comment on it, and ask us one after another if we understood. I liked Dasgupta's explanations so much, and I took so many notes, that I always answered that I understood.

I had arrived in Bengal at the most beautiful time of the year. Each morning I awoke to the same blue sky, the same mild and gentle sun. I did not see the first cloud until about four months after my arrival, on the eve of the monsoon. And until March, I did not complain of the heat. When I went for walks in the evening, I had to put on a jacket.

During that winter, Mrs. Perris's boarding house enjoyed its era of glory. Besides myself and Lobo, there were two Frenchmen— Abadie and Vairat—among the boarders, who had undertaken to travel from Saigon to Paris in a small but seemingly durable automobile. They liked Calcutta so much that instead of staying a few days as they had planned, they remained several weeks. They left with heavy hearts toward the end of January—and we never heard from them again. Thus we never knew how far they managed to go. I don't know if they succeeded even in crossing India. But Mrs. Perris was proud and happy, because the Frenchmen had been photographed standing beside their car in front of the house on Ripon Street, and the picture had appeared in *The Statesman*.

Mrs. Perris had three sons and three daughters. John, about five, Verna, who was seven, and Gertie, ten, slept in their grandmother's room. The eldest girl, Norinne, who was sixteen, slept in the next room with three (sometimes four) girls who were older than she. That winter her roommates were three dancers from the Globe Theatre. I became friends with one of them in particular, Catherine.

About a week after my arrival at Mrs. Perris's boarding house, Dasgupta called to say he was coming to get me in the car. The Maharaja had arrived the evening before and wanted to see me. I still remember very vividly that first meeting (a second one took place a year later at Dasgupta's house, after I had begun to speak Bengali). He was a small, thin, elderly man, dressed in a dhoti, wearing only slippers on his feet. He was waiting for us in the courtyard, seated on a chair. The house did not seem very pretentious, and perhaps it was not his. Besides, as Dasgupta had explained to me already, the Maharaja was not at all concerned about outward indications of grandeur. He had expended almost all his

wealth in donations and subsidies to various cultural and benevo-
lent institutions. He helped all religions likewise, and without distinction. In addition to these things, he had given a number of
scholarships to industrious and deserving students. He was continuing even then the subsidizing of Dasgupta's library, which permitted my professor to build the richest collection of books on philosophy and religion that I had ever seen.

I spoke very little, because my English was still imperfect and
especially because Dasgupta (who, like every great man had his
vanity and naivetés) tried to impress his patron by discoursing with
me in French and then translating the conversation into Bengali.
But Dasgupta could scarcely speak French, so the discussion did not
last long. The Maharaja assured me once again of his interest in my
study of Sanskrit and Indian philosophy. Upon our leaving, Dasgupta informed me that my stipend would be 90 rupees per month.
This was exactly the amount of my room and board at Mrs. Perris's
house! With the stipend that I expected to receive from Romania, I
would be able to clothe myself, buy books, and travel.

From then on I received regularly, on the first of every month, a
letter with a wax seal, in which I knew I would find nine 10-rupee
banknotes. After about two years, unfortunately, the Maharaja suddenly died. His eldest son wrote to me that although the State of
Kassimbazar was head over heels in debt (because the generosity of
the Maharaja had exceeded all bounds), he would continue sending
my scholarship as long as I wanted to remain in India to study. But
after six months he wrote again, regretfully stating that it was beyond his power to keep his promise. The debts were so large that
Kassimbazar had disappeared as a semiautonomous state and had
been taken over by British India. He himself had become a functionary in one of the industrial concerns that formerly had belonged to
his father.

By the time I received this bad news, I had passed through so
many other trials and I knew India so well, that I hardly noticed the
absence of the 90 rupees. For one thing, I had learned that I could
live very well, and without spending even one rupee a year, in an
ashram in the Himalayas.

/   /   /

I heard the ship's dinner bell sounding. My cabin-mates had not
come below, and I went looking for them on deck. A strange wind

was blowing, now hot, now cool, as though a storm were brewing. Bombay still glimmered, half-hidden by the waters of the bay. I found my cabin-mates in the dining hall, impatient and curious. It was their first European meal. I had made the acquaintance of one of them a few days before on the train. He, like myself, had come from Calcutta. A native of Bengal, he was going to study engineering in Germany. The other was to be enrolled at the London School of Economics. Both had chosen this Italian ship, which would take them to Venice, in order to be able to visit several European cities en route. The two of them were wearing European clothes for the first time that evening. They had purchased top coats, but not gloves. Two weeks later, on a gray morning with an icy wind blowing, when we went out on deck to look at Venice, my companions turned up the collars of their coats and blew on their hands to keep warm.

At the table I found a list of the passengers. We were in third class, but casting my eyes at random over the list of passengers in first class, I came upon the name of Giuseppe Tucci. It had been a long while since I had seen him because, after he left Dacca, he had been continually on the road: Kashmir, Nepal, and western Tibet. But it seemed as though my whole Indian "past," that entire fabulous era of "beginnings," came to mind again—all the memories linked to my first visits in Dasgupta's home in Bhawanipore.

It was there I had met Tucci, one afternoon in the winter of 1929. I found him surprisingly youthful, vigorous, full of vitality, working on several books at the same time: a history of Indian logic, the Tantric liturgy of the goddess Durgā, the symbolism of Tibetan temples, and so on. He had come to consult Dasgupta about a detail of Indian logic. At that time, Tucci was translating back into Sanskrit several Buddhist treatises on logic that had survived only in Tibetan and Chinese translations.

In those days I was going to Dasgupta's house twice a week. He would help me resolve difficult problems of Sanskrit grammar, but, more particularly, he was following the progress I was making in the study of Sāṃkhya-Yoga philosophy. Sometimes we took tea together in his study upstairs. I began to become acquainted with his family: the kind, young, and beautiful Mrs. Dasgupta, their two daughters, Maitreyi and Chabu, and their son of about five or six, with whom I labored to converse in Bengali.

At the end of winter, the stipend from Romania for five months arrived, and thus I was able to travel in Central India: Allāhābād, Benares, Delhi, Agra, Jaipur, and Ajmer. Some of those cities I was to see again several times in subsequent years. But I think I have never been more overwhelmed than I was on that morning when the train rolled slowly onto Dufferin Bridge and I saw Benares for the first time—and the ghats with their steps of white marble leading down into the waters of the Ganges. Never since has the Asi-Ghat seemed more gorgeous, or more laden with flowers. In the evening, in a room at a modest hotel owned by an Anglo-Indian, I wrote diligently in my journal and composed long, pathetic letters to my family at home and to friends now scattered in many European countries. I recall that in Jaipur I was so overwhelmed, feeling that never would I be able to describe the nature—and above all the mystery—of the beauty that confronted me on every hand, that I wrote to Ionel Teodoreanu. I confessed that I had never envied him so much his gifts of describing a landscape. Only he could have succeeded in expressing through words the infinite variety of shapes and arabesques and colors.

From the time I moved into Mrs. Perris's house, I sent articles to *Cuvântul* with some degree of regularity. I had much to say about that inexhaustible Calcutta, about Belur Math, about Chandernagore and environs, which Dasgupta showed me. But I returned from Central India so heavily laden—I had taken so many notes, had met and talked with so many interesting people—that I supposed that I should have material for at least ten columns.

I don't believe I ever wrote more than a few. On the one hand, I began to realize that I knew too little about India, that I was running the risk of writing like a tourist who spends a few days in Benares and thinks he knows all its "secrets." On the other hand, I had plunged with such fury into scholarly reading that I did not find time for newspaper articles. After three months of uninterrupted work, during which time I had concentrated exclusively on Sanskrit and Indian philosophy, I allowed myself to read other kinds of books, and not just books about India, but also about Tibet, Central Asia, and the Far East. My library grew larger before my eyes. Besides what I bought, I began to write to various Indian publishers, requesting their publications, and I always received them: everything from classical Sanskrit literature to the collections of the Cama

Oriental Institute in Bombay. I had purchased a bookcase long before, which I rapidly filled, and now I piled the books on top of the two suitcases.

Gradually, without my being aware of it, the weather had become hot. In my room the ceiling fan, with its broad wooden blades, ran night and day, and the windows were kept closed during the daytime. The walk through the sunshine to the street car that took me downtown or to the university or to Bhawanipore became harder and harder. I had to change shirts three or four times a day, and just as often I shut myself in the bathroom, drew water in the tub, and splashed it over my body, because showers didn't exist on Ripon Street. I waited for night to come in order to be able to breathe freely, to take refuge in the garden, or to go for a walk in the park. But I persisted in spending at least twelve hours a day at my work table, learning Sanskrit roots and translating from Kalidasa, to the amazement and anxiety of Mrs. Perris, who warned me repeatedly that I was in danger of ruining my health.

And it is probable that I should have ruined it eventually if I had not become involved in several happenings about that time, which snatched me suddenly out of my program of inevitable overexertion. The first was an excursion into the region of Fardipur, when I accompanied Mr. Perris, who was a supervisor of the telephone and telegraph communications system in Bengal. A long time before he had proposed that I go with him to the edge of the jungle, on one of the inspection trips he made periodically. It had always happened that such inspections took place on days when I had to go to Bhawanipore. But in April, on a morning that promised a torrid day, we set off for Fardipur. In an article in *Cuvântul* entitled "110° Fahrenheit, Cyclone Direction Southwest," I related the story of this adventure, dramatizing it, emphasizing the spectacular details, and exaggerating the dangers we experienced. But, as a matter of fact, it was difficult *not* to exaggerate. I suffered a sunstroke, which brought on a serious hemorrhage. Fortunately, being only half-conscious, I did not realize what was wrong, and I had started looking for Mr. Perris's group just as the cyclone was approaching. Mr. Perris assured me later that I had been very fortunate. We were almost picked up by the cyclone, and our pith helmets, thermoses with water and whiskey, and all the equipment we had brought from Calcutta disappeared in a few moments. We all fled in the same direction, but although we shouted at the top of our lungs, we could not hear one another. We managed somehow to protect ourselves from branches and brambles driven by the wind by holding our arms in front of our eyes. It was a miracle I didn't stumble over a fallen tree trunk. How I reached home the next morning, I don't remember very well, because I did not come to my senses until several days later.

The consequences of this adventure broke my study schedule, which I had followed religiously for almost four months. I set the Sanskrit grammar aside and started reading adventure novels, while in the evenings I dined with our little group in the Chinese district or went to the Globe Theater. There was a bizarre week in which I met all sorts of strangers, both men and women, and I let myself go with them to their houses, where there was dancing and drinking of whiskey and where serious fights often broke out, some of us leaving with faces bloodied. Once, with such a group, I visited a house in China Town where one could smoke opium for a modest fee. I discovered that even Mr. Perris permitted himself such a fantasy once in a while. I also discovered that one of our friends from the boarding house, a dancer at the Globe, enjoyed prominent protectors. And I entered for the first time into houses I had never suspected existed in Calcutta, brilliantly and grotesquely luxurious, where I found men dressed in dinner jackets and women in evening gowns gathered around a glass cabinet of Chinese jades, or standing enraptured before Indo-Tibetan bronzes, and then signaling to barefoot, turbaned servants to bring them champagne and black caviar, and speaking to one another in Russian, German, and French.

We would return home toward morning. In the car one of the girls, Catherine or Norinne, would warn me again not to tell anyone where we had been, but to say only that we had been enjoying ourselves with friends in a bar in China Town. My mind was rather confused anyway. I could not always distinguish between what had really happened to me and what I had imagined or what I had been told by one of those mysterious strangers with whom I sometimes held conversations lasting several hours. I was exhausted, my head felt heavy, and my eyelids seemed weighted with lead. When, in the late morning, Mrs. Perris or the grandmother would come to waken me, bringing a cup of greenish-black tea to my bed, I would try to convince her that my condition was due to drinking a glass of whiskey too fast.

Perhaps that was true, but it did not explain the state of semiconsciousness and fantasy in which I found myself almost all the time. I felt that something had happened to me, but I could not manage to remember exactly *what*. I had not forgotten the sunstroke at Fardipur, and I had tried to pry something out of those around me, but they all assured me that, since I had not died on the spot, I had escaped all danger. The afternoons became more and more torrid. Sprawled on the bed, I tried hard to grasp what was happening to me. Sometimes, when I was alone, a girl entered on tiptoe and kissed me. I told myself that it must be some girl to whom I once had confessed my love (but when? in what circumstances?). Often I shuddered. I remembered vaguely having asked her to marry me. But who was this bride I had chosen? Other times, it seemed to me that the marriage had taken place several years previously, that it all had happened long ago, in the past—but when? *When?*

In order to keep from thinking, I wrote *Isabel şi Apele Diavolului*. I began the novel one evening, almost at random. The plot of the book was very vague in my mind. It had to do with some of my experiences in India, but projected into a milieu about which I knew almost nothing. Several images from my trip through South India, the family of the Swedish pastor with whom I stayed in Madras, elements from Mrs. Perris's boarding house, and later a few names and faces encountered in my nocturnal wanderings with Catherine and Norinne. The plot disclosed itself to me as the novel progressed. On the other hand, I wrote deeply engrossed, almost spellbound, as if I were continuing a "dream" into which I had slipped without noticing it. What is even stranger is that, although apparently an autobiographical book, the novel was invented from one end to the other. It is probable that what fascinated me was just this process of invention. In a sense, I dreamed a life that was not mine and that I should not have desired, but which nevertheless tempted me by its fabulous and demonic qualities and its brutality. Sometimes I seemed to be identifying myself with the "Doctor," that strange character who had come, as had I, to India to study—but to study Asian art, rather than Indian philosophy. However, the Doctor and I were different in almost every way: I had never believed in the Devil nor ever suffered an obsession with sin, and I was indifferent to the "problem of evil," at least as the Doctor understood it.

Little happenings at the boarding house were transfigured, characters were obsessed by problems that were not only inaccessible, but were also foreign to the Anglo-Indian spiritual climate. Because I wanted at all costs to hold "sin" in the central position in the novel, I involved the Doctor in improbable pan-sexual adventures; among others, I introduced into his friendship with Tom an erotic scene for which, later in Romania, I was suspected for years. Another central theme of the novel, "sterility," was one equally foreign to me. I have never felt "sterile," either in the physiological sense of the word or in a spiritual sense. Why, then, that strange behavior of the Doctor, who, loving and being loved by Isabel, drives her nevertheless into the arms of soldier number 11,871; and after finding out that she is pregnant, asks her to marry him and declares the child to be his? I don't know. Perhaps I wanted at any price to invent something "new" and "tragic." Perhaps it was the recollection of lectures of Nae Ionescu and discussions with my friends, Vulcănescu and Sterian, about "man's powerlessness to create."

Of course at that time, late spring 1929, I did not ask myself such questions, because I did not yet know how the novel would end. What fascinated me then was the "dream of a summer's night" that I had experienced and that I tried to reconstruct from a few fragments. This "dream" permitted me to imagine myself living in the future: sometimes I imagined my life ten or fifteen years hence, and I could continue it, starting from that age, knowing for example the melancholy of a European stranded in India who remembers his homeland after thirty years. I was enthralled by the possibility of an obscure and unfulfilled existence: an existence unfulfilled because squandered inauthentically among Anglo-Indians in a banal and sterile milieu of petty colonial functionaries; in a word, the life of a man who lives in that India I loved so much, on the margin of its "mysteries," who turns his back and ignores the very thing that attracted me most: the true Indian life.

In the meanwhile, the monsoon had been unleashed, with lightning such as I had never seen, so that I thought sometimes the same bolt kept flashing continuously for an endlessly long minute. On the first day the abundant tropical rain fell heavily and rapidly without letup—but soon one could distinguish a sort of daily timetable: it did not begin to rain until a certain hour and the deluge lasted for a certain period. The rest of the time we contended with unbearable heat and humidity. My shirt became saturated as soon as I stepped outside the house. I could work hardly at all. Dasgupta took refuge with his family somewhere in the region of Chittagong. In the second week in May, I decided on the spur of the moment to go to Darjeeling.

I stayed in the Himalayan region until the end of June. My lodging place was a modest hotel in Darjeeling called The Sanatorium. In the mornings I strolled around the area, afternoons I spent on Sanskrit grammar, and in the evenings I tried to continue the novel. Sometimes a group of us would go to Ghum for two or three days to visit one of the Buddhist monasteries, or just to be able to look at daybreak, from Tiger Mountain, upon the glassy white crest of Mt. Everest, almost 200 kilometers to the west. I was with a few friends, but I kept to myself as much as possible; it had been a long time since I had enjoyed so much solitude. Sometimes it was cold and foggy, and I found the wind there like that of the Carpathians. I wrote long letters to the family at home, while for *Cuvântul* I tried to describe Kurseong, Darjeeling, and towns of Bhutan in the vicinity, in particular Lebong, a small mountain village where for the first time I attended a Lamaistic funeral. Without being aware of it, I was becoming captivated by the Himalayan landscape, and especially by this new type of "Asiatic man" that I met, who set me dreaming of Tibet and Central Asia.

I knew that, for the time being, Tibet was forbidden to me. But I did not resist the temptation to visit Sikkim, although I realized the expedition would exhaust my savings. Indeed, in order to reach Sikkim, I had to hire a serdar, a guide who would also be the leader of the caravan, and buy a little camping tent and food for us and the eight coolies who were to carry the baggage. On May 31, in rain and fog, we reached Jorepokri; the following day we were at Tonglu (11,000 feet), and on June 2 in Sandakphu we sighted Kangchenjunga. That night we stayed at a bungallow. It was an unforgettable evening, looking at the line of glaciers lying white and glassy many kilometers further on. On the following day we set off for Sabargham, but the fog was dense, rain began to fall again on the mountain hard and steadily, and we were covered with leeches. We encountered them on the paths, and they fell on us from trees and rocks. The sirdar and I protected ourselves from the rain as best we could. But the coolies were barefooted and although they did the same, their feet were soon covered with blood. We had to return to Sandakphu.

For years after that, I would wake up in a cold sweat from this nightmare: it seemed I was trying to climb a steep slope, slippery from rain, and I would lose my footing and not be able to rise. Then I would feel I was being followed by a slimy, living mass formed of tens of thousands of leeches, advancing slowly and relentlessly toward me. In reality, what happened that day was this: tired, harassed by the stinging bites of the leeches, we tried to take a short-cut, descending toward the valley by cutting straight through the jungle. All of a sudden everyone stopped. Like a carpet of moss a column of leeches was approaching us. We did not actually see them, but I seemed to hear their massive crawling. The others understood what had happened. The monsoon had swept through the valley earlier, and the jungle floor was covered with leeches climbing slowly to higher ground. I felt the blood drain from my heart, and I was about to flee running into the valley when the serdar seized my arm and pointed toward the slope we had just descended. The coolies abandoned their loads and began scrambling up the mountainside. I followed them, almost unconscious, trying to hurry but stumbling again and again. There was no time now to burn off the leeches with the tip of a lighted cigarette. I felt them on my face, feet, and body. In haste I tried to jerk them loose, in the process tearing pieces of skin from my chest. At the same time I tried to protect my eyes by continually wiping my hand across my face.

I reached the bungallow late, with my shirt and socks in shreds. A few days later, having returned to Darjeeling, I wrote (with the inevitable exaggerations) the article "When the Monsoon Came," which frightened everyone at home terribly. But all my acquaintances in Darjeeling were amazed at the irresponsibility of the serdar in agreeing to start for Sikkim on the eve of the monsoon. Everyone had heard about the carpet of leeches that is set in motion at the beginning of the rains, but no one was so naive, or so ill-advised, as to risk meeting them. Some even wondered if there were not, at the back of it, a scheme on the part of the serdar: to start down toward the jungle in order to convince me of the danger, and then to flee— so that a week later he could return and recover the baggage and boxes of canned goods, sugar, and tea that had been abandoned on the hillside.

The adventure demoralized me. I spent the last weeks in Darjeeling, stubbornly continuing to work on the novel, but writing listlessly and with a great effort. And because the rains intensified, I did not dare leave my hotel very often. Toward the end of June I returned to Calcutta.

I found there the Bengalese summer again, but it seemed less torrid with those few daily hours of rain. In the gardens and parks the vegetation had become luxuriant, and when we went walking at night around the lakes, the strong fragrance of flowers and fresh fruit intoxicated us. Whole bundles of letters, reviews, and newspapers from Romania were waiting for me. In an interview, Cezar Petrescu declared, among other things, that the situation of Romanian writers had changed, that today a young author could find a publisher if his work were indeed of value. Full of doubts after my experience with Meny Toneghin of Cartea Românească, I wrote him that I was on the way to finishing a novel, and I asked him to recommend a publisher. After about four weeks I received his reply. Petrescu wrote that he was well pleased with a new publisher, Ciornei, who had already brought out several novels, and he urged me to send him the manuscript as soon as it was finished.

This news heartened me. I had begun long before then to correct and transcribe the text. But I had not succeeded in finishing it. Each page cost me a tremendous effort. I had written several friends about *Isabel*, and Ionel Jianu offered to take care of the proofreading and publicity, once Petrescu had arranged the contract with Ciornei.

With a supreme effort I finished the book in early August. I had lost interest in literature by this time, and I had plunged anew into my Indian studies. Each hour spent on the last chapter seemed endless. When I reread the manuscript again, I didn't know what to think. I was irritated by some things that now sounded terrible to me, but I felt it was too late to do anything about them. The "foreign" character of the novel also bothered me: it falsified the structure and orientation, emphasizing problems and conflicts that had never interested me. The only pages I liked were those in which I recapitulated "the dream of a summer's night."

I breathed easily only after I had taken the package to the post office. I had regained my freedom.

Early in the morning I went out on deck. I remembered the column I had written three years before on board the S.S. *Hakone*

Maru, which I had entitled "On the Indian Ocean." Such a title brought a wry smile to my lips now.

I went looking for Tucci. But the way from third class to first class was long and complicated. I had to obtain permission from some functionary or other. There was an iron grille separating our deck from the upper deck of the second class, beside which I waited for the necessary papers.

"How fortunate to be working with Dasgupta at twenty-two!" Tucci had said to me one day. "What I wouldn't have given to have been associated with such a man at your age!"

He said that to me in the autumn of 1929 in Bhawanipore. Dasgupta had just found a pandit from his city with whom I could read Aniruddha's commentary, and who could help me to advance in conversational Sanskrit beyond the elementary stage at which I had arrived several months ago. The pandit came three times a week and stayed sometimes four or five hours. Mrs. Perris did not appear overjoyed by these frequent and interminable visits of the pandit. Anglo-Indians at that time guarded against having relations with "natives." While she was very proud to count among her boarders a European whose skin was as white as mine, she was equally embarrassed to be out on the veranda and see that Bengalese pandit entering her house, barefooted and dressed in a dhoti. Although he would greet her politely, bringing both hands to his forehead, and would try, sometimes, to speak a few words of English to her, Mrs. Perris would reply always in curt, icy Hindustani.

Sometimes the pandit would see one of the girls dressed in shorts, and then his eyes would sparkle. Soon I observed that he was prolonging his sessions until he had succeeded in catching sight at least once of Norinne. Only after he told me he was a poet and had brought me some poems in Bengali and Sanskrit—which had to do with a woman of matchless beauty, described in all the clichés of Kalidasa and Kumaradasa—did I understand that he was enamored of Norinne. When I questioned him, he acknowledged that I had guessed it. He was, of course, married and the father of several children, but he let it be understood that he had never known true love until now. I don't know if he fancied that he would be able to approach Norinne someday, or not. He asked me only to translate the poems into English and show them to her.

In September, Dasgupta took me to Shanti Niketan with him to meet Rabindranath Tagore. It was one of the decisive experiences of that year. I found myself suddenly in the midst of "the true Indian life," for which I had been longing. Everything about that university enchanted me. Classes were oftentimes held in the garden, under a tree. All the students and all the women I met seemed to me beautiful and enigmatic. Dasgupta was lodged with Tagore, but I was given a little white room in the guest house. To that room, with its terrace, I returned several times a day to record things in my journal, such as a conversation with the scholar Vidyashagar Shastri or an account of another indiscretion in the legendary life of Tagore. In a special notebook I set down almost everything I heard said about the poet concerning his unlimited powers of seduction. As an administrator put it one day, half the feminine population of Bengal was in love with him.

I met him only after two or three days. Dasgupta accompanied me, and this interfered with our conversation somewhat. Dasgupta admired Tagore as a poet, a musician, and a creator of cultural institutions, but he did not have much faith in his capabilities as a theorist. Whenever Tagore would begin to talk about the "meaning of Life" or "knowledge of Truth," Dasgupta would shift his gaze vaguely toward the window. Tagore noticed this and seemed annoyed. Happily, a few days later I lunched with Tagore, without Dasgupta. Only then did I come to know the atmosphere of the mystic sect in which the poet lived—although certainly against his will. A whole ritual accompanied his appearance at the table on the terrace in the garden. Tagore's presence was charismatic. One recognized his genius even in his manner of living. One guessed that Rabindranath Tagore enjoyed and profited from living as very few of his contemporaries were capable of doing. Every hour was "pregnant," "fruitful." No time was wasted, he was always *present*, as if every object, every flower, every patch of light were an epiphany. His life was, in fact, a continuous "creation." When he was not meditating or writing, he composed melodies (at that time he was the author of some three thousand songs), painted, or conversed with friends who came to see him—but in a way people do not converse in a modern society: as if he were experiencing a continuous revelation.

I returned to my room spellbound. That evening and the day following I wrote feverishly in my journal. I was to see Tagore again in March of 1930, and I reproduced a part of the conversation we had then in a chapter of my book, *India*. But my first visit to Shanti Niketan shook me. I realized the vulgarity of the Anglo-Indian life in which I had let myself become involved. Dasgupta had spoken to me about the possibility of coming to live with him, and this prospect helped me fight against despair.

The night I returned to the boarding house on Ripon Street, one of the landlady's sons found a small python in the parlor. Very likely I had brought it from Shanti Niketan, hidden between the sheets of my folding bed. The boy discovered it in a corner of the room, fighting with a rat. "Don't anyone come—there's a snake in the parlor!" he screamed. Keeping it in the beam of his flashlight, he killed it with a stick.

The next day was Sunday, the day when the mail from Europe came—"home mail," the Anglo-Indians called it, although many of them had had no relatives in England for several generations. I was the only one who received letters and packages of journals, reviews, and books. I spent Sunday afternoons reading my mail. There was usually news from friends who had gone to Paris for their doctorates. Petru Comarnescu was preparing to leave for the University of California in Los Angeles. Haig Acterian had published a small book of verses under the pen name of "Mihail." (He was the "Mihail" in the dedication in *Isabel*: "To brother Mihail and blind Lalu, the beggar on Babu Street." This dedication embarrassed me later by its pretentiousness and fervor; and yet, one torrid afternoon in May, that beggar had helped me to shake off an attack of melancholia and dejection. It was so hot that no one would stop to throw a copper penny in his lap. He seemed to be asleep. Approaching him, I thought for a moment he was dead, and I put my hand on his arm. He awoke and smiled, then talked to me a long time, thanking me for the money I had given him. I spoke to him too, in the smattering of Bengali mixed with Hindustani I had learned. When I reached home, I was at peace. It seemed to me that at the Last Judgment I would be saved, thanks to Lalu.)

That autumn Mrs. Perris's boarding house took on a new appearance. Catherine and the girls from the Globe Theater had gone and other boarders took their place. Among them was Frank, a very dark-skinned young fellow from Madras, with whom I eventually became friends. He was a curious man. Several years previously, at a restaurant in Madras, in a furious rage, he had thrown a small marble table at a native "boy" whose behavior he had considered insolent. The boy tripped fleeing down the stairs, and the table caught him on the back and broke his spine. Because this incident had happened during the height of the Gandhian agitation, the English judge wanted to make an example of the case, and he sentenced Frank to pay compensation to the boy for the rest of his life. More than half his salary as a telegrapher went for the compensation. Frank retained a savage hatred for Indians and for Gandhi, but after that episode he controlled his temper and he no longer drank, except at home.

We went out together to the Chinese quarter, or we went to one of his friends' places, but Frank almost never touched alcohol. Nevertheless, due to him, I was drawn into a series of awkward adventures. Frank liked to strike up conversations with strangers and then do everything he could to get himself invited to their homes. About two years after we met, he asked me to lend him some money; he had to pay the compensation and he had spent almost all his salary. He assured me he would pay me back in a few weeks. The truth was, he knew he had been transferred to the Andaman Islands, and he wanted to get revenge on anyone handy. Since we had become friends, he took out his spite on me. A few days later he left, vowing that he was going to see a friend and would return very shortly—and I never heard from him again.

In November, Dasgupta began to come now and then to Ripon Street in the late afternoons. He liked to get out of his car and stride haughtily through that house of Anglo-Indians toward the room where he knew I would be found. He likewise enjoyed conversing with the girls, proud of the fact that his English accent was as good as theirs, and he read Shelley to them. It would have pleased him greatly if someone had initiated a discussion of philosophy. Then he would have been able to amaze the girls on Ripon Street with his knowledge of Western thought, and in particular of Hegel, which his professor at Cambridge, McTaggart, had taught him.

But the girls did not prolong the conversations, and Dasgupta spent the remainder of the time with me. On the road to Shanti Niketan, without my asking him, he had promised to initiate me into the practice of yoga. But in the visits that he made to me on Ripon Street, he concerned himself more with the technical vocabu-

lary of Sāṃkhya-Yoga, on which I had begun to work, and with my
doctoral thesis. Dasgupta preferred me to concentrate on the history
of the doctrines of yoga, or on the relationships among classical
Yoga, Vedānta, and Buddhism. I, on the contrary, felt attracted by
Tantrism and the different forms of popular yoga; that is, as it is
found in epic poetry, legends, and folklore. I knew that Dasgupta
had said everything essential on the subject of Yoga philosophy and
its place in the history of Indian thought. It would have been useless for me to review this problem again, even if I should have
brought out certain new points. On the other hand, I had learned
enough by now about Indian philosophy to realize that Yoga is not
very interesting *as a system of philosophy*. Beside Vedānta or Ma-
hayana, Yoga "philosophy" seemed to me rather commonplace.

On the other hand, that which seemed to me original, and that
which tended to be neglected by the Indian elite as well as by Western scholars, was Tantric yoga. I discovered in the Tantric texts that
India was not entirely ascetic, idealistic, and pessimistic. There exists
a whole tradition that accepts life and the body; it does not consider
them illusory nor the source of suffering, but exalts incarnate existence as the only mode of being in the world in which absolute
freedom can be won. From then on I understood that India has
known not only the desire for *liberation* (*eliberare*), but also the thirst
for *freedom* (*libertate*); India has believed in the possibility of a
blessed and autonomous existence, here on earth and in Time. I was
to develop these ideas in my doctoral thesis (which was written
between 1930 and 1932, and appeared in print in 1936). At that time,
Tantric studies were still at the stage in which Sir John Woodroffe
had left them. It seemed to me that in presenting Yoga and Tantra
in the vast compass of Indian religion, I should be making a significant contribution to the understanding of Indian spirituality as a
whole.

Little by little, Dasgupta let himself be persuaded. His reserva-
tions were mainly of a practical nature. It seemed to him that I was
in danger of being drawn into many domains in which I could not
always master the documentation at first hand. He was right, of
course, but in the fall of 1929 I had an infinite faith in my capacity
to learn. I was sure, for example, that I would learn Tibetan and
even some Dravidian and Australasian languages. Before a year had

passed, I realized that I did not enjoy the linguistic genius of a Tucci or Paul Pelliot.

Dasgupta also came to Ripon Street in order to find out about the kind of life to which I had become accustomed in Calcutta, and to see to what extent living in Bhawanipore would be suitable for me. And so now, at the end of autumn, it was decided that I should go to live in his house. The moving date was set for the first of January. The Perris family and the boarders were disconcerted, and they looked at Dasgupta quite coldly. I told them I wanted to stay in Bhawanipore only five or six months, so that I might learn Bengali more quickly and become accustomed to speaking Sanskrit. Inwardly, however, the decision had long since been made: I would stay in Dasgupta's home as long as he would have me, and after that I would seek lodgings in a Bengali neighborhood.

In November I began receiving letters from Romania having to do with *Isabel.* Ionel Jianu and Mircea Vulcǎnescu sounded enthusiastic. Cezar Petrescu had presented the manuscript to Ciornei, and the publisher had accepted it without reading it. Jianu had even obtained an advance of 20,000 lei, which he cabled to me. This unexpected sum enabled me to buy Christmas presents for the Perris family, and to make the rounds of China Town with the group of young people who were left at the boarding house. Christmas was not so sad as I had feared it would be, because the Perris family were sure that I would not be able to live very long in a "house of natives." I moved on the morning of January 2, 1930. As she confessed to me later, Mrs. Perris expected me to return in March. I did return, for just a few days, in September. But I returned against my will.

10. *A Hut in the Himalayas*

ON THE steamer I enjoyed speaking Bengali with one of my cabin-mates. I had already begun to forget it, because after leaving Bhawanipore I spoke it less and less often. And yet how enthusiastically I had learned it originally, repeating whole sentences by heart, memorizing poems of Tagore, talking with children and neighbors. . . .

My room at Dasgupta's house was right beside the entrance. I had brought with me my bed, bookcase, and writing table. On the ground floor of the house were Dasgupta's enormous library—occupying several rooms—the kitchen, and a dining room. Dasgupta's study, the living room, and the bedrooms were on the upper level. And above the second floor, extending over almost the whole house, was the rooftop terrace, flanked by palm trees.

From the day I moved to Bhawanipore, my happiness knew no bounds. It seemed that only then had I truly "arrived" in India. Everything enchanted me: the strange noises that kept coming from the rooms overhead, the strong spicy odors that announced the approach of mealtime, the voices that came from neighboring houses. Early in the morning I would go up to the terrace for an hour of Sanskrit grammar with Dasgupta. Then I was free for the rest of the day, except for classes at the university, to which I went in the car with the professor. I spent at least eight or nine hours a day at my writing table, because I had now added Bengali to the Sanskrit and Indian philosophy I was studying. In the evenings, before dinner, I would go for a walk through the neighborhood. In the spring and summer I took long rides in the car with the family around Calcutta. Quite frequently we went to Chandernagore. As often as possible I conversed with Chabu, who did not know English, or with Mrs. Dasgupta or the relatives and neighbors who came to the house to see how a European looked in Bengali lodgings.

At first, Dasgupta made his family eat at a table with knives and forks, to accustom themselves to European manners. On the first evening after my arrival, Mrs. Dasgupta even tried to prepare some kind of soup, because the professor had told her that a European dinner always includes soup. Soon, however, the silverware disappeared and I began to eat with my fingers like everyone else. And when I lunched for the first time seated on the floor with a large leaf for a plate, I felt I was beginning to be a part of the family.

Toward the end of winter I went away for a few weeks on a trip through North India. I stopped at Allāhābād to see the Kumbh-mela, that enormous procession of ascetics, yogis, and sadhus that takes place once in twelve years. I spent a few days at Benares—on that occasion to consult the manuscript collection at Sanskrit College. Then I saw Delhi again, and Agra, Fatehpur-Sikri, and Jaipur—and I journeyed farther, to Bīkaner, Lahore, and Amritsar.

It was as though I were seeing India with another pair of eyes than in the spring of 1929. It seemed to me that I was beginning to understand its secrets, that I was discovering beauty and meaning that had been inaccessible to me a few months previously. This was because I had had the good fortune to have lived in the house of the most illustrious historian of Indian philosophy, and because I had begun to become accustomed to Indian life and to speaking Bengali.

It did not seem to me now that I was a "visitor" in India. I felt completely at home, and if I had an intense desire to visit important cities, temples, and monuments, it was because I wanted to become acquainted with my adoptive country. I hoped to be able to stay in India for many years, and I was not thinking only of my doctoral thesis and my career as an Indianist. Even more than scientific enthusiasm, what attracted me was the quality of life that I felt I could know in India. I liked everything: the landscape, the climate, the people, their languages and beliefs, their manner of living, their clothing, and their foods.

It is not surprising that I was excited by the civil revolution unleashed by Mahatma Gandhi at the beginning of May all over India, through a series of nonviolent demonstrations. The arrest of Gandhi on May 5, 1930, as well as the sentencing of Jawaharlal Nehru and the mayor of Calcutta to six months imprisonment, provoked demonstrations and *hartal* (locked shops and strikes) all over India. As was expected, Muslim troublemakers and fanatics provoked more violent clashes between Hindus and Muslims. In spite of the heroic intervention of Gandhi's volunteers, these intercommunal conflicts rapidly degenerated into real massacres.

Following several assaults organized by students, the University of Calcutta was closed indefinitely. Dasgupta was somewhat uneasy about my long walks in the city. He was afraid that I would let myself be drawn into some street demonstration and be arrested. Since I was living in his house, such an event could have had serious consequences. He kept telling me over and over that I had not come to India to assist in the political liberation of the Indian people, but to study Sanskrit and Indian philosophy.

I knew, however, that the danger of my becoming involved in a street demonstration was minimal. I was white, and on the streets and in the streetcars the Bengalis looked at me with contempt and hatred. In Bhawanipore children shouted after me, "white monkey!" and sometimes threw stones. This contempt and aggressiveness fascinated me. I realized the gulf that had been created between the British and the Indians. I realized that the attitude of the Indians had changed: no longer were they paralyzed by the prestige of the whites; basically, they were no longer afraid of them. When I said this to the Perris family during my short visit to Ripon Street— adding that the "British Raj" already belonged to the past—everyone made fun of my naiveté. Mr. Perris assured me that Indian independence was a utopian dream, that the English language and Western culture constituted the only unifying elements, that in fact this so-called thirst for the freedom of India was an invention of "Mister Gandhi," that the majority of Indians were satisfied with the British Raj and would continue to be, for at least a hundred years.

Soon the newspapers announced that fifty thousand Indians were in jail. Several of my fellow students at the university had disappeared. I recorded in my journal everything I learned from the newspapers and everything I heard being said around me, in the hope of someday writing a book about the civil revolution. At the same time I collected material from publications to which I had access. But that book was never written. Later, I contented myself with publishing passages, annotated and expanded, from my Indian journal in the book *Şantier* (Work in Progress), which was published in 1935.

In June, the civil disobedience campaign abated. When Gandhi, in jail, was informed about the excesses that had taken place, he gave orders to suspend the demonstrations (especially the collective marches to the sea where salt was prepared and distributed free of charge by Indians; this commodity was quite expensive and constituted an extremely heavy burden on the poor). In order to keep me at home, Dasgupta asked me to assist him in the preparation of the index for Volume II of *A History of Indian Philosophy*. Sometimes he invited me into his work room and dictated to me, either a chapter of Volume III or something concerning his book on the Upaniṣhads. Also, he gave me *Bhāmātī*, Vācaspatimiśra's commentary on the *Vedānta-sūtra-bhāṣhya*, to translate, and every day he checked and corrected the paragraphs I had translated that morning. Since classes were not being held at the university, he occupied himself now more closely with my particular studies. He admired my power to work because, although it had become hot, he saw me at my writing table all the time. At night I fell exhausted into bed. But I could not go to sleep immediately. I now shared the room with a cousin of the professor who was preparing himself for the master's degree in political economics and studied at night in the usual Indian fashion: that is, he would read over a few sentences, repeating them several times aloud, until he had memorized them. The young man, moreover, was on the point of being married. He had not yet seen his fiancée, but he knew approximately what she looked like. He talked to me a great deal about that stranger with whom he had fallen in love in a moment, when he had found out that she was destined for him, and of the happiness that he anticipated.

Due to the political agitation, Dasgupta had decided to spend the summer in Calcutta, and he persuaded me to stay too. It suited me perfectly. To go back to living with English and Anglo-Indian people again would have been very difficult for me. I knew that I should be unable to restrain myself from bringing up the subject of the civil revolution. Further, it suited me better to remain for the summer in Bhawanipore, because I had gradually begun to dream of a new novel. The beginning of the novel fascinated me: a learned librarian, Cesare, has stayed after the hour for closing the library. The smell of smoke arouses him from his painstaking work. He realizes that a fire has broken out somewhere in the stacks, and he runs to the head librarian's office to telephone for help. To his surprise he meets Dr. Weinrich, professor of Slavic, in the doorway, quite frightened. And upon entering the room Cesare sees Melania, Dr. Weinrich's young assistant, standing naked beside a man Cesare doesn't know. All three have lost their heads and probably would have perished in the flames if Cesare had not broken down the only door through which they could escape, and if he had not carried the nude Melania in his arms through the lobby, which had by now caught fire too. But a blow on his forehead, probably from the same rafter which set Melania's hair on fire, blinds him.

Thus the novel begins. Although Cesare recovers his sight, the doctor gives him to understand that it is only a matter of time: in a year or two he will become blind permanently. . . . The way I imagined the novel from there on, Cesare's secret drama emerged from the fact that although he wanted at all costs to enjoy these last years of light, he did not succeed: his mind kept returning continually to the scene that he had burst in upon at the head librarian's office. He did not understand what mysterious rite could have taken place between a frigid girl, a pedantic professor, and Manoil, a fantastic and possibly insane young man. All the investigations by the police failed to uncover the cause of the fire. Manoil claimed that it had broken out through a magical ritual, but since Cesare could not accept such an explanation he kept wracking his brain, struggling alone and in vain with the mystery. All the adventures that constituted Part I of the novel were provoked by Cesare's desperate attempts to find out the meaning of the "mystery" that had so radically altered his life, destining him to an imminent blindness.

I wrote mostly in the early part of the torrid afternoons, when I knew the whole household would be asleep, or else at night, after my roommate had gone to bed. I did not know exactly what was going to happen to Cesare until his final meeting with Manoil, when this demoniac would try to persuade him to commit suicide, and failing to do so would take his own life. And it is probable that at the time I was furtively writing the first chapter I was not yet aware of the full significance of those improbable adventures. Several magical and philosophical conceptions were presented without the author's betraying his preferences. In addition to some reflections about the "magic deed"* that I had entertained for several years, there now appeared elements that could be only "Tantric" (for instance, Melania's ritual nudity). But the crux of the difficulty, as it was revealed to me later when I started to write Part II, lay elsewhere: it was the pathos of an existence radically transformed as a result of that incomprehensible "deed"—the orgiastic ritual and the fire—and nevertheless remaining, basically, a meaningless and artificial existence even in the shadow of impending blindness, but at last acquiring an unsuspected depth at the moment when Cesare takes upon himself the "sin" of Manoil (who had committed suicide) and confesses, "I killed my brother."

Perhaps this word with which the book closes could constitute the true "key" to the novel, prompting the wise reader to reread the book from the beginning. But I doubt that this experiment was ever attempted. When the book appeared in 1934 with the title *Lumina ce se stinge* (The Light That Fails), almost all the critics and many of my friends agreed that it was a failure. Only one critic, Ion Biberi, deemed it my most significant literary work, probably because it was the first Romanian novel in which the technique of interior monologue was employed and in which, sporadically in Part II, one could discern the influence of James Joyce. What surprised me later, when I tried to reread and correct it, was the artificiality and false affectation of the language I had used. I don't think this was due to my long estrangement from Romanian, although I had not uttered a word of it for a year and a half. It was, rather, the result of an attempt to write in a "foreign" manner, about "foreign" people, living in an unidentifiable city, possibly Italian, but with people like those of Bucharest or some Romanian or Central European provincial city. After the fervor of the first days, when I wrote very fast, fascinated by the events I was inventing, there followed weeks of stubborn labor, time when I forced myself to describe little by little that world which seemed to be nowhere, yet was not a world of fantasy. Was it perhaps an exemplary Europe with synthetic land-

---

* "Faptul magic" was the title of an unpublished article Eliade had written in late 1928. The word *fapt* can mean "action," "deed," "event," "fact," and so on, and is difficult to render precisely into English.—Tʀ.

scapes, cities, and characters, imposing itself upon me without my realizing it, out of my repressed longings and nostalgias—trying to make its way into my consciousness, which had been wholly conquered by India in order to defend me from the enchantment of Asia, to hold onto me? Or, on the contrary, did those exemplary European landscapes and faces mask my own drama, which I did not yet suspect, but which was presaged by the "mystery" of *Lumina ce se stinge*?

Because, exactly as in the novel, the drama in which I unknowingly found myself involved also began in a library. Seeing that the index was progressing very slowly, although I worked at it several hours each day, Dasgupta asked his daughter Maitreyi to help me. We worked together in the library. In the month just prior to this we had become friends. I gave her lessons in French and she helped me with Bengali; together we translated some poems of Tagore. I knew she venerated Tagore, whom she called *gurudev* (divine teacher); I knew also how complex and suspect the admiration of an Indian woman for her *gurudev* can be; but being deeply engrossed in Sanskrit and the novel, I was not jealous. I did not realize that, in spite of myself, I was already in love. I say in spite of myself, because I thought the whole family was conspiring to cause us to be together as much as possible, and this suspicion put me on the defensive.

But, although I believed I was beginning to know the Indian soul, I was mistaken. There was no such conspiracy. It is probable that Dasgupta had something entirely different in mind: namely, to introduce me into his family by a kind of "adoption." It is probable that he was planning to relocate to Europe. King Carol II was then on the throne in Romania, and Nae Ionescu had become one of his intimate counselors. Dasgupta had written the king, describing me as one with a great future in Indian studies, and suggesting that the king establish an Oriental institute at Bucharest. He had written likewise to Nae Ionescu, insisting that he allow me to stay three or four years in India to study with him. Perhaps Dasgupta had in mind to come to Romania for some length of time as a guest of the institute. The political situation in India was being aggravated constantly, and the climate of Bengal did not agree with him (he suffered from hypertension and was threatened with the loss of his right eye). He would have liked, certainly, to have settled in Europe—to live in Rome, where Tucci had invited him, or in Bucharest, where he would have had me, his favorite pupil and, in a certain sense, his adoptive son.

I didn't understand all this until much later. At the marriage of Dasgupta's nephew I seemed to decipher mysterious allusions in what was, undoubtedly, proof that I had become, spiritually, a part of the family. At the wedding, as at other celebrations, I wore a dhoti—that Bengalese costume which can hardly be called flattering, but which nonetheless pleased me tremendously for the simple reason that it was the apparel of the people with whom I wished to become one.

I received the first copies of *Isabel*, and Maitreyi, who was a poet, began looking upon me with different eyes. I had become her equal; I had become a part of the same spiritual family as Rabindranath Tagore. I told her about the new novel I had begun, asking her not to say anything about it to the professor. And then, in those hours spent together in the library, while the rest of the household was resting upstairs, we copied on cards the technical terms in *A History of Indian Philosophy* and classified them alphabetically. One day our hands met over the little box of cards, and we could not unclasp them.

Despite all the hesitations and resistances, despite all that could separate an Indian sensibility and culture from an Occidental one, despite all the clumsiness, brashness, and boldness, love grew and was fulfilled as it was destined to be. In the winter of 1933, when I wrote in my attic on Strada Melodiei the novel that I intended to submit for the Tekirghiol-Eforia Prize, I reread for the first and last time the journal of those months. I even used some of the pages, incorporating them directly into the text of the novel. In spite of the pathos of the narrative, I tried to hold as closely to reality as possible. But, of course, this "reality" had become mythological from the very moment I had lived it. I lived again a long, blessed, and yet terrifying dream of a summer night. But this time I did not live it alone.

I woke up on the morning of September 18. In fact, I had begun to awaken during the night. I had scarcely closed my eyes. Maitreyi had managed to send me a note informing me that her parents had found out everything, and that she had been forced to confess. In the morning, Dasgupta summoned me to his study, told me that his precarious health would not allow him to offer me hospitality any longer, and gave me a sealed envelope that I was to open only after I had returned to Ripon Street. I must leave that very morning, immediately. My books and other things would be transported during the course of the day. Mrs. Dasgupta, her beautiful face frozen, distant, inaccessible, forced me to eat breakfast there, in her presence. I could not leave their house without eating. With great effort I swallowed, furtively wiping my eyes now and then.

None of us ever saw one another again after that. But Maitreyi managed to telephone me—by what miracle I've never understood—and, among other things, she told me I must save myself at all costs, to show the world that I was truly "a man." I had just time to say that I was going away to a monastery in the Himalayas. Then our conversation was broken off.

′   ′   ′

The Perris family pretended not to understand that I was upset. They were delighted to have me again as a boarder. The daughters tried to make me forget Bhawanipore, inviting me to the movies and to restaurants in China Town. But on the third day I gathered up a few books, a Sanskrit grammar and dictionary, and left for Delhi. I saw Fatehpur-Sikri again, as in a dream. People stared at me in wonderment and sometimes with suspicion. I had let my beard grow, and I looked hairy and wild. I sensed the Anglo-Indians and the police following me with their eyes.

I was suffering terribly, all the more so because I knew that, along with the friendship of the Dasgupta family, I had lost India itself. All that had happened had arisen out of my desire to identify myself with India, to become truly "Indian." After I read Dasgupta's letter, I knew that I would not soon be forgiven. This India that I had begun to know, about which I had dreamed and that I had loved so much, was now permanently forbidden to me. Never would I be able to attain an Indian identity. Our hope—mine and Maitreyi's—that we could be married, had been born of an illusion. I had learned enough Indian philosophy to know how hard it is to free oneself from illusions, to waken oneself from dreams. In rare moments of complete lucidity I realized very well that I had been deluded by my own hallucinations. I had allowed myself to be bound and enchanted by mirages, and there was nothing else for me to do but tear asunder the veil woven by māyā and become again free, serene, and invulnerable.

I had known this for a long time, but it was very hard for me to awaken. "Liberation," at the price I knew I should have to pay, left me almost indifferent. Moreover, Vedānta had never held much attraction for me. I liked Tantric yoga because it had hammered out a technique of liberation in which life was not sacrificed, but was transfigured. Meanwhile, however, I was so discouraged, so tormented by remorse, and so exhausted by insomnia that this technique of absolute liberation was beyond my reach. First, before all else, I had to find myself again. I set off for Hardwār and Rishikesh, that fabled Himalayan region, the choice of Indian ascetics and contemplatives for millennia. What seemed so tragi-comic about this was that I was going to the place I had yearned so long to see. For almost an entire year I had wanted to go to Hardwār, but Dasgupta had urged me to postpone the venture. He advised me to learn first all that I could in an Indian university, especially from a scholar like himself, and only then to spend several months in an ashram trying to practice techniques of meditation. And now, owing to that tragic misunderstanding, the positions were reversed: Dasgupta rejoiced to know that I was in a Himalayan ashram, as far as possible from Calcutta, while I longed to be still living in his house.

I made my way with difficulty from Delhi to Hardwār, because it was just the season of the Pūjā holidays, when millions of Indians go on visits to holy places, especially those in the Himalayas. The Ganges barely squeezes between the close-pressing mountains, swirling swiftly along; then it becomes calm and serenely descends into Hardwār. I installed myself in a dok-bungalow in the vicinity of the railway station, and spent the day strolling around the city, visiting temples, and descending the steps of the ghats. Since I was the only European who bathed ceremonially in the Ganges and offered rose petals to the goddess Lakṣmī, a crowd of curious onlookers followed me everywhere. That same day I went by horse-drawn carriage (*tonga*) to Kankhal, at the other end of Hardwār, to visit a temple surrounded by gigantic poplars and locust trees in which monkeys were swinging. The Ganges flows directly in front of the temple, and the stillness was deep, unnatural.

On following days I visited other temples and libraries and also the Gurukul College, an important Ārya Samāj center, located several miles outside the city. But I had not come to Hardwār for such excursions and visitations. I went on to Rishikesh, farther upstream. The Śiva temple, built that very year, impressed me profoundly. It was white with a gate of the same color and with a crystal globe on the tip of a shaft, which took flight from the center of the dome. With considerable difficulty I found lodging at a dok-bungalow, right on the bank of the Ganges. Rishikesh has long been the paradise of hermits and contemplatives. Virtually all the buildings there are either ashrams or guest houses for pilgrims. On the street I met an unending stream of sadhus in saffron-colored robes, *nāga* ascetics with their naked bodies smeared with ashes, all manner of swamis, as well as bands of pilgrims who had come with their families to visit the holy places and pay homage to those who had embarked on the road of renunciation.

On the second day I looked for a suitable place to stay, but my heart urged me not to remain. I went on still farther then, only a few kilometers beyond Rishikesh, but on the other side of the Ganges, to Svarga Ashram—and as soon as I set foot there I knew that this was the place. The Ganges flows swiftly between the rocks here, the jungle grows almost up to the riverbank, and the dense woods are full of monkeys, snakes, peacocks, and wildcats. In the late autumn, when the springs in the mountains would become dry, the jackals would come to the edge of the ashram and I would hear their howling from my hut.

On the very day of my arrival I met Swami Shivananda. Someone conducted me to the dwelling of the Mahānt, and I received permission to stay in the ashram provided that I shed my European clothing and dress in a yellow or white robe, wear sandals, and adopt a vegetarian diet. Then the Mahānt showed me the *kutiar* he was placing at my disposal: a small, solitary hut with a cement porch, a wooden bed, and an oil lamp. The next day I brought my baggage from Rishikesh and settled myself. I thought I would be staying for several months. Toward Christmas I decided to remain until May, when the road to Badrīnāth would become passable again. But I left in March, just as abruptly as I had come, after having lived the life of a hermit for nearly six months.

The huts were spaced about a hundred meters apart. At the third hour of the day, when the bell was rung, I would set off with a brass bowl and a cup to "beg" food from the *chetra*: rice, boiled beans, milk, and sometimes cakes made of rice and honey. I awoke at daybreak and bathed in the Ganges, just a few meters from my *kutiar*. At the beginning of fall, the jungle was fresh and luxuriant.

Seated on his haunches in his hut, the hermit was protected from the heat in summer and from the icy blast in winter. It was peaceful beyond imagination. There was no sound but the rippling of the waters of the Ganges and the short, gutteral cries of the monkeys. If I wished, I could spend the whole day alone; but, especially in the beginning, I liked to converse with Swami Shivananda or other hermits. I recorded as much as I could of these conversations, and in this way I regained my appetite for philosophy and Sanskrit. In the evenings I would sit for several hours on the porch, listening to the Ganges, searching for myself, trying to collect myself, to understand myself.

After a few weeks I realized that I was beginning to be in better spirits. At the same time I was beginning to understand the reason for the events that had provoked my breakup with Dasgupta. If "historical" India were forbidden to me, the road now was opened to "eternal" India. I realized also that I had to know passion, drama, and suffering before renouncing the "historical" dimension of my existence and making my way toward a trans-historical, atemporal, paradigmatic dimension in which tensions and conflicts would disappear of themselves. Later I understood that my drama itself followed a traditional model: it was necessary that my relations with Dasgupta pass beyond the phase of candor and superficiality and know the tensions and conflicts that characterize the beginning of true rapport between guru and disciple. Mar-pa, for instance, persecuted his favorite disciple, Milarepa, for years. I told myself that I was now in the phase of "trials." Although I had been banished in a brutal way from Bhawanipore, Dasgupta would acknowledge me someday as his true disciple—but this would take place on another plane, *in aeternum* and not *in saeculum*. (In the spring of 1939, after I had published *Yoga* and the review *Zalmoxis*, when he was en route to England, Dasgupta telegraphed me from Rome that he wanted to see me. But due to conditions beyond our control, we were unable to meet.)

The last events in Bhawanipore now seemed to me like a long wandering in a labyrinth. I felt that I should not be able to get out of that labyrinth until I should have returned to the "center." I must at all costs "concentrate" myself, regain my true center. The yogic meditations and techniques that I had studied with Dasgupta in the classic texts, which I was now applying under the guidance of Shivananda, had convinced me once more that they were the result of an extraordinary knowledge of the human condition. Only someone who knew truly the passions, temptations, and distractions of those "caught in the net of existence" could have evolved all those psycho-physical techniques that constituted yoga. Also, the very fact that I had arrived in the Himalayas at the end of my wits, exhausted, stupefied, permitted me now to "master" myself and to "break the bonds" more quickly than I should have hoped to do if I had been in a "normal" condition. The paradox was only an apparent one. I had proved for a fact what I like to call the "camouflaged optimism" of Indian spirituality, the belief that an excess of suffering provokes a thirst for liberation, that, actually, the more "lost" you feel, the closer you are to "salvation," that is to liberation; that the truly tragic situation is that of "happiness" and "self-satisfaction." (That is why, in the Indian view, the gods cannot know absolute freedom: precisely because they live a blessed existence.)

By Christmastime, I was a "changed" man. I shall not try to repeat here the steps of that inner transformation. What can be said about the results of the various preliminary exercises, I have described as precisely as I can in my works on yoga. The other exercises and experiences must be passed over in silence, because I am bound to remain faithful to the Indian tradition that agrees to communicate the secrets of initiation only from guru to disciple. Besides, I doubt that I should be able to describe exactly—that is, in scientific prose—certain experiences. The only means of expression approximately exact would be a new poetic language—and I have never had that gift. Later, in 1939, I tried to evoke some yogic experiences in a novella, *Secretul Doctorului Honigberger* (The Secret of Doctor Honigberger). The freedom of the artist to "invent" allowed me to suggest more, and to do it with more precision, than it would have been possible for me to do in a strictly scientific description.

Swami Shivananda marveled at how quickly I mastered the rudiments of yoga practice. He predicted for me a sensational career: I would become a second Swami Vivekananda, destined to shake the Western world and bring it back to its spiritual wellsprings, now well on the way to being forgotten. Personally, the comparison with Vivekananda did not flatter me. Although I admired Sri Ramakrishna, I did not feel attracted to the suave, moralizing writings of Vivekananda; I considered his works of propaganda and "popularization" to be hybrid and non-Indian. I had decided to penetrate as far as I could into the secrets of Indian contemplation, but aside from the thesis on which I had begun to work again I vowed not to make myself the bearer of any "Himalayan message." Besides, fate was to intervene in time to ensure the triumph of my secret wish not to dedicate myself to any "mission," not even that of "liberation."

In January, the vacant hut near mine regained its master: a *nāga* ascetic from the south, returning after I don't know how many months from a pilgrimage. Although it had become cold, the ascetic rigorously maintained his ritual nudity. He spent a good part of the day and night meditating, but if I happened to find him in front of his hut when I was going to the *chetra*, he would salute me, bringing his hands together in front of his face and smiling. We became friends quickly, and although we could barely communicate in Hindi, a language we both spoke badly, he was of help to me in some practices. Now, after having spent better than three months at the ashram, I had met a goodly number of ascetics and had learned much from my conversations with them. The strict regimen of my earlier life I had imposed upon myself again. I was restricting myself to only a few hours of sleep, and I was able to do a great many things without becoming tired or bored. Outside of the hours devoted to meditation and yogic exercises, I read Sanskrit texts every day, I worked on my thesis, I wrote articles for *Cuvântul*, and at nights I continued *Lumina ce se stinge*.

Sometimes I went alone to the caves at Brahmapura. I spent several days once in the hut of a swami whom I met on my first excursion to the region in the company of Shivananda. The recluse had built his cabin out of bamboo canes in the midst of a stand of bananas, which he cultivated with great difficulty because a whole tribe of monkeys (they were gray, with white faces) had taken up residence in the trees directly behind the hut. Every morning the swami brought out several leopard skins and spread them over some stumps. When the monkeys saw the hides they were seized with panic and took refuge in the tree tops, spying at us from among the branches. The swami told me once that he had watched them closely for a month, and he had marveled at their inexhaustible vitality, especially the sexual capacity of the males. This seemed all the more remarkable inasmuch as the monkeys ate little and at random. The swami was convinced that this extraordinary vitality was due to a certain root known only to these simians. He had decided to follow them and see what tubers and bulbs they gathered. The hermit hoped to discover the miraculous root one day— and then man would regain the vitality and sexual exuberance of the monkeys!

For an Indian ascetic, this curiosity seemed to me excessive. I visited him as often as I could because, although apparently he was applying a "scientific" method (he observed, he gathered, and tasted the roots which he supposed the monkeys ate), the swami was, in reality, searching for the "plant of life," the "fruit of youth and longevity," of which so many myths and legends speak. I was fascinated by the power of the manifestation of this archaic myth, now disguised in the form of a scientific preoccupation. Moreover, this was not the only example. Before arriving at the bamboo hut, I stopped at the dwelling of a Nepalese brahmācārin who spent part of his time gathering and tending medicinal plants. Long before I had learned about the "fruit of the *rishis*," some bulbous root on which recluses feed. The brahmācārin showed me a whole garden of the "fruit of Brahmā," a plant having small round fruits with a medicinal taste, renowned for its fortifying qualities. The plant was known thousands of years ago in the Ayur-Vedic pharmacopoeia, and recently it had been adopted by the Bengal Pharmaceutical Works in Calcutta for treatment of exhaustion from overwork.

But I especially liked to visit the hermits in the caves that stretched along beside the Ganges from Brahmapura to Lashmanjhola. The small caves, hidden among the rocks, had been hewn at random, one atop another, in the steep cliffs above the Ganges. I entered with difficulty and sat down on the cool sand of one of these caves, awaiting permission to go farther inside. A true hermit's cave, picturesque and roomy, it was the dwelling of an aged swami from Malabar. Among his bedside books, besides the *Bhagavad-Gītā* and Śaṅkara, he had *The Imitation of Christ*, which he considered the most profound work of Christian spirituality after the Gospels. Sometimes our conversations would last for hours, and once I spent a night in a niche of his cave.

Not very far from there was the cave of an old female ascetic. I could never find out who she was or where she had come from. Her whole body was smeared with ashes, including the top of her shaven head. Night and day she remained in meditation, always in the same yogic posture, seated on a bed of ashes. She almost never spoke, but I felt that she knew I was there beside her long before she uttered her first word. When Swami Shivananda brought me to her, she looked at me with piercing eyes, and then smiled. All at once I felt serene, reconciled. It was as though I had discovered, unexpectedly, a certainty that could change my life. I saw her again some months later, at the beginning of spring. She looked at me and her gaze suddenly became cool, stern, distant. I knew she had divined that I was no longer the brahmācārin whom she had seen at first, and in chagrin I withdrew from her. I understood that the road I had taken, although highly praised by a great many Indian spiritual masters, profoundly repulsed her. My old woman of the ashes certainly did not believe that any road existed other than that of asceticism and prayer—the one she had chosen.

For a long time no one knew of my whereabouts, neither my family at home nor Mrs. Perris. I lived for several weeks without any news from anywhere. Only after I felt I had returned to my senses did I write Mrs. Perris, requesting her to forward my mail to Svarga Ashram. One day the postman climbed up to my *kutiar* laden with letters, newspapers, and magazines from home. Thus I learned one October evening, on the rocks where I liked to sit and listen to the rippling waters of the Ganges, about the harsh review which Nichifor Crainic had published in *Gândirea* and of Mircea Vulcănescu's defense of me in *Cuvântul*. Mircea had entitled his article "Carte pentru 'Isabel'" (A Book for *Isabel*), and there were also letters for me, informing me of the storm that *Isabel* had stirred up, and explaining why N. Crainic had made the mistake of judging my novel immoral. (Crainic had written bitterly and regretfully: "So much intellect and so much talent buried under the ground!" and from then on my name was no longer included among the contributors to *Gândirea*.) Mircea Vulcănescu sought to penetrate beneath the camouflage that the author had erected, to decipher the secret intentions of the book. For him, *Isabel* was above all a "book with a key" and must be judged as such. From a letter of Ionel Jianu, I learned that F. Aderca had praised the novel in *Adevărul*, writing among other things: "In a country of great culture, such a debut would have brought glory, fame, and riches to the author."

Long before, I had sent the first part of *Lumina ce se stinge* to

Ionel Jianu, and he had suggested publishing it in serial form in *Cuvântul*. It appeared in the winter of 1931, but I doubt that anyone had the patience to read all the installments. I was now writing the second part. I wrote at night in an even more "foreign" style, as though someone else were writing it. Nevertheless, as I wrote I was fascinated by the "mystery" that I believed I was revealing more and more as I neared the end.

Sometimes at night, after laboring over the manuscript of *Lumina ce se stinge* for several hours, I would feel that I could not go to sleep without returning to my Indian "springs." At such times I would translate, into the most poetic Romanian of which I was capable, portions of the *Bhagavad-Gītā* or poems from Tagore's latest book. But for me India was, and has remained ever since, an integral culture in which different and often antagonistic currents of thought are articulated. I was interested not only in the techniques and philosophies through which the Indian spirit had said the most formidable No! to life and the whole universe, but also in the creations in which I discerned a positive valorization of cosmic and vital realities. I had discovered long before the exalted and transfigured paradox of sexuality that Tantric theologies and techniques had evolved. I was discovering now the spiritual roots of the interest in the organic world. Only an Indian scholar like Sir Jagadis Bose could have succeeded in demonstrating scientifically the homology between the animal and vegetal kingdoms. I do not know to what extent the theoretical implications of Jagadis Bose's experiments are accepted as yet; but for me the important fact was that modern science has recorded such a hypothesis of the fundamental unity of life, and that it was formulated and illustrated by an Indian, in conformity with the philosophical traditions of India (which Bose, moreover, ignored—a fact that makes his scientific work all the more significant).

In my *kutiar* in Svarga Ashram I meditated often on the possibility of writing a history of Indian sciences, but not in the apologetic sense in which certain Indian scholars understood it—those who tried to show that India too had been capable of "rigorous observations and objective, scientific experiments"—but one that would show very simply that the Indian spirit had applied methods that were suitable for describing, classifying, and explaining natural phenomena. I wrote at that time, working at night in my *kutiar*, a long study, "Cunoștințele botanice în vechea Indie" (Botanical Knowledge in Ancient India), which was published in 1931. I planned several other monographs, but I actually undertook to write later only a short text on "The Qualitative Nature of Indian Physics" (unpublished) and the chapters on Indian metalurgy and alchemy published in *Alchimia Asiatică* in 1935.

At the end of October I met Arthur Young, an Englishman in his late twenties or early thirties, who wore the orange-colored robe of a hermit. He was returning from Badrīnāth, walking with difficulty because his feet were swollen; from time to time more hardy pilgrims would carry him on their backs. He had been a soldier in the army in Mesopotamia, and after innumerable unverifiable and improbable adventures, he had attempted to commit suicide by driving his motorcycle into the ocean. He had been rescued, and in despair and exasperation one evening he had thrown his European clothes into a lake, put on a yellow robe, and set off toward the Himalayas, begging from town to town. He had spent some time in Rishikesh and Svarga Ashram, had taken the name of Jñānananda, and then had left with a group of pilgrims for Badrīnāth.

I don't know to what extent he had been transformed by the monastic discipline. At any rate, he seemed to be a man reconciled with life. He had regained the curiosity and appetite for adventure of his early youth. After only about ten days of rest at Svarga Ashram, he persuaded me to accompany him to Peshāwar, since from there we could enter Afghanistan through the Khyber Pass. Because both of us were dressed oddly (he in a yellow robe and I in the white one of a brahmācārin), and my beard had become long, red, and overgrown, and since our journey coincided with a new assault against the British in North India, we were considered suspect and followed all the time by the police.

At the train station in Lahore we were even arrested and interrogated—very politely—by several police. We had to leave our passports with the station master and take the first train for Peshāwar. Fortunately, the station master at Peshāwar was related to Mr. Perris, so we stayed at his house and thus escaped from the watchful eye of the police.

In order to cross the Khyber Pass, it was necessary to obtain a special permit. Mr. Perris' relative succeeded in procuring it for us, and three days after our arrival in Peshāwar we boarded the train for Landi Kotal. In the forty kilometers that separated us from the frontier we passed through more than thirty tunnels. But what fantastic views: that narrow desolate valley through which the train climbed from Lalabegh to Landi Kotal, with its walls of reddish stone rising vertically on both sides! On the jagged summits the forts of Ali Masjid, Jamrud, and Landi Kotal were silhouetted. But in Landi Kotal we were informed that the frontier was forbidden even to persons with special permits. Discouraged, we returned to Peshāwar. But the optimism of our host was inexhaustible: he assured us that we could cross into Afghanistan through another point on the frontier, and two days later we set out again, this time for Durgai. But we had no luck here either. Meanwhile, two of Young's fingers, which had been nearly frozen on the road to Badrīnāth, became infected. They were dressed by a medical attendant in a little railway station, and we returned to Peshāwar. I left then for Rishikesh, stopping at Lahore to retrieve my passport, but Young went to see a friend, a Father Brown, in Roorkee.

On Christmas Eve a female cellist from Johannesburg arrived at Svarga Ashram. Swami Shivananda took her under his wing, and to everyone's surprise she was allowed to live in a house built by a Maharani, right on the bank of the Ganges. Jenny had left Johannesburg and her music forever to go in search of "the Absolute" in India. Dressed in a simple white sari, she would sit in meditation on her terrace or listen to Swami Shivananda explaining the rudiments of Vedānta philosophy. An old Indian woman from Hardwār had lent her a gramophone and a few records. Sometimes in the evenings Shivananda would come to listen to the *Unfinished Symphony* or the *Jupiter Symphony*, and Jenny would serve us cocoa.

I believed I had made my position clear, but destiny had decided otherwise. Swami Shivananda left for Benares and Jenny begged me to continue her Vedānta lessons. I replied that I could not do it: on the one hand I didn't have time, and on the other hand, Vedānta wasn't my interest. I explained why. I told her about Sāṃkhya-Yoga, about my thesis and Tantrism, adding that Tantric yoga in particular interested me, but I did not go into detail. Having come to India to search for "the Absolute," Jenny was not going to be put off by my reserve and indifference. Discreetly but very adroitly she managed to draw me into discussions in which she always learned something more about Tantric rituals. She continued to invite me for cocoa on her terrace, and although I refused as often as I could, I agreed to go once or twice a week.

Once I had promised to come and I forgot. That evening I heard a timid knocking on the door of my *kutiar*. Blushing, embarrassed, with tears in her eyes, Jenny confessed that she had waited all afternoon until at last she had burst into tears, feeling humiliated and scorned. I excused myself as best I could, but because I saw she was quite depressed I said I would come after a little while so we could listen to *Peer Gynt* together.

I realized later how an ordinary detail, an event without any apparent significance, can radically alter your life, thrusting you onto a course which, only a few hours before, had seemed improbable or of no concern to you. My life in India would have been entirely different had I not gone to visit Jenny that February evening. As I entered, I sensed that something had *changed*—in the atmosphere of that large, white-walled room with its windows overlooking the Ganges, and in Jenny's appearance and behavior. It was not only the fact that for the first time she was wearing lipstick and was dressed in a sari of transparent silk. It was especially the premonition that a difficult ordeal was awaiting me, and that this ordeal was of an initiatory order; that is, that a later fulfillment or a lamentable failure would hinge upon it.

In the hour that had elapsed since I had found her, tearful and humiliated, at my door, Jenny had undergone a total transformation. By what miracle she had recovered the mystique of her own body, and had acquired an almost ritualistic seriousness in her voice and a secret light in her eyes, I never understood. But for *this* Jenny I did not feel sorry! Indeed, she almost frightened me. In place of the meek, timid, lovesick girl who had bored and confounded me, there now appeared a being whose mere presence provoked a confrontation with myself. I felt that whatever course I might take, I would never be able to regain the serenity and plenitude that I had won through such great effort in the past five months. If I should return at once to my *kutiar*, I would have to say that I had been afraid of the first real temptation that had crossed my path and I should feel humiliated for the rest of my life. But if I accepted what appeared to be the inevitable, my stay in the ashram would become ridiculous and humiliating.

As at so many other times in life, a solution was found between the two alternatives. Actually, it was after Jenny had brought me a cup of cocoa, when she asked me if I had ever seen a flesh and blood *nāyikā*, that I understood. The sensation of a ritual atmosphere that had disturbed me ever since I had entered the room was this: without realizing it, Jenny was embodying a *nāyikā*, the consecrated partner in certain Tantric ceremonials. I replied that, not being initiated, I was not allowed to look upon a *nāyikā* in her ritual nudity. "Couldn't we be initiated together?" Jenny asked. "It's impossible without a guru," I replied. "We could look for one," Jenny persisted, "and until then. . . ."

I knew what she meant. Until we could find a guru (and I knew in advance that we would not find one in this ashram) we could try the preliminary rituals of which I had once spoken to her. But such rituals also entailed a great deal of risk. It was, however, beyond my powers not to brave them. . . .

From then on I came late, after midnight, and returned to my *kutiar* an hour before dawn. I succeeded in preserving my lucidity and self-control, not only in the "preliminary rituals," but also in all that followed. Jenny was astonished, but I sensed that I was on the road to becoming another man. Sometimes I slept only two or three hours a night, yet I was never tired. I worked all the time, and I worked better than ever before. I understood then the basis of all that vainglorious beatitude that some ascetics, masters of Haṭha-yoga, proclaim. I understood, too, the reason why certain yogis consider themselves to be like the gods, if not even superior to them, and why they talk about the transmutation and even the immortality of the body.

Upon returning to my hut one morning in March, I found my *nāga* neighbor waiting for me in the doorway. "I know where you've been," he said as soon as we had entered the *kutiar*. "I believe you could be compared with Maha Bhairava! But do you have enough *vīrya* (energy) to proceed on this path? People of today are impure and weak. Very soon you will feel a strong fever in the crown of your head. You will know then that you do not have much time. It is better that you stop before this happens."

He had spoken as clearly as he could, using whole clauses of Sanskrit so that I could understand him. I understood him.

"But what if I find a guru?" I asked.

"You already have a guru," he said, smiling. Then he saluted me, bringing his palms together in front of his face, and returned to his hut.

I did not go to bed. For several hours I remained motionless, seated beside the wall where I had learned the first yogic postures and had accustomed myself to rhythmic respiration, concentrating on a single mental object. Little by little I began to understand. For a second time in less than a year I had let myself be deceived by my own imagination—in Indian terms, by illusions created by māyā. Just now, when it seemed to me that I had "awakened," I had fallen prey to the first magical temptation that an unresting māyā had produced along my path. Actually, I was not in love with Jenny, nor was I even attracted to her physically. And yet I had consented to know her body in a "magical" manner, that is in a lucid and detached way, as only an initiate is allowed to do—and I knew full well that initiation does not exist without a guru. I had let myself be drawn into a senseless "magical" game, and as the *nāga* had warned me, an extremely dangerous one.

Once again a young woman had embodied a secret that I had not known how to decipher. And once again my ignorance or incomprehension had closed a road to "India," the land with which I wanted to identify myself. I had failed my "adoption" by Dasgupta and had, therefore, lost "historical" India. And now, as soon as Swami Shivananda's back was turned, I had also lost my chance to integrate "eternal," trans-historical India. I had no right to remain in that ashram. It would be necessary to start all over again from the beginning in another such place, later on. But in the meantime I had to leave immediately.

I could not know it then, but eternal māyā, in her blind wisdom, had set those two girls on my path in order to help me find my true destiny. Neither the life of an "adopted Bengalese" nor that of a Himalayan hermit would have allowed me to fulfill the possibilities with which I had come into the world. Sooner or later I should have awakened from my "Indian existence"—historical or trans-historical—and it would have been difficult to return, because by that time I should not have been only twenty-three. What I had tried to do—renounce my Western culture and seek a "home" or a "world" in an exotic spiritual universe—was equivalent in a sense to a premature renunciation of all my creative potentialities. I could not have been creative except by remaining in *my* world—which in the first place was the world of Romanian language and culture. And I had no right to renounce it until I had done my duty to it: that is, until I had exhausted my creative potential. I should have the right to withdraw permanently to the Himalayas at the *end* of my cultural activities, but not at the beginning of them. To believe that I could, at twenty-three, sacrifice history and culture for "the Absolute" was further proof that I had not understood India. My vocation was culture, not sainthood. I ought to have known that I had no right to "skip steps" and renounce cultural creativity except in the case of a special vocation—which I did not have. But of course I understood all this only later.

Calm, cheerful, I went to inform Jenny of the decision I had made. She registered astonishment—then burst into tears. Next I went to the Mahānt, thanked him for his hospitality, and—dressing in European clothing for the first time in six months—I left for Hardwār, where I caught the first train to Delhi. On the morning of the third day I was in Calcutta. At 82 Ripon Street I created quite a sensation with my sunburnt skin and short red beard, which gave me the air of a student from one of Leonida Andreiew's plays.

On board the liner, in the evenings after dinner, I often went to see Tucci. He had recently been made a member of the Italian Academy, which allowed him to travel first class without charge on all Italian vessels. He was returning to Rome after almost six years, bringing with him an immense collection of manuscripts, art objects, and rare books. But he was already planning new expeditions to Tibet, which he was to undertake in subsequent years with the support of the Italian government.

As we strolled on deck, Tucci spoke to me about the Oriental institute that he was planning. It was to be not merely an academic institution, but above all a workshop in which young scholars in Asian studies could labor—not only on ancient history and archeology, but also on problems of culture and contemporary history. He felt that we must draw Asia out of the museums and libraries where the Orientalists of the past century have buried it. Asia constitutes a complex of *living* civilizations, he said.

How well I understood him and how enthusiastically I agreed with him! Tucci, with his prodigious experience and authority, confirmed and validated the conclusions that I too had reached, especially in the time just past, in the nine months that had elapsed since my return from the Himalayas. I have felt ever since then that this period was different from the other phases of my life in India. I found other friends, I frequented other places, I was engaged with other problems. After the lessons I had learned in Bhawanipore and Svarga Ashram, I turned instinctively toward other springs of that inexhaustible India. From then on I no longer tried to become a different person, imitating an Indian model, but I let myself be drawn by the mystery of the many obscure or neglected aspects of Indian culture.

Immediately after my return, I immersed myself completely in my work. I spent the mornings at the Imperial Library, afternoons at the library of the Asiatic Society, and nights working until late in my room, preparing the second part of my thesis, the comparative section. A year earlier I had finished the second chapter about Sāṃkhya philosophy and yoga psychology and had sent it to Rădulescu-Motru, who had published it in the *Revista de Filosofie*. I had written two articles for the *Ricerche Religiose*, Ernesto Buonaiuti's review. I had kept up my correspondence with Buonaiuti, as well as with quite a number of other Italian scholars. They continued to send me all their publications, and whenever I had experienced attacks of melancholia—especially during my first year in Calcutta—I had written to them. They always replied with the same promptness and warmth that I had known from them for so many years.

Now, in the spring of 1931, trying to compose a comparative history of yogic techniques, I realized that Sanskrit, Bengali, and Pali were not enough. I should have to learn at least Tibetan, if not also Chinese and even the rudiments of several Dravidian and Australasian languages. I wanted to integrate my analysis of the meditative techniques into the total history of Indian culture, and if possible that of Eastern Asia. I began learning Tibetan, encouraged by Van Manen, librarian of the Asiatic Society, who provided me with the manuals and dictionary I needed and offered to help me. I didn't think it would be very hard. But after only a few weeks I realized that if I did not apply the method I had used in studying Sanskrit—that is, working night and day on nothing but Tibetan—I would not be able to progress with sufficient speed. But now I was so enthused over all the discoveries I was making, especially in Indian and Southeast Asian ethnology, that it was impossible for me to concentrate exclusively on Tibetan.

Moreover, unexpectedly, new difficulties arose. Mrs. Perris telephoned me one morning at the Imperial Library to say that someone wanted to talk with me. It was Jenny. She had given up the life of an ascetic at Svarga Ashram and had come to see me. Worse than that, she had taken a room in the boarding house on Ripon Street. She stayed for about two weeks, during which time I worked only sporadically. I told her quite frankly that all that had happened between us belonged to the past. But Jenny still had hope. One day she declared that since she had failed to find "the Absolute," she was going to become a tart. She put on her most elegant dress, made up her face, and went to drink cocktails in the most fashionable spot in Calcutta. An hour later she returned, discouraged and dejected. She consoled herself by going out every evening with the group from the boarding house—to movies, China Town, and bars. Finally, she decided to try asceticism again. She left for Pondicherry, for the ashram of Aurobindo Ghose. A week later she wrote that she was happy, that "the Mother" had given her courage to search for "the Absolute" again, that she had donated what little she had to the ashram, since she had decided to stay there for the rest of her life. She wished me success in finding my "true path" as soon as possible. After that, I heard no more from her.

After Jenny's departure, I set to work even more furiously. The study of Tibetan was put aside and I began concentrating on East Asian ethnology. Since I had decided to stay two or three more years in India, I promised myself I would return to Tibetan after I had become familiar with the folk culture of India and Southeast Asia. An excursion to Sahibganj where I lived for a week among the Santal, and journeys to villages around Calcutta, had greatly stirred my interest in the pre-Aryan aborigine population. It seemed to me that I was beginning to discern elements of unity in all peasant cultures, from China and Southeast Asia to the Mediterranean and Portugal. I was finding everywhere what I later called "cosmic religiosity"; that is, the leading role played by symbols and images, the religious respect for the earth and life, the belief that the sacred is manifested directly through the mystery of fecundity and cosmic repetition and not through events of history. Of course, the peasant cultures of Europe had been transfigured by Christianity, but Eastern and Mediterranean Christianity was also at the same time a "cosmic liturgy." The incarnation, death, and resurrection of Christ had in a certain sense transfigured Nature. The world was again "good," as it had been before the Fall. In the case of the peasant population of India, the world was not an illusion and life was not reduced to a series of sufferings as the post-Upaniṣadic philosophers and ascetics represented it. The world, life, and pleasures were divine creations and "sin"—that is, "ignorance"—consisted not in not accepting them as such, but in believing that the world and life represented ultimate reality.

Indirectly, the understanding of aboriginal Indian spirituality helped me, later on, to understand the structure of Romanian culture. I recognized even more the importance of pre-Aryan, autochthonous elements in the makeup of Hinduism. The most specific characteristics of Indian religiosity—above all, the cult of and the mystic devotion to goddesses of fertility—were the contribution of the aboriginal population or the result of a synthesis between autochthonous spirituality and that of the Indo-Aryans. I was to understand soon that the same synthesis had taken place in the history of Romanian culture. The Dacians—the "autochthonous base" of which Blaga spoke following Pârvan and Hasdeu—played the role in Romanian culture that the pre-Aryans played in Indian culture, with this difference: while in India these pre-Aryan strata and their cultural expressions are still observable, the contribution of the Dacians can be only partially and approximately reconstructed. Undoubtedly, however, among the elements of unity in the peasant cultures of Southeastern Europe, the most important was the Thracian substratum. Upon this substratum, in the course of time, the cultural influences of the Greeks, the Roman Empire, the Byzantines, and especially Christianity were superimposed. But if, as I became convinced still later, Romanian folk traditions preserve a part of the Geto-Thracian heritage, then it seemed to me that historical and philosophical problems of Romanian culture must be debated on another plane. In the first place, Romanian folk creations were articulated in a much broader perspective, because they were not only "Romanian"; more precisely, their dimensions were not "provincial," nor were they confined to the borders of the Romanian nation. A certain type of civilization was illustrated by Romañian folk culture and also by the other cultures of Southeastern Europe, despite their diversities and variations (which characterize, moreover, the genius of folk creations everywhere in the world).

In the second place, the recognition of the validity, authenticity, and universality of this mode of existing and being creative in the world allowed the contemporary Romanian elite to understand other expressions of the same mode of being, in particular the values of the Indian folk culture. That is why, in 1937, after I had published *Yoga* and several other studies concerning pre-Aryan civilization, I was surprised by certain articles in the right-wing press in which I was rebuked or mocked for my "exotic" preoccupations. From my point of view, in presenting the contribution of pre-Aryan elements in Indian culture or in commenting on the symbolism of the temple of Barabuḍur, I was nearer the universe of the Romanian peasant than I should have been, for example, in translating Kant, as one of the young theoreticians of the right was doing at that time!

But there was something else that made me feel an urgency to understand Indian spirituality and Asian culture in general. I knew that Indian independence was imminent, and that very shortly the whole of Asia would reenter history. On the other hand, in the not-so-distant future a number of archaic peoples would take their places on the stage of world politics. It seemed to me that we Romanians could fulfill a definite role in the coming dialogue between the two or three worlds: the West, Asia, and cultures of the archaic folk type. To me it appeared useless to repeat certain Western clichés or discoveries—but likewise it seemed sterile and dangerous to take a stand in an antiquated "traditionalism." It was precisely the peasant roots of a good part of our Romanian culture that compelled us to transcend nationalism and cultural provincialism and to aim for "universalism." The common elements of Indian, Balkan, and Mediterranean folk culture proved to me that it is *here* that organic universalism exists, that it is the result of a common history (the history of peasant cultures) and not an abstract construct. We, the people of Eastern Europe, would be able to serve as a bridge between the West and Asia. A good part of my activity in Romania between 1932 and 1940 found its point of departure in these intuitions and observations made in the spring and summer of 1931.

I became friends with Van Manen, who loaned me rare publications from his prodigious Tibetan library, and with Lucian Bogdanov, a Russian Orientalist who had settled in Calcutta after spending four years in Afghanistan. Van Manen loved India as much as Bogdanov hated it. The latter could tolerate only Islamic India, and he could never approach the art and culture of Hinduism (in which he saw nothing but "idolatry"). He would have given anything to have been able to leave India—where he made a poor living by means of a post at the French Consulate and by doing translations for the Cama Oriental Institute. I spoke to him once about the possibility of his coming to Bucharest as professor of Oriental languages at the university, and this suggestion revived his hopes. Both of us wrote to Nicolae Iorga, but we received no reply.

At the library of the Asiatic Society I met all sorts of scholars, among them the Tibetanist Jacques Bacot, and the "sexologist" Maurizius Hirschfeld. The latter was returning from Japan with a tremendous collection of phallic stones. He was accompanied by a young Japanese assistant who was possessed of the notion that one day his country would become famous for its erotic creations and perfections. Van Manen sometimes invited me to his home. He liked to converse with his cook in Tibetan, leaving the guests to guess what new sort of Himalayan food to expect.

Through Bogdanov I became acquainted with an attaché of the French Legation who had spent two years in Bucharest. Andre came sometimes to Ripon Street, invited the girls to tea at Firpo's, and dated Norinne. At that time Norinne was engaged to a young Anglo-Indian, Ernest Mann, who worked in a jute plantation in East Bengal. Whenever he came to Calcutta, he invited the Perris family to a restaurant, and took Norinne dancing afterward. One night I heard voices in the front hall and a scream—and when I went to see what was the matter, Mrs. Perris shouted to me, "Ernest has drowned!" His brother and brother-in-law had come to bring the news. They had received a telegram from the head of the firm where Ernest worked. He had been hunting crocodiles on a branch of a river, the boat had overturned, and Ernest, not knowing how to swim, had drowned. Another brother, Cyril, had gone that very night to try to find the body, or what might be left of it in a region infested with crocodiles.

Mrs. Perris suffered a blow, the consequences of which were visible for a long time afterward in her face. Ernest Mann was, indeed, an unexpected match for Norinne: 600 rupees a month, a bungalow at the jute plantation, and a house in Calcutta. Norinne was quickly consoled, however. And just as quickly she accepted invitations to the city; but after a little while she took a position at the home of a very rich Parsi, which allowed her to escape the watchful eye of her mother.

I did, and in a way I did not, take part in all these happenings that preoccupied the boarders on Ripon Street. Aside from my work, I lived without a schedule. I no longer imposed anything on myself; I did not force myself to become anyone or do anything now. I learned to accept life in Calcutta as it unfolded itself: sometimes sublime, pure, affecting me like a refining fire; at other times mediocre, insipid, banal, but no less mysterious for all of that. I learned not to let myself be elated or depressed by encounters and relationships into which I was drawn, often involuntarily. A certain indifference toward those events which might have seemed constitutive of my biography began to make its way into my soul from that time on. It was not, properly speaking, an indifference toward life in all its aspects; but I no longer took seriously what happened or did not happen to me. I began to feel that the deep dimensions of existence are beyond the ebb and flow of the tides of events. I perceived that if I should succeed in situating myself in such a dimension, I should become in a certain sense "invulnerable." That is, whatever might happen, I should continue to remain *myself*, and as such I should be free to fulfill my destiny.

The dry season had passed, the monsoon had begun, and although it was still rather hot, I decided not to leave. I had planned to go to Almora, then proceed to Kashmir for five or six months, but I didn't want to leave until I had gathered a great deal more material for the comparative chapter of my thesis. I wanted to take advantage of the documents I had at hand in the two large libraries before betaking myself again to the Himalayas.

Then all at once, in the middle of June, I felt I had to write a novel. At first I called it *Victorii* (Victories), then *Petru şi Pavel* (Peter and Paul). It was different from anything I had written before: it was not autobiographical like *Romanul adolescentului miop* and *Gaudeamus*, nor was it written in the third person like *Isabel*, and yet it was not a "fantastic" novel like *Lumina ce se stinge*. The setting was Bucharest immediately after the First World War. Apparently, it was the history of a family: Francisc Anicet and his two sons, Petru and

Pavel. In reality, I wanted to write the history of two generations: the generation of the war and the one that followed it—the "young generation," which I had praised so highly three or four years previously in my *Cuvântul* articles. When I began it, I "saw" clearly only the first chapters: Francisc's youth, his impatience in waiting for the war, the estate that he lost after the agrarian reforms, the decadence and poverty of the Anicet family, and the childhood and adolescence of the two sons, whom I perceived as different but complementary. The title, *Victories,* could be taken either ironically or symbolically, because the novel consisted of a series of "downfalls" and "defeats"—in the first place, the disintegration of Francisc Anicet's fortune and his social degradation, having gone from a great landowner to a simple clerk in a bank owned by a former classmate from school.

I wrote furiously night and day, and in three days' time I had filled a hundred pages. I interrupted it then, taking it up again a week later at a slower pace, writing only at night and no more than two or three hours at a time. But very soon I felt that the theme had escaped my hand, that the novel was threatening to become a "sociology of the generations," and so I broke it off completely. A good part of the manuscript I eventually destroyed, saving only about fifty or sixty pages, which I used later in *Întoarcerea din Rai* (The Return from Paradise), published in 1934.

This happened at the end of June. In August I made several excursions to the Ganges Delta, stopping as often as I could at Puri. In September a young Indian whom I had met at the Asiatic Society took me one day to the residence of his spiritual master in Howrah, a suburb of Calcutta. The guru was a rather young man who spoke perfect English. He impressed me from the start by his lucidity and originality. Almost without my confessing them, he guessed all the trials through which I had passed. I don't know to what extent he divined the actual content of my adventures, but he was aware of their nature and their consequences. He discovered and evaluated unfailingly the experiences I was having in connection with the techniques of meditation; and from the second meeting with him he helped me to recover everything he calculated I could use out of my Himalayan lessons. It was indeed paradoxical: I had found in Howrah, just a few miles from Ripon Street, that guru for whom I had sought in the far-off Himalayas! Not that he was "superior" to Swami Shivananda and the other ascetics at Svarga Ashram and Lash-manjhola from whom I had learned so much; but he was the spiritual master *I* needed, the one who could help me better, and more, than all the others.

I went to see him regularly, every week, and each time I spent several hours with him. He was married, had children, and every day dozens of people came to him—and not only from Calcutta. They came for *darshan:* just to gaze upon him, to touch him; because according to Indian belief, it is enough for one to *contemplate* in order to be lifted and purified spiritually. The guru accepted only a few disciples, and I had had the good fortune to be accepted at our first meeting, when after a brief introduction by my friend, he had invited me into his house and we had begun to converse.

I postponed my departure for Almora. I thought I had postponed it for just two or three months when, one Sunday morning, a letter arrived from my father. It was necessary that I return as soon as possible for military service. The news struck like a bolt of lightning. My first reaction was to reply that I was ill and could not return. I thought I could get a medical certificate from a doctor with whom I was well acquainted. But after a few days' reflection and discussions with friends, I decided it would be better to return now, and then come back to India after I had completed my military duty and had presented my thesis. At the maximum, I should be able to return to India in two years with my doctorate; then I should be free to stay as long as I liked. Even if I did not obtain a stipend from the Romanian government again, it would not be hard for me to find a subsidy in India. In any event, I knew I would need very little money in a Himalayan ashram. So I wrote home that I was returning, but without specifying a date.

The last three months I spent in Calcutta have remained in my mind as a fabulous interval. I had a kind of premonition that I would never return to India because I would never again find a way. When I was not at Puri or Chittagong, I would spend hours at a time in the Museum of Indian Antiquities, or take long walks through the villages around Calcutta, or go to Belur Math or Chandernagore. I went as far as Uttapara, at the invitation of a zemindar who owned a splendid collection of English novels in first editions. I took advantage of every hour. At the library of the Asiatic Society I ransacked the shelves in a desperate effort to complete my documentation. Sometimes at night I would go walking through the native sectors to which my first memories of India were linked: I walked in the direction of Bhawanipore, but I did not dare approach it very closely; I circled around it, listening to the noises of the neighborhood as the wind carried them—now muffled and suppressed, now suddenly animated, near, threatening . . .

After I had dispatched my library by mail, there began the farewell parties, prolonged until morning, in China Town. It was as though I had returned to the "dream of the summer's night" of 1929. Memories of those last days soon became hazy, and after a few years they vanished completely, except that they return to me now sometimes in dreams. Then I waken, exhausted by an incomprehensible sadness.

In the railway station on that bright, clear December morning I told everyone, "I'll be seeing you! I'll see you in 1933!"

At Port Said I found that the Romanian ship had left Alexandria the night before. The next ship would not arrive for another twenty days. I decided then to continue the voyage to Venice, and from there take a train to Bucharest. The Adriatic was gray and murky. Tucci disembarked at Bari. We set a date for India in 1933. (I didn't see him again until 1950 in Rome, almost twenty years later.)

Having spent all my money, I waited in Venice for a money order to be telegraphed from home. Lodged in a shabby hotel next to the station, I tried to ward off melancholia by reading Papini's latest books, *Gog* and *Sant'Agostino.*

I arrived on Strada Melodiei on Christmas Eve, 1931. It was as though I were struggling to awaken out of a dream, but could not. The evening was cold, damp, strange. In the attic a fire was burning in the stove, but still I was cold. During the night it began to snow.

PART III

The Promise of
the Equinox

11. The Return to the Attic

IT WAS incredible, and yet I had to admit that it was so: I was speaking Romanian badly and with a foreign accent! I couldn't think of the right words. On the day following my arrival, when the whole family was crowded around the table and everyone was listening to my stories, I caught them casting glances at me out of the corner of their eyes, trying to hide their smiles.

My sister Corina, whom I had left a schoolgirl in her last year at the lycée, had been married recently to a magistrate; but all the others appeared virtually unchanged. Mother seemed the same; time's passage had not touched her. She still maintained, undoubtedly, the faith she had always had in me, but she gave no sign of it. It pleased her to listen to the others praising me, but she always pretended to be plagued with doubts. It was as though she were afraid it would bring me bad luck if she were to acknowledge openly that I was now what she had dreamed, ever since my early youth, that I'd become: an "eminent young man." Father was past sixty, but still as robust and indefatigable as ever. A month earlier he had carried to the attic, by himself, the thousand or so books I had shipped home in boxes from India.

It was with a thrill that I found those books there, just as my father had stacked them, in piles leaning against the wall. And on awakening in the morning I found again the stove in the wall, still hot, and saw again the little attic windows. I gazed out, feasting my eyes on the fresh snow and the houses across the street. It was as though I were trying to awaken from a dream. I couldn't understand what was wrong: everything seemed the same, and yet all was different. For several weeks, ever since leaving Calcutta, I had been living only in anticipation of this homecoming, but now that I had arrived, I still didn't *feel* that I was there. It seemed that I ought to have farther to go, to travel another long road, before reaching home again and being among my loved ones. I stared half-consciously at that house across the street, which once upon a time had seemed so huge and luxurious, and so full of mystery because the blinds were almost always drawn and the lights lit only a few days a year when the owner, Trandafir Djuvara, returned from abroad. The house was still there, but it seemed smaller, aged, with its shades drawn, waiting for the ambassador's return. (At that time I had not yet learned that the ambassador had died and that the estate was being processed in the courts.)

That same morning I went to see Nae Ionescu at the editorial office of *Cuvântul* on Pasajul Imobiliara. He gave me a long look, smiling and shaking his head. "It's good to see you home!" he said. He appeared younger and more relaxed than I had left him in the autumn of 1928, exhausted from the long struggle he had carried on, almost singlehanded, to save *Cuvântul*. And he had saved it. Moreover, since the return of King Carol II in June of 1930, *Cuvântul* had become the semi-official newspaper of the regime.

Very soon I was to discover that Nae was in the midst of a *malentendu*, while his influence at the palace, which so many envied, was a myth. King Carol listened more to the advice of Wieder or Urdăreanu than to that of Nae Ionescu. At that time, 1931–1932, the political prestige of the professor was in decline. The "government of technicians" presided over by Nicolae Iorga, which Nae had supported, had already become unpopular. I had arrived in time to witness the gradual discrediting of the professor in "palace circles" that was to lead, in 1933, to a rupture and eventually to the suppression of *Cuvântul*.

A little while after my arrival at Nae's office, three other men came in: Gheorghe Racoveanu, Mihail Sebastian, and Ion Călugăru. They had heard I was back and had come to see me. I knew them all from their writings, but I met them now for the first time. Gheorghe Racoveanu, hale and hearty, quickly burst into laughter, and he laughed so hard that he had to wipe tears from his eyes. Ion Călugăru was a small man with sharply chiseled features, puffing furtively on a cigarette, speaking first in a whisper, then loudly, sometimes uttering short propositions that one didn't know how to take because they sounded like quotations from Urmuz or Saşa Pană (and sometimes they were). Mihail Sebastian was not as I had imagined him. I had admired him ever since reading his first article in *Cuvântul*. In my mind I had pictured him rather impertinent, perhaps even a little snobbish, and in any event older than he was. His age at that time was twenty-four, but he did not look to be more than twenty. He was not tall, his complexion was pale and flushed, and his expression distant. He was so discreet and delicate that he might have been taken for timid. Only after you knew him better did you discover his charm, his generosity, his impossibly complex *presence*.

From then on we met one another every day at the *Cuvântul* office. Nae wanted to know if I would finish my thesis in the course of the year, while doing my military service. If so, I should be able to defend the thesis and obtain the doctoral degree in the spring of 1933. With a little luck, the University Council would agree to let me assist him in his course on metaphysics and his seminar on the history of logic, thereby leaving Nae to teach only the course on logic. I did not dare confess to him then that I had made up my mind to return to India in the fall of 1933. The professor assured me emphatically that he had maintained his faith in my potential for science. Since he doubted that a chair in Sanskrit or the History of Religions would be easy to establish, he had chosen this route—an assistant for his chair in Logic and Metaphysics—in order to hasten my entrance into the university faculty.

Meanwhile, I had a year of military service to perform. However, I postponed as long as possible the day of my appearance at the regimental base. The holidays came and I could not bear to celebrate them another time far from family and friends, quartered in army barracks. I told myself that at the last moment I'd find a plausible excuse to justify my tardiness.

And so I used my last days of freedom to maximum advantage. Several of my friends had gotten married, and it pleased me to think that I discovered in them new dimensions that I had not suspected only three or four years previously at the university. Mary, wife of Mihail Polihroniade, was an English girl who of late had been teaching English in a boys' lycée. She was tall, robust, and redheaded, and her freckles seemed to add a masculine strength to her open, honest face. She always looked you straight in the eye, and she spoke loudly, precisely, and efficiently. We became friends quickly; in fact, I was soon well-acquainted with the wives of two other friends of mine also, Marga Jianu and Mariana Viforeanu. News of the beauty of Marga had reached me even in India: friends had written me about her. She always remained the same as the day I met her: calm, serene, smiling constantly, looking as though she had descended from a da Vinci canvas.

To my surprise, Mariana turned out to be an excellent classicist. While she was still a child her father, Istrati Micescu, had taught her Greek. She was perhaps the only person in her generation who had read Pindar and Plato in the original before reading fashionable French novels. But Petre Viforeanu had remained just as I had known him in lycée: sociable, scholarly, and ambitious. He wanted to live several lives at once: to become a great jurist and university professor, but also to triumph in politics without renouncing the social life and friends from lycée days. He was so much in demand in so many circles that I could not meet him as regularly as I met with Polihroniade and Jianu, or with Haig Acterian and Marietta Sadova, who were living together now in an apartment on Bulevardul Elisabeta.

I had known about their romance while attending the university, when Marietta, an actress, was on the verge of separating from Ion Marin Sadoveanu. But at that time it was a great secret—so I had never had occasion to meet her, although I had seen her on stage. I met her one evening in late December. She looked just the way she had on stage the first time I had seen her. Her face was "foreign," more like that of a Scandinavian than a Transylvanian from Bistriţa, from whence she had come several years earlier to enroll at the Conservatory of Dramatic Arts. Only after we became friends did I realize how much kindness, intelligence, imagination, and energy resided in that woman who seemed frail, almost chlorotic, who made you think she might fall gravely ill at any time, whom you expected to find preoccupied with her health and other personal problems. I discovered later that Marietta lived exclusively for others and that, apart from her great passion for the theater, her life was nourished by the pleasure she gave to other people.

I had scarcely begun to penetrate into this new world revealed by my married friends when it became necessary for me to present myself at the Antiaircraft Artillery Base. It was located on the far side of the city, at Ghencea. To reach there required half an hour's ride on the tram and another twenty minutes' walk. Of course, I had been adjudged a "draft-dodger" long before; however, I was not incarcerated immediately as some had warned I would be. The colonel knew I had returned from the "Far East," and until the day when I would appear before the Disciplinary Council, he accorded me the favor of my "extenuating circumstances." However, I was confined to the base, in accordance with the rules. For two solid weeks I never set foot off the grounds. Much to my surprise, I did not feel exiled. There were still plenty of cadets (men of education who had been given reduced terms: *teterişti* as they were called), but now, after three months of training, they had permission to go to town for their evening meals and sleep off base. So at nightfall I was left among the privates, the great majority of whom were peasants. In my adolescence, during the summers, I had knocked around villages from the mountains to the Danube, I had slept in houses of peasants, and I could say that I was not completely a stranger to the world of the villages. But only at Ghencea, while I was billeted with the troops and slept in the same barracks with them, did I come to know well the peasant life. I did not feel in the least "strange" among these peasants, and with some of them I even became friends.

Nevertheless, I was counting the days. From my awakening in the morning until after dark, till "lights out," time passed very slowly. I took part in the training sessions, but since I had come three months late, I had not yet been assigned to a battery. A second lieutenant offered to initiate me, but I did not succeed in learning much from him. At our first lesson he assured me that being an "intellectual," a "man of books," I would become familiar very quickly with the mechanism of the antiaircraft gun ("As quick as you can snap your fingers!" he declared). And so he preferred to let me tell him stories about India. The two of us would stand beside the cannon, he questioning me about the heat and the monsoon, the temples and the women of India—and I answering. For me to have learned to operate an antiaircraft gun would have been useless anyway; my eyes were too weak to have sighted hostile aircraft in time to do any good. Soon afterward, I discovered that due to my myopia I had been assigned to the auxiliary service, and I was given only elementary military instruction.

In the evenings I watched melancholically as my friends picked up their passes and left for town. I could see Bucharest, seemingly very far away, blanketed with snow, smoke rising from the chimneys of several factories. I returned in thought to my little hut in Svarga Ashram, and the memory of that fabulous solitude lifted my spirits. Long before, I had discovered the almost magical valences of my Himalayan images. Just as I had invented, in adolescence, a series of "spiritual exercises" by means of which I entered into certain imaginary universes and took refuge in them, so now it was enough to recall precisely, down to the last detail, my hut or the rocks on the bank of the Ganges, in order for me to find myself once more whole, serene, reconciled, and invulnerable.

One morning I was summoned to appear before the colonel. Four other officers were present. My turn had come to be judged for failure to submit to conscription on time. The guard who escorted me removed my belt at the beginning of the proceedings. The colonel asked me several questions. The prosecuting officer pointed out, rather gently, the gravity of my deed, reading from the Military Code the articles that pertained to my case. I ought to have been sentenced to I don't know how many weeks in the guardhouse. But he had quashed the indictment by pleading extenuating circumstances because, he added, this was a matter of an "eminent licentiate in philosophy who has studied three years in India." A young captain had been appointed counsel for my defense. He pled my case with obvious satisfaction. I was, of course, acquitted—and I was given back my belt. It would be necessary, however, for me to make up my three months' absence. So, instead of being discharged in October along with the other *teteriști*, my turn would not come until close to Christmas.

I was thrilled one evening in February to receive my first pass to leave the camp. A group of us *teteriști* set off together. I didn't dare separate myself from the group for fear of meeting some commissioned or noncommissioned officer and failing to salute him. Many times we saluted at a distance any man we saw in uniform—not only police captains and sergeants, but also firemen. We always saluted according to regulations: stamping one foot heavily on the pavement.

Not yet having purchased a dress uniform, I was wearing the tunic, cape, and boots issued at the camp. When I presented myself for the first time at the *Cuvântul* office, Nae Ionescu and all the editors were dumbfounded. They could hardly believe that I had come all the way from Ghencea to Calea Victoriei in those oversized fatigues, with those boots that threatened to slip off my feet if I should make an abrupt movement. Neither could they believe that some police sergeant had not stopped me on the street to ask for my identification papers. They said I looked exactly the way a deserter ought to look, as though I were wearing someone else's clothing!

But I was used to the outfit. Probably many people stared at me on the street, but since I was intent only on watching for uniforms, I took no notice of the inevitable ironic smiles of the passersby. All that winter, as soon as I reached home, I would change clothes, and once dinner was over, be off for a friend's place. I became acquainted with Ionel Jianu's sister, Leta Stark, and her friend Vera. They were architects. I liked spending evenings with them, and sometimes our conversations lasted until well past midnight. We discussed alchemy and Asian philosophies, in particular, and the history of religions.

I also went gladly to Bulevardu Elisabeta, to Haig Acterian and Marietta Sadova's apartment. One evening, without understanding why, I told them the whole story of what had happened in Bhawanipore and the reason why I had not set eyes on Dasgupta since. Up until then I had tried to think as infrequently as possible about Maitreyi. But I lived all the time with my memories of India. Wherever I went, whatever house I might visit, I would be required eventually to talk about India. Probably I looked forward to it, because I never declined an invitation. I also spoke about India with my comrades in arms, sitting around the stove, on nights I spent at the camp. But despite all this, there were whole blocks of memories concerning which I never spoke, things that, even if I had wished, I should not have known how to communicate: secret, inaccessible continents, like some Atlantis sunk in the depths of the sea. In a way, the more I dwelt upon images, characters, and events from what I called "historic India," and which constituted, ultimately, the elements of a two-dimensional biography, the more deeply I was thrust into that secret, other world, made up of incommunicable meanings and discoveries.

When I went to visit Rădulescu-Motru, I expected him to question me mostly about Indian philosophy. He had written me once in Calcutta that he had tried repeatedly to read the Upaniṣads and Vedāntan texts, but without success; he said he hoped I would be able to explain to him, when I returned, why such writings are considered to be of great interest *philosophically*. I found him younger, in better health, and more lucid than when I had known him in the first year at the university, in the fall of 1925. But he asked me very few questions concerning Indian philosophy. Instead, every time I visited him, Rădulescu-Motru would want to talk about my experiences in Bengal and the Himalayas, and about the political situation, about Gandhi and the nationalist movement in particular.

The one who never missed an opportunity to bring up the subject of Indian philosophy was Mircea Vulcănescu. He still lived in his parental home on Strada Popa Soare, but he was married (for the second time), and he and his wife Marguerite already had a little girl. He had grown rather stout in recent years, but his face was still quite handsome, dominated by large, black, deep-set eyes. He remained the same up until the last time I saw him ten years later—growing ever stouter, yet walking with a lively step, pacing the floor constantly, and talking incessantly but brilliantly on any topic with the same amazing coarseness and clarity. He read everything in all fields, and anything he undertook he did as well as anyone else. When he decided to learn to play bridge, he studied it methodically and stubbornly for several weeks—and then he became a champion. He wrote with equal facility and competence about problems of Eastern theology, the economics of banking, and modern novels. Once there fell into his hands a French review that was sponsoring a contest having to do with a detective novel it was publishing serially. Mircea read the novel and replied on the spot. And of course the solution he found was the right one. A few weeks later his name appeared at the head of the list.

He wrote a great deal but published little and only when forced to do so by friends or circumstances. He was, as he reminded us

Goethe had been, an "occasional writer." Thus he would intervene in some polemical exchange, or he would write an article in defense of a friend unjustly attacked. His writings appeared mainly in *Cuvântul*, not only because he liked the paper, but especially because of his great admiration and affection for Nae Ionescu—feelings he preserved to the end, even when, several years later, he was no longer in accord with the professor's political activities. Most of the time, however, Mircea wrote for himself and a few friends: essays, little studies on obscure or unfamiliar problems, elaborate plans for future treatises on theology, ethics, or political economics.

That year he was director of customs. I don't understand by what miracle he was able to maintain himself in that office for so many years, because he was more than just incorruptible: he was a man of rigid honesty, sometimes out of touch with reality. He confided to me once that he had no other criteria than the customs regulations, which he did not permit himself to interpret, but applied *ad literam*.

From him I learned that Stelian Mateescu had recently been confined to a mental institution. During the past few years he had somehow fallen into a religious mania, but in spite of this he had written several extraordinary novellas. Then, suddenly, he had gone to pieces. He burst into Mircea's place one evening, drew a large kitchen knife from underneath his overcoat, and rushed at him, ready to stab him. His plan had been to assassinate his best friends—to save them, as he thought, from the temptations of the Devil.

With the exception of Nae, Mircea was the only person with whom I discussed Indian philosophy to any great extent. He was interested especially in soteriology and aesthetics. With his prodigious memory, he quickly mastered the whole technical vocabulary. Other friends were astonished to hear him interrupt me to add a detail or to correct an expression. Since he had plenty of time, not only did he read my columns in *Cuvântul*, but he also listened to my talks, which I had begun giving over the radio. Adrian Maniu was at that time director of cultural programming at the radio station. He sent word through Ionel Jianu that he wanted to meet me. Accompanied by Jianu, I went to see him on Strada Edgar Quinet. He proposed that I read two papers per month of some twenty minutes each on the subject of India. I would receive 800 lei per lecture. I accepted gladly because, apart from my modest salary from *Cuvân-tul*, I had no other source of income, and at twenty-five I was ashamed to ask my parents for money.

It is probable that these radio talks, many of which were published in 1934 in the book *India*, contributed considerably to my popularity. When Ionel Jianu invited me to speak at the King Carol I Foundation about Rabindranath Tagore in the series of lectures of the Forum group that he had organized, the hall was packed. I spoke without notes and, unfortunately, without preparation—but my reception was all the more successful. I let myself be carried away more or less by "inspiration": I evoked the torrid nights of Bengal, trees laden with glowworms in Chandernagore, meetings and conversations with the poet at Shanti Niketan. I don't think the audience learned a great deal, but without my intending to do so, I transported them to Tagore's doorstep—and their enthusiasm knew no bounds.

At the exit, waiting for me with other friends, was Constantin ("Dinu") Noica. I had known him for a long time, ever since lycée. But since I was three or four years older than he (he entered the university the fall I left for India), we had never become friends. He had written me several letters while I was in Calcutta that excited me. The shy boy I had left behind had matured with surprising speed. Soon after my return I learned from friends about C. Noica's experiences at the university. During the first year he had attended classes irregularly and had read haphazardly, whatever came to hand. He was at that time, as he admitted smilingly later, quite "sociable." He liked to dance and he never missed a party. But at the end of the school year, in the summer, he realized he had gained nothing. He decided then to organize his life and his studies in an intelligent manner. As he said, "We know nothing except what we learn." He made up his mind to study philosophy in a thoroughgoing way. He followed the program he mapped out for himself all the way to the doctorate. Thus in the fall, when classes reopened, Dinu Noica was there, in the front row (he had come half an hour early to be able to choose the best seat), with his notebook in his lap. He attended with inflexible regularity the courses he had chosen. He undertook to learn Greek, and every day he read for a certain number of hours from some classic of philosophy. In this fashion he read *The Critique of Pure Reason* four times. No longer did he read to gain information, but to understand, to learn how those great philosophers *thought*: Plato, Aristotle, Kant, Hegel.

He was preparing now for the licentiate with P. P. Negulescu, but he did not plan to go abroad for his doctorate. On the one hand, he said that he had more to learn at home; and on the other he was planning to be married soon to Wendy Muston. I found out about these matters later, after we had begun to be friends. On the evening of my Tagore lecture he had come with a fellow university student, a young man from Sibiu with blond hair falling over his forehead—Emil Cioran. I remember that I saw him again soon afterward that spring at my attic, together with other friends—because, at the end of March, Rădulescu-Motru obtained a month's furlough for me to enable me to work on my thesis, and thus I resumed the life of a student. The dissertation was partly written, but in the English language; I was now laboring to translate into Romanian those chapters I considered would be of interest to the professors on the doctoral committee. (I set aside, for instance, much of my analysis of popular forms of yoga practice that later, in the French edition of 1936, was to attract the interest especially of Orientalists and historians of religions.)

At last I had regained my attic. I was able once more, as of old, to remain at my writing table without the worry that I would have to awaken at four the next morning in order to be back at the base on time. I bought and installed new shelves for my books from India. I found again the files and notebooks from Ripon Street and Bhawanipore. In the bottom of my heart, like a holy secret, I still cherished the decision to return as soon as I had obtained the doctorate. On the other hand, the Bucharest to which I had begun to become accustomed again still held a strong attraction for me. It seemed to me that I found myself in a city still unknown, full of resources; that I was living in a privileged moment when all of us could create, as I liked to say, "major works." I should not want to return to India before having *finished* something, before having published at least a part of my manuscripts.

That winter I transcribed from my notebooks a series of jottings and commentaries that were to appear a few months afterward in a little book of less than a hundred pages, *Soliloquii*. Mihail Sebastian, Ion Călugăru, and I decided to publish a series which we entitled *Cartea cu Semne* (The Book with Signs). I believe it all started with the assurance given us by Zaharia Stancu that Torouțiu, director of the Bukovina Printery, was willing to publish our collection under unusually favorable conditions. Torouțiu was satisfied with a modest advance; the balance we could pay after selling the first five or six hundred copies.

It was in this way that Zaharia Stancu had begun his publication of *Azi*. For the appearance of this review, in which I was later to be attacked repeatedly, I myself was to some extent responsible. Not only did I collaborate on it from the start (the first number opened with excerpts from *Soliloquii*, and in the second or third number I published pages from my Indian journal under the title *Șantier*); but in order to collect the sum needed for the advance, Stancu arranged to hold several public lectures and literary soirées in cities of Dunărea, and he asked me to speak (on India, of course). I agreed because George Mihail Zamfirescu—the author of *Madonă cu trandifiri* (Madonna with Roses), a book I very much liked—was coming along too. I remember Oltenița, Roșiorii-de-Vede, the amazing snowdrifts and the mud when the snow melted. I remember the poorly lighted auditoriums crammed with all sorts of people, from the mayor and the priest to lycée girls and boys. There were the families of the politicians and the inevitable young intellectual with the vague ambition to become a writer or scholar, who would come up after the lecture and bemoan his failure, which he blamed on his "environment." (I remember how rude I was once—and perhaps even unfair—when, while making my way through the mud under the pale, shadowy light of a gas street lamp and listening to my companion complaining, I interrupted him almost brutally: "Don't suppose that the Russian writers of the last century had any better streets. But they certainly had more talent!" I don't know whether or not I was right in rebuking him that way. But I was echoing my "Letters to a Provincial," I was repeating what I had proclaimed from the year 1927 onward: that nothing, *absolutely nothing*, can sterilize spiritual creativity so long as a man is—and realizes himself to be—*free*. Only the loss of freedom, or of the consciousness of freedom, can sterilize a creative spirit.

I don't know if Zaharia Stancu succeeded in underwriting the first issue of his review with what he earned from his "literary soirées" in Dunărea, but *Azi* appeared in the winter of 1932. Mihail Sebastian and Ion Călugăru, who contributed to that first number, each prepared also a volume for the collection, *Cartea cu Semne:* Sebastian, *Fragmente dintr'un carnet gasit* (Excerpts from a Notebook that was Found); and Călugăru, a volume of short stories. All three books appeared simultaneously in the spring of 1932. I remember entering Nae Ionescu's office one morning and presenting him suddenly with autographed copies of the three. Mihail Sebastian in particular was happy. It was his first book, and the fact that it had been published so quickly encouraged him to prepare another: a smaller volume of short stories, *Femei* (Women), which appeared the following autumn at Editura Ciornei.

Our books were favorably received by the critics. But with the Bukovina Printery handling the distribution, the readers had difficulty locating copies. We announced some ten titles for the series, with Mircea Vulcănescu, Dan Botta, and Paul Sterian among the contributors. The only other volumes to appear, however, were books of poetry by Sterian and Ilarie Voronca. Neither we nor Toroutiu were satisfied with the results, so by mutual agreement we abandoned the project.

That winter, at Mircea Vulcănescu's place, I met Dan Botta. He gave me a copy of his book of poems, *Eulalii*, about which I became quite enthusiastic. After that, he came to visit me from time to time. He was a tall man, blond haired and good-looking. When he was declaiming, he would hold his right arm as high as he could, shaking his index finger (the "apodictic finger," he called it) in a threatening way. The first time he set foot in my two rooms crammed with books, he exclaimed, "This is an Alexandrian library!" Although he read very little, and only "classics" (from folk poetry to Proust), he admired libraries containing instruments of specialized study: dictionaries, grammars, philological studies, critical editions, and such. He liked tracing down etymologies—the history of words excited him; and when he discovered a rare word, a forgotten adjective, an archaic expression, he would repeat it lovingly, pronouncing it slowly, in different tones, and murmuring from time to time, "How beautiful!"

The attic became again, as formerly, a place of meetings. Mircea Vulcănescu stopped in often on his way home, while Paul Sterian came with his wife Margareta in order to "recover his studious youth" of Paris. Margareta liked to peer through the porthole-like window while Paul was unveiling projects (a detective novel or a book of prayers). He had a way of breaking out suddenly with that shrill laugh of his, which you hesitated to believe was genuine—and then you would wait to see what he would say next, to see if he were going to laugh again—and it was this very thing which delighted him: to disorient his interlocutor and read bewilderment in his face. Like Mircea Vulcănescu, Sterian could write a great many things—but unlike Mircea, he wrote rapidly in those days, "making the pen fly," as he liked to say. Sometimes, in the course of one night, he would write several fine poems. At other times he would dictate a detective novel in the space of a week. He liked painting, but he had given it up, so we heard, on Margareta's account. "We copied each other unintentionally," Margareta was supposed to have said. But several years later I found out that Paul had rented a room somewhere in which he had set up an easel; and whenever he had a few free hours he would shut himself up there and paint. I never knew if the discovery of that secret room contributed to the crisis that erupted about that time, in 1935, which led later to the breakup of their marriage.

One who came often was Petru Comarnescu, and I remember that at first we conversed in English. Comarnescu had spent two years in California, where he had obtained a doctorate in philosophy, and he was determined at all costs not to forget the English language. He was then writing a series of articles about the American man and American civilization, which he later collected in a volume, *Homo Americanus*. But ordinarily he published literary, graphic arts, and musical reviews in various newspapers and magazines. He was indefatigable, kept himself up to date with everything going on in social, political, and artistic circles, and was always full of projects. He organized literary soirées and a series of public lectures. Thanks to him there would come into existence the following autumn the group known as Criterion.

,   ,   ,

After the month of furlough, I was moved to the translating service of the General Staff Headquarters. I worked in a large, well-lighted room on the top floor along with several other *teterişti* and two officers. Our job was to translate articles from British, American, and Italian military publications. I remember once translating a handbook on chemical warfare and methods for defense against it. Anxiously and sadly I translated it, because the methods of defense seemed illusory to me. Working at the same table with me was a young Bessarabian. He began giving me lessons in Russian, and he translated for me a long and difficult article by Stcherbatsky on the history of Buddhist logic.

The month of May had come upon me unawares, and when I returned home in the evenings I felt that the whole world was mine. I always stopped at the *Cuvântul* office to see Nae Ionescu. I had become friends with Mihail Sebastian and Gheorghe Raco-veanu, and often we ate together. It became our custom to gather on Sunday afternoons at the home of Floria Capsali and Mac Constantinescu. They had an old house in the Crucea-de-Piatră neighborhood, with a garden as large as an orchard. In one section of the garden Mac had made a volleyball court. A number of people came regularly, arriving early enough to play volleyball: the Polihroniades, the Vulcănescus, and the Sterians, along with Dan Botta, Petru Comarnescu, Mihail Sebastian, Haig Acterian, and Marietta Sadova. Every Sunday new faces would appear: Marioara Voiculescu and her son the magistrate, Lily Popovici, Harry Brauer, Sylvia Capsali, Gabriel and Adrian Negreanu, and many others. Another frequent attendant was Nina Mareş, a girl who occupied a room on the top floor of the same building on Pasajul Imobiliara in which the *Cuvântul* office was located. We were all acquainted with her. At that time she was an employee of the telephone company. Nina was a petite blonde and good company, and although (as I learned later) she led a rather hard life, she was always laughing and never mentioned her troubles. She was an especially good friend of Mihail Sebastian, for whom she typed novels from his manuscripts: pages of tiny handwriting with many obliterations, which no typographer would have been able to decipher.

In the evenings we would all go to eat at a tavern in the neighborhood. Sometimes there were more than twenty of us. And because we came from related, though different, worlds—the theater, graphic arts, dance, journalism, literature, philosophy—we got along very well together. When I spoke to Nae about our get-togethers and meals, he marveled and expressed envy. In his youth, he said, there had not been such intimacy among artists, journalists, and scholars. What interested him most was the fact that our meetings included painters like Mac Constantinescu and Marcel Ianscu, sculptors such as Miliţa Patraşcu, actresses like Lily Popovici, Sorana

Ţopa, Marietta Sadova, Marieta Rareş, and Marioara Voiculescu, as well as writers, philosophers, and musicians. "You'll have to invent a new language," he said, "but since you have Mircea Vulcănescu with you, you'll succeed!"

One Sunday evening while we were eating at the tavern, Comarnescu proposed that we organize a series of public lectures-symposia, to be held at the King Carol I Foundation, on the subject either of great contemporary personalities or a number of current issues. Five or six speakers would participate at each symposium, the majority of them chosen from our group. To preside over the sessions, we would invite a scholar somewhat older than ourselves. Everyone began to suggest names and subjects. The discussion continued until well past midnight in Mac and Floria's garden. But although we all showed enthusiasm for it, the project might not have been carried out for several months—perhaps not even till fall—had not Petru Comarnescu taken it upon himself to rent the auditorium at the King Carol I Foundation, and to concern himself with the compilation of the programs and the printing and distribution of advertisements. He asked us each for 1,000 lei in order to be able to make the deposit on the auditorium. It was understood we would put the finishing touches to the whole program the following Sunday.

Without our realizing it, the Criterion group had come into being. None of us suspected on that summer night, when on our way home we continued searching for names and subjects, that we were planning the most original and significant collective manifestation of the "young generation." (I believe that we could still consider ourselves young: the average age of the responsible nucleus of the group was at that time twenty-eight.) And certainly no one could have imagined the tremendous response our undertaking was to receive. We hoped to attract an audience large enough to cover our expenses. We never suspected that we would be forced to repeat certain symposia as many as two or three times!

The next Sunday we soon came to an agreement as to which cultural and political personalities four or five of us would discuss first, from different but complementary perspectives: Gandhi, Lenin, Mussolini, Charlie Chaplin, Proust, Gide, Freud, Bergson, Picasso, and Stravinsky. We projected another series of symposia centering around several problems: the contemporary Romanian novel, modern Romanian art, America and American culture, Asia as seen from the West, and several others.

And on that same Sunday we made plans to go hiking in the Bucegi mountains and spend a week at Casa Pesterii and Bulboki.

It was the first of July, and thanks again to Rădulescu-Motru I had obtained a furlough from the General Staff. We stopped for a day at Breaza where Mac and Floria had rented a house for the summer. Besides myself, the group included Sebastian, Comarnescu, Botta, Vulcănescu, Lily Popovici, Marietta Sadova, Haig Acterian, the Polihroniades, Adrian Negreanu, and Sylvia Capsali. The next day we took the train to Sinaia; from there we began our climb toward Pietrele Arse. And so, after four years, I saw the Bucegi again. I was back once more, with a different group of friends, in the mountains of my adolescence. It was amazing to me how precisely I remembered certain shortcuts along the path. I told my companions in advance about cliffs that lay ahead and springs we were approaching. And, as I had done in former times, I went swimming in the icy waters of the Ialomicioara.

We stayed a week. With the assistance of Mary Polihroniade I translated *Pygmalion*. Mihail Sebastian and Petru Comarnescu wrote articles when they felt like it. But every morning we took long hikes in the direction of Bulboki or Piatra Craiului. Evenings we kindled a fire of dry wood and branches. Dan Botta recited fragments of folk poetry on which, though continually being interrupted by Polihroniade's jokes, Mircea Vulcănescu gave commentaries from unexpected, improbable perspectives. We all talked, by turns or at the same time; and between the laughter and interruptions, we listened to one another and understood.

Each of us, in his or her own way, was reliving vacations of childhood and adolescence. We were acquainted well enough not to be self-conscious about enjoying one another's company, and well enough to succeed in being spontaneous without bombast or vulgarity. That week spent in the Bucegi delighted us so much that we decided to return every summer. And we held to our word for a number of years, although the group that climbed Pietrele Arse was not always the same.

Back in Bucharest, the attic was hot as an oven, and I remembered with melancholy the ceiling fans on Ripon Street. Toward sunset I would come home from the General Staff, but the oppressive heat in the attic was no inducement to work. As often as I could, I met with friends in the evenings. Frequently I went to eat at an outdoor restaurant ("summer garden") with Haig and Marietta, and with Sorana Topa, whom I had met recently. I had seen her playing in Zamfirescu's *Domnişoara Nastasia*, and although it seemed to me she overacted her part (sometimes I had the impression I was watching a Russian drama), I liked her. Sorana insisted on citing to me what Nae Ionescu had written about her: that she was the most precious gift Moldavia had given us since Eminescu. She was, indeed, a Moldavian from head to toe. Rather tall, robust, with a round, almost chubby face, she had hair the color of ripened grain. Although she read all sorts of learned books and had recently discovered—and come to venerate—Krishnamurti, she was proud of the fact she had been born and reared in the country, uncultured, playing in the dust along with other peasant children. She had much charm, and yet she could be exasperating. She was good company, generous with her coworkers at the theater, engaging in self-analysis and analyzing her interlocutor for hours on end. I was soon to realize that she never ran down.

I don't believe I really liked her, but I always enjoyed meeting her at Marietta's. Then she invited me to tea in her little apartment near Cişmigiu. We talked a long while, and certain observations and intuitions of hers impressed me. On another occasion she read me the beginning of a play, *Genesis*, which I thought surprisingly original. I came then as often as I could after leaving the General Staff. She told me about her experiences at the Conservatory of Iaşi and she spoke of the nights in Iaşi. Only when she tried to persuade me that Krishnamurti was the greatest genius of the twentieth century did I lose my patience. She had met Krishnamurti that summer at Ommen, in the Netherlands, and she had returned enthusiastic. She did not doubt that Krishnamurti alone understood "Life" (and she pronounced it with a capital letter). Sorana, too, was fascinated with "Life." She spoke of nothing else: the miracle of "Life" and the crimes we commit daily, every one of us, against ourselves and "Life" by refusing to live simply, spontaneously—sterilizing ourselves with clichés, formulas, and systems. Actually, she was right, but she always spoke in the name of "the Absolute," of "Life" and "Love," and this pretentious, spiritualistic jargon, presented with all the pathos and skill of an authentic actress, drove me out of my wits. Never have I felt more strongly the necessity, the magnificence, the *healthiness* of vulgarity than I did after a few hours of talking with Sorana. I realized, of course, that I was dealing with an actress who had known considerable success, but now was on her way to destroying her career—because, perhaps without realizing it, she had become detached from the theater and was refusing to make the effort to obtain an important role, sometimes allowing a whole season to pass without appearing on stage, or appearing in roles worthy of a novice. And she had done all this because she believed she thirsted for the "Absolute" and believed she had discovered the way to reach it. The price Sorana Țopa had paid for having the right to speak about "Life" as if she understood it was so great that her friends at least ought not to have lost their patience while listening to her. Only after returning home, sometimes rather late at night, did I realize that I had been wrong to interrupt her sarcastically—sometimes even abusively—in her spiritualistic, Krishnamurtian monologues. I would promise myself then to be more understanding the next day.

. . . For now, in September, we were meeting daily. Sometimes we went out to eat at a nearby restaurant and continued our discussion. She had read *Isabel*, but she didn't like it. She read everything I published in *Cuvântul* and *Vremea*, and sometimes she praised me excessively, while at other times she criticized me quite frankly. She was unpredictable, especially in her moods. She would burst out laughing immediately after a pathetic tirade; she would become sad to the point of tears in the middle of a hymn to Life. While attempting to detach herself from everything, she remained nevertheless aggressively feminine, capricious, bizarre. In spite of all her strident ways, she still possessed much charm. And that charm, added to her beauty and talent, would have been truly irresistible if she had not annihilated herself, furiously and stubbornly, in trying to become something other than what she was.

／　　　　　／　　　　　／

I cannot believe that after two months of meeting with her almost daily, I did not realize what was about to happen. Sorana asked me once, tactfully enough, if there was "anyone in my life." I was content to reply that there *had* been someone, and that the experience had been such a bitter and unhappy one that I felt no need to repeat it. As far as I could judge, there was no one in her life for the moment. In a way, I had been forewarned, and yet I continued seeing her with regularity, every evening. I told myself, probably, that not being in love with her I was running no great risk—although the affair with Jenny ought to have put me on my guard. On the other hand, in a vague way, I felt attracted to her, perhaps to about the same degree that her presence exasperated me. I felt I *had* to see her every day, although often from the first word I regretted having come. But I knew if I should leave immediately, I would rue it. At other times I would tell myself it was useless to resist: I was alone and I did not like being alone; on the other hand, no matter what might happen, in a year I'd be back in India, and then I'd smile about my scruples and hesitations. From the perspective I chose to assume, whatever might happen would be of no great importance.

And at first I believed that it really would *not* have any great importance. As I descended the stairs of her apartment one morning in October, I said to myself that all it meant was that now I too, like every other young man of my age, had a "relationship." I continued going to her place as soon as I left the General Staff. Then, in addition to the permission I had to speak at the Carol I Foundation, I obtained another furlough, and we could meet in the afternoons. Mornings I shut myself away in the attic and worked. Evenings our group met at various friends' places, putting the final touches to the first Criterion symposia.

I believe it was I who inaugurated the cycle on Freud. Among other speakers for that symposium I remember only Mircea Vulcănescu and Paul Sterian, but there were five or six of us, including a psychoanalyst. When I entered the hall I could hardly believe my eyes. The auditorium was full and overflowing. Seats on the main floor had been sold out well in advance, and people were crowded into the balcony and galleries. They sat wherever they could: on the stairs, on the railings. And then, because no one could hold them back, they had pushed into the main auditorium and were leaning against the walls and even sitting on the stage. Likely we should not have been able to begin if Petru Comarnescu had not announced in the auditorium and foyer that we would repeat the symposium a few days later, and that with the cooperation of the fire department we would close and bolt the entryway door.

I had agreed to speak about Freud because I thought I could decipher in his work a final phase in the desacralization of Old Testament monotheism and propheticism. Freud's certainty that he had found a unique and universal meaning for psychomental life and human creativity, that he had forged the magic key that would unlock all enigmas from dreams and *actes manqués* to the origin of religion, morals, and civilization—this certainty, I said, betrayed the monotheistic fervor of the Hebraic genius. In the same way, the passion expended by Freud in promoting, imposing, and defending psychoanalysis from any "heresy" is reminiscent of the intolerance and frenzy of Old Testament prophets. In a certain sense, Freud believed that his discoveries were destined to transform mankind, to "save" it. Psychoanalysis satisfied the thirst for the absolute, characteristic of the Judaic genius, the belief that there is a *single* royal road to the Spirit, and it betrays the specifically Hebraic revulsion against pluralism, polytheism, and idolatry.

I don't know how clearly and articulately I said these things that evening. Like the other participants, I was rewarded with loud, prolonged applause. I learned later that Emil Cioran had been so impressed that he had come to hear us the second time when we repeated the symposium. (We repeated it twice, and then we gave it I don't know how many times in provincial cities.)

The other symposia followed, two per week, with equal success. A half hour ahead of time the auditorium of the King Carol I Foundation would be full to the last seat, and the participants would have difficulty making their way through the crowds gathered on the sidewalk. With great effort, assisted by the police, they would gain entrance to the crowded foyer. The municipal police had found it necessary to send a dozen sergeants and several captains to ensure traffic circulation in front of the Foundation, and to defend the entrances from the throng. This unprecedented success disturbed the Minister of the Interior, irritated a goodly number of journalists and writers, and gave rise to all sorts of envy and jealousy. And of course our risks increased as the personalities we discussed became more controversial. Just as we feared, the symposium on Gide gave rise to incidents. André Gide had visited Soviet Russia a short while before and was considered a Communist. That evening about a hundred nationalist students tried to gain entry to the auditorium. Halted by the police, they began to sing and raise a clamor. The symposium began, but the hall was charged with electricity. Several of our group went outside to talk with the head of the demonstrators. They parleyed for better than an hour. The students claimed they had not come to provoke a disturbance, but only to listen, to be sure that no apology for communism was made. Finally, we let them inside. The symposium came to an end soon afterward, but I do not think it ended that evening as it had been planned. Shortly after being admitted into the crowded hall the students began shouting, and the moderator closed the session with a few ironic, sarcastic remarks that were lost in the tumult.

A less serious incident, and one that ended in our favor, occurred at the symposium on Charlie Chaplin. Among the speakers was Mihail Sebastian. When his turn came, someone shouted from the gallery: "One Jew talking about another Jew!" Mihail was on his feet, holding several sheets of paper on which he had written an outline of his remarks. He became very pale. Tearing up his notes, he took a step forward and began to speak in a voice choked with emotion. "I had planned to speak about a certain aspect of Chaplin's acting," he said, "but someone out there has called attention to our Jewishness. So I shall speak as a Jew about the Jew, Charlie Chaplin."

Suddenly the audience burst into applause. Mihail Sebastian raised his arm. "Thank you!" he said, and then he improvised one of the most moving and intelligent lectures I have ever had the opportunity to hear. He presented a Chaplin whom only someone from Eastern Europe could imagine and understand. He spoke about the loneliness of man in Chaplin's films as a reflection of the loneliness of the ghetto. When he finished speaking twenty minutes later, he was rewarded with a tremendously enthusiastic ovation. Part of the audience rose to its feet. We had won a battle, and we knew it. In the office that connected with the speaker's box, there was exultation. For joy, Nina Mareş began to dance and hug us one after another.

For the symposium on Lenin, we invited both Belu Silber and Lucreţiu Pătrăşcanu to take part. We wanted to have two Marxists to participate along with Mircea Vulcănescu and Mihail Polihroniade, who were prepared to criticize communism in the name of democracy and nationalism. Belu Silber I had met some time before at the editorial office of *Cuvântul*. He and Racoveanu had been friends ever since the latter had written an article in his defense when he was on trial two years earlier, accused of espionage. Belu Silber had been moved greatly by the article and immediately after his acquittal he had come to thank Racoveanu. From then on he visited the editorial office rather frequently. He became good friends especially with Mircea Vulcănescu, Ion Călugăru, and Paul Sterian. Small in stature, Silber was a brilliant, well-educated man, and although he repeated constantly that he was a Marxist, he seemed neither dogmatic nor intolerant. He admired me in particular because in my articles on India I attacked colonialism and the British Raj.

Lucrețiu Pătrășcanu I met only that evening, I believe. I liked his face, which was kind and at the same time grave. He spoke without éclat, but sincerely and with a wise sobriety. Interruptions by students in the audience didn't bother him. He waited until the uproar died down, and then he took up his exposition again, calmly and intently. In contrast, the students interrupted Polihroniade with applause every time he spoke of the necessity of a nationalistic revolution. And when he referred to the expression of Lenin's that the bourgeois state is a cadaver that will topple at a single blow, he was applauded as much by the nationalistic students as by the groups of Communist sympathizers who had been drawn to the Foundation by the scheduled appearance of Pătrășcanu.

Following this symposium the rumor was spread, especially among the security forces, that the Criterion group was crypto-Communistic. The truth was that the only Communist among us was Belu Silber. But the audacity we had shown in inviting the secretary of the Communist Party himself to speak at the Carol I Foundation had been misconstrued. We had tried to be "objective": *audiatur et altera pars.* We said that, in a major culture, all currents of thought can be presented. We felt strong enough not to be afraid of confrontations with ideologies and systems contrary to our own beliefs. Likewise, we felt that we could not get beyond cultural provincialism except by annulling the inferiority complexes and infantile defense mechanisms inherent in any minor culture. Having come to believe in the creative possibilities of the Romanian genius—as the majority of us did, although for different reasons—we no longer feared "evil influences" or "subversive ideas." On the other hand, we considered ourselves adults; we were unwilling to have people shout at us, "Don't play with fire!"—because we knew very well that we were not playing.

That which was later called the "spirit of Criterion" became clearer and more articulate the longer the program ran. But even from the first few symposia, the public discerned that this was a significant cultural experiment and one of great proportions—and they remained faithful to us until the end. Even when the subject was not a sensational one like Lenin, Freud, or Gide, the auditorium was full. In the symposium about the contemporary Romanian novel, Mihail Sebastian executed Cezar Petrescu *con molto brio*, and he was extremely hard on Ionel Teodoreanu, the most popular novelist of the day—reserving all his plaudits for Hortensia Papadat-Bengescu, Camil Petrescu, and Matei Caragiale. But Vulcănescu showed in what sense Cezar Petrescu's novels are integrated into a Romanian literary tradition and are significant even if they are not artistically valuable. What excited the enthusiasm of the audience was the dialogue between members of the Criterion group. Very seldom, and only in the case of sensitive subjects—for instance, Lenin and Mussolini—did the speakers get together beforehand and make rigorous preparations for the symposium. Ordinarily, each one would announce the observations he had in mind to develop. Only if we saw that two or more of the participants intended to make the same points did we ask them to modify their plans. In any event, the spontaneity of the dialogue was almost always assured. This gave rise, at times, to amusing scenes. For instance, when we discussed America vis-à-vis Europe and the Far East, Comarnescu, who identified himself to some extent with the American man and American culture, endured rather calmly the criticisms I made in the name of Oriental spirituality, but he lost his temper when Sebastian derided *Homo Americanus* in the name of the French spirit, and he tried to interrupt him several times during his presentation. Even after being called to order by the moderator, he continued to shout, to guffaw, or to turn his back abruptly in his chair every time he thought Sebastian went too far.

For the members of Criterion, the symposium did not end in the auditorium of the Foundation. We all gathered at the Cafe Corso, where we occupied a whole corner of the second floor and continued our discussion until after midnight. Usually Dan Botta, who rarely took part in the symposia, expressed his opinions then, succinctly and mercilessly. He never forgot to remind us of the responsibility we had toward the public. For him, this meant above all the duty to lift the public, not up to our level, but beyond, to our *ideals*. Dan believed that Criterion could effect, in the minds of the more intelligent members of the audience, an operation of Platonic *anamnesis*. In attending our symposia, where many points of view were presented and debated, the public actually was witnessing a new type of Socratic dialogue. The goal we were pursuing was not only to inform people; above all, we were seeking to "awaken" the audience, to confront them with ideas, and ultimately to modify their mode of being in the world.

Of course there ensued long, animated discussions. Not because the others did not share Dan's ideas about the role of Criterion, but because they were not always in accord with the methods he advocated. Botta insisted that at least one of the participants ought not to make any concessions to the average listener, but instead ought to use the technical vocabulary of metaphysics, science, poetry, or whatever the subject might be. Usually it happened that way anyhow. But as some of us saw it, the very fact that we were debating difficult problems was courageous enough without aggravating the difficulty by employing excessively technical language. But of course we were all agreed that every speaker was free to use whatever style he pleased.

Sorana Țopa was always with us. Accompanying her home, I would have to listen once again to her criticisms of the symposium—her criticisms of me in particular, if I had happened to have spoken that evening. Sometimes her observations were just and invaluable, but at other times they seemed irrelevant and pretentious. On the first of December, 1932, I concluded my military service and received my discharge papers. Now Sorana and I could spend even more time together. This concentrated and prolonged intimacy was not always to my liking. For one thing, Sorana's presence was exhausting. With her it was necessary to be unceasingly intelligent, profound, original—and above all, "spontaneous." Love, for her, was a constant "burning at white heat," as she liked to say. This meant, among other things, that any prolonged silence, any banality uttered out of weariness or inattentiveness, constituted evidence of indifference or absentmindedness, and thus required to be interpreted laboriously in order to be understood and assumed as such, and at last corrected.

Often I breathed a sigh of relief when I regained the solitude of my attic. I still had much need of that solitude. The thesis was almost finished and Nina Mareş was typing the chapters as fast as I took them to her. But in addition to the translation and reworking of the thesis, and in addition to the articles I was writing, and the radio talks and symposia presentations I was preparing, a new project had begun to tempt me. I had read in the papers the announcement of a literary prize being offered by Cultura Naţională for a previously unpublished novel. Among the judges were Perspessicius, Şerban Cioculescu, and G. Călinescu. These names encouraged me to contribute. I told myself that at least I should be judged by authentic literary critics. At first I planned to start over again with my novel begun in Calcutta, *Petru şi Pavel*—but the portions I reread discouraged me. It was then that I decided to write *Maitreyi*. On the one hand I felt that I had to relive, in order to consume it forever, the drama that had changed my life so radically, requiring me to renounce all the projects I had planned for my stay in India. On the other hand, I felt I could finish the novel by March 15, the deadline for submission of manuscripts—whereas *Petru şi Pavel* might require at least six months of work. Since the manuscripts had to be submitted anonymously, I spoke to no one about my decision.

One evening in December I sat down at my writing table and, with a thrill, opened the envelope in which I had collected in the fall of 1930 several relics: the notes Maitreyi had sent me after we could no longer see each other, the letters from Dasgupta, an old photograph, a few dried flowers, and a lock of hair. Then I began reading my journal for those years, even the pages that I had not dared to reread before. I did not realize that evening that my decision to write *Maitreyi* would cost me my one last chance to return to India.

12. *"Man without a Destiny..."*

IN ORDER to obtain freedom to be alone in my attic, I had to confess to Sorana that I was writing a novel. Just as I expected, she was fascinated when she learned the subject of the book. I had long since told her about what had happened in Bhawanipore. She had listened sympathetically and gravely, but, as she admitted later, she had not really taken seriously this adventure of tender youth. It had not been a *true* passion, a "burning at white heat" comparable, she implied, to our current relationship. Still, she could not allow herself a retrospective jealousy because, as she specified after telling me about her great passions of the past, our lives had had a new beginning from the moment we met. Together we were living a new life, and not even our common past counted for very much. The only thing having value or meaning was the "present"—more precisely, that which she had learned from Krishnamurti to call the present. Nevertheless, she regretted that I did not want to submit revised and corrected versions of *Romanul adolescentului miop* and *Gaudeamus*, which she had read recently and considered exceptional works—much more interesting, for instance, than *Isabel.*

I wrote mostly at nights, when I knew no one would be coming to knock on my attic door. The first chapters were penned quickly, almost without difficulty. But little by little I found myself again in that fabulous time in Bhawanipore, and I realized that no longer was I writing a novel as I had intended, but a confession. Often I copied whole pages from *The Journal,* and if that journal for the summer of 1930 had been more extensive, perhaps I would have transcribed it in its entirety. Not for a single moment did I stop to consider what an indiscretion I was preparing to perpetrate. Sitting in front of those blank pages, writing about people and events that had played such a decisive role in my youth, it was impossible for me to "invent." I changed the names of the characters, of course, except for Maitreyi and her sister Chabu, but I let myself give correct dates, addresses, and telephone numbers. Likewise, I changed the occupations of Dasgupta and the narrator, and I drastically modified the conclusion, as if I wished to separate myself definitively from Maitreyi. And of course I bathed that faraway world in a pale golden light, radiated from memories and melancholia. But it is no less true that if it were to have been read by certain persons in Calcutta, the novel would have needed no key to have been deciphered. I never thought, however, about the possibility of its being read in Calcutta. In fact, I never thought about its being read by strangers in Bucharest where I was writing it. I simply did not "visualize" a public. At most, I wondered what my friends would think, should the novel have the luck to receive the prize and be published. I could not even say that I wrote it for myself or for Maitreyi. I wrote it somewhat "impersonally," as a testimony *in aeternum.*

At that time, on the eve of Christmas of 1932, I had not yet become aware of all these things. I was still living in the euphoria of beginnings. After a year and a half, I was once more writing a novel, and this time it was an autobiographical one. I could be alone again, day and night, because Sorana had gone away for two weeks to Moldavia, to spend the holidays with her people. I also spent Christmas with my family, but as often as I could I met with friends. We had decided to get together on New Year's Eve at Mia Steriade's place—or rather, in the rooms occupied by Mia's father, the painter, at the Kalindera Museum. Almost the entire Criterion group was there, plus a few other guests. Everyone had contributed a certain sum, and several had taken it upon themselves to decorate the halls, purchase wines, and prepare a buffet. We hired a pianist, so that those who wished could dance until dawn. Truly, it was the most successful New Year's Eve party our group had ever had.

As far as I was concerned, however, I didn't know what to think of myself. I examined myself and tried to understand—in vain. A few days earlier, something totally unexpected had occurred. It was so unexpected that it would have been impossible for me to have imagined its happening even half an hour before. Three days after Christmas, in the evening, I was at Floria and Mac's place with several friends, among them Nina Mareş. I don't know why, but I looked at her hands, and they seemed remarkably small. I took her hands in mine. Her fingers were as tiny and delicate as those of a child. I couldn't bear to let go of those hands. Nina smiled, a little embarrassed—and some of our friends regarded us curiously. She, as well as several other friends, knew about Sorana. Often at the *Cuvântul* office, or upstairs in her little room where Mihail Sebastian and I frequently went to drink coffee, I had confessed how difficult Sorana could be, and Nina had consoled me, at the same time showing amusement. The three of us had become very good friends, and as often as we could we would take dinner together. We were such good friends that a "relationship" between Nina and one of us men would have seemed a crime against our common friendship. I knew how fond Nina was of Mihail, and he knew how much she thought of me.

But on that evening I didn't understand what was happening to me. Neither did I understand when I escorted her home and kissed her good night. Back in the attic, I tried to write, but I didn't succeed. I fell asleep very late. The next day and the day after I remained shut in the attic, writing. I told myself I ought not to see her again, but I went to her room that same evening. We ate dinner together, we went to a movie, and then I spent the night with her.

But at the New Year's Eve party I tried to conduct myself as I had before, as a very good friend.

I had learned Nina's life story some time before this. When very young, she had married an army officer, Ionescu, who by now had attained the rank of colonel and was garrisoned in a town in Bessarabia. Five or six years later, while they were living in Braşov, Nina had fallen in love with a young lieutenant who was quite handsome, and as I realized after meeting him later, surprisingly intelligent and cultured. Eventually their relationship provoked a scandal. The husband would not under any circumstance agree to a divorce, so Nina left home. The lieutenant's father, a general with a famous name, tried to rescue his son by sending him on a mission to Paris. He considered, probably, that a marriage preceded by such a scandal might ruin his son's career. The young man obeyed, but he announced to his family and his superiors that as soon as he returned from his assignment he would marry Nina. (Ionescu, meanwhile, had agreed to a divorce.)

And probably that is what would have happened if at the last moment a tragi-comic incident had not intervened. On the eve of his departure from Paris, the friends of the lieutenant gave him a farewell dinner. Several Romanian girls were invited, including one who had just arrived from the homeland. I don't know whether or not it was a plot arranged by the general, but the young woman, with the help of the lieutenant's friends, succeeded in getting him drunk. The next day, in her hotel room, with the lieutenant still befuddled and in bed, a civil marriage ceremony was performed before the consul and the required witnesses.

When the newspapers in Brasoy announced the marriage, Nina suffered such a shock that she required hospitalization. In vain did the lieutenant telegraph that he had been the victim of a farce and that he had filed a request for a divorce. In vain did he return alone, leaving his wife in Paris. For a long time Nina refused to see him. And for a long time the doctors doubted she would retain her sanity. She stayed at the clinic for three or four months. After learning that the lieutenant had obtained a divorce, she agreed to see him. She confessed to him that her love had grown cold, and she told him he was free to do anything he wished. Of course, the young man couldn't believe it. He continued visiting her at the clinic, and later at the German boarding house to which she moved. He assured her that he would wait for her, that he would follow her everywhere, that he could not believe she wouldn't forgive him some day, and that he was determined to wait for that day—if need be, five, ten, or fifty years. She replied that she had forgiven him, but that she did not love him any longer—that she *could not* love him any longer, no matter how hard she might try. But he continued to come, laden with flowers and presents. They sat talking, and Nina disclosed her plans: since it had been necessary for her to give up all she owned to her husband in exchange for the divorce, she must now think about a way of making a living. She had decided to go to Bucharest and enter a secretarial school. At first, until she could find work, she would live with an uncle, General Negreanu. And that is what she did.

A year later the lieutenant was promoted to the rank of captain and moved to Bucharest. He could not believe his eyes when he saw Nina living in a little room on the top floor and working eight hours a day. He spoke to her again about their love, and Nina interrupted him dreamily: "Yes, truly it was a great love. I'll never regret it!"

Then the captain tried to win her by a different tactic. He began to drink heavily and would come in the evenings, drunk, to wait for her at the entrance to her apartment house, begging her to take pity on his youth, his career. Very kindly, Nina would try to persuade him to go home. It was useless. "I'll go to the prostitutes!" he shouted, seeing her start for the elevator. "It wouldn't be the first time," she replied. (I myself witnessed such a scene one evening when I was leaving the *Cuvântul* office. Nina became paler than normal, but she smiled with her usual self-control. The captain had tears in his eyes.) Once, late at night, he climbed the stairs to the top floor and began pounding on her door—until the neighbors came out and, by means of threats, forced him to leave. On those rare occasions when she found him sober, Nina tried to talk with him seriously, urging him to seek a wife worthy of him. She always received the same reply: he was waiting for her. (He did wait for her, indeed, some five or six years, and he did not take a wife until after Nina had married.)

That autumn, when Nina told me the whole story, she added, "I regret very much that it turned out like this. I'd like to be able to love him again, at least a little—because I forgave him long ago—but I can't. Probably I can never love anyone again. From here on I shall have to be content just to know men as friends." That is why Sebastian, Racoveanu, and I believed that Nina could be such a perfect friend.

′ ′ ′

Days passed, and still I didn't understand. Sometimes I told myself that the recent events would count more in Nina's life than in mine, that perhaps this was destiny's way of drawing her out of her solitude. With perfect discretion, Nina never told me that she loved me, nor did she ask me what my intentions were. But once Mihail Sebastian returned from Brăila, it was necessary to confess to him. He declared that he would forgive us only after he had been convinced that the three of us would remain friends as before and, in a few months' time, he was convinced.

However, I didn't know whether or not I ought to confess to Sorana what had happened during her absence. It was not only the inevitable cowardice of an "inexperienced" youth who did not know how to break off a "relationship." As the days passed I discovered that the situation was more complex than I had imagined it. I discovered, for instance, that I didn't want to "lose" Sorana, that I needed her, that actually I was fond of her, no matter how much her presence at times wearied me. I told myself that since Nina had never mentioned love, she might decide any day now to break off with me, and I did not consider that I should have any right to object.

Meanwhile, I continued to cherish the hope of returning to India immediately after receiving my degree. That hope gave me strength enough to endure the difficulties into which I was sinking ever more deeply as time passed. Both women knew I had to finish the novel by the fifteenth of March, so I was free to visit them only when I wished. Since Nina worked at the office until evening, I met Sorana in the afternoons. I had an excuse ready now when she asked me to take dinner with her or spend the night: I had to go home and work. And in truth, each night, after separating with difficulty from one or the other of them, I would stay at my writing table until long past midnight. Only at night did I succeed in finding myself again—although never entirely. I should have realized that in retelling the events of 1930 for others, those who would read the novel eventually, I was letting myself be drawn again, almost involuntarily, into an adventure in which I might be lost. (For me, at that time, "lost" meant, above all, not being able to return to India.) But concerning *this* danger I was unaware. Reliving my passion at Bhawanipore, I asked myself if all that had happened so recently, from Christmas on, did not constitute a lie, aggravated by a blasphemy. To my astonishment, I was forced to admit it was not. It might be something else, but it wasn't a lie. These two women *existed*. If, by some miracle, I had been able to leave immediately for India, undoubtedly I would have gone, but it would have pained me deeply to separate from them.

I thought about these things and they tortured me when, toward dawn, I tried to go to sleep after having written for five or six hours without a break. I would awaken exhausted, and for some time I would lie there in bed, trying to remember where I was, what year it was, trying to remember what had happened to me. Sometimes I felt I was being tested, that fate was preparing me again for something new, something that would alter the trajectory of my life once more. Then, for several moments, I would see *signs,* like beacon lights suddenly lit in the darkness and quickly extinguished—too quickly for me to be able to grasp their meaning. I would raise myself on the bed, knowing that *signs* were being given me—but how was I to decipher them?

I kept postponing the denouement, the choice I knew was inevitable. In February I deposited at the office of the Faculty of Letters three copies of the thesis, as required. The chairman of the committee was D. Gusti; P. P. Negulescu and Rădulescu-Motru were also readers. I waited for the date of the public debate of the thesis to be set. But I did nothing to prepare for my "entrance into the university," for which Nae had worked so persistently. True, I had published in recent years three lengthy studies in *Revista de Filosofie,* another three in *Ricerche Religiose,* and my article "Cunoştinţele botanice in vechea Indie" had appeared in *Buletinul Societatăţii de Ştiinţe din Cluj.* I had prepared the doctoral thesis for publication in the event I should decide to publish it in Romanian. But since my return from India, I had been engaged in a frantic and multilateral life: articles for *Cuvântul* and *Vremea,* radio talks, the Criterion, and lectures in the provinces; and this frenzy bothered some of my professors. They wondered, probably, if I were not spreading myself too thin. Learning that I was on the way to completing a second novel, Nae smiled. "I shall have to explain to Rădulescu-Motru that you need money again," he said. I tried to protest: a *true,* authentic university of today extends itself far beyond its classrooms; the newspaper, the lecture platform, the radio—all these participate in a general studies curriculum. Besides that, there is the tradition of the Romanian university, I added. Hasdeu wrote poetry, novels, and plays, and he was a great and prolific journalist, the greatest after Eminescu. It is unnecessary to mention N. Iorga's activities. But Rădulescu-Motru himself wrote plays and political articles in his youth, Vasile Pârvan was an extraordinary essayist, while you, *domnule* Professor....

Nae interrupted me gently. "That's exactly what I mean. Forget about me. After ten years I'm just what I was the first day: a wretch of a university lecturer. And that's not because I'm too 'bright.'

There were other 'bright' young men who joined the faculty and in time became full professors. But I have a great defect: I publish a newspaper. In other words, it can be said of me that I'm not a serious scholar."

"But there are plenty of other professors who publish articles in newspapers," I reminded him.

"Yes, but no one reads them," Nae rejoined. "They can always say that they write for posterity, that they're addressing mankind in general, for centuries to come. Meanwhile, I write for the present, because fundamentally that's what being a journalist means: to interpret and criticize the world as it appears *today, here and now*. If what you write now will be valid tomorrow or ten years from now, in France or in India, so much the better. And in fact that's what will happen in the case of certain first-class journalists. But you mustn't think of that while writing an article—what readers will say about it ten years hence. If the opinion of posterity matters that much to you, then you'd better write a monograph or a book!"

I had been, of course, familiar with the professor's ideas about journalism for a long time, but I enjoyed hearing him talk about what he called "the decipherment of events in the course of their unfolding."

"To return to our point of departure," he resumed. "It has never occurred to me to say to you: write this but don't write that, publish more philosophy and less literature. And even if I should say this, granting that I should consider it my duty to say such things to you, don't you listen to me! Because, if you were to listen to me and do what I say, then you wouldn't be *you*, Mircea Eliade, but one of our 'eminent' students—Posescu, for instance. But if you were Posescu, you wouldn't interest me, and therefore I'd continue giving you all sorts of practical advice and I'd stop reading what you write.... So, write and publish what you feel you must—nightingales must sing!—nothing else matters. Nevertheless, I want to warn you that by choosing to remain as you are, you'll have a lot of trouble, especially at the university. As a friend of mine says, life will crown you with hindrances and reward you with obstacles. But then, what would we accomplish without hindrances and obstacles?"

I believe I finished the novel a few days before March 15. The typist had kept up with me all along, so I was able to submit copies on time. There was nothing left for me to do but wait. The enthusiasm of the young typist encouraged me. She assured me that she had never before in her life read a novel "more heartrendingly beautiful. It makes you want to cry," she added. "In fact, I cried typing it," she admitted finally.

I was free again. But I soon realized that this freedom, so long desired, also made my life more complicated. Not long after March 15, Nina confessed to me one evening that she loved me.

"I didn't want to tell you before, because you were writing. For a long time I didn't know it myself. At first, I couldn't believe it. But now I'm convinced." Then she added, "I don't think I can share you with another woman. Up till now, it was hard, but I accepted it—for your sake and Sorana's. But from now on, I won't be able to. You must tell her."

Probably Sorana had suspected something, because several times that winter she had tried to find out more about Nina from me. I replied always that we were very good friends. Sometimes I was ready to break up with her on the spot. Among her many other talents, Sorana had a knack for irritating and insulting me without giving the appearance of doing so—a talent for creating all kinds of painful scenes. For instance, she once asked me why I had said that such and such young writer was the same height as I, because, when she had met him, she realized immediately that he was taller—adding, with a mysterious grin, that she had invited him to tea and that he might arrive at any moment. And when I started for the door, resolved to vanish before being confronted, and probably measured back to back with my colleague, Sorana became pale and implored me not to go, embracing me and assuring me that she loved me as she had never loved anyone else in her life, that it was absurd to imagine I could be compared with someone else, that I was a unique genius, that the invitation to tea had been made only because she had recently read a wonderful article by my colleague that had excited her. And when I informed her that I had also read the article and that it had not seemed so exceptional to me, Sorana put on a very different countenance: she had not suspected, she said, skewering me, that I could be so egocentric, that I could not tolerate talent, intelligence, genius, and culture in others besides myself. I defended myself by reminding her of all my friends and colleagues at Criterion, whose genius, talent, and intelligence I had acknowledged with my own mouth. "That's not the same thing," she interrupted me. "They're all friends of yours. The admiration you proclaim for them is proof of your egocentricity!" I put my hand on the latch, but at that moment the doorbell rang: the young writer had arrived. He seemed surprised and vexed to find me there. And of course Sorana stood us back to back—and I was shown to be in the wrong: he *was* taller than I!

Several times after such an ordeal I returned home determined to separate from her. I would write to her, as calmly as I could, explaining why our relationship could be prolonged no further: we were not made for each other, we were not happy together, we tormented each other without meaning to. She would reply, begging me to come see her, or she would even come herself and knock timidly on the attic door. She would say she hadn't slept for twenty-four or forty-eight hours, and I'd believe her. She would have aged, seemingly, ten years. Once again she would assure me that I was free, that never had there been "a freer man than I," that she would do nothing to hold me back, that whatever might happen she would always remain grateful that I "existed."

I could not resist. It wasn't only weakness, cowardice, and horror of extravagant gestures and heartrending scenes. I was really troubled, but at the same time humiliated by my ready compliance and my lack of imagination. Because, in truth, Sorana's experience of love was of a totally different dimension from mine. I saw traces of insomnia and tears on her cheeks, and I was ashamed of myself. If I had said I didn't love her any longer, that I loved another, I have no doubt that Sorana would have disappeared from my life. But this I could not say, because, especially in such moments of tension, confronted with the possibility of separation from her, I felt I loved her very much. Of one thing alone was I certain: that we would never be happy together, that we would torment each other to no avail until one of us would drop exhausted, and then the other would fall upon that one, embrace him or her, raise a lament, and beg forgiveness; and then, amidst tears and sighs from a love too great, commit suicide. I tried to tell her this, but far from discouraging her, such a denouement only reconfirmed her ideas about love. And a few minutes after repeating that I was the freest man in the world, she would explain to me why our love, since it was a "burning at white heat," implied torture and did not exclude death, of whatever nature that death might be: physical, spiritual, or social. Without the presence of death, or at least the risk of it, one could not speak of love. And, of course, I agreed with her.

I might have said to her that although I still loved her, I was also in love with another woman at the same time. I don't know how she would have reacted to that. Probably she would have said that I just *thought* I loved someone else, that I was a victim of an illusion, a passing fancy, since anyone who was in love with *her* could not possibly love another woman. And if she had told me this, probably I'd have believed her. Looking at her as she was then: pale, red-eyed, with a vacant look on her face, seemingly ten or twenty years older, knowing I had before me a beautiful, adoring young woman, a great actress, who would sacrifice not only her whole career, but also her youth, health, and peace—would sacrifice all that might be required in order to be allowed to love in the way she dreamed, "burning at white heat"—it would have been impossible for me to doubt that I loved her, or that she alone deserved to be loved.

Several days before the results were to be made public, I suspected that I would win the prize. Şerban Cioculescu came to see me, enthusiastic. The anonymity had been, in my case, a fiction: all the members of the committee knew that I was the only person who could have written with such pathetic "authenticity" about Maitreyi and life in Calcutta. When I read in the papers that I had won first prize, I went immediately to Cultura Naţională. The director of the publishing house, Alexandru Rosetti, congratulated me and presented me with a check for 20,000 lei. I thought I was in another world. Now, among other things, I was able to buy myself two new suits.

Maitreyi appeared on May 1 with a handsome cover: a head of a young Indian girl, inspired by a fresco of Ajaņţă. The first readers were enthusiastic. Mihail Sebastian wrote an ecstatic column in *Cuvântul.* The few friends who knew the story back of it were baffled by my indiscretion—but eventually they were won over by the literary quality of the confession. It was, after all, written in the mode of "authentic" literature, the autobiographical novel. *Maitreyi* was lauded by the entirety of the critics. Among my friends, only Mircea Vulcănescu was less than enthusiastic. It was not because he did not like the novel, but because, as he told me privately, "There's nothing you can say about it. The book is transparent, devoid of enigmas; it tells all—and after you've read it, you can't add anything, you can't *comment* on it." (This in contrast to *Isabel*, which fascinated him because of the multitude of enigmas and the variety of symbolism in it.)

After about two weeks, Isaia Răcăciuni called me to the publishing house to tell me that, to his great surprise, sales were not going well. "Perhaps readers hesitate on account of the title," he suggested. "They don't know how to pronounce it, and they're ashamed to go into a bookstore and ask for a book by pointing."

On the other hand, Răcăciuni acknowledged, he had not met a single reader who was not enthusiastic. Liviu Rebreanu, for example, had bought a large number of copies and had given them to friends and acquaintances. A steady stream of favorable reviews appeared, and yet the book made headway exclusively through the oral propaganda of the few, but enthusiastic, readers. I understood this during Book Week, which was held for the first time that year, at the beginning of June. A month had elapsed since the publication of *Maitreyi*, and according to Isaia Răcăciuni, only six or seven hundred copies had been sold.

"That means a thousand or more readers," he interpreted, "enthusiastic readers who will advertise for us."

Indeed, on the very first day of Book Week, I was besieged by a large crowd of customers at the table where I was autographing books. A few hours later, Răcăciuni had to send a messenger to the warehouse to fetch another hundred copies. From the second day on, the stand where *Maitreyi* was being sold and autographed was the most crowded one. By the end of June the first edition was sold out, and a second printing was exhausted before the end of summer. The third printing appeared in the fall. By Christmas, nearly ten thousand copies had been sold. Many people were predicting I'd become as "popular" as Ionel Teodoreanu or Cezar Petrescu. But the books I was to publish over the ensuing years at an ever increasing rate would sharply check this popularity.

A short while after the novel appeared, I defended my doctoral thesis. I remember that the chairman of the committee, Gusti, who was also minister of education and the arts, congratulated me before the conclusion of the session and withdrew because he was "expected by His Majesty." P. P. Negulescu made several observations that annoyed me concerning Sāṃkhya philosophy. I regretted for years afterward that I responded to my old professor more vehemently than he deserved. And indeed he never forgot it. While Posescu, his favorite pupil, received *summa cum laude*, I was awarded my degree *magna cum laude*. And in later years, whenever any of the professors proposed in the Council the creation of a lectureship for me in Sanskrit or History of Religions, P. P. Negulescu vigorously opposed it. The committee, however, released me from the obligation of publishing the Romanian version of the thesis that I had submitted, and allowed me to publish, either in French or English, my original thesis. This meant I had to go to work. If I had published the English version, I should have had few readers in Romania. I was obliged, therefore, to translate it into French, and since I did not dare translate it by myself, it was necessary to seek help. The reworking, completion, and translation of the thesis was to require two years.

At the end of June I was a Doctor of Philosophy, I had been made assistant to Nae Ionescu in a course and a seminar, and I was a "famous writer"—and even rich, because, in addition to the prize, I had been paid as royalties for the first edition of *Maitreyi* a total of 36,000 lei. (In those days a university lecturer received between 12,000 and 15,000 lei per month.) I ought to have been content. On the contrary, I was disoriented, frustrated, and unhappy. And the more time passed, the more I realized there was no way out of my dilemma. The only solution would have been to go away again, anywhere, for at least a year. But Nae had been to a great deal of trouble to have me named his assistant, and if I should have withdrawn at the last moment, all my professors would have believed that I did not consider myself capable of conducting classes. They would have thought that I considered myself good enough to lecture at the Foundation and on the radio, to write articles and novels, but that I was not made for the university. If I had admitted to Nae the difficulty in which I found myself and why I had to go away again—to Paris, Oxford, Calcutta—he would have understood and would have forgiven me; but he would have asked me, certainly, why I hadn't told him this long ago, why I had let him take so many measures to obtain an assistantship for me. I didn't dare disappoint him again. (I knew how much I had disappointed him a few years earlier, when I had written him that I could no longer work with Dasgupta.) Besides, I was giving him enough headaches

with my extracurricular activities, which he had to explain and justify every time he met Iorga, Rădulescu-Motru, or Negulescu.

If it had been a matter of myself only, perhaps there might yet
have been a way out. Eventually, I should have made a choice, and
even though I would have suffered in giving up either woman, in
time I would have become resigned. But now I realized that choosing one meant destroying the other. And it was my fault alone that
things had come to such a pass. I did not have the vocation of a Don
Juan. I didn't know how to break things off in time. With respect to
Nina, I was especially guilty. We had been very good friends. I
knew she had passed through a great ordeal, but she had regained
her calm and peace and was content the way she had been living,
certain that she would never fall in love again. Without meaning to,
I had done everything possible to take away that certainty, robbing
her at the same time of the peace and calm of which she had such
need. She asked nothing of me except that I not share her with
another. And she asked this because I myself had told her many
times how much Sorana wearied me, how much she exasperated
me. She imagined, with good reason, that I did not love her—and so
she wondered why I prolonged a relationship that confounded all
three of us. She wanted to see things simplified, brought out into
the light of day, so that we could cease avoiding others. (Since all
three of us had the same friends, it was necessary for me to find out
in advance of a party whether or not Sorana was coming, in order to
know if Nina could come.)

Several times I lied to her, assuring her that I had broken off
with Sorana. Probably I even believed myself oftentimes that our
separation was final. I had written her a clear, precise letter, or I had
said (for the umpteenth time) that we could not remain together,
that one day I'd lose my head and choke her, if she didn't succeed
in killing me first. I hoped in vain—because sooner or later she
would come again. And the more days that had elapsed between
my ultimatum and her reappearance, the more Sorana's presence
was freighted with revelations and presentiments. I would ask myself then, How can I leave and forget such a creature? I had had the
undeserved good fortune to meet and be loved by an extraordinary
woman, of a kind so rare that only a few are born in any century.
What did it matter if, due to her mode of being, she tormented me,
drained me, and would eventually destroy me? Only one thing mat-

tered: that I had had the luck to be chosen for this exceptional experience. The months or years we would spend together would more than compensate for all that would follow—even if this should be failure or death. (If Sorana could have read my thoughts she would have wept for sorrow; she believed me to be the "freest man living." She imagined that with her beside me, I could not help but "burn at white heat," that I certainly could not "fail," that on the contrary her presence was a stimulus for all sorts of things: from novels and philosophy to scholarship, criticism, and pamphleteering.)

I succeeded in resisting her, however, whenever she raised the subject of Krishnamurti. Sorana kept imploring me to accompany her to Ommen so we could listen together to Krishnamurti resolving the riddles of existence, so we could learn from him the secret of happiness and wisdom. I refused. I tried to explain why Krishnamurti did not interest me. I admired him for his courage in breaking away from the Theosophical Society, for renouncing the "Order of the Stars" and the whole mythology that had been erected around him ever since, as an adolescent, he had been proclaimed the Messiah by Annie Besant and C. W. Leadbeater. But judging from the expositions he had made at Ommen and the way he had replied to questions that were put to him, I realized I had nothing to learn from him. He was, undoubtedly, an intelligent and honest man who was able to help many people. But I could see no reason for me to meet him. Heartbroken, Sorana again went alone to hear him.

Those two weeks in July when she was away were like a blessing to me. Our group continued to meet on Sunday afternoons at Floria Capsali and Mac Constantinescu's place, playing volleyball and eating at a tavern, preparing the first Criterion symposium for the fall. Then we went to Breaza, and a few days later we climbed the Bucegi. This time Nina was with us. I found again the serenity and beautitude of the previous summer's vacation. I could live freely, without any problems, without any regrets. I knew that very soon I would have an enormous amount of work to do, but these few days of peace and relaxation gave me faith in myself again. On the one hand, I had to prepare the course and seminar for the autumn. But above all, I had to finish another novel, because, impressed by the success of *Maitreyi*, the publisher Ciornei had offered me a contract under terms very favorable to me. (I received in the form of advances, prior to the time I submitted the manuscript of a novel, a sum equal to half the royalties on four thousand copies.)

I decided to take up again *Petru și Pavel* under a new title, *Întoarcerea din Rai.* It was the story of Pavel Anicet, whom—although very different from me—I understood. Like me, Anicet was in love with two women. True, his Una and Gigi did not resemble Sorana and Nina, but Anicet's perplexities and inhibitions were familiar to me. I wanted, on the other hand, to write a novel of the "young generation," as I now understood its destiny. "The return from Paradise" meant the loss of the beatitude, illusions, and optimism that had dominated the first twelve years of "Greater Romania." Along with a part of my generation, I had lived my adolescence and early youth in this atmosphere of euphoria, faith, and indolence. I knew now that this "Paradise" lay behind us. We had lost it before becoming aware of it. Ours had been, in fact, the first and only generation which could enjoy the "paradise" established in 1919–1920. (Of course this paradise was of a spiritual order: it was simply the beatitude resulting from the fulfillment of a collective ideal. It did not imply a paradisal syndrome manifest in social, economic, or political life.)

When I began writing *Întoarcerea din Rai* one oppressively hot night in July, the entire structure was not yet clear to me. I knew only that this would be the first volume of a trilogy presenting the story of Pavel Anicet interwoven with a series of episodes concerning activities of the group of "intellectuals" to which he belonged. The action was to take place in Bucharest in the years 1932 and 1933; that is, in the time that had elapsed since my return from India. I abandoned the idea of writing the history of the father, Francisc Anicet, of the decay of the family following the expropriation of the country estate, and the poverty into which the two sons, Pavel and Petru, had fallen. In this first volume of the trilogy, Petru would appear only occasionally, but the other two volumes would be devoted in large measure to him. Because I also wanted to present a fresco of the "young generation," I could no longer write in the first person as I had in *Isabel* and *Maitreyi*, but neither did the style of *Lumina ce se stinge* suit me. I wanted to write an apparently realistic novel, but utilizing the interior monologue and some technical devices learned from John dos Passos.

The writing went hard at first, requiring more effort than I had anticipated, and I wondered what was wrong with me. Why was I making such slow progress, and why was I writing such strident prose, studded with unnecessary neologisms, with a pretentious, artificial, aggressive syntax? I told myself that, very likely, I was too tired. I slept badly and very little, because I went to bed at dawn and sometimes awoke only late in the day, after the attic had begun to grow hot. It was then that I decided to go to the mountains again. Nina agreed that it was a good idea, in spite of her regret at not being able to go along with me. But of course, I didn't tell her I wouldn't be alone.

Sorana had returned from the Netherlands. Marietta and Haig had discovered an inn on the outskirts of the village of Săcele. They praised the solitude, peacefulness, and beauty of the surroundings. The innkeeper rented several rooms on the upper floor and provided meals. I should be able to work the whole day in front of a window with a view of the mountains. I couldn't resist. On the other hand, I sensed that the experiment I was about to attempt—to live with Sorana, in the same room, day in and day out, for two weeks—could be decisive. The inn was just as I had imagined it. We arrived in a little mountain rain shower, ate dinner with a few transients, and then went for a walk along the road in the rain. I looked at Haig and Marietta and envied them. They had been in love for a long time, seven or eight years. At first it had been necessary for them to hide from the world, but after Marietta separated from Ion Marin Sadoveanu, their relationship became public—and they were happy together. No longer did they need to lie to others, and neither did they lie to themselves. I too could have had that serenity, that plenitude of peace, if one Christmas holiday evening I had not looked at Nina's fingers, if they had not fascinated me, if they had not seemed like something painted in miniature—or if, on the other hand, on an October's evening, when Sorana asked me if there were someone "in my life," I had answered in the affirmative and said that I would visit her rarely or that I would not come again.

Every time I had fallen in love or had thought I was in love up till ther· something had intruded that had diminished and even destroyed my joy, and eventually I had awakened to find myself alone again, suffering and at the same time furious at myself for feeling that way. When no exterior obstacle had existed, I had invented one.

Nothing need have kept me from remaining with Rica—but I chose to go away to India, knowing I'd lose her forever. Now I was condemned anew to suffer in an absurd way—and I alone was to blame. After all I thought I had learned from my experiences in India, less than two years after my return I was wandering once again in the labyrinth. I believed I'd learned at least not to be deceived by the mirages and snares that I well knew *she* was producing continually—"the Mother of us all," māyā. Not only had I not learned anything, but I had shown myself more irresponsible than I had been in my Indian experience of a few years earlier.

And despite all this, I sensed that the trials through which I was passing were pursuing an end that was for the time being indecipherable, but one that I did not despair of deciphering some day. As much as my suffering was due to a situation of my own creation, I had to acknowledge that, in the bottom of my heart, there was something I wanted very much: namely, to be able to love—simultaneously and with the same intensity and sincerity—two women. Logically, this desire seemed absurd, but I sensed at the same time that logic had nothing to do with such an experience. I tried to make sense out of it by saying that I wanted to live a paradoxical experience, impossible to formulate in rational terms, because I wished to attain to another mode of being than the one we are fated to live. If I had had a mystical vocation, probably I should have wanted—and attempted—to become a saint. But, in spite of assertions of a great many friends and foes, I did not have a mystical vocation. In a way, I was closer to "magic" than to mysticism. Even in adolescence I had tried to suppress normal behavior, had dreamed of a radical transmutation of my mode of being. My enthusiasm for yoga and Tantra was due to the same Faustian nostalgias. Perhaps my yearning to love two women at the same time was none other than an episode in a long secret history that even I myself did not understand very well. In my way, I was trying to compensate for my fundamental incapability of becoming a "saint" by resorting to a paradoxical, nonhuman experience, which at least opened for me the way to the mystery of totality.

Of course, on those summer days of 1933, writing *Întoarcerea din Rai* with Sorana beside me, I did not understand the profound meaning of this longing. Often I felt nothing but the torment, remorse, and resentment that she provoked, which nourished the ambiguity of my situation. Only later did I understand that this ordeal had been part of my destiny, which demanded that I live "paradoxically," in contradiction with myself and my era; which compelled me to exist concurrently in "History" and beyond it; to be alive, involved in current events, and at the same time withdrawn, occupying myself with apparently antiquated, extra-historic problems and subjects; to assume the Romanian mode of being in the world and at the same time to live in foreign, far-off, exotic universes; to be simultaneously an "authentic Bucharestian" and a "universal man." Not *les extrêmes me touchent*—but *coincidentia oppositorum*. It was not, I think, an inclination toward extravagance and paradox. It was rather—camouflaged in biographical incidents and creations of a cultural order—my religious mode of being in the world. *Coincidentia oppositorum* is just as integral to folk religiosity in Eastern Europe as to the religious experience of an Oriental or archaic type. I should go even further and say that the paradox of the coincidence of opposites is found at the base of every religious experience. Indeed, any hierophany, any manifestation of the sacred in the world illustrates a *coincidentia oppositorum*: an object, a creature, a gesture becomes sacred—that is, transcends *this* world—yet continues to remain what it was before: an object, a creature, a gesture; it participates in the world and at the same time transcends it.

But these things were not part of my thinking at the time. I was trying to figure out how Pavel Anicet would solve his problem—which was at the same time my problem. After only a few days, Sorana's presence began to tire me. The rain fell almost without ceasing, and Sorana was obliged to spend a good share of the day in the same room with me, reading. But whenever she would see me getting up from the table or pausing to light a cigarette, she would inquire how the novel was going and if I could write with her near by, or she would ask me to read her what I had written. I promised to show her the manuscript as soon as I finished Part I. But on returning to the room one day from a walk in the woods, where I had gone alone on the pretext of having to resolve some problem or other provoked by one of the characters, I found her sitting at my work table with the manuscript before her, crying.

"So you've been suffering all this time with me around!" she exclaimed. "I didn't realize. . . . "

And she pointed to the first lines, the scene with which the novel opens: "When he heard the bathroom door closing, Pavel jumped out of bed and took a long, deep breath, as if he had been afraid until then to breathe naturally. For almost ten minutes he had pretended to be asleep, covering his face with his arm and breathing slowly, rhythmically, trying to avoid attracting the woman's attention. When he sensed she had gotten out of bed, his heart began to pound: would he be able to be alone for a few minutes?"

"Was it so hard for you to stand me?" she asked (and I had only to look at her to know she was suffering: again she had aged ten or twenty years).

I tried to lie. "It's not you," I told her. "Or it's not *just* you. This is the reaction of any man—and probably of any woman too. *To be able to be alone*, at least for a few minutes, away from the creature you love. A companionship of two improperly prolonged is demonic. You remember what Goethe said. . . . "

She interrupted me to remind me once again that I was the "freest man that ever lived." If her presence was oppressive to me, that meant I didn't love her. But *that* was impossible, because she knew very well I *did* love her. Therefore, the cause must be something else. We must discover together *now* what it was about her presence that tired me, when it ought, on the contrary, to inspire me.

"Let's discuss this another time," I suggested. "I have to write now."

With good reason my egotism exasperated her. In a moment she had become again the Valkyrie I knew all too well. Now she was thirty, and pacing the floor she flashed like lightning. I was, undoubtedly, an impossible man to understand. An enigma. Here we were together in the mountains—we who had had the luck to meet and love as we did—and instead of climbing together the "summits of the Spirit," analyzing them, explaining them, and helping each other attain perfection, I was writing a novel. This only a few months after publishing *Maitreyi*, which had enjoyed such great success. Why this hurry? Why did I take refuge again in a book, instead of living "Life" with her?

As usual, I realized as I listened to her that, in a way, she was right. If Nina had not existed, perhaps I should have accompanied Sorana to the "summits of the Spirit," despite all the risks that I foresaw. But now Nina *also* existed. That is, Pavel Anicet had to find the solution to his problem, in order to help me find mine. I had to write *Întoarcerea din Rai*. I reseated myself at my wooden table, and Sorana returned to her book. From time to time I heard her sobbing softly. She heard me sigh, and inquired the reason.

"It's going hard. I can't figure out what's happening in the mind of the main character. He thinks he's in love with two women at the same time."

She paled suddenly, but she replied with a smile, in an unexpectedly gentle voice. "That's impossible."

"I think so too," I continued. "But he's convinced he loves them both. He can't make up his mind to choose between them."

"Then he's a coward!" Sorana exclaimed.

I realized then that the solution Pavel Anicet was beginning to frame was the right one. In a sense Anicet was, like myself, a coward—or at least he would appear so in the eyes of others when he would take his own life. For him, suicide was the only possible solution: only through suicide would he be able to keep them both. Ordinarily, death restores that unity which is broken in any existence—broken by virtue of the fact that any existence is contingent, limited, diminished, fragmented. In the case of Anicet, however, who had obtained this unity here on earth by loving two women at the same time, death would preserve it *in aeternum*. If he were to choose one or the other, the unity would be broken and he would live alone, frustrated, continually thinking of death, awaiting it.

"You're right," I said. "Pavel Anicet *is* a coward. In the end he'll commit suicide."

One fine day I could stand it no longer and I returned, alone, to Bucharest. Sorana went to Sibiu to meet Emil Cioran. As I learned later, she confessed everything to him; she told him I wanted to break off with her, that for a whole month I'd been doing nothing but trying to find a pretext. Cioran was extremely impressed by Sorana's sufferings and, with good cause, indignant over my cruelty and inconstancy. He couldn't understand how an intelligent man who had been lucky enough to have been loved by such a woman could desire and provoke a separation. The only possible explanation was my spiritual inertia, my inability to accept the risk of a passion at the end of which madness or death might await me; in a word, it was my mediocrity and hypocrisy. In articles in *Vremea*, which Cioran published that summer and fall, I could read between the lines repeated allusions to my lack of imagination and courage. In September or October there appeared an extraordinary article, *"Omul fără destin"* (The Man without a Destiny), in which I recognized myself immediately—and which, no doubt, comforted Sorana like a magic balsam.

I was to learn of all these things only later. For the time being, I returned with the intention of concentrating all my attention on the novel. But I went to see Nina. She paled when she set eyes on me, but I could tell she was happy I had come. Of course she had found out that I had been not only with Haig and Marietta, but also with Sorana. However, I had no desire to open *that* discussion again. At her first words, I interrupted her, starting toward the door.

"If I make you suffer too, I'll disappear, and you'll never see me again. I'll lose myself somewhere in the wide world, because I can't bear to make people suffer."

Nina became even more pale and begged me to stay. I stayed— and then, for a long while, she asked me no more questions. . . .

It was still very hot in the attic and I worked mainly at night, almost naked. The novel progressed rather slowly, but even so it went faster than it had in the mountains. I wrote without enthusiasm, depressed by all the horrors of an erotic or other kind that I felt constrained to introduce at all costs, as if I wished somehow to infuse "life" into a basically "cerebral" novel dominated by intellectuals—a novel whose characters launched into interminable discussions as soon as they met. (As a matter of fact, this is approximately what we members of Criterion did.) Although I borrowed traits and peculiarities from some of my friends, the characters had no models in reality. Probably that is why they seemed pale and artificial to me later. What interested me were their ideas, their tendencies, their gestures—above all, their ideas. I was reacting, perhaps unintentionally, against the traditional Romanian novel, in particular against the worlds of Cezar Petrescu and Ionel Teodoreanu. I reacted by presenting almost exclusively young Bucharestian intellectuals, preoccupied by what they considered then to be "essential problems." The strike at the Grivița Shops in February, 1933—that siren whose sinister whine we heard for a whole day—played an important role. When Mihail Polihroniade read *Întoarcerea din Rai,* he declared that politically the novel was "completely mistaken," because I had accorded too much attention to an episode devoid of political importance. But, for me, that strike illustrated in a pathetic and artificial fashion our "loss of Paradise," our thrusting into history.

Although camouflaged in various mediocre pseudo-ideologies, the same problem kept returning like a leitmotif: the finding of a valid "post-paradisal" meaning for existence. All those loquacious, pretentious, aggressive intellectuals were terrorized, without realizing it, by the specter of "failure." The theme of the intellectual who fails had been a rather familiar one in Romanian novels, from Vlă-huţa to Cezar Petrescu. Ordinarily, however, the "failure" is due to the opacity and inertia of the provincial milieu in which the characters are forced to live, or to a personal accident (alcohol, drugs), or, especially, to the temptation represented by politics. The characters in *Întoarcerea din Rai,* however, lived in Bucharest, not a provincial town; they were in a sense free to choose what occupation they wished, and they did not seem paralyzed by economic or political contingencies. Despite all this, however, they lived a hybrid, chaotic life, in the majority of instances abnormal, each one trying to the best of his abilities to defend himself from the despair that threatened him, to "save" himself; that is, above all, to save his life from failure, to live an *authentic* existence. For some of them, "authenticity" meant revolt, at all costs, against parents, against the "old ones," bourgeois society, and contemporary values. Almost all were obsessed, and even more so inhibited, by "problems."

The only one who didn't let himself become intimidated by "problems" was Petru Anicet. That is why I was to name the novel about him and his comrades *Huliganii* (The Hooligans). Petru Anicet was no longer terrified by the specter of failure. On the contrary, he had confidence in his genius and his destiny. He was sure he would be the first Anicet who would not let himself be felled either by historic conjecture or personal "problems." Totally indifferent toward moral life, he would become, in the eyes of some, a demoniac or a true "hooligan." But by this means Petru Anicet believed he could be creative: by freeing himself from all the inhibitions, problems, and frustrations that had ground down and eventually crushed the lives of his father, Francisc, and his brother, Pavel. With him would begin a "New Life" (*Viaţă Nouă,* the title of the last volume of the trilogy), when the Anicets would triumph in "History"—not because Petru would take History seriously, but because he would no longer fear it, as such, and no longer oppose it (more precisely, he would not risk his life in order to oppose or modify History; he would know how to "adapt") and he would not be ashamed, because, in his belief, this was the only alternative available to the Romanian people for creatively surviving the terrors of History. But of course all these things were to become clear only in *Viață Nouă*, on which I did not begin work until four years later, in 1937.

Meanwhile, at summer's end I found myself at the halfway point in the novel, and the editor, Ciornei, expected the manuscript by October 1, so he would be able to publish it just before Christmas. Probably I should have been able to finish it in four or five weeks if, on Sorana's return to Bucharest, I had not found myself caught anew in the vortex. By no means did Sorana want to lose me; not only because she was more enamored of me now than ever before, but also because she wanted to save me. She felt that if we were to separate, all my creative possibilities would be squandered. Only with her beside me would I be able to become what she alone knew I was capable of becoming: more than a great writer, savant, or philosopher—a genius and a prophet combined. She had learned for certain from friends about my relationship with Nina, and she did not doubt that it could be fatal.

My family as well as my friends wondered what was wrong with me, what I was intending to do. I was a "successful writer," the author about whom everyone was talking that summer (I had received hundreds of letters, especially from female readers), and yet my behavior was worse than ever. I ran away from people. Mother, especially, did not understand. Sometimes I didn't spend any time at home for days in a row; I would come in just long enough to change clothes or grab a book or two. At other times I would shut myself in the attic and not come down for meals, asking only for coffee and more coffee. And sometimes when a friend would come, he would talk for a while with Mother, asking her what I was doing. (In vain would he climb the wooden stairs and knock at the attic door. I wouldn't answer. Probably I didn't hear, because I worked nights and slept a good share of the day.)

It seemed to me that the only possible solution was to separate from both women. In a way, this "death" of love corresponded to Pavel Anicet's suicide. I knew I'd suffer, but any amount of suffering seemed preferable to the situation in which I found myself. At the end of September I had a long talk with Nae Ionescu. He had recently returned from Germany and seemed very impressed by the "revolution" that had begun there. He believed that a similar revolution would have to take place some day in Romania. By this time, he was in constant and obvious opposition to the Palace. Long before, King Carol had ceased heeding his advice, and in articles in *Cuvântul* Nae was criticizing eloquently, but frankly, royal politics, and making clear allusions to the court clique. At the end of the conversation he looked at me again, frowning.

"What's the matter with you?" he asked. "You seem to be living in another world. Can it be you're writing another novel?"

I had to admit he had guessed correctly.

"What is it called?" he asked, smiling.

"Întoarcerea din Rai."

He gave me a long look, as though he could not believe his ears. The silence was prolonged, and I began to feel embarrassed. I was afraid I had disappointed him again.

"So soon?" he exclaimed finally.

How right he was! I repeated to myself on the way home, *So soon.* Less than two years had elapsed since my return from India. It was not even a year since my release from the army. That time seemed like a blessed interlude, and yet it was impossible for me to recover it now—the time when I was free, available for any adventure, hoping and dreaming of an imminent return to India. That freedom I myself had annulled through a series of unpremeditated acts. I repeated over and over to myself that I alone was to blame. There remained to me a supreme solution: to try to be forgiven and forgotten; and to separate from them both.

I remember that evening in September, in Nina's little room. There I tried to explain my decision to her. She listened to me, standing by the open window, looking very pale. She had stepped to the window during the time I was speaking to her. I had said the essential, but I continued talking, fearing an awkward silence. Then she spoke.

"I don't think I can stand a second time," she said. "I'm afraid I can't stand it again."

She looked out the window, spellbound. I remembered then about her life story, her misfortune. Now she had loved for a second time, and for a second time the man she loved let himself be caught up in a game that meant, for her, the end. This time, here on the eighth floor, an open window existed. But even if the window had not been there, all that I had said to her might have turned her love to ashes again—and in vain might I return a few days hence, laden with flowers and presents, because she would reply, as to the lieutenant earlier, that she no longer loved me, that even if she should try, she could not love me again. . . . Whatever might happen, I had brought her misfortune a second time. It was as though a curse followed us.

In a flash, I knew that all I had said to her was a last, demonic attempt of māyā to destroy me, that far from bearing her bad luck, I would be able to give her all that she had not had before in her life, that my destiny was to make her happy, whatever price I might have to pay.

"All right," I said, "I won't leave you. But we can't continue this way. We'll have to start living together."

She looked at me, smiling as though it were a dream.

"I know this means a great sacrifice for you," she said. "But don't regret it. I have a secret to confess, something I've never told anyone. I haven't much longer to live. I know I'm going to die young."

*   *   *

That evening I wrote Sorana a long letter, explaining the decision I had made. I let a day pass, then went to see her. It was just as I had expected: she hadn't closed her eyes all night. She said she had known for a long while what was the matter with me, but she had tried everything in her power to prevent me from making the decision I had made—and this for my own good.

"I'd like to ask you one thing," she added. "If you had to choose, why didn't you choose me?"

I didn't dare repeat again what I had said so many times before, that we could never live together, that we would destroy each other.

"You know the reason why," I replied. "You have enough strength and imagination to forget me. . . . I chose the weaker one."

After that we never met except by chance, and each time my heart ached. Why had I brought her so much misfortune? Why had she fallen in love with me, of all people, and why couldn't she forget me? Why did she wander like a phantom through places where we had gone together, frequenting circles of mutual friends in order to see me, knowing full well I would hide as soon as I caught sight of her? For many years thereafter I did not dare be happy: I knew that the thing I should be able to call happiness was built on a monstrous, absurd sacrifice, which no man could accept with an easy conscience. Because, indeed, Sorana had made a sacrifice and continued to make others for years afterward. She gave up, one after another, all our mutual friends, she withdrew from the Criterion circle, she kept only her friendship with Marietta Sadova, but she saw her less and less frequently. Her name appeared hardly ever on playbills of the National Theater. She lived more and more to herself. And she found her only support and consolation in the teachings of Krishnamurti.

My decision broke other hearts besides Sorana's. It seemed equally catastrophic in the eyes of my family. My parents had dreamed of someone entirely different from a telephone company secretary, a divorcée with a little girl in an obscure boarding school. Several years earlier Nicu had married a poor girl, and I well remembered how the whole family had received the news, with tears and lamentations. Nicu was still a student, and they were afraid he would give up the idea of a doctorate in chemical engineering in order to take a second-rate job as soon as he graduated from the university. I was their last hope. They wanted to be able to avenge themselves on the other branches of my father's family who were more well-to-do, more fortunate, by my having a brilliant career and marriage. They had begun to believe in the possibility of my "career" after I was named assistant to Nae Ionescu's chair. They did not doubt that I would know how to make a "match" that would console them for the choice Nicu had made. They tolerated sympathetically my relationship with Sorana, and although the advent of Nina perplexed them, it did not upset them too much. On the one hand, Sorana was still in the picture, and on the other they remembered that I had known how to break off with Rica. As they saw it, I was involved in one of those irresponsible adventures of youth, from which I should know enough to disengage myself eventually.

When I confessed to them that I was going to move into an apartment with Nina, it was as though the sky had fallen on them. Corina was also present, and the three of them were stricken dumb, out of fear, indignation, and fury against fate. I believe they were convinced at that moment that a curse was hanging over our family. From the war onward, all of Mother's brothers, my uncles, had gradually become poor, and the little wealth that still remained had been consumed in recent years through hasty and extravagant weddings. The house on Strada Melodiei now belonged to Corina, and it was burdened with mortgages. The only income was my father's pension. But they had borne it all with dignity and faith in the future—because of *me*. They had trembled many times for my foolish acts and adventures, they had trembled on learning of the dangers I had undergone in India, they had trembled thinking I would never return—but lo and behold, I *had* returned, I had finished with the army, I had become a famous writer, I had been named a lecturer at the university—and I was not yet twenty-seven. One fine day, soon, I would introduce them to my chosen bride, a girl without peer for beauty, the daughter of a minister or an ambassador; or a banker, a general, a university professor; or perhaps even a foreigner; but in any event bearing an illustrious name or belonging to a family of great political prestige and, of course, rich, even extremely rich. Because they did not doubt I deserved all these things—I, because I was so gifted and had worked like a madman, had read so much that I risked losing my sight—and also *they*, because they had sacrificed everything in order to permit me to buy books, to travel, to go to India. But all the sacrifices they had made, and the poverty and frustration in which they had lived for the past ten years—all would be rewarded by my career, my marriage, my success. Even if I should not immediately have those millions that were my due, I should have other satisfactions—and these satisfactions would be theirs also.

These images and scenes had their source in more than just nostalgia and dreams. On several occasions in the past year, Mother had spoken to me about such and such a "match." Men had come to see her, asking if I had decided to get married. They told her of villas, of millions; they showed her photographs of beautiful girls, some of them still in the university. My answer was always that I had no intention of getting married now—and she believed me. Likely she said to herself that there was no hurry, that it was better I play the fool while I was young, rather than later. And now, all of a sudden, like a bolt from the blue, I gave them the news that I was moving in with Nina. I didn't tell them I was marrying her, because I wasn't thinking of marriage, but it amounted to the same thing. Once we were living together in the same apartment, the chance for the brilliant "match" would vanish. No daughter of an ambassador, general, or banker would come to talk of marriage in an apartment I had prepared to share with Nina.

They simply couldn't believe it, and between tears and lamentations they labored to convince me I was committing a great folly, that moreover (and this I knew myself) I was darkening their old age, I was extinguishing the only light and consolation yet remaining to them. It was impossible for them to understand me. And I didn't even attempt to justify myself. What could I have said to them? That I loved Nina was not enough. They knew I'd been in love with Rica and Maitreyi (they had read the novel), they knew I loved Sorana—and yet either freely or otherwise I had broken off with those girls. Could I have told them that it all began six or seven years earlier, one evening in Paris, when a handsome and infatuated lieutenant had been made drunk by friends and had awakened the next day in bed with a strange woman, with the consul by his bedside and witnesses for a marriage? Could I have told them it all began one evening during Christmas holidays when I suddenly became aware of the fact that Nina's fingers were extraordinarily slender? And above all could I have told them that if, in adolescence, I had escaped drowning once on the Danube Delta and a second time later on the Black Sea, if I had escaped from the leeches in the jungle of Sikkim, if I had not lost my mind in September of 1930, and if I had succeeded in finding myself again in my *kutiar* in Svarga Ashram, that if I had learned so much and written and gathered so much—all these things had happened in due course only so that now, in the fall of 1933, I would have enough intelligence and strength to be able to make this apparently demented gesture in order to prove to Nina that *it will not happen a second time*, that this time, with me, and because of me, her destiny will be fulfilled, a destiny that had been suspended by a stupid incident one drunken evening some years before in Paris?

I could not tell them that. Instead, I repeated wearily, at the end of my strength, that I had decided to move into an apartment with Nina. And yet I knew very well that Nina did not ask me to do this. All she had asked of me, earlier, was to break off with Sorana. Later, she had dropped even that condition and had asked only that I not leave her. The rest was my own decision—and that decision did, indeed, seem demented. I had managed to make a break with Sorana. I might have prolonged things as they were—and Nina would have been happy. But I wanted more than Nina's happiness: I wanted to fulfill her destiny by a *restitutio ad integrum;* everything that she had had and had lost in an absurd manner had to be restored *by me.* I realized very well what this would mean for me, but I was prepared to make any kind of sacrifice. What pained me even more than the sacrifice of Sorana was the sacrificing of my family. I sensed that in the bottom of their hearts my parents felt that they had lost me forever. Not only had I swept away all the hopes they had concentrated on me, but I had become estranged from them. I realized all this, and I suffered terribly—all the more so since there was no one in whom I could confide. They had given me their all, and in exchange I could not give them even my physical presence. (I foresaw what was to happen later: they would not accept Nina, and I would not agree to live without her. Nevertheless, I went to see them now and then: on holidays we ate together; I came on New Year's Eve with two bottles of champagne and stayed an hour. But that was all. No longer was I their child. I was a phantom who materialized from time to time for a few moments, then disappeared, having returned to his own world. Four or five years were to elapse before normal relations were reestablished. But by then it was too late.)

On St. Dumitru's Day, when the movers came to transport my books from the attic to the apartment, I had the sensation that I was attending my own funeral. I walked about among relics and recollections, and I knew this was the last time I'd ever find them there. I placed in boxes the copybooks and notes written in adolescence and bundles of published articles, and I relived in a dizzy whirl the whole story of myself and my attic. I saw myself as an adolescent, forcing myself to read by the lamp with the blue bulb, my eyes continually watering because of the new lenses that were too strong. I saw myself with classmates from the lycée, then later with fellow students from the university. I saw Thea and Rica; more recently my friends from Criterion; I saw Sorana and Nina from the early days of our friendship when we all were free, when everything was possible, when life tempted me with a thousand roads. From among those ten thousand roads, I had chosen the hardest one. . . .

I heard the movers groaning as they descended the wooden stairs, bent under the burden of the boxes, and it was as though I heard them carrying my own coffin.

13. We Must Hurry...

THE APARTMENT house was on Bulevardul Dinicu Golescu, not very far from the North Station. I believe it had been built that very year. Our apartment was on the top floor, the fourth. We had chosen it in particular because, in addition to an enormous dining room and two bedrooms, it had a spacious living room with windows covering one whole wall, in which I could place my desk and bookcases. But when we moved in, the desk and bookcases that I had ordered seven weeks earlier still had not arrived. The men transported the five or six thousand volumes up the stairs and stacked them on the floor. The proprietor, who lived in one apartment where he also had his law office, lent me a kitchen table on which I began writing that very evening. I had so much and so many different things to write, that sometimes in despair I wondered if I ought not to sign another three or four more contracts! But I should have known that it was simply *impossible* for me to finish on time all I had pledged myself to write, and realizing this, perhaps I would have stopped worrying.

Still I had not finished *Întoarcerea din Rai*, although I devoted the nights to it, from 11:00 P.M. till 4:00 or 5:00 A.M. Ciornei wanted at all costs to publish the novel before Christmas, and he forced me to hurry, especially since I had made the mistake of giving him, at the first of October, all that I had written up till then, and the manuscript had been handed over immediately to the printer. I had received the galley proofs, and the printer was waiting for the remainder of the book. Ciornei had begun to lose patience, and I had to placate him at any price, because it was in large measure thanks to him that I had been able to rent and furnish the apartment. That autumn I had signed a new contract; and in addition to the sums already received for *Întoarcerea din Rai,* Ciornei had given me another 50,000 lei in advance for two novels, which I committed myself to write in 1934 and 1935. Of course, not even this amount was enough to cover expenses, so I signed several promissory notes with due dates three and six months hence. In order to augment my income, I sought all sorts of expedients: translations, proofreading, editing of classics. Alexandru Rally gave me Colonel Lawrence's *Revolt in the Desert* to translate for the Foundation of Literature and Art of King Carol II, which was then in the process of being established. And when, soon afterward, Alexandru Rosetti replaced Rally, he proposed that I undertake the editing of Hasdeu's writings—and I accepted enthusiastically, especially because I could get a sizable advance. I continued writing my two columns weekly for *Cuvântul* and articles for *Vremea,* but I accepted every other invitation to contribute for remuneration.

In addition to all these things, I had to begin teaching on the first of November. Fortunately, I had announced a course on "The Problem of Evil in the History of Religions," and a seminar about "The Dissolution of Causality in Medieval Buddhist Logic." I had given much thought to these problems, and I knew the documentary material rather well, so there was nothing for me to do in preparation except draw up the outlines for my lectures. But when I arrived for my first lecture at the Faculty of Letters one Friday afternoon (my lecture was to be from 5:00 to 6:00 P.M.) and headed toward the Titu Maiorescu Lecture Hall, I wondered if there were not some mistake. I couldn't believe that all those people crowded into the corridor had come to hear me. It was a repetition of the surprise that I had had on the first night of the Criterion symposia. I made my way with difficulty to the faculty lounge. Fortunately, Nae was there. I was embarrassed to have a larger crowd at the opening of my course than he had—although I knew very well that the majority had not come to learn what constituted the problem of evil and salvation, but to see and hear the author of *Maitreyi.*

I was not mistaken. When I entered the lecture hall, I was impressed not only by the throngs of people crushed against the walls, but above all by the fashionable character of the crowd. The rows in front were studded with elegant matrons and misses, whose perfume diffused itself overpoweringly all the way to my chair. The feminine public, moreover, constituted the majority. Probably there were also many students from Letters, but—with the possible exception of Nae's—I don't think they were taking other philosophy courses. I was sufficiently versed in the subject that I succeeded in speaking for almost an hour without consulting the notes I had in my pocket, and although I presented Indian conceptions of evil and salvation in a rather scholarly way, the audience listened to me as to an oracle and applauded afterward as at a political rally.

When I left the speaker's platform and started toward the faculty lounge, a crowd of ladies—young and old—followed close behind. The lounge filled to capacity and other "fans" waited their turn outside. The majority had come just to meet me or to invite me to a tea or a concert, or to tell me they wanted to learn more about India. Several inquired about *Maitreyi* and even produced copies from briefcases in the hope that I would autograph them. But I told them, rather brusquely, that here at the university I did not discuss my literary works, and I did not sign books except on Book Day. I had to spend almost half an hour talking with everyone who had gained entry into the lounge (there were a few students who had come to ask timidly for bibliographical references). Then I excused myself, saying that I had an appointment on the other side of town.

On the way, riding the tram, I smiled to myself: how many of those elegant and wealthy ladies would have believed that I was hurrying home because, if I didn't write an article before 11:00 P.M.—at which time I had to go to work on the novel—I wouldn't receive that 500 lei from *Vremea* or *Cuvântul*, and I'd have nothing to give Nina for food for the next three or four days? I smiled, but I felt no regrets. I sensed that only now was the great ordeal beginning. I was, perhaps, a little apprehensive, but not for anything in the world would I have turned back.

              ′   ′   ′

The majority of my friends were heartsick when they learned of my decision. For them, I had committed a mistake that might well prove fatal to my career. It was not only the fact that Nina was poor (and they were even more amazed when they found out I had made her give up her job at the telephone company), but she was also several years my senior, she had a child, and above all she did not belong to the milieu of "artists" and "intellectuals" in which we moved. Everyone wondered, with apprehension, to what extent an ex-wife of an army officer would be able to assist, support, and "inspire" a writer who doubled as a scholar, and especially someone like myself, so eccentric and unbridled. To them, my act seemed both absurd and dangerous. After having told them time and again that I had no intention of getting married, I had taken an apartment with Nina, which for many implied either a secret or an imminent marriage. And I had done this now, of all times, at the start of a tremendous literary career, just when I could have been having an unlimited number of "adventures" that, at least, would have enriched me with "experiences" so valuable for a writer. Knowing I was without money, my friends imagined I should be forced to renounce many of my principles in order to pay for the rent and furniture: I would, for instance, write popular novels and produce second-rate books—because how else could I continue buying expensive books, how could I travel?

Some of my friends even tried to have talks with me and offer advice. Of course, I could not tell them that, at least for a while, the chief aim of my life would be to make Nina happy by means of a *restitutio ad integrum*. And neither could I speak to them of love, because they, like my parents, would have asked me what possible relationship love could have with the "bourgeois" program on which I had embarked: an apartment too large for my needs, bookcases that were too expensive, the self-contradictory existence that I had assumed: on the one hand, working like a convict in order to pay the rent and the debts, and on the other hand following the model of any other bourgeois householder. The life I was preparing to live on Bulevardul Dinicu Golescu depressed them by its banality, its lack of "style." The fact that they, my married friends, had assumed such a way of life several years previously was something altogether different. They had not had my luck: to have gone to India at age twenty-one, to have been loved by Maitreyi, to have practiced meditation in a Himalayan monastery, and then, as soon as I returned home, to have "launched" myself as a novelist, to have been named an assistant professor at the university at twenty-six, and so forth. Because of this, they should like to have seen how a lucky man like me would live his life. It would have pleased them to have seen me prolonging in Bucharest the adventure begun five years before when I departed for India: to see me, for instance, frequenting sophisticated circles, appearing at our meetings with exotic or extravagant mistresses, continuing to be what they had known me to be since adolescence—an original, a bizarre man. They were, of course, disappointed and at the same time annoyed that I was behaving like a provincial student who marries directly after graduation and "settles down" in an apartment with a part of the dowry (with the difference that Nina had nothing; as I liked to boast later, her only dowry had been a little girl of seven or eight, Adalgiza). They wondered if I would be able to be "creative" in such an environment. They wondered if I would not become a failure. Several of them confessed confidentially that I was already "washed up," adding that this belonged somehow to the destiny of the Romanian people; Romanian men of talent and genius have a meteoric trajectory: either they die before their time, or they fall into failure.

Part of these reflections and worries I learned at the time from the mouths of friends who were trying to save me *in extremis*. The rest I found out later. In a sense, they were right. I could not deny that I had taken a great risk. Even if it were to be granted that in the future I should succeed in the *restitutio ad integrum* and in the fulfillment of Nina's destiny, the danger remained that I might fail my own destiny. But on the other hand, it was impossible for me not to accept that risk. For a long time I had been convinced and I had repeated it in articles, lectures, and discussions, that *nothing* can make a truly creative person fail, short of his loss of freedom. I refused to believe that poverty or wealth or the "environment" could sterilize a creative spirit. If a writer "fails," it is not owing to his environment or biographical circumstances, but simply because his potential had been modest or nonexistent. Although I sensed in the depths of my being that nowhere would I ever find again the "atmosphere" of my attic, I could not believe that I would ever be unable to write in the apartment on Bulevardul Dinicu Golescu. Although I was sure that if I had been allowed to live alongside Maitreyi I should have written several "great books," I could not believe that I would be unable to write them living with another woman, for instance with Nina. There were, to be sure, certain extreme situations in which the possibility of my "failure" as a writer and man of letters might have had a positive meaning; that is, the renunciation of an irrelevant objective (to write books, to "make culture") in favor of an "absolute" goal: spiritual perfection. This is what would have happened, very likely, had I remained forever in the Himalayas—or if I had succeeded in surviving as Sorana's companion. But in both instances, "failure" would have meant only my fulfillment on another plane than that of literature or science.

And so, despite all the risks I knew full well I was taking, I could not believe that my acceptance of an apparently banal and bourgeois life style would result necessarily in "failure." I could not believe that an existence is modified according to scenery and characters, that in an attic or a studio you become and remain an artist, while in an ordinary apartment you are transformed into a "bourgeois." For me, the style of one's existence was a continual inner creation that had nothing to do either with material conditions or with the surroundings or setting in which circumstances had placed one.

On the other hand, the life I had decided to live seemed interesting to me from another point of view. For several years I had wondered: what would have become of Goethe if he had married Lotte or Lili Schönemann? What would have happened if Kierkegaard had not renounced Regine Olsen? (The meaning Kierkegaard had given this act had helped me five or six years earlier to renounce Rica. But I wanted to know if this action had indeed guaranteed his creativity or had only channeled it in the direction that we know. In this case, I wanted to know what *other sort* of Kierkegaard there might have been. . . .) I wondered how certain writers whom I admired might have evolved if, in their youth, they had accepted a "banal existence."

So far as I was concerned, banal existences attracted me. I said to myself that if the fantastic or the supernatural or the supra-historical is somehow accessible to us, we cannot encounter it except camouflaged in the banal. Just as I believed in the unrecognizability of miracle, so I also believed in the necessity (of a dialectical order) of the camouflage of the "exceptional" in the banal, and of the transhistoric in historical events. These ideas, which I was to formulate later in *Şarpele* (published in 1937), *Noaptea de Sânziene* (The Forbidden Forest, written between 1949 and 1954), and in several works of the history and philosophy of religions, sustained me in the experiment that I had begun. Actually, when instead of returning to India I accepted a situation that inevitably led to marriage, I was consenting to do in Bucharest that which I knew I'd have been forced to do in Calcutta or Benares: namely, to camouflage my "secret life" in an existence apparently dedicated to scientific research. But with this difference—that at this point a somewhat tragic element was introduced, my certainty that I understood my destiny: precisely because my marriage to Nina seemed, *apparently,* to be a disaster, it must, if I believed in the dialectics and mystery of camouflage, mean exactly the opposite.

Not all my friends were so pessimistic. Mihail Sebastian avowed that I could not have made a better choice. Those who were well-acquainted with Nina seemed delighted. Nae Ionescu listened to the news with the same interest he showed in all the predicaments and adventures of those he loved—but he made no comment, at least not then. His own marriage had not been a happy one, and for many years he and his wife had lived in a state of separation, although they were not divorced. The professor believed only in love; as he expressed it, love is both "an instrument of knowledge" and a "means of salvation." And at just that period his current great passion was passing through another grave crisis.

But after only a few months, my friends began to be convinced that their fears had been for nothing. On the one hand, I had not changed, I had not given up a single one of my objectives. On the other hand, they discovered in Nina a warm, intelligent friend, and her disarming sincerity won them over in the end. As time passed they came to believe that, thanks to Nina's love and devotion, I had become "invulnerable." Knowing that she would be at my side, they were no longer fearful about my future. Whatever might happen, they were sure that Nina would know how to extricate me from the difficulty. After a few years, Nina became in the eyes of my friends more than an ideal wife—she became a legendary figure, without whom it was hard to believe I should have been able to accomplish what I had. They especially admired her extraordinary energy, which was surpassed only by the discretion and humor with which she camouflaged it. I remember asking Camil Petrescu once, in 1934 or 1935, why he had not married, and his answer was that he had never had the luck to meet a Nina Mareş. He was especially impressed by the fact that, although Nina lived exclusively for me, she hid her devotion so well that it required some time to discover it. As Camil admitted to me once, an overly obvious love and devotion embarrassed him; and yet, he added, he could never marry a woman unless he were sure she would not only love him exclusively, but also identify herself *totally* with all his beliefs, plans, and dreams.

I wondered later what would have happened *if.* . . . If, for example, we had not been together that day during Christmas holidays, or if instead of me, Nina had fallen in love with Mihail. I realized very well that this game, "What would have happened if—?" was pointless, but I continued to wonder. I don't know to what extent the hypotheses I made then were valid, but I said to myself that no matter how long I might have prolonged my relationship with Sorana, eventually we would have separated anyway. Very likely I should have taken advantage of my "freedom" by living more or less the life of a "successful" young writer. During those years I should have produced less, probably, because I would not have needed money, but perhaps I'd have written better books. I find it hard to believe that I would not have married sooner or later. But, as well as I know myself, I'd have separated from my wife after the first "scene," or after the first misunderstanding, or at her first attempt to change my way of living. I doubt that many wives would have been able to preserve their love, trust, and serenity living with the man I was then: paying for an order of books from London or Leipzig with my entire salary from the university, and discovering on arriving home that we had exactly enough food for two days; returning from the city often with one or two friends and forgetting to telephone that I was bringing them for dinner; inviting sometimes ten or fifteen people to a party and talking until the wee hours; leading a disorganized, fantastic life: writing all night till dawn and sleeping mornings (during which time I must not be disturbed by the ringing of the doorbell or the phone, or by footsteps in the apartment); constantly receiving letters and telephone calls from feminine admirers—letters that I found on my desk, and calls to which Nina replied with humor, asking the unknown female voice to wait a moment, then coming to inform me: "An admirer is on the line; do you want to speak to her now, or shall I tell her to call back an hour later, when you've finished your article?"

I wonder, too, what would have happened if my wife had been wealthy or had had the idiosyncrasies of an aristocrat. Probably I'd have left her at the first mention of her wealth or the prestige of her family. Likewise, it is probable that I should not have gotten along well with her friends, although I should have sought to impose on her all of *my* friends, the majority of whom were bohemians: writers, actors, painters, and journalists. This would have given rise to "scenes," and since I have a horror of "scenes," I should have left. But even if she had accepted my way of life and my friends also, probably we should not have been in agreement on a central problem: the matter of children. For various reasons, I did not want to have children—not for a good many years at least. It is hard to believe that my reasons would have been convincing to a young wife. (In this connection, Nina accepted a great sacrifice also, and this secret tragedy of hers constitutes a key to the novel *Nuntă în Cer.*)

However I imagine things, I should have known a different life—a happier or less happy one—but a different life. I should not have had, in any event, the consolation that, however egocentric my existence, I had succeeded in at least one thing: that *restitutio ad integrum*, which I had promised myself to give her one evening in September, 1933. Nina never hid from me the fact that she was happy, but she always added that this happiness frightened her. All this she recalled on her deathbed in 1944; but then she was no longer afraid. Just as she had anticipated, she died young. Her last year was very hard for her to bear, not only on account of her illness, but especially because she was afraid I'd discover she had cancer. She implored the doctors, my family in Bucharest, and our friends in Romania and Lisbon not to tell me, lest it cause me to suffer, to worry, to be unable to work. To the amazement of everyone, the secret was kept. I did not learn the true nature of her illness until a few days before it killed her.

／　　　　　／　　　　　／

In November, the desk and bookcases arrived. The shelves covered all the walls, from floor to ceiling. Once the books were in place I regained to some extent the peace and solitude of my attic, and I was able to work at nights on the last chapters of *Întoarcerea din Rai.* The Criterion symposia had begun again at the King Carol I Foundation, but we had rented also the hall of the Dalles Foundation for a cycle of lectures devoted to the history of music. The subject assigned to me was Asian and primitive music. Since the lectures were accompanied by choral and instrumental illustrations, it was necessary for me to locate as many recordings and printed scores as possible. I possessed only a few essays on Bengalese folk and religious music, plus a very few examples of Balinese melodies. A good share of the materials I found at G. Breazul. Several young musicians offered to adapt melodies from Africa, Asia, and Oceania to the instruments available to them, and to improvise a chorus that would attempt to reproduce both equatorial African rhythms and melancholic Indonesian monotones. The performance enjoyed an extraordinary success. I spoke for ten or fifteen minutes on Indian music, and then withdrew. From behind the curtain there appeared the instrumentalists and the chorus; and in the auditorium of the Dalles Foundation, perhaps for the first time in Romania, arias from Travancore and Puri resounded. I reappeared and attempted to evoke the mythologies and religious spirit of certain archaic peoples; then I disappeared and the audience listened in fascination to Bantu ritual songs, Melanesian chanting, and the syncopated shouting of some Australian tribe. The entire series of lectures, as a matter of fact, was followed by an enthusiastic public, with larger crowds each successive night. Petru Comarnescu concluded the series with a lecture on jazz, abundantly illustrated by the best jazz music in the capital at that time.

My course on "The Problem of Evil and Salvation" continued drawing a sizable audience. Several lectures were devoted to Buddhism; and I recall that once, having gone directly to the podium and announced, "Today I shall expound the Law of the Twelve Causes," the audience murmured a moment, then froze in such an unnatural, ecstatic hush that I hesitated a few moments, not knowing quite how to begin. Many friends—and also enemies—of mine were now coming to listen. Once, following a lecture on the Upaniṣads, Emil Cioran came to the faculty lounge and declared that I had spoken with such passion and in such a rhythmic way, that if I had continued lecturing ten minutes longer he would have exploded—or else committed suicide on the spot!

Not everyone, however, was so enthusiastic. After a lesson on Buddhism, Oscar Lemnaru—about whom, two years earlier, I had published the first articles in Cuvântul, for which he never forgave me; for years he attacked me whenever he could and in any way he could—said that he could not understand what I said, that I talked too fast, that I cited too many technical terms. Posescu, who was upset and worried about the throng of students in my course, came to listen and afterward advised me not to speak so freely and from a standing position, but to do rather as he did: sit on a chair, rest my elbows firmly on the desk, and slowly, calmly, and without gestures, follow an outline worked out in advance (of two or three pages, no more). Fortunately, after my lectures several students of philosophy, medicine, and theology also came to see me, and these reconfirmed my own opinion: that I was good at delivering lectures in a certain way, and that it was useless for me to try to change. This was my "style": spontaneous, unsystematic, personal; not aiming primarily to inform the students (because the best information is to be found in books), but to confront them with essential problems, and above all to surprise them, "awaken" them, by the shock of projecting them abruptly into a horizon heretofore unsuspected (the *anamnesis* of which Dan Botta spoke).

To some extent I belonged to the category of lecturers so brilliantly represented by Nae Ionescu: those who do not repeat a prepared text, but "think problems" as they speak, standing on the podium in front of the students. But there was this difference—an enormous one—that I did not have Nae's unique gift of making himself understood even while expounding extremely technical matters, and neither did I have his genius for constructing a lecture like a symphony, with nothing superfluous, summarizing in the last five minutes all the themes discussed in the course of the hour and bringing them together, explaining each in the light of the whole. My lectures had a less systematic character and could even appear improvised, because I let myself be drawn into reflections and commentaries provoked by reactions from my audience. (I could tell instantly if the audience had or had not understood what I had said; likewise, I sensed what ideas and observations interested them. Of course, for me, the "audience" was constituted of those several dozen students whose intelligent facial expressions I followed.) Often, while speaking, I "discovered" aspects or meanings that I had not seen previously, even though the problem was a familiar one that I had studied for many years.

I finished *Întoarcerea din Rai* early in December. The rest of the book was already in type, and when I sent the printer the last pages, I hoped the novel would appear by Christmas. But Ciornei considered it to be too late for that, and he postponed publication until early January.

December of 1933 was, for our group, a month of tensions. Nae no longer concealed his blatant hostility toward royal policy. In a series of outspoken articles against the Duca government, he drew attention to the dangers involved in the dissolution of the Iron Guard, an action he deemed not only illegal but also unnecessary. As he said, either it was a matter of an artificial movement without roots in the life of the Romanian populace (in which case the ban was unnecessary because the movement would disappear of its own accord), or else, on the contrary, it was an authentic, powerful, growing movement, and then it would be impossible to annihilate it by means of a ministerial decision. Sometime in the course of the autumn, Nae met Codreanu, and later he visited him at Casa Verde. Captain Corneliu Z. Codreanu was the founder of the Legion of the Archangel Michael, also known as the Legionnaires or the Iron Guard, a nationalist movement. Nae was impressed by the fact that he had *made* something—in this case, a house. He told this to Codreanu, and when the latter replied that Ionescu himself had made many things, the professor interrupted him.

"No, all I've 'made' up till now are two sons. It's not much, but it's something. For the rest, I've made nothing; in politics I'm only a gardener: I've watered the trees, flowers, and vegetables. But I haven't made the fruits. I've just helped them to grow—protected them from the cockleburs."

That year we celebrated New Year's Eve at Ionel Jianu's place. But the evening before, I. Gh. Duca, the Prime Minister, had been assassinated on the platform of the railway station at Sinaia. Although Ionel Jianu had asked the guests not to discuss politics, that night we talked of nothing else. Only the next day did I realize the consequences of the attack. *Cuvântul* was suspended and Nae was arrested. Also arrested were the leaders of the Legionnaires (from the Criterion group, Mihail Polihroniade and Alexander Tell). Martial law was declared and censorship was reintroduced—not only for newspapers, but also for books. *Întoarcerea din Rai* was to have appeared that very week. With an anxious heart, I deposited several copies of the novel at the office of the Censor. I remembered many passages that might result in the book's being banned: above all, the description of the strike at the Grivița Shops, and allusions to the brutalities of the military police and army officers.

We met at the *Cuvântul* office and asked one another what might happen to Nae, to the paper, and to us. A few days later we learned that Nae had been interned at the Cotroceni barracks and that a military prosecutor was questioning him. They wanted at any price to implicate him in the case; and on the basis of several articles in *Cuvântul*, they charged him with instigating the assault.

Several weeks later I heard that he had asked for *Sein und Zeit* and *Dichtung und Wahrheit* to be brought to him from his library. All sorts of rumors were flying about the dictatorship King Carol was preparing to establish. Perhaps some of these rumors had a basis in fact. But the verdict given by the military judiciary reminded the King that he still could not depend on the army: the assassins of Duca were sentenced to life imprisonment. But Corneliu Z. Codreanu and all the other leaders of the Legion were acquitted of having had any part in the assassination. All were returned to their homes with much pomp and circumstance. Nae's friends and fellow workers on *Cuvântul* assembled to celebrate the professor's release (he had been freed a few days earlier, without having been implicated in the case).

But in vain did we gather each day, as usual, at the editorial office. The newspaper continued to be proscribed. The "palace" was taking what revenge it could for the time being, in anticipation of the final settling of accounts. Although many other papers and reviews of the right and extreme right were appearing regularly again, *Cuvântul* had to wait four years. And when, in January 1938, it succeeded in reappearing, its voice was virtually a swan song, because censorship had been reintroduced and Carol was planning again—this time with much cunning—to impose the dictatorship. *Cuvântul* survived as best it could for three months until being suspended forever in March, 1938.

A few days prior to Duca's assassination, Sandu Tudor began publishing a new paper, *Credinţa* (The Faith). I remember that, in November, Tudor asked me to accompany him to the home of a very wealthy man whose name I have long since forgotten. He was a gentleman approaching old age, with rather ordinary features and slow gestures. Quoting the saying, "In a windstorm the trash rises too high," he asked us if we would be willing to publish an "honest and courageous" newspaper. Sandu Tudor accepted immediately. I replied that, given the existence of *Cuvântul*, I could not collaborate on a second newspaper. The old man, however, was determined on having my cooperation at all costs, "at least at first, until the paper is launched." Tudor insisted also, begging me to help him, "so that we young people will have our newspaper too." I agreed to collaborate for the first three months, but only under a pseudonym. I was convinced that the project would never get off the ground, or that in any event it would not hold up for more than five or six months. I was mistaken. Thanks to political circumstances, and thanks especially to the scandals which it provoked, *Credinţa* was to enjoy an extraordinary ascent.

I wrote articles for *Credinţa* at the newspaper's office, and signed them "Ion Plăeşu." I wrote them with a feeling of culpability mixed with fury. Nae Ionescu now was imprisoned, *Cuvântul* had been suspended, while this cheap tabloid was allowed to appear. Tudor's articles were unreadable: pretentiously and "poetically" written, aggressively moralistic, they vaguely criticized vice, injustice, the state of things in general, and so forth. When he became convinced that I would not abandon *Cuvântul*, Tudor took Petru Manoliu as his chief editor, and later Zaharia Stancu, E. Jebeleanu, and others joined him.

Întoarcerea din Rai appeared at the end of January. Nae read it while still in prison, and he told me I had written a very "fumbling" book. He asked me when I had had time to gather so much sadness and bitterness, and whence had come this bent toward cruelty, brutality, and despair. It was difficult for me to talk about the autobiographical content of the novel. But I asserted that the "atmosphere" of *Întoarcerea din Rai* was something I sensed all around: tensions, conflicts, cruelties, and especially the ineffable feeling that we had entered upon a "broken-off" era—this I sensed now more than ever, since Duca's assassination and all that had followed. Criterion continued with the same degree of success, but seemingly something had been "broken" there too. It was hard now to bring together on the same platform Legionnaires, Democrats, and Communists. The members of Criterion remained friends, but some of them—for instance, Polihroniade and Tell—no longer could, or no longer wished, to discuss certain problems in public with certain speakers.

Întoarcerea din Rai was as much a surprise to some of my friends as to a good share of the critics. After the fervor and transparency of *Maitreyi*, this book of four hundred pages, with characters too numerous and too similar, with pretentious theoretical dialogues and long interior monologues, with many violent scenes, and above all with Pavel Anicet's singular and unnatural problem—the book could not but baffle its readers. In a sense, this was the effect I had sought. I couldn't accept with an easy conscience the glory of being a "successful young writer." *Maitreyi* represented only one aspect of a literary *oeuvre* which had begun with *Romanul adolescentului miop* and which I saw unfolding itself on several planes. I considered *Întoarcerea din Rai* my first truly "epic" novel. As such, I believed I had the right to introduce as many characters and "problems" as I wished; I believed likewise that I had the right to employ any literary technique I found convenient.

Scarcely had the discussion concerning *Întoarcerea din Rai* died down when, in March, *Lumina ce se stinge* was published by Cartea Românească. The novel bewildered the great majority of the readers. Those who had hoped to understand the book after reading the second part (Part I had appeared serially in *Cuvântul* in 1931) were disappointed. The second part seemed even more mysterious, with the interior monologue giving place to the "stream of consciousness" technique, which made certain pages unreadable. Only Ion Biberi wrote enthusiastically about it, because only he among the critics of that time had read *Ulysses* and portions of *Şantier*. So far as I was concerned, I had realized long since that *Lumina ce se stinge* was a failure, and I had published it because it belonged to a history of my literary experiments, it completed the epic universe that I had inaugurated with *Romanul adolescentului miop*.

I saw Mihail Sebastian frequently. The suspension of *Cuvântul* had been a hard blow for him, although Nae was struggling to pay the editors a part of their salary. Much earlier, Sebastian had begun a novel, *De două mii de ani* (For Two Thousand Years), and the professor had promised him a preface. Recent events warned him what sort of preface to expect, but Sebastian would not give up the idea for any reason. He loved and admired Nae Ionescu too much to let himself be swayed by his present political orientation, however much it disturbed and grieved him. Sebastian often came to eat lunch with us, and he complained that he had not succeeded in finishing the novel. Recently, he had begun writing reviews and articles of other sorts for *L'Independence Roumaine* and *Rampa*; thus he was obliged to produce five or six articles per week, and this corvée of futile writing exhausted him.

That spring, Criterion was convulsed by a new "crisis." Gabriel

Negri had arranged at the Opera House a dance performance that enjoyed a sudden, great success. During the intermission Floria Capsali, who had been his teacher, could not control an upsurge of jealousy, and she declared in front of a group of reporters that Gabriel Negri had interpreted *L'après-midi d'un faune* through the spectacles of a pederast. The handsome program that Gabriel had printed contained, among other things, texts by Mircea Vulcânescu and Petru Comarnescu. The next day, *Credinta* published a note which left the impression that Criterion encouraged pederasty. Chancing to meet Sandu Tudor in the Café Corso, Vulcănescu demanded of him a reckoning. I don't know how Tudor answered him, but in the course of the discussion Alexandru Tell, who was also present, slapped him and provoked a duel. This unleashed a long and odious campaign against Vulcănescu, Tell, Comarnescu, and Negri. Actually, as was quickly realized by the Minister of the Interior—who encouraged it with all his might—the campaign was aimed at discrediting Criterion. All the envy and jealousy provoked by our unprecedented success could now avenge itself. In particular, the articles (not always signed) by Zaharia Stancu and Petru Manoliu exceeded all bounds. The campaign was detestable, because it had been launched by a few journalists and writers against other writers and actors, in the full knowledge that the charges were unfounded. But thanks to this sensational journalism, *Credinţa* increased its circulation tenfold and became one of the most popular afternoon gazettes. The scandal constituted a very useful diversion for the government. On the other hand, the Minister of the Interior wanted at all costs to paralyze the activity of Criterion, in its eyes an extremely suspicious group of intellectuals, whose growing popularity was making them ever more dangerous.

Just as was expected, *Credinţa* and Sandu Tudor were found guilty in the slander suit brought by Tell and Vulcânescu. But of course very few readers ever learned about the decision, because the newspapers published the announcement of it in places where it would not easily be noticed. Moreover, Tudor appealed the decision to the higher courts, so that when he was finally sentenced to pay the symbolic 1 leu damages, the scandal had been forgotten. In the meanwhile, Criterion had ceased activities. The occasion of its closing was a student demonstration, which the Prefecture Police tried to disperse—after letting it assume its full size—by bringing to the Carol

Foundation a company of military police.

The results of the *Credinţa* campaign were disastrous. Friendships old and new were broken; Negri suffered a nervous breakdown that kept him off the stage for many years, while Petru Comarnescu did not dare, for some time to come, to give public lectures, and his limitless potential for being a cultural entertainer remained from that time onward neutralized. Owing to the *Credinţa* campaign, the unity of the Criterion group was shattered, and the political tensions of 1935 to 1939 only served to deepen the rift.

On Book Day, 1934, Editura Cugetarea published *India,* a volume consisting of some of the articles which had appeared previously in *Cuvântul* and several texts of talks I had given on the radio. It was on Book Day also, I believe, that Sebastian's novel *De două mii de ani* appeared, with the preface by Nae Ionescu. I remember Mihail came to me one afternoon, his face pale, almost disfigured.

"Nae gave me a preface," he said, "but it's a tragedy! It's a death sentence!"—and he thrust the professor's manuscript into my hand.

I read it with great excitement, but also with a heavy heart. "Judah suffers because he must suffer," Nae had written. And he explained why: the Jews had refused to acknowledge Jesus Christ as their Messiah. This suffering in history reflected, in a certain sense, the destiny of the Hebrew people who, precisely because they had rejected Christianity, could not be saved. *Extra Ecclesiae nulla salus.*

For someone who had written that "the Jews are a people who have been delayed on the road to salvation," for one who had studied the Cabala and Jewish mysticism, who had said (in 1927 or 1928, when I was his student): "I've been tempted for a long while to give up both journalism and politics and devote myself entirely to Hebraic studies"—this newly written preface constituted a retreat to a position considerably more rigid. Of course, both Sebastian and I understood the origin and meaning of this rigidity. The professor knew now that he would be read by a certain public on the extreme right, and he wanted to show in what sense he saw the "Jewish problem": he saw it, above all, in religious terms—which allowed him to judge it on a plane other than political or social.

Mihail Sebastian did not question the professor's right to think this way. The thing that grieved him was that Nae had chosen *this* occasion—the preface to his first novel—to expound conclusions that he had reached only recently. But, he kept repeating, he had asked him for a preface, he had waited for it many weeks while the novel was ready to go to press, and he had been unwilling to refuse what Nae had written, no matter how much this fidelity might cost him.

None of us suspected then how much it was to cost. The novel was attacked by the majority of the press, from the extreme left to the extreme right. The whole left reproached it for encouraging an age-old red herring, accepting Ionescu's interpretation that antisemitism has a religious explanation and origin. Belu Silber wrote a violent article in *Şantier*, which forced Sebastian to sever relations with him for a long time. On the other hand, Petru Manoliu wrote in *Credinţa* that "Mihail Sebastian must be prevented from breathing," for what reason I no longer remember. Mihail carefully saved all these articles, reviews, and insults, because he had decided to write that very summer a book entitled *Cum am devenit huligan* (How I Became a Hooligan), in which he would reply to each one, at the same time explaining the meaning of the novel and his motive for publishing Nae Ionescu's preface. Those months of summer and fall, 1934, constituted a great ordeal for Sebastian. We saw him almost every day and tried to give him encouragement. As he testified later in his dedication in my book, he had found in me his only support at a time when "everything around [him] was collapsing."

I saw Nae, of course, and discussed with him the presuppositions of his preface. The argument "Judah suffers because he must suffer" (an argument of the Hegelian type) no longer convinced me, I told him, because it started from a historical fact—the suffering of the Jews—and sought the origin and meaning for it in a holy mystery, the Incarnation. I told him I didn't understand how we could assert that the Hebrews, or any other non-Christian people, would not be saved; this means we are putting ourselves in the place of God, and no theologian can possibly know what God will decide. No man can claim that he knows what will happen *in the absolute*, beyond History. I added that I should like to discuss all these matters in an article for *Vremea*, and Nae encouraged me to write it. It will be hard for me to write, I told him. Not because I'll be criticizing you, but because it's the first article I shall have written about you, and it will be a negative one.

"That's the way it always is," Nae consoled me. "If a disciple has something to say, he begins by saying why he is not in agreement with his master, and only after that does he declare where, and up to what point, he agrees. Of course someone or other will come and ask me, 'Hey, did you see what your good disciple and admirer has done to you?' But I'll pretend I haven't seen."

That summer I published two long articles in *Vremea* (in numbers 346 and 347) which upset Racoveanu. Racoveanu had been angry with Sebastian after reading his novel. Now it seemed he had become angry with me also. He had not liked my gesture (criticizing the professor!) and he attacked rather sharply the theological presuppositions of my thesis. Racoveanu published articles in *Credinţa* and I replied, without losing my temper, in *Vremea*. For some time our friendship underwent a crisis, though I did everything possible to save it. But from then on Racoveanu came to visit less and less frequently, being afraid he might encounter Sebastian.

Toward the middle of August I went to Berlin, in order to complete the recent bibliography related to my thesis and to consult periodicals not available in Romania. The Stadtbibliothek in Berlin was the nearest large library, and I had learned, moreover, that living was cheaper in Germany than in France or England. I went directly to the lodgings a friend had found for me on Berlinerstrasse, in Charlottenburg. The city captivated me from the first day, without my knowing why. It was my first trip to Germany; and enamored as I was with Italy, Greece, and the Orient, I was afraid I'd be disappointed. My surprise and delight were, then, all the more unexpected. I found here again the mystery and charm of the Berlin of *Remember*, by Matei Caragiale. I was troubled, however, by the red flags with swastikas flying over the buildings, and the brown and black shirts I saw on the streets. From morning to late evening I worked in the Stadtbibliothek. As in the old days in Rome and Calcutta, I worked from the opening of the library until its closing. And always I returned to my room laden with a satchel of books that I consulted or read during the course of the night. In those five or six weeks I stayed in Berlin, I completed the recent bibliography for *Yoga* and gathered enough material for *Alchimia Asiatică* and *La Mandragore*. Other than a Romanian student who was living in the same guest house, and Nicolaie Argintescu, I saw no one. Certainly I ought to have tried to meet several of the Indian specialists and historians of religions in Berlin, but I was afraid I'd become involved in visits, meetings, and discussions, and my time was limited. I promised myself to meet them the next summer when I returned to Berlin (because I had enjoyed the experience so much that I had decided to repeat it every summer).

I had not seen Nicolaie Argintescu since leaving for India. He and I had become well acquainted in the summer of 1927, when the two of us, plus Radu Cotaru, spent almost two months together in Geneva. He had been living in Berlin for several years, working vaguely on a doctoral thesis in aesthetics. But as he himself admitted, the important thing was the research, not the results of the research. I do not know if he ever undertook to pass his doctoral thesis in Berlin, although he remained there another four or five years. So many things interested him that it would have been hard for him to concentrate on a single subject. Besides, he wrote with much difficulty, laboriously, continually going back over the pages already written, correcting and "purifying" them. Formal perfection obsessed him. He admired Dan Botta especially for his extraordinary stylistic rigor. Argintescu showed me a long article he had written about Botta, which I liked; and I suggested he publish it in *Azi*. And because he confessed that he knew no one, I assured him that I myself would present the article and correct the proofs. (Later, I almost regretted having made this offer. Several times Argintescu asked for the article to be returned, so that he could change a word or add a comma. Then he wrote me many letters at Bucharest, indicating how the article must be printed, what sort of type should be used, already trembling at the thought of typographical errors, asking if the editors would be willing to publish an errata sheet, and so forth. And after publication of the article—which I had corrected personally and more meticulously than I had ever done with any of my books—Nicolaie continued to write me, asking about "echoes" of his article and what I thought after rereading it, specifying that such a text can be deciphered only after repeated readings, and so on.)

I encountered Argintescu almost every day at the library, and sometimes in the evenings we went walking together in Charlottenburg. I always listened spellbound when he talked, not so much for the interesting things he said, but mostly for the fantastic opinions he held about himself. I was fascinated by his boundless pride and the imaginary universes in which he lived (he confessed to me that he had the vocation of a Don Juan and that all sorts of extraordinary adventures had happened to him). His absolute confidence in his own genius delighted me. He was then thirty years of age and had written nothing except a few articles—but I realized he valued them more than all else that the "young generation" had written. And I realized, too, that he was happy to be alive, that he had not yet awakened from the stupor provoked by his own epiphany: he discovered himself each day more gifted, more brilliant, more unique. I would part company with him regretfully, especially on those nights when he had given me to understand that, actually, the project on which I was working was not a major one; that my experience in India had been, culturally speaking, peripheral, and knowledge of the Sanskrit language was irrelevant; that *Maitreyi* was a failure; that my method of supplying Nae Ionescu's chair was an uninteresting one, and if he had it, he would give it a completely different scope—as he would have done with Criterion also, had he been in Romania. . . .

I've wondered for a long time why I am fascinated by men who have an exalted opinion of themselves and proclaim it, and why I am attracted by megalomaniac failures—writers who suffer from delusions of grandeur, obscure, second-rate men bursting with pride, in whose eyes you read nothing but the cold intoxication of absolute triumph. I don't think I've ever found a satisfactory answer. But I am constrained to note here this strange attraction because, I suspect, it too has its meaning.

I returned at the end of September, and on that long journey in a third-class train car from Berlin to Bucharest, there came to my mind the plot of a novel that I imagined while looking through the window at the forests enveloped in the mists of evening. Before the First World War, in 1910 or 1912, two young people meet during a summer vacation at Tekirghiol or Movilă, they fall in love, and they even become secretly engaged. For various reasons they cannot marry, and they separate. Several years later, each marries someone else, they have children, they become caught and carried along by life. The war comes and goes. Years pass. Then, after twenty years, they meet again. Both are free now, and their original love is rekindled. Only now can they marry. Only now does their true life begin.

I should have liked to have been able to write that novel then, but I did not dare begin something else before having finished the *Întoarcerea din Rai* trilogy. The theme continued to haunt me for a long time. I recalled it anew in June of 1949, in Paris, when I began writing *The Forbidden Forest*. I was undoubtedly gripped even then, when I was barely twenty-seven, by the mystery of the recovery of "lost time," the hope that all can be saved if we know how to begin life *ab initio*. And perhaps this belief in the possibility of "rebirth" through a return to "the beginnings" allowed me, a few years later, to understand the essential character of the man of archaic and traditional societies that I analyzed in *Le Mythe de l'éternel retour* (The Myth of the Eternal Return).

No sooner had I arrived home than I undertook to prepare the volume of essays, *Oceanografie*, which I had promised Virgil Montaureanu, owner of Caetura Poporului, the favorite bookstore of writers, where we often held meetings. Virgil Montaureanu was a great supporter of modern Romanian literature at a time when, apart from a few exceptions (M. Sadoveanu, Ionel Teodoreanu, Cezar Petrescu), customers asked exclusively for French novels or translations of British or American fiction. Montaureanu endeavored to promote books by younger Romanian writers. When he suggested I edit a volume of my essays, I agreed gladly. I very much wanted to gather my recent essays into one place, because they had been written with that end in view. I believed then, as I do today, that certain articles and essays gain in value if they are read, or reread, together in one book. They gain—that is, they reveal dimensions that were not evident on first reading in the periodical in which they appeared. Certain allusions or lateral observations in one article are taken up again or find their completion in other texts written later; but this is not seen unless the articles are collected in a single volume. With this thought in mind, I had written a series of articles for *Vremea*, the titles of which began with "About . . ." ("About an Aspect of Eternity," for example). I was thinking not so much of the readers of *Vremea* when I wrote it, as I was of those who would read it in a book later on.

The selection and correction of the texts that were to constitute *Oceanografie* did not take very much time. At the same time, I wrote "A Preface Properly Speaking," which occupies some seventeen pages in the book and is not devoid of interest. I confessed there that, had I been able, I should have written a preface for each of my earlier books, even my novels, because only in this way can an author converse *directly* with his readers. But I also confessed many other things, with a boldness that might pass as irresponsibility— because what I said about myself was not at all flattering. I confessed, for instance, that: "Although by nature a very calm, quiet person, I am seized with panic whenever I have to write something for the public or when I must speak before a certain public. (Those who have had occasion to listen to me know how awkwardly I stammer and how hard it is for me to maintain my train of thought.) On such occasions I have the feeling that people are expecting from me a truth of which they have urgent need . . ." And I continued: "And then I hurry, I leap over obstacles, make errors of language and logic (but what matter all these things?) only in order to reach the point the sooner."

For years these confessions were repeatedly reproduced and misinterpreted. I never replied to these critics. I knew very well that I myself had encouraged them, that in fact I had provoked them, once I had entered the arena "with my guard down." Anyone could strike me, using for a weapon my own indiscretions. But I had confessed all these things, above all my "haste," in order to awaken my readers, to force them to understand that "we don't have time." I repeated that "we are cursed to consume time uselessly," that we do not know how to "control time and make it fruitful."

With equal imprudence, I confessed there might be errors, contradictions, and incoherent passages in my book—but I added that this was of no consequence. The opening essay in the book is entitled "Invitation to Ridiculousness," and I wrote about "Truths Found by Accident," about "concrete happiness," the "masculine mode," sex, the detective novel, "superior women," and many other things of that sort, which baffled my professors and colleagues and made several grave and severe spirits indignant.

Despite all this, the book was rather successful, especially among the young people. To some extent, *Oceanografie* inaugurated a new type of Romanian literature: personal prose, carelessly and rapidly written, liberated from academic interdictions and inhibitions. The book was reminiscent of Nae Ionescu and Eugenio d'Ors, and it anticipated somewhat the philosophic and essayistic prose of the eve of the Second World War, when authors like Gabriel Marcel and Jean-Paul Sartre did not hesitate to philosophize, taking as their starting point personal happenings and everyday events. I republished in this book "Five Letters to a Provincial," written between 1932 and 1933, and a large number of "fragments" published in *Cuvântul* and *Vremea* in the same period, the majority of which actually were extracts from my journal and notebooks. I concluded the volume with the article "Invitation to Masculinity," which was in fact an invitation to joy and hope. "So many dead lie all around me that I do not know how to contain my wild joy that out of all these corpses there will arise tomorrow another world."

In a certain sense, it was true. These dead, these corpses, I knew. But more particularly, I foresaw them in a very near future. I had not forgotten the siren from the Grivița Shops, nor the bullets of December 30 on the station platform at Sinaia, which took the life of I. Gh. Duca, the Prime Minister, nor the students and military police who had invaded the Carol Foundation auditorium, nor the sundering of friendships and the "parting of the ways" that had put an end to the "Criterion experiment." Some of us, rather few of us in fact (Camil Petrescu, Sebastian, Vulcănescu, and one or two others), were troubled by Hitler's rise to power. But my uneasiness and fear were connected not only with such political events. I had had the premonition long before, in adolescence, that we would *not have time*. I sensed now not only that time was limited, but that soon there would come a terrifying time (the time of the "terror of History"). I sought to defend myself by a paradoxical overturning of all values: I accepted the dead around me, and I accepted also the dead I knew would come, as symptomatic of a new world that would have to be born. For me, personally, this meant that first of all I would have to "hurry," to undertake to say what it seemed to me I must say in the time I had, as much as I should be allowed to say.

*   *   *

In November I opened the course on "Metaphysics and Mysticism," and the seminar in which I discussed *De docta ignorantia* by Nicolaus Cusanus. For the initial lesson, the lecture hall was quite as crowded as in the previous year, but after a few months the fans and admirers began to withdraw, leaving me with my faithful students. I was beginning now to know the students very well. Many were in polytechnics, theology, and medicine. Among those who participated in the seminar I remember Mihail Sora and Mariana Klein (who became husband and wife soon afterward), Axente Sever Popovici, and several others whose names I've forgotten, but not their faces, their intelligence, and their humor. (For instance, that young law student who declared that Cusanus's Latin was too simple for him, and that, probably, was the reason why he could not understand him; also that mysterious, intelligent lady, a fanatic admirer of Nae Ionescu, who followed all our courses and seminars, and published a surprising article on *Întoarcerea din Rai.*)

It was during that fall or winter that I met Lucian Blaga. Marietta Sadova brought him with her one evening. He gave me a very cordial smile, and confessed that he had read *Maitreyi* mainly because he had known for a long time about Maitreyi, the wife of Yājñavalkya in the *Bṛhadāraṇyaka Upaniṣad*, and he had wanted to see if in my novel, even in a camouflaged way, I had reiterated the metaphysical lesson Yājñavalkya had given her to reveal to her the mode of being of *ātman*.

The circle of friends remained the same, and we continued to see one another regularly. Camil Petrescu and I had begun to be friends, in spite of the fact that he seldom liked anything I wrote. I had become rather close to Belu Silber, and thus was all the more pained by an article of his, published in the journal *Şantier*, in which among other things he called me "a little mystic, a little agent of the Secret Service." A few days after the article appeared he came to dine with us, as if nothing had happened. I said to him, "Belu, you know me, you know how I earn my living, you know how hard I work to be able to pay the rent, buy books, and invite friends to dinner. How could you write that I'm a 'little agent of the Secret Service'?"

He began to laugh. "You're even more naive than I thought," he replied. "This is of no consequence. It's just a part of the jargon of Marxist journalists. I'm obliged to attack your ideological position, and I do it by employing classical clichés—but I like you as a man and I cherish your friendship."

I looked at him sadly. "I'm sorry," I said. "I have a different conception of friendship, as well as of journalism."

I believe we stopped seeing each other from that time on.

／　　　　／　　　　／

The winter of 1934–1935 seemed very short. I had hoped to be able to complete the revision of the thesis, making use of the documentation I had gathered in Berlin. I had hoped as well to finish the volume *Alchimia Asiatică* and to make some headway with the editing of Hasdeu. I succeeded only in finishing the first section of *Alchimia*, in which I discussed Indian and Chinese forms of alchemy. Part of the text appeared in *Vremea*, while the book was published, again by V. Montaureanu, in the spring of 1935. In succeeding fascicles I proposed to present Babylonian, Greco-Egyptian, and Arabian alchemy. Of these, only the first ever appeared as a book, in a volume of 1937 entitled *Cosmologie şi Alchimie Babiloniană*, in which, as one may surmise from the title, the horizon was considerably broadened. (In the chapters about cosmology, I discussed the symbolism of the "center of the world," and the ideology implied in the exemplary models of cities and temples—problems with which I would deal again in *Traité d'histoire des religions* [Patterns in Comparative Religion] and *The Myth of the Eternal Return*.) The enormous quantity of material on Greco-Egyptian and Arabian alchemy that I had been collecting ever since the last year in lycée remained, unused, together with a great many other notes and manuscripts which were eventually left behind in my library in Romania. (In 1955, when I was writing *The Forge and the Crucible*, in which I made use of some of the documentation for the books published in 1935 and 1937, I pondered for some time whether or not to present Arabian alchemy also. In the end I decided against it.)

Outside of Nae Ionescu, Octav Onicescu, and a few others, I don't believe my researches concerning alchemy interested very many. Camil Petrescu asked me quite frankly why I had wasted time on such a dry and irrelevant subject—why I had not studied, for instance, the problem of aesthetics. Twenty years after the appearance of *Alchimia Asiatică*, the interpretation I proposed was almost universally accepted. I sought to show that alchemy is not a prechemistry, not an elementary science, but a traditional technique implying a cosmology and a soteriology. To the extent we take account of this fact, alchemy can become an interesting problem, because its study can illuminate an obscure phase in the history of the spirit. Considered a pre-chemistry, an embryonic science, or a science in an infantile state, the study of alchemy loses any cultural value and becomes simply an erudite curiosity. Six months after the appearance of *Alchimia Asiatică*, C. G. Jung gave a lecture at Eranos valorizing alchemy psychologically, which was published in 1936

and became the point of departure for a series of studies he concluded a quarter of a century later.

I did not succeed, in that winter of 1935, in completing *Yoga,* but
the first chapters had already been translated into French, from English and Romanian, by Lydia Lax and Wendy Noica. Of the editing
of Hasdeu, I finished only the text of *Poezii* and the two versions of
his wonderful novella *Duduca Mamuca.* I had promised Ciornei *Huliganii* for that year, but I soon realized that I would be able to write
that novel only during summer vacation. At the same time, however, I had a great need of money. (From *Oceanografie* and *Alchimia
Asiatică* I received no royalties, but I ordered books constantly
through Virgil Montaureanu and did not have to pay for them.) I
accepted the proposal of Georgescu-Delafras to furnish one volume
for his publishing house, Cugetarea. Because excerpts from my Indian journal published in *Azi* had been read with great interest, I
decided to add another 100 to 150 pages, annotate them, and publish
them under the title *Şantier* (which means, literally, "shipyard" or
"construction site"; figuratively, "work in progress").

I later regretted that I chose this solution to my problem of paying the rent for six months. Not because I considered it excessively
indiscreet to publish excerpts from a relatively recent diary (so far as
I was concerned, no indiscretion was excessive!); but Delafras believed I was going to give him a novel. Indeed, I spoke of *Şantier* as
an "indirect novel" (and I wrote a preface to explain what I meant
by the term). This forced me, on the one hand, to jettison a number
of observations, notes, reflections, and travel impressions, which
constituted an important and characteristic side of the journal. On
the other hand, I was obliged to accentuate the "novelistic" element,
underscoring and "enriching" certain episodes and adding in paren-
theses all kinds of details about Mrs. Perris's boarding house—
which damaged the journal's stylistic unity. Because a rather large
number of pages had been reproduced or at least utilized in *Maitreyi,* I was forced to omit the most dramatic periods: Bhawanipore
and Svarga Ashram—that is, to suppress precisely those pages in
which I had recorded my most authentic Indian experiences. *Şantier*
presented almost exclusively my life in an Anglo-Indian boarding
house, and it emphasized and exaggerated the most external aspects
of it. Several years later, when I had begun to rue the solution I had

chosen, I told myself that I ought to publish *The Journal* in its entirety, with a minimum of notes and without trying to turn it into an "indirect novel": that is, without those more or less pathetic additions with which I had salted it in order to make it more sensational.

I never forgave myself that in that year when I allowed myself all liberties, I chose the hybrid solution of the "indirect novel." If I had published it whole, my Indian journal would have been a significant book. It would have inaugurated in Romania a genre of literature that probably will become popular in European literature in the near future. I believe, indeed, that the multiple crises through which the novel, the theater, and systematic theology have passed will encourage a new "literary genre," hard to define for the time being, but which will be as far from the traditional expressions of philosophical writers, essayists, and critics as from the intimate journal of the type of Goncourt or Amiel—writings apparently hybrid, tending as much toward notebooks and intimate journals as to the style of erudite monographs, correspondence, philosophical reflections, and sociopolitical or historiographic problematics.

*   *   *

That spring, together with Mihail Sebastian, Dan Botta, and several other young authors, I became a member of the Society of Romanian Writers. Everyone hoped for a radical renewal of the society. Since Book Day had been established and the Royal Foundations for Literature and Art had begun publishing activities, writers had attained a certain prestige. Until then, only a Rebreanu or a Mihail Sadoveanu had succeeded in living exclusively by writing. Although their works enjoyed an enormous circulation, Ionel Teodoreanu continued to practice avocations and Cezar Petrescu did newspaper work. But the Royal Foundations for Literature and Art announced a number of series: essays, philosophy, critical editions, novels, poetry, translations, and others, and almost all writers of any worth, even the young ones, began to receive advances for future books or translations. General Condeescu, himself a writer and a great friend of writers, had been named director of the Royal Foundations. Several young men, foremost among whom was Mircea Damian, convinced him to offer himself as candidate for the presidency of the Society of Romanian Writers. They hoped by this means to obtain much more for the "writers' guild": pensions, grants, assistance in illness, and so on. When Damian came to ask me to participate on the board of which Condeescu would be chairman and N. I. Herescu secretary, he said, "We must choose the General! He'll build us a palace!" And indeed the Palace of Writers was placed on the program of the Society that same year. Soon the Book Stamp Law was passed, and funds began to accumulate. The palace was to have been built in the fall of 1939. But by that fall the Second World War had already begun.

As was expected, the new board was chosen by an overwhelming majority. On the occasion of the election, I met or renewed acquaintances with a number of writers, young and old, whom I had not seen before except on Book Day. I did not frequent the cafés—Capşa's and Corso's—nor the literary clubs, not only because I didn't have time, but especially because the writers usually met before noon or toward evening, times when I had to stay home and work. I remember that Mircea Damian would ask me every time we met, "Why don't you come to the café and sharpen your wits a little?" I replied that I went to Corso's now and then, in the evenings and late at night. "Nights we spend at taverns," Damian explained. "What the devil, haven't you learned that at your age?" I didn't want to tell him that I did the same myself, with friends, whenever I could, especially at this time of the year, early summer.

Later, after I had left Romania, I was sorry I had not frequented the cafés and literary circles. But my meetings with my friends and associates from the Criterion group, *Cuvântul*, and *Vremea* satisfied my need for dialogue and literary confrontation. I regretted, nevertheless, that I had not participated in the Sburătorul Club, although I knew Eugen Lovinescu and often had conversations with him at Montaureanu's or the Alcalay Bookstore. Since Lovinescu read everything, he also read my books, but I suspect he thought of me more as a man of learning and a journalist than as a novelist. However, the fact that I wrote and published much, pleased him. "I know that others criticize you," he told me once, "but I always say to such people: the writer must write."

I met rather often with Liviu Rebreanu, who liked *Maitreyi*, but liked *Întoarcerea din Rai* even better, despite the fact he considered it imperfect from an artistic point of view. "It's a shame," he said to me once, "that you turned it loose as fast as you wrote it. If you'd worked on it a year or two, if you'd copied it over several times, it would have been a great book."

It saddened me to hear him say this, because I knew he was right. I recalled his sleepless nights, the pains he took to write, correct, and recopy, never hurrying, never agreeing to submit a manuscript until the day he was truly satisfied with it. I knew, on the other hand, that I could not write except in a fever, hastily, almost in a frenzy; that, in itself, *this* kind of writing is not improper to literary creativity (Dostoevsky wrote, or dictated, several novels in the same manner); that if my productions did not attain to a high plane it was not the fault of my haste, but of my deficiencies. Then, too, I knew one thing more: that we did not have much time ahead of us. At that time I had plans for some twenty books: novels (three or four volumes in the *Întoarcerea din Rai* cycle; the novel I had "seen" on the way home from Germany); several books of literature in the fantastic genre; *La Mandragore;* a book about myth; another on religious symbolism; *Muntele magic* (The Magic Mountain, about archaic symbolism); *Comentarii la legenda Meşterului Manole* (Commentaries on the Legend of Master Manole); the completion of the work on Oriental alchemy; a history of Indian philosophy; a monograph on Hasdeu and the encyclopedic tradition in Romanian culture (from Cantemir to Nicolae Iorga); a book on the conception of death in the beliefs and customs of Romania; and others which I have forgotten. Some of them I was unable to undertake until after leaving Romania, but instead I wrote others that I did not then have in mind to write (for instance, *Şarpele, Mitul Reintegrării, Nuntă în Cer,* etc.).

And so I hurried. Not only because I always needed money, but also because I wanted to succeed in presenting the beginning of an *oeuvre*—that is, a series of books from which it would be possible to understand what I thought, what I loved, what I believed and hoped would become the Romanian culture—if we should be given time, if we should be left in peace. But I was afraid I would not be able to present the *oeuvre* in its entirety. I wondered often if it would not be necessary for me to proceed in this fashion: to concentrate on one, or at the most two, books. But this would have meant abandoning the whole, selecting just a few fragments from a work that would not be fully understood unless judged in its totality. On the other hand, I was not at all certain that, even by making an effort to "concentrate," I should be able to write a masterpiece. Insofar as a writer of my age then is capable of understanding the structure and intention of his own creativity, I was inclined to believe that no formal perfection could save my writings from being merely transitory. I preferred to be guided by instinct, that is, to write as I had written up till then, whatever the risk might be. And I knew the risk was considerable.

I asked myself, how would Goethe's *oeuvre* look if he had not lived past forty? And what would the *oeuvre* of Eminescu or that of Hasdeu be like if one or the other of them had been creative for another twenty years? (Hasdeu's creativity was mutilated if not actually paralyzed by the death of Julia when Hasdeu was scarcely fifty.) Of course, any *oeuvre*, however complete and "rounded out" it may be, is "saved" only by the exceptional worth of a few of the writings that constitute it. Had it not been for ten or twelve masterpieces, Balzac's *La Comédie humaine* would long since have been forgotten. We read with interest *Physiologie du mariage* or *Les Employés* because of the existence of *Le Cousine Bette, Le Père Goriot,* and a few other such great novels. And in the case of Goethe, we are interested in *The Metamorphosis of Plants* and texts about minerals and theories of color, and even *Egmont,* only because he also wrote *Faust, Iphigenie auf Tauris,* and poetic masterpieces. Thanks to these summits, any fragment from the vast and polymorphous *oeuvre* of Goethe gains weight and significance. I told myself that if I could succeed in writing a single exceptional book, whether a novel or a work of philosophy or history, my whole production could be "saved," in the sense that it would continue to be read, at least by a handful of people, who in this case would be able to decipher the message revealed by the whole.

The risks, of course, I knew very well. I had not forgotten, for instance, the long period of literary sterility that Goethe had experienced in the midst of his maturity, probably owing to his excessive preoccupation with scientific problems. It was Goethe's great luck to have lived after that for another thirty years, during which time he recovered his creativity and wrote several additional masterworks. I asked myself if the passion, time, and energy I had expended on my extra-literary researches would not, eventually, nullify my potential as a writer. I could not answer; but I knew that whatever the answer might be, there was nothing to be done. I could not abandon these aspects of my *oeuvre*, even as Goethe could never abandon his scientific researches. There was also the chance that I might die before my time, as had happened in the case of many Romanian writers and scholars. (And among the scholars I was thinking not only of Pârvan, dead at an early age—though after he had published *Getica* and *Memoriale;* but also of V. Bogrea, "the most learned Romanian," as Iorga called him, who died at forty without having published a single book—he had published only extraordinarily erudite book reviews and short articles.) But in my case, there was nothing to be done. I only hoped that I should be more fortunate than a great many of my predecessors.

There was one thing I knew, however: that I had to write at least one "great book." Unfortunately, every time I would start writing a new book, I would say to myself: It won't be this one. Not this one, but the next. . . .

As soon as I finished with my course at the university, I set to work on *Yoga*. General Condeescu had spoken to King Carol, who knew about the years I had spent in India and who had, it seems, read *Maitreyi* enthusiastically. The King suggested that *Yoga* be published by the Royal Foundations. I had planned to have it published in France, and had written to this effect to Paul Geuthner. But Alexandru Rossetti assured me that everything could be arranged: the book would be printed by the Royal Foundations and distributed abroad by Librairie Orientaliste Paul Geuthner. In a few additional weeks of work I completed the manuscript. The final chapters remained to be translated, however. Since I was in a hurry and since I didn't dare ask Wendy Noica and Lydia Lax to work during their summer vacations, I had recourse to S. Rivain, who had been recommended to me by Alcalay. Rivain had lived in France for several years and had even wanted to translate *Maitreyi.* He translated the last 150 pages in less than a month—and I sent the manuscript to the printer with a sigh of relief. I had worked on that book, off and on, for almost six years.

As we did every summer, we went with a group of friends to the Bucegi and set up residence for ten days at Casa Pestera. We returned early in August, and I began immediately on *Huliganii.* I knew the plot in broad outline, but there were still a considerable number of details to be specified. Only the reactions, ideas, and adventures of Petru Anicet were clear to me, from the scene with which the novel opens—the piano lesson in Vila Tycho Brahé—to the last, at the cemetery, after the burial of Petru's mother. The action, moreover, is centered on Petru and his friend Alexandru Pleşa. Each of them illustrates, in his way, a mode of being in the world that I designated "hooliganic," because it implies at once an unconscious impulse to brutality and an absolute self-confidence. In the then-current meaning of the term, "hooligans" referred to groups of young antisemites, ready to break windows or heads, to attack or loot synagogues, to burn books. None of this happened in my novel. The political context—that is, more precisely, the antisemitic connotation of hooliganism—was entirely absent. Nevertheless, the behavior of the principal characters was quite as violent and irresponsible as that of any ordinary hooligan. What distinguished the characters of my novel from other young people before them or contemporaneous with them was, on the one hand, the brutal way they entered into life, and on the other hand, their certainty that if they were "victorious," they would be in the right.

Of course, it was not a matter of an external victory obtained by methods of a parvenu or by political opportunism, but by the fulfillment of the characters' own destiny. For Petru Anicet, for example, "victory" meant the realization of his musical genius and at the same time his social triumph. He believed in his creative possibilities, and if one day he should have discovered he was a second-rate composer, probably he would have given up composing. But precisely because he did not doubt his genius, he would not agree to live the modest life of an "artist." When his opus would begin to be written and then recognized, he would *have* to have all he believed a genius deserved to have: glory, notoriety, and wealth. Meanwhile, he was still very young and he made his living by giving piano lessons and by various other expedients. He did not shrink from taking money from a semi-prostitute whom he called Nora, and he accepted without hesitation gold coins and jewels that Anişoara Lecca, a girl who loved him, had stolen from her home.

This strident amoralism made some critics, in particular G. Călinescu, speak about my "Gidism." I don't believe they were justified. Like all young people of my age, I had read several books by André Gide, but for my part I admired him more as the critic and essayist of *Pretextes et nouveaux pretextes* than as the author of immoral novels. Rather, the behavior of Petru Anicet is explained by my recent personal experiences and by ideas I held then with respect to Romanian culture. Two years previously, I had passed through a great ordeal that I had resolved by assuming a certain responsibility. I did not in the least regret my action, but I wanted to present several characters in whose eyes such an act as mine would have seemed ridiculous. On the other hand, I wanted to give a certain existential and axiological prestige to a type of Romanian behavior that, until then, either had been interpreted sociologically or else condemned moralistically in literature. There were plenty of "immoralists" and opportunists around who had triumphed, but their triumph was almost exclusively of a political, social, or economic order. Moreover, with rare exceptions, these conquerors had not cared about anyone else. Notions of destiny, work, interior freedom, were matters of indifference or else inaccessible to them. My "hooligans," however, existed on a different plane. What mattered to them above all was the obtaining of a mode of being that would allow them on the one hand to "create," and on the other to "triumph in History." My hooligans bore more resemblance to heroes of the Italian Renaissance than to heroes of Gide's novels.

I believed in the possibility of a Romanian Renaissance, and for that reason I allowed myself to portray such heroes. But I was also afraid that "History" would prevent us from bringing it into being. In desperation, I tried to imagine what might be done. Of one thing I was certain: the excessive intellectualism of the characters in *Întoarcerea din Rai*, their obsessions and idiosyncrasies, their fear of "failure"—all these were obsolete. Retreat from confrontation with History, the acceptance of the traditional destiny of the Romanian intellectual—to "fail" or to survive humbly on the periphery of society—did not seem to me a solution. The eternal defeat of the poet, the eternal victory of the politician—the leitmotif of the Romanian novel from Vlahuţa to Cezar Petrescu—depressed me, although I knew that sociologically the presentation was correct. I said to myself that, for the present, I must break out of this vicious circle: the "intellectual" who cannot "win" because a victory would imply the nullification of his mode of being as "intellectual." My hooligans succeeded in resolving the dilemma through what I called then the

"Gordian solution." They showed in this way that they participated in another mode of *Romanian* existence than that of the intellectuals of Cezar Petrescu's novels.

,   ,   ,

I wrote from 2:00 to 8:00 in the afternoons and again at night from 11:00 P.M. to 3:00 or 4:00 A.M. Sometimes I would produce as many as twenty or thirty pages in twelve hours, and the chapters written at that rate seem to me today to be the most successful ones. But there came days and nights of sterile torpor, when I didn't know how to extricate some character from the predicament into which I had projected him by leading him into unforeseen and absurd adventures.

Mihail Sebastian often came to dinner and would ask, "How's it going?" He marveled and envied me when he heard that twenty or thirty pages had been written in the past twenty-four hours. He himself wrote with difficulty, sighing, often getting up from the table and pacing the floor desperately, continually crossing out and correcting. I, on the contrary, if I saw after a few hours of effort that I had not gotten beyond the first page—which, on rereading, proved to be rather mediocre—would tear up the paper and give up trying to write any more that day. It was not just a matter of "inspiration," but more especially of the presence, intensified to the point of hallucination, of the characters. I could not write well except when I *felt* the characters, with an almost physical intensity, present before me, beside me.

After four or five weeks, I found myself in the middle of the novel. I knew that it would be a somewhat longer book than *Întoarcerea din Rai*. Only if I allowed my characters to "exist" for five to six hundred pages did I feel they would succeed in becoming "incarnate." Since the majority of them were intellectuals, ready at the drop of a hat to analyze themselves or break into a long discussion, such characters would have seemed artificial if I had limited the novel to three hundred pages. They could obtain depth and autonomy only if I let them remain on stage for a long time. On the other hand, I tried to present four groups of characters, moving in different worlds that, at least in the beginning, were unrelated. Toward the end of the book, these groups would have to meet and certain characters be drawn into common actions. This implied *duration*—

that is, many hundreds of pages. (And no doubt the novel would have profited considerably by being two or three hundred pages longer than it is.)

The last part I wrote with difficulty, while almost ill. The brutality of certain scenes, the cruelty of some of the characters, sickened me. But it was impossible for me to jettison them or to attenuate their savagery. I had set out to write a novel of "the hooligans," and I could not retreat. All those atrocities would have to be avenged later, in *Viaţa nouă*. It was the price some characters paid in order to become themselves.

I finished the novel with a great effort, tortured—as it has been my fate to conclude the writing of almost all my books. By that time Volume I was already in print, and the first half of Volume II had been set to type while I was composing the last chapter. Fortunately, my teaching did not begin until November, and I had announced a subject about which I was quite excited: religious symbolism. My seminar was to deal with Book X of Aristotle's *Metaphysics*. But by St. Dumitru's Day we had to move. We were no longer satisfied with the apartment on Bulevardul Dinicu Golescu, and we had found another on Strada Palade, a quiet street with many trees. There was a garden in front, and the apartment consisted of several rooms that were surprisingly large and light, about which I was enthusiastic.

Huliganii appeared a few days after we had installed ourselves in our new lodgings. The book's success with the public, and in part with the critics, was rather great. The original printing of four thousand copies was quickly exhausted, and after Christmas a new edition appeared, printed in one volume.

But the cruelties and excesses of all sorts upset many readers. Eugen Lovinescu confessed to me one day that, while he was reading *Huliganii*, he worried constantly that he might suffer a heart attack. From such persons, he said, you can expect anything, and yet they always do precisely what you don't expect. As in *Întoarcerea din Rai*, the erotic scenes were unnecessarily coarse, at least for the era in which the novel was written. N. I. Herescu, with whom I had begun to be acquainted, testified that although he was neither a prude nor a puritan, his conception of art forced him to protest against the excess of eroticism. What we do in everyday life is another story, he said, but in a novel there is no need to tell everything.

I realized that in a way they both were right. But, on the one hand, *Huliganii* was, and had to be, a violent book; while on the other hand, unconsciously, I was avenging myself by writing against the quiet settled existence that I had accepted. It was a protest of one part of me against the part that had decided to live that sort of life. But as I realized later, for the present it was preferable for such protests to find expression in a novel.

14. When a Writer Reaches Thirty

At No. 43 Strada Palade, we had an apartment on the third floor—the top floor—of a house, in front of which was a beautiful rose garden. The street was melancholic and peaceful, with lovely old houses, built around the turn of the century, still well-kept. In 1935, I believe the only modern house in the neighborhood was the one in which we were living. I liked it especially for its large windows, which occupied whole walls, and because it was situated about fifteen meters back from the street. In the most spacious room I had set up my library. The success that *Huliganii* had enjoyed at the bookstores allowed me to buy new bookcases, so that now all the inner walls were covered with my library.

In the winter of 1936 the final chapters of *Yoga* were set in type and the book appeared at the beginning of spring, published by the Royal Foundations and Librarie orientaliste Paul Guethner. Seven years had elapsed since I had begun writing the first chapter one torrid afternoon in a large room on Ripon Street, before having been invited by Dasgupta to live with him in Bhawanipore. Despite all its omissions and imperfections—some explicable by youthful inexperience, others due to the double translation of several chapters (from English to Romanian, and from Romanian to French)—*Yoga* was considered to be an important contribution to the understanding of Indian mystical techniques. Nearly all the great Orientalists of the time, from Jean Przyluski and Louis de La Vallée Poussin to Ananda Coomaraswamy, Heinrich Zimmer, V. Papesso, and G. Tucci, declared themselves in accord with my interpretations. Only Paul Masson-Oursel published a somewhat ambiguous notice in the *Revue Philosophique*. Later I understood why: he himself was preparing a book on yoga (which, however, he only undertook to write some fifteen years later). What is even more interesting is the fact that, as soon as I arrived in Paris in the fall of 1945, Masson-Oursel invited me to give a course of lectures on yoga at the Institute of Indian Studies of the Sorbonne. From that time until his death almost ten years later, in all his publications about yoga he cited me as "the great world authority," alongside Dr. Jean Filliozat.

But, of course, only the half-negative review was known in Bucharest, and I did not doubt that its discovery had been received with a sigh of relief, if not indeed with rejoicing, by several of my former professors and many of my colleagues at the university, to say nothing of numerous essayists and journalists who, for different reasons, did not take my scholarship seriously. I suspect that the majority of my detractors could not believe that the author of successful novels and the prolific journalist that I was then could be at the same time a "savant." Probably the young men were also somewhat envious. They felt I had been too lucky, from the time of my trip to India up to the success of *Maitreyi* and the popularity it gained me in the Faculty of Letters. At any rate, long before the publication of Masson-Oursel's review, there had appeared several unfavorable notices about the book in Romanian periodicals of both the left and the right. For nationalists, *Yoga* fell short of interest because it did not deal with "Romanian realities." For left-wing journalists, on the other hand, *Yoga* had no value because *I* had written it—I, an assistant of Nae Ionescu and a writer for *Cuvântul:* hence, a "right-winger."

I recall an article by Oscar Lemnaru: he said that upon entering a bookstore he had caught sight of my book, had leafed through it, and had recognized immediately that it was of no interest; therefore, he had not even bothered to read it. This gross unfairness angered Constantin Noica and moved him to write an article for *Revista Fundațiilor Regale* (Review of the Royal Foundations), entitled "*Yoga* and Its Author." Noica invited Romanian critics and journalists to concern themselves exclusively with my literary productions and essays, adding that my Orientalist works and those of the history of religions were—and would remain—inaccessible to them. He spoke of my library, reminded them of my years of study in India, and reprimanded them in his inimitable way for trying to judge *Yoga* with a smattering of "experience of India obtained from reading *Maitreyi.*" Then he added, as another illustration of his celebrated refrain: "We do not know anything except what we have learned."

I dedicated *Yoga* to the memory of the Maharaja Mahindra Chandra Nandy, Professor Nae Ionescu, and Surendranath Dasgupta, the only persons I considered my "masters." Dasgupta did not acknowledge receipt of the copy I sent him; but two years later he telegraphed me from Rome asking if we could meet, either in Bucharest or in Italy.

Nae breathed easily only when he saw the thesis published. He insisted then that I finish editing Hasdeu, so that I might be able to consecrate myself wholly to the investigation of Oriental philosophy and spiritual techniques. He was very pleased with the first fascicle of *Alchimia Asiatică,* he knew I was working on *Cosmologie și Alchimie Babiloniană,* and he showed interest in the interpretation I was giving to those pre-empirical sciences. He told me that such studies could constitute a very useful and suggestive introduction to the philosophy of culture.

I did not understand this until later, but I do not doubt that the unexpected literary popularity that I enjoyed between 1933 and 1938 was detrimental to my scientific creativity. Not because I devoted too much time and energy to literature, but because, without realizing it, I was influenced by the negative attitude of the majority of my professors and colleagues. Consequently, I felt constrained to prove, at all costs, that I was not only an accomplished writer, but likewise a "man of science," a scholar. Since the majority of them had no means of checking the validity of my research in the history of Eastern religions and philosophies, I was obliged to show them the "documents" on which I based my interpretations. I have always loved erudition—and I believe that I should not have been deceived by it had I not known that only a massive presentation of documents and bibliography could convince the university people. If I had not been a successful writer from my youth, very probably my subsequent scientific and philosophical works of that period would have been more elegantly presented. Precisely because I had written *Maitreyi*, I did not permit myself in *Yoga* or *Alchimia Asiatică* to write "beautifully," clearly, and with few footnotes. What is even more serious: I did not let myself carry to their conclusions the results at which I had arrived. I was afraid of being accused of generalizing too quickly or of reading a "personal interpretation" into the documents I used. Nearly all the ideas that I expounded in the books published in French after 1946 are found *in nuce* in studies written between 1933 and 1939. But outside of a handful of readers—persons, it is true, of the caliber of Nae Ionescu, Lucian Blaga, Mircea Vulcănescu, and Constantin Noica—no one realized that in those books of extravagant erudition there was being elaborated a new interpretation of myth and symbolism, of archaic and Oriental religions.

I continued to assist in all of Nae Ionescu's courses, which seemed to increase in popularity in the university after the professor's political ideas became known. He and I met almost every day also in the *Cuvântul* office. Although the newspaper had been suspended for two and a half years, Nae continued paying the rent on the office and the salaries of several editors. The professor was unchanged: serene, ironic, generous, listening to our problems, optimistic, curious about everything that was going on, interested in everything any of us was doing. I never understood on what he based his hope that sooner or later *Cuvântul* would be able to appear again. He was on the worst of terms with "the palace." He had enemies not only among the politicians and journalists of the left, but even more among those on the right.

I wondered sometimes if the professor had not let himself be deceived by that vain hope due to the publication of the book *Roza vânturilor* (Compass Points). Its appearance was my doing. As I was speaking one day to Alexandru Rosetti about Nae's articles of drama criticism, he assured me that he was ready at any time to publish a book of them at *Cultura Națională*. I consulted the professor, and much to my surprise he gave me his consent (I knew that he didn't want to publish a book made up of articles). But after I had collected a good part of his articles on current events from *Cuvântul* for the years 1923–1925, I realized that the volume was in danger of being a disservice: it would represent only one facet of his many-sided activity as philosopher, critic, and journalist. I persuaded him to allow me to include a number of articles on theology and on historical and social criticism. In this fashion I put together a rather thick volume, to which I appended an epilogue. Nae himself selected the title of the book. I supposed that it would have a great success on the market, but I was mistaken. The first edition of four thousand copies was not exhausted until several years later. Fate willed that this collection of articles and columns would be the only volume of Nae Ionescu's writings to be published in his lifetime.

, , ,

Summer had come, the season when I liked to write "literature": it was my way of relaxing, of dreaming, of enjoying vacation time. On the other hand, I needed money in order to be able to work for five or six weeks in the Stadtbibliothek in Berlin—in order to finish *Cosmologie şi Alchimie Babiloniană.* A contract with Ciornei obligated me to give him yet another novel. I had promised him *Viaţă nouă,* the sequel to *Huliganii.* After beginning to write, I realized that this last novel of the trilogy would require several volumes. I was working now on the first, *Stefania.* As usual, I would write from the beginning of the afternoon till evening, then between 11:00 P.M. and 3:00 or 4:00 A.M. I would go to bed at dawn, sometimes after sunrise, and sleep until noon.

Mihail Sebastian came often to eat with us. He was now editor of *Revista Fundaţiilor Regale,* and he was wrestling also with a novel, *Accidentul.* He asked me how my book was going, and I didn't know what to say. I was writing with much difficulty, as at other times, but that was not what was bothering me. Rather, it was the tempo of the action, which was too slow. It seemed I was not writing a novel, but a monographic presentation of a group of rather ordinary persons, in the center of whom I must exalt Stefania, as if she were a person descended from another world. I wanted, by all means, to avoid the nervous, hasty rhythm of *Huliganii.* Since *Viaţă nouă* might comprise from twelve hundred to fifteen hundred pages, I told myself that if the action at the beginning of the first volume were too fast-paced, the novel would be lacking in density. I must, therefore, "put the brakes" on the characters as much as possible, to slow down the action. As I imagined her, Stefania was an exceptional personality, but I kept postponing the episodes that would reveal this to the readers. Above all, I postponed her meeting with Petru Anicet. Perhaps this was because, without my realizing it, I was frightened by the brutality of this "hooliganistic" episode, and I was trying to prolong as much as possible the "paradise" in which Stefania lived.

Indeed, until her meeting with Petru Anicet, Stefania seemed like a character from a *roman rose*—all good qualities were hers. She was not only beautiful and intelligent, but she had a husband quite as exceptional as she, with whom she was deeply in love. She was rich, and she loved the wealth in which she had been reared, which allowed her to travel, to buy costly paintings and books, and to enjoy friendships with the many people she admired in Paris, Rome, and Barcelona. All this she must renounce, and renounce as in a dream, knowing that her husband will be destroyed and her children alienated, yet hoping that by some miracle everything will remain the same, as at the beginning. And after confessing everything, she will run away to the appointed rendezvous with Petru—and she will wait in vain. Petru will be meeting Nora, a prostitute from the slums, with whom he has had a relationship since youth; but she is now a very successful courtesan, maintained by an eccentric landowner, and is preparing for her debut in a theatrical review. He will accompany her to her apartment, and afterward they will carouse until dawn, wandering from bar to bar.

Thus it was necessary to begin with the end, with Stefania's great love for Anicet, since of course—after that night of waiting—Stefania would break off her affair with Petru, but she would continue to love him. For years to come she would help him, encourage him, and sustain him, especially in his creative work, although threatened all the while by his relationship with Nora. The following volumes of *Viaţă nouă* would describe Petru Anicet's struggle (and also Stefania's) with his own genius, which tempts him with an endless number of possibilities for the composition of *Ereticii* (The Heretics), a symphony of which Petru has dreamed since adolescence, which must "proclaim" in musical language the liberation of contemporary man from any dogma, law, or pre-established pattern of behavior. The demon possesses him sometimes with such fury that he writes like a man in a daze. Stefania and the rare listeners hear fascinating fragments—but sometimes even in their presence Anicet knows that he has failed or that he must do better, and he starts over again from the beginning with another technique, using other methods.

Almost miraculously, *Ereticii* is finished a few years after his meeting with Stefania (he had worked on it for some fifteen years). But it is only thanks to Stefania, who has succeeded in stealing fragments of rejected versions (Petru burned the manuscripts once he lost interest in them) and has shown them to several musicians— only thanks to her is *Ereticii* performed one evening in November at the Opera House in Bucharest. In one of the boxes on the third row, calm, serene, except that she is twisting her handkerchief in her hands, sits Stefania, observing the triumph. That same night she will disappear without leaving a trace.

But all that would happen later, in Volumes II and III of *Viaţă nouă*, together with many other things; because, besides the characters from *Huliganii*, there would appear in this flowing novel a considerable number of characters from various strata of society (I was trying at all costs to rid myself of the "intellectuals" of *Întoarcerea din Rai*). *Stefania* comes to an end on the night when Petru meets Nora and goes out with her to make the rounds of the bars in Bucharest. (This episode would have to occupy a third of the book, because in that adventure—grotesque and yet "initiatory," resembling a wandering in a labyrinth—those two would meet all sorts of people and would be witnesses to scenes that would have their importance in subsequent volumes.)

In one month I wrote about two hundred pages in which almost nothing happened—at least, not the meeting of Stefania and Petru. I let myself become involved in a laborious presentation of the family of Stefania's husband, and in interminable dialogues between Stefania and her children. In particular I lingered too much over groups of picturesque and sinister characters gravitating around Nora's protector—strange, lewd old men who fascinated me by their unpredictable behavior. Whenever I reread a chapter, I wondered what would be the reader's reaction: if, perhaps, he would not be tempted to lay the book aside. The original inspiration had begun to fade, and I broke off my writing. I had to stop, in any event, at the end of July, when I had decided to leave for Berlin.

One day I received a telephone call from Professor Gusti. He said that King Carol was interested in the Oxford Group Movement and that he wanted to send me as an observer to the congress, which was to take place in a week. I was selected because I spoke English and was somewhat familiar with religious problems. I knew that Carol had known about me ever since I had been in India, because

Nae had spoken to him about me. I also knew that he had read *Maitreyi* enthusiastically. However, I did not suppose that I was of interest to him now, since his break with Nae. Although it would mean losing two weeks of work at the Stadtbibliothek, I accepted. On the one hand, I wanted to see London and Oxford; on the other hand, the sum that Gusti put on deposit for me would allow me to buy clothes and a great many books.

I left alone, Nina staying behind in order to meet me in Berlin two weeks later. I cannot say that in the summer of 1936 I became well acquainted with London. I stayed there only a few days, spending my time in art museums, libraries, and second-hand bookshops. I was fortunate in buying almost all of Frazer's works, with which I had been familiar for a long time, but only a part of which existed in the libraries of Bucharest. I also purchased two suits of clothes, somewhat by accident: I had stopped in front of a shop window, hesitating as to whether I should enter or look further, when someone from the shop appeared and invited me inside. I bought the latest book by Aldous Huxley, *Eyeless in Gaza,* which I read on the train in one breath. I remember finishing it a few minutes before reaching Oxford.

About the Oxford Group Movement, I knew almost nothing. I had read only one book on it, which Yvonne Wright had given me before my departure. (It was she, as a matter of fact, who had spoken to King Carol about the movement and persuaded him to send an "observer" to the congress.) Their sessions of meditation and prayer, with sudden and dramatic public confessions, fascinated me. After a few days, Frank Buchman summoned me to his office and asked me if the movement he had initiated could have any success in Romania. I answered quite frankly that I doubted it, and I tried to explain why. The revolutionary techniques that the movement used—above all, confession and meditation-prayer with notebook in hand in anticipation of messages (which Buchman believed were dictated, directly or indirectly, by God)—were not designed to make much impression on Romanians. On the one hand, confession constituted, among the Orthodox, one of the principal sacraments, and it was hard to believe that public confession could be made a substitute for it. On the other hand, prayer and meditation constituted part of the liturgical life of the communities of love; they could scarcely be materialized in "messages" recorded by believers in pocket notebooks. But of course, I added, such techniques adapted to the conditions of modern Western man could be somewhat useful for those who had separated themselves long since from the living tradition of Orthodoxy, who existed far from any religious life. For such, the Oxford Group Movement, or any similar experiment, could constitute the initial shock that would introduce them into the religious sphere.

I believe Alice Voinescu, who arrived a few days after I did, had the same reaction. In any event, so far as I was concerned, the meeting with the Movement in Oxford was very instructive. I began to think about the possibility of awakening the interest of modern, desacralized man in religious realities. The Oxford Group Movement was also significant from another point of view: it brought together not only nonbelievers of all sorts and believers from different Christian denominations, but theists from other religions as well. In this way I met a Jew of Romanian origin, Philip Leon, professor at the University of Manchester and author of several books, among them *The Ethics of Power*. For Philip Leon, the Oxford Group Movement was the only, and the last, chance modern man had of finding God again. Thus he refused to discuss any other theological problem than that of the relationship between God and man.

In Berlin I returned to the room on Berlinerstrasse in which I had stayed in 1934, and I followed virtually the same schedule: mornings and afternoons at the Stadtbibliothek, nights working at home. Since Nina had come this time, we went out sometimes for a stroll around Berlin with our landlady. I saw Argintescu again and found him unchanged. Those weeks of August passed swiftly. I finished the documentation for *Cosmologie şi Alchimie Babiloniană* and began to collect material for a monograph on the origins of the legends of the mandrake. At the beginning of September we left for Leipzig, where I met with Anton Golopenţia. He urged me to read Karl Jaspers' *Philosophy*, and he gave me a wonderful analysis of the strengths and weaknesses of National Socialism. He told me also that unless something unexpected should intervene, in a few years we would be at war; and then we Romanians would have one great problem: to find a way to "hibernate," to survive this new cataclysm.

We stopped next at Munich, which I saw then for the first time, and when we reached Vienna I had only a few shillings in my pocket. I went to the Romanian Legation to look for Lucian Blaga and ask him for a loan, but Blaga was on leave at Cluj, so that day we had to make do with a sandwich on a park bench. We had nothing else to eat until after the train had crossed the Romanian border.

*   *   *

At home again, I reread from the beginning the manuscript of *Stefania*. It was hard to imagine that I was capable of writing anything so insipid. I believed that whatever a "writer of talent" might do, he could not fall below a certain level. Now I had to admit I was mistaken. A good part of the text was unusable. Mihail Sebastian did not want to believe me; he said it was probably a matter of an attack of discouragement, and he asked to see the manuscript that he might read it and judge it for himself. Perhaps I might have given it to him if I had not known that, good or bad, I would still have been unable to finish the novel in time for it to appear in the fall. It was necessary, therefore, that I write something else, another novel.

I wondered if I could not publish those two manuscripts from adolescence and early youth, *Romanul adolescentului miop* and *Gaudeamus*, if I were to rewrite and correct them. But Mihail urged me to abandon that easy solution. I had no right, he said, to publish now, when I was nearing literary maturity, the efforts of an immature period. Those manuscripts must be published someday, for their historic-literary interest, but not now, when I had not yet reached the age of thirty.

I quickly realized that he was right, and I decided to write a short novel, one quite unrelated to the "atmosphere" of the *Întoarcerea din Rai* cycle, but, on the other hand, without autobiographical incidents. After so many years of writing "realistic" literature, I felt attracted to the "fantastic" again. A story obsessed me in which the principal character was a young woman who had died thirty years before. Obviously, it was a matter of a *strigoi* (vampire), but I did not wish to repeat any folkloristic theme, so popular in Romania and neighboring countries, nor yet the romantic motif of the haunting ghost (of the genre "Lenore"). Actually, I did not feel attracted by *that* aspect of the problem. What fascinated me was the sad and hopeless drama of the dead youth who cannot separate herself from the earth, but who persists in believing in the possibility of *concrete* communication with the living, hoping that she can love and be loved as people love in their incarnate modality.

My character, Miss Christina, was the daughter of a landowner, killed during the peasant uprising of 1907, but who returns continually to the places where she had spent her childhood and where she had never had time to live her youth. Obviously, being a *strigoi*, she cannot prolong this precarious phantom post-existence except with fresh blood from the inn and the village. But it was not this folkloric motif that constituted the point of departure of the plot; rather, it was the fact that Christina succeeded in "corrupting," spiritually speaking, her niece Simina, a little girl of about ten or eleven; she succeeded, that is, in communicating with her in a concrete way, teaching her not to be afraid of her "physical" presence. Though but a child, Simina becomes, thanks to these strange experiences, "mature" in all ways. Thus, when Miss Christina wants to make love to one of the guests at the inn, when she tries to conquer him by bewitching him at first in dreams, then preparing him not to emerge from the spell even after he awakens from sleep, Simina reflects the same "passion" and she behaves toward Egor like an adult woman. It was not a case of "precociousness"—sexual or otherwise—but of an absolutely abnormal condition, created by the corruption that resulted from the overturning of the laws of Nature.

I was well aware of the "horribleness" of that character, but this was just what I wanted to show: that any lingering, contrary to Nature, in a paradoxical condition (a "spiritual" being behaving like a living body) constitutes a source of corruption for all around it. Beneath an angelic exterior, Simina conceals a monster, but this is due not to some unknown abnormal instinct or impulse, but on the contrary to a false "spirituality," to the fact that she lives entirely in the world of Miss Christina, a spirit that refuses to assume its own mode of being.

Going to the Cultura Națională office, I spoke to Isaia Răcăciuni about my ideas for *Domnișoara Christina* (Miss Christina) and, captivated by the title, he asked for the book. I believe I took him the manuscript two weeks later. The book came out at the end of autumn and rapidly acquired admirers and detractors, both equally fanatic. Among the admirers were poets such as Dan Botta and passionate skeptics of the political phenomenon like Mihail Polihroniade. Several friends recognized that I had succeeded in creating a much more authentic atmosphere of the fantastic than had previous

Romanian writers who had attempted it, but they regretted that I had not used traditional folklore motifs. With a few exceptions, the literary critics appeared favorable. The success at the bookstores was, however, far from that of *Huliganii*.

Soon *Domnişoara Christina* became the object of an attack by the editor of *Neamul Românesc*, Georgescu-Cocoş, who for a long time had been leading a campaign against "pornography." Day after day, Cocoş reproduced in *Neamul Românesc* fragments of scenes that showed Simina's "precociousness." Taken out of context, the quotations often appeared uncouth. More serious was the fact that Nicolae Iorga had also attacked "pornography" in literature, and I expected him to intervene again, this time opposing me exclusively, employing not only citations from *Domnişoara Christina*, but from all those other novels that, as I had heard, a team of Cocoş's was now reading with red pencils in hand. Since *Neamul Românesc* circulated mainly among the universities, I knew that many would gain knowledge of my literary works exclusively through the "pornographic" fragments, and I also knew how terrible the indignation would be.

Thus on the eve of Christmas, 1936, the situation was threatening to become tragi-comic. Almost no one spoke any longer about the "fantastic" novel that I had written—about its merits or faults, or about the possibilities and limitations of fantastic literature in itself—but rather about the "pornography" of *Domnişoara Christina*. What is more amusing is that, in the spring of that same year, at a special session of the Society of Romanian Writers, I had declared myself opposed to pornography as a means of creating scandal and publicity. Of course, we also opposed all advance censorship, and we proclaimed once again the right of writers to create according to their own aesthetic conceptions. At the time of the discussion, nevertheless, I made a point of specifying that in the case of pornographic writings a problem existed, although, fortunately, there were no such products signed by responsible authors. I recalled a few examples in which it was clearly understood that certain authors, the majority of them young scandal seekers or else suspicious dilettantes hiding under pseudonyms, used graphic and erotic scenes exclusively for their shock value. I said, then, that we could not make common cause with any author of pornographic prose. Many members of the society were not pleased by this intervention of mine. They were afraid that by introducing distinctions between authentic writers and scandalmongers, we were encouraging the idea of advance censorship.

So now, in the winter of 1936–1937, when I had become the object of Georgescu-Cocoş's attack, writers not only did not take up my defense, but they confessed satisfaction that I was the first victim of a campaign in which I, naively, had tried to introduce nuances and distinctions. Şerban Cioculescu published an article in *Adevărul* entitled "Every Bird . . . ," recalling my intervention at the society's meeting and showing through my own example that the distinction I wanted to make between "writers" and "opportunists" was an impractical one. The article did not convince me. I knew that many of my novels contained scenes of aggressive and savage eroticism, but I understood their purpose. My characters were mainly intellectuals, living somewhat on the margins of "life"; their sporadic outbursts and sexual excesses were, in fact, their desperate attempts to embody and obtain a vital dimension that they did not possess. I don't believe I ever wrote a single erotic scene simply to "shock" or to unleash a literary scandal that would "launch" my books—as was the case not only with obscure Romanian "opportunists" in the years 1936–1937, but also with other writers of unknown talent. In my case, the situation was exactly opposite. The popularity that *Maitreyi* had brought me was an embarrassment, and I sought to reduce it to tolerable proportions not only by publishing difficult novels, such as *Lumina ce se stinge* and *Întoarcerea din Rai*, but also volumes of essays and scholarly works. What interested me was not success at the bookstores, but the creation of a public of my own that would follow all my activities; I was seeking readers of my entire *oeuvre*, not people who were fans of the novelist or the "man of science" only.

, , ,

The "scandal" of *Domnişoara Christina* was to have unexpected consequences a few months later, in the spring of 1937.

That winter, I had concentrated with all my might on the Hasdeu book. I had copied several thousands of pages, collated the variants in the poems, and constructed a rather extensive bibliography. I was working now on the arrangement of the texts and on the general introduction. The hours spent at the State Archives, where I found boxes full of papers brought from "The Castle" at Câmpina, impressed me tremendously. There were hundreds of thousands of pages, some containing only a few words: "messages" sent from Julia during spiritualistic seances. I found innumerable journals of linguistics, history, and folklore, with their pages uncut. In his old age, Hasdeu renounced completely all the interests of his youth and mature years. I had the impression sometimes that I was wandering through a ruins.

I should have liked to have written a whole book about Hasdeu and his contemporaries. But because it was necessary that the critical edition be published that year, I had to be content with composing a lengthy introduction in which I presented his biography and his historical, political, and philosophic thought. The second volume of *Scrieri literare, morale și politice de B. P. Hasdeu* I had begun to assemble during the winter. I recall now my desk covered with proofs and manuscripts, and the long, exhausting work of correcting and checking references. If I could have worked day and night on nothing but the editing of *Scrieri*, I could have finished it by March. But there was also the course and the seminar at the university; I had to write at least one article per week for *Vremea* and one a month for *Revista Fundațiilor Regale*; and I had, besides, lectures to give in the provinces—many of them arranged by the Royal Foundations—while the innumerable books I was receiving on Orientalia, the history of religions, and literature could not remain unread for long.

Ever since my student days, I had been receiving books and reviews from many Orientalists and historians of religions, for the most part Italians. After my return from India, the number of authors who gave me their publications increased appreciably. Now, however, since the publication of *Yoga*, I had established relations with another twenty or thirty Orientalists, ethnologists, and historians of religions, and not a week passed in which I did not receive at least one book or bundle of offprints. I corresponded in particular with Ananda Coomaraswamy, Jean Przyluski, Carl Hentze, and C. Clemen, all of whom were to contribute to the first volume of *Zalmoxis*. In addition, my Parisian publisher, Paul Geuthner, would give me almost all his new publications, and I took them in at a single breath, frequently writing long reviews or critical articles in *Revista Fundațiilor Regale*. The majority of these articles, later republished in *Insula lui Euthanasius* (Euthanasius's Island, published in

1943), were written in the years 1937–1938. I had been invited to contribute to several foreign Orientalist reviews, and I had already published in G. Tucci's *Asiatica*, E. Buonaiuti's *Ricerche Religiose*, and the *Journal of the Indian Society of Oriental Art*, published in Calcutta by Stella Kramrisch. Of course, very few Romanians knew about these scholarly activities, owing in part, perhaps, to my own indifference, since I did not send offprints of my published studies to any but teachers and colleagues in foreign lands. At home, I was content to give them to Nae Ionescu and a few friends.

On the ninth of March I reached thirty years of age. As usual, all my friends gathered—from those of long standing, such as Haig Acterian and Mihail Polihroniade, to the newer ones, Mihail Sebastian, Dinu Noica, and Petru Țuțea. I remember that N. I. Herescu, V. Voiculescu, and Camil Petrescu came also—Petrescu was quite surprised to learn that I was only thirty. Did I feel that I had come to the end of a cycle? I knew only that I was ready to begin a new stage of life in which I could no longer allow myself certain freedoms, negligences, and errors. I had published twelve books and edited *Roza vânturilor*, and Hasdeu's *Scrieri* in two volumes was about to appear; I imagined that I would need to publish just a few books more—some of them already in progress—in order for the contours of my *"oeuvre"* to be defined. Only after that, I told myself, would I have the right to "concentrate," to try to write one or two books in a leisurely manner. But there was one thing that disturbed me: the failure of *Stefania*. I knew that I had three volumes of *Viață nouă* left to write in order for the whole *Întoarcerea din Rai* cycle to reveal its true dimensions. I could not write much except during the summer vacation periods. I must have another two or three summers for "literature" only; but I began to doubt that I would have them, as in the past, in their entirety.

By April, the two massive volumes of *Scrieri* were already collected and corrected, in part even in type, but I had not yet finished the introduction and bibliography. The director of the Royal Foundations, Alexandru Rosetti, intended to publish it on Book Day, at the end of May. But Ciornei also wanted to publish a novel of mine for the same occasion. Perhaps I could have managed to put him off until autumn had I not needed the money for the trip abroad. I assured him, therefore, that he would have *Șarpele* in time for Book Day. This meant that I had to give him the manuscript in two weeks.

I don't believe I shall ever forget that spring of 1937. Every day, except Friday and Saturday when I held the class and seminar at the university, I sat down at my desk immediately after lunch, at two o'clock. If I had any articles to write that day, I wrote them first; then I began working on Hasdeu, writing from five to fifteen pages (of introduction, annotations, or bibliography) until 10:00 or 11:00 P.M. After that, I cleared the desk and returned to the novel. I wrote until 3:00 or 4:00 A.M., fifteen or eighteen pages, which—sometimes without even reading them over—I put into an envelope and left beside the entryway door so the boy from the print shop could pick them up in the morning. Each day he collected the chapter I had written the night before.

Şarpele is my only book written without a plan, without knowing how the plot was going to unfold, and without knowing the ending. It is, undoubtedly, a product purely of the imagination. I did not make use of anything I knew or could have learned concerning the symbolism and mythology of snakes. When I began that story I knew only one thing: that a group of people from Bucharest, with no inclination toward the fantastic, was going to spend a night at a monastery, and that a stranger, Andronic, whom they had met on the road, was going to say at a given moment, "Please, don't be frightened, but here, very near us, there is a snake." The rest I imagined, or more precisely I "saw," in fourteen nights, as the story unfolded itself little by little. When, in the morning, I went to deposit the manuscript in front of the entryway door, I knew only vaguely what was going to happen in the next chapter. I had almost no time during the day to think about Andronic and his snake. When I resumed the writing, I had nothing at hand except a few notes sketched in haste the night before; the rest of the manuscript was already at the printer. I would spend some time staring into space, sipping my first cup of coffee for the night and trying to catch the thread of the story. Sometimes I began writing full of doubts, because I did not remember exactly the ending of the preceding chapter.

When I received the galley proofs, I could scarcely believe my eyes. The story unreeled itself, without a break or repetition, and it showed a stylistic unity that few of my books had achieved. What delighted me even more was the fact that I had succeeded in creating the "fantastic atmosphere" I had desired, without anything "occult" or "symbolic," and without folkloristic echoes that are as inevitable as death in Romanian *littérature fantastique. Şarpele* was written as I had "seen" it from the beginning: a story with banal characters who go on an outing to a monastery park and become involved involuntarily, almost without realizing it, in a series of strange happenings that eventually bewitch and transfigure them. The "fantastic" is disclosed gradually, imperceptibly, and in a sense "naturally," because nothing extraordinary occurs, no supernatural element intervenes to abolish the world in which my characters have been born and have lived up to that time. In fact, the "fantastic" world in which, thanks to Andronic, they find themselves after midnight, is the same as the everyday one—with the single difference that it discloses now an added dimension, inaccessible to profane existence. It is as if the everyday world camouflages a secret dimension which, once man knows it, reveals to him simultaneously the profound significance of the Cosmos and his authentic mode of being: a mode of perfect, beatific spontaneity, but which is neither the irresponsibility of animal existence nor angelic beatitude.

Unconsciously and unintentionally, I succeeded in "showing" in *Şarpele* something I was to develop later in my works of philosophy and history of religions: namely, that the "sacred" *apparently* is not different from the "profane," that the "fantastic" is camouflaged in the "real," that the world is what it shows itself to be, and is at the same time a cipher. That same dialectic—of course, in the context of an epic fresco of grand proportions—also sustains *The Forbidden Forest,* begun twelve years later in 1949, with the difference that at this time no longer was it a question of the profound meaning of the Cosmos, but of the "cipher" of historical events. The theme of the "fantastic" camouflaged in everyday occurrences is found again in several of my novellas written still more recently, for example: *La Ţigănci* (With the Gypsy Girls, written in 1959) and *Podul* (The Bridge, written in 1964). In a certain sense, one could say that this theme constitutes the key to all the writings of my maturity.

Şarpele appeared as I had promised Ciornei on Book Day, almost simultaneously with the two volumes of Hasdeu's *Scrieri.* But I don't believe I had any time to enjoy the fact that I had written a book that satisfied me completely, and that I was at last delivered from the nightmare of the Hasdeu project. A few days before, Constantin Kiriţescu, Director-General of the Ministry of Public Instruction, had published in all the papers an official communique in which he drew the attention of the Rector of the University of Bucharest to the fact that I, an assistant lecturer in Metaphysics at the Faculty of Letters, was the author of certain "pornographic" writings. Obviously, it was the natural consequence of Cocos's campaign against *Domnişoara Christina.* The tragi-comic part of the minister's communique was that it had been drafted by a man who was nicknamed "the director with the couch." I was forced to bring charges against him for slander, demanding a symbolic leu as compensation.

Those summer months I count among the most invigorating and glorious of my youth. For, from everywhere, voices were raised in my defense. N. I. Herescu, director-general of the Society of Romanian Writers, arranged a banquet in my honor at Capşa, with the president of the society, General Condeescu, and Liviu Rebreanu, V. Voiculescu, Ionel Teodoreanu, and other writers present. He also invited the dean of the Faculty of Letters, Rădulescu-Motru, and many other professors, among whom I remember Nae Ionescu, C. C. Giurescu, Al. Rosetti, and O. Onicescu.

Among my witnesses at my first appearance before the tribunal were Nae, Motru, Rosetti, and Herescu. I do not remember the names of the minister's lawyers, but the attorneys who offered themselves in my defense were numerous. When I went to the tribunal together with Nae for my first appearance, I met one of my brightest students, Mariana Klein, pacing absently in the hall. Her blond hair was disheveled, streaming down her back, and she looked that morning like a Valkyrie in despair. Running up to Nae, she caught hold of his arm: *"Domnule* professor, you must save him!" she exclaimed with tears in her eyes. Nae calmed her, patting her shoulder. When we were alone he said, "If you've succeeded in arousing such devotion among the students, I no longer have any doubts about your future!"

"If only the minister will leave me in peace," I replied. (I never suspected how truly I had spoken. . . .)

Soon after the official communique appeared, *Vremea* published several pages of student protests from the Faculty of Letters and Philosophy. They were unexpectedly bold declarations, with hundreds of signatures attached. After that, almost all summer, "manifestos" continued to appear in *Vremea:* from students, from the Faculties of Theology, Polytechnics, and Science and Medicine, so that it might have been suspected that a campaign had been organized by myself or the editors of *Vremea*. I asked Vladimir Donescu, the director of the review, about it once. He assured me that he had not intervened anywhere, and he showed me the pile of letters he had received that week. "Impossible to publish all of them," he added. "It would take too much space. I'm publishing only the signatures."

I no longer recall all the particulars of the trial. I remember it was postponed twice; then, after hearing the pleas of several of my lawyers, the tribunal ruled in my favor. The minister of instruction appealed. That autumn, when I opened my class, I was met with such enthusiastic applause that I raised my arms and begged the students to be quiet, for fear that the rector would think it was a political demonstration. I was to have another hearing at the end of November, but the case was postponed again. Then the royal dictatorship was imposed, and in the spring of 1938, A. Călinescu was named minister of public instruction. One of his first directives officially suspended all the cases pending against members of the teaching profession instituted by the former minister. And so I never received that symbolic compensation for damages I had requested. But by 1938 it would not have meant anything anyway. . . .

I had learned long before that Kirițescu was by no means satisfied by the way things had developed. The aim of the communique had been to have me removed from the university "for scandal." But the dean, Rădulescu-Motru, had testified in my favor at the trial, and no one was found in the University Council who would request my expulsion. On the other hand, the sudden, massive spontaneous intervention of the students from all the faculties impressed the rector and the minister of instruction alike.

. . . And yet, I sensed that we were on the verge of entering upon the period that I had foreseen and feared ever since my student years, the era that I named inwardly "the time when we will no longer be free to do what we wish." It was not a matter of an anarchic, antisocial liberty, but of the freedom to create in accordance with our callings and potentialities. Fundamentally, it was the freedom to "make culture," the only thing that, for the time being, seemed to me decisive for us Romanians.

Index